THE BOER WAR

THE BOER WAR

London to Ladysmith via Pretoria

Ian Hamilton's March

by

Winston S. Churchill

W·W·NORTON & COMPANY
New York   London

Originally published by Longmans, Green & Co. in 1900
Copyright © 1989 by Octopus Publishing Group

First American Edition 1990

Printed in the United States of America.
Library of Congress Cataloging-in-Publication Data

Churchill, Winston, Sir, 1874–1965.
[London to Ladysmith via Pretoria]
The Boer War / by Winston S. Churchill.
p. cm.
Reprint (1st work). Originally published: New York : Longmans, Green, and Co., 1900.
Reprint (2nd work). Originally published: New York : Longmans, Green, and Co., 1900.
Contents: London to Ladysmith via Pretoria—Ian Hamilton's march.
1. South African War, 1899–1902—Personal narratives.
2. Churchill, Winston, Sir, 1874–1965. 3. South African War,
1899–1902—Prisoners and prisons, Boer. 4. Escapes. 5. Buller,
Redvers Henry, Sir, 1839–1908. 6. South African War, 1899–1902—
Journalists—Biography. 7. Hamilton, Ian, Sir, 1853–1947.
I. Churchill, Winston, Sir, 1874–1965. Ian Hamilton's march.
II. Title.
DT1916.C48 1989
968.04'88—dc20
[B] 89-23168

ISBN 0-393-02815-1

W. W. Norton & Company, Inc.
500 Fifth Avenue, New York, N.Y. 10110
W. W. Norton & Company Ltd.
37 Great Russell Street, London WC1B 3NU

1 2 3 4 5 6 7 8 9 0

FOREWORD

London to Ladysmith and *Ian Hamilton's March* were published in book form by Longmans, Green on 15 May and 12 October, 1900, respectively, in editions of 10,000 and 5,000 copies. The American issues were subsequently published in New York by the same house, in editions of 3,000 and 1,533 copies, respectively. Copp, Clark of Toronto published Canadian issues in both hardback and paperback in 1900. Aside from the 1974 Centenary Edition of the Collected Works of Sir Winston Churchill, and a 1982 South African Edition of *London to Ladysmith*, both works had been out of print for nearly 90 year prior to this new edition.

Both tell of Churchill's adventures in South Africa during the Boer War and both are based on the despatches he sent to the *Morning Post* between November, 1899, and July, 1900. When the Collected Works were published by the Library of Imperial History in 1974 it was decided to issue both books in a single volume, since both are quite short and the one follows straight on from the other. The combined volume was called *The Boer War* and the same practice has been followed in this edition, but it must be borne in mind that Winston Churchill never actually published a book under that title.

In March, 1899, Churchill left his Regiment, the 4th Hussars, in India and returned to England, having already "sent in his papers" and resigned his commission. This was an act of bravery bordering on rashness, as he had no means of support except his pen; but, as he pointed out in *My Early Life*: "... the two books I had already written, *The Story of the Malakand Field Force* and *The River War*, had already brought in about five times as much as the Queen had paid me for three years of assiduous and sometimes dangerous work."

Scarcely six weeks after his return to England he was adopted as Conservative Candidate for Oldham, a cotton town in Lancashire, then in the throes of a by-election. In this, his first attempt to gain a seat in Parliament, he was defeated by 1,499 votes. Six weeks later negotiations between the British Government and the Boer Republics of South Africa broke down and Alfred Harmsworth, proprietor of the *Daily Mail*, telegraphed to Churchill asking him to be their correspondent in the war which was now inevitable.

Randolph Churchill's life of his father takes up the story: "Churchill immediately telegraphed to his friend Oliver Borthwick of the *Morning Post*, telling him of Harmsworth's invitation. Churchill suggested to Borthwick that he should go to South Africa for the *Morning Post*, after all his earliest backer, in return for expenses, copyright of his work and £1,000 for four months' shore to shore (£250 per month) and £200 a month thereafter. Within hours Churchill's offer was accepted and he told his mother (September 18), 'I am at their disposal'. This was probably the most lucrative contract into which any newspaper war correspondent had entered up to this time; and it served to elevate the scale of journalists' salaries in general." (RSC, Vol.1. p.451).

The first shots of the Boer War were fired on 12 October and Churchill sailed from Southampton on the *Dunottar Castle* on the 14th, arriving at Cape Town on the 31st. The story of his capture by, and escape from, the Boers is told in *London to Ladysmith* but it is worth mentioning that it was this incident which first made him famous: "The headlines of the world's press screamed the news: telegrams poured in upon him: he was hailed in Durban as a popular hero." (RSC, p.505).

On 6 January, 1900, he was given a Lieutenancy in the South African Light Horse, while still retaining his status as a war correspondent. This was all the more remarkable in view of the fact that it was on account of his activities as an officer-correspondent in the Nile campaign of 1898 that it had been laid down that the two jobs could not be embodied in a single person. "Churchill was the first and as far as is known the only individual for whom it was relaxed." (RSC, p.517).

On 4 July, 1900, he sailed for home in the same ship which had taken him out, the *Dunottar Castle*.

London to Ladysmith, as mentioned above, had been published six weeks before he returned to England and the first edition was soon sold out. In an undated letter to his brother Jack, written while on board ship, he says, "My book *London to Ladysmith* had sold when I left Cape Town 11,000 copies exclusive of American sales and as it is still going well it should bring me in a good return.... I am bringing out another book almost immediately *Ian Hamilton's March* which is a reprint of the rest of the letters plus one or two I have finished on board ship." In another letter to his brother dated 31 July, 1900, he says, "About the books, *London to Ladysmith* had not gone so well as I expected but I have sold altogether about 13,000 copies. A new edition is going out shortly with a full account of my escape in it."

When *Ian Hamilton's March* appeared on 12 October, 1900, Churchill was just short of his 26th birthday and already had four books to his name, which had all received no small measure of critical acclaim.

Tom Hartman

LONDON TO LADYSMITH

CONTENTS

MAPS AND PLANS

MAPS

PLANS

INTRODUCTORY NOTE

THIS SMALL book is mainly a personal record of my adventures and impressions during the first five months of the African War. It may also be found to give a tolerably coherent account of the operations conducted by Sir Redvers Buller for the Relief of Ladysmith. The correspondence of which it is mainly composed appeared in the columns of the *Morning Post* newspaper, and I propose, if I am not interrupted by the accidents of war, to continue the series of letters. The stir and tumult of a camp do not favour calm or sustained thought, and whatever is written herein must be regarded simply as the immediate effect produced by men powerfully moved, and scenes swiftly changing upon what I hope is a truth-seeking mind.

The fact that a man's life depends upon my discretion compels me to omit an essential part of the story of my escape from the Boers; but if the book and its author survive the war, and when the British flag is firmly planted at Bloemfontein and Pretoria, I shall hasten to fill the gap in the narrative.

WINSTON S. CHURCHILL.

March 10, 1900.

CHAPTER ONE

STEAMING SOUTH

R.M.S. *Dunottar Castle,* at sea: October 26, 1899

THE LAST cry of "Any more for the shore?" had sounded, the
last good-bye had been said, the latest pressman or photo-
grapher had scrambled ashore, and all Southampton was
cheering wildly along a mile of pier and promontory when at 6 p.m.
on October 14, the Royal Mail steamer *Dunottar Castle* left her
moorings and sailed with Sir Redvers Buller for the Cape. For a
space the decks remained crowded with the passengers who, while
the sound of many voices echoed in their ears, looked back towards
the shores, swiftly fading in the distance and the twilight, and
wondered whether, and if so when, they would come safe home
again; then everyone hurried to his cabin, arranged his luggage, and
resigned himself to the voyage.

What an odious affair is a modern sea journey! In ancient times
there were greater discomforts and perils; but they were recognised.
A man took ship prepared for the worst. Nowadays he expects the
best as a matter of course, and is, therefore, disappointed. Besides,
how slowly we travel! In the sixteenth century nobody minded
taking five months to get anywhere. But a fortnight is a large slice
out of the nineteenth century; and the child of civilisation, long
petted by Science, impatiently complains to his indulgent guardian
of all delay in travel, and petulantly calls on her to complete her
task and finally eliminate the factor of distance from human calculations. A fortnight is a long time in modern life. It is also a long
time in modern war—especially at the beginning. To be without
news for a fortnight at any time is annoying. To be without news
for a fortnight now is a torture. And this voyage lasts more than a
fortnight! At the very outset of our enterprise we are compelled to
practise Mr. Morley's policy of patience.

We left London amid rumours of all kinds. The Metropolis was shrouded in a fog of credulous uncertainty, broken only by the sinister gleam of the placarded lie or the croak of the newsman. Terrible disasters had occurred and had been contradicted; great battles were raging—unconfirmed; and beneath all this froth the tide of war was really flowing, and no man could shut his eyes to grave possibilities. Then the ship sailed, and all was silence—a heaving silence. But Madeira was scarcely four days' journey. There we should find the answers to many questions. At Madeira, however, we learned nothing, but nothing, though satisfactory, is very hard to understand. Why did they declare war if they had nothing up their sleeves? Why are they wasting time now? Such were the questions. Then we sailed again, and again silence shut down, this time, however, on a more even keel.

Speculation arises out of ignorance. Many and various are the predictions as to what will be the state of the game when we shall have come to anchor in Table Bay. Forecasts range from the capture of Pretoria by Sir George White and the confinement of President Kruger in the deepest level beneath the Johannesburg Exchange, on the one hand, to the surrender of Capetown to the Boers, the proclamation of Mr. Schreiner as King of South Africa, and a fall of two points in Rand Mines on the other. Between these wild extremes all shades of opinion are represented. Only one possibility is unanimously excluded—an inconclusive peace. There are on board officers who travelled this road eighteen years ago with Lord Roberts, and reached Capetown only to return by the next boat. But no one anticipates such a result this time.

Monotony is the characteristic of a modern voyage, and who shall describe it? The lover of realism might suggest that writing the same paragraph over and over again would enable the reader to experience its weariness, if he were truly desirous of so doing. But I hesitate to take such a course, and trust that some of these lines even once repeated may convey some inkling of the dullness of the days. Monotony of view—for we live at the centre of a complete circle of sea and sky; monotony of food—for all things taste the same on board ship; monotony of existence—for each day is but a barren repetition of the last; all fall to the lot of the passenger on great waters. It were malevolent to try to bring the realisation home to others. Yet all earthly evils have their compensations, and even monotony is not without its secret joy. For a time we drop out of the larger world, with its interests and its obligations, and become the independent citizens of a tiny State—a Utopian State where few toil and none go hungry—bounded on all sides by the sea and vassal only to the winds and waves. Here during a period which is too long while it lasts, too short when it is over, we may placidly reflect on the busy world that lies behind and the tumult that is before us. The journalists read books about South Africa; the politician—were the affair still in the domain of words—might examine the justice of the quarrel. The Headquarter Staff pore over maps or calculate the sizes of camps and entrenchments; and in the meantime the great ship lurches steadily forward on her course, carrying to the south at seventeen miles an hour schemes and intentions of war.

But let me record the incidents rather than their absence. One day the first shoal of flying fish is seen—a flight of glittering birds that, flushed by the sudden approach of the vessel, skim away over the waters and turn in the cover of a white-topped wave. On another we crossed the Equator. Neptune and his consort boarded us near the forecastle and paraded round the ship in state. Never have I seen such a draggle-tailed divinity. An important feature in the ritual which he prescribes is the shaving and ducking of all who have not passed the line before. But our attitude was strictly Erastian, and the demigod retired discomfited to the second class, where from the sounds which arose he seemed to find more punctilious votaries. On the 23rd we sighted a sail—or rather the smoke of another steamer. As the comparatively speedy *Dunvllur Custle* overtook the stranger everybody's interest was aroused. Under the scrutiny of many brand-new telescopes and field glasses—for all want to see as much of a war as possible—she developed into the *Nineveh*, hired transport carrying the Australian Lancers to the Cape. Signals were exchanged. The vessels drew together, and after an hour's steaming we passed her almost within speaking distance. The General went up to the bridge. The Lancers crowded the bulwarks and rigging of the *Nineveh* and one of them waggled a flag violently. An officer on our ship replied with a pocket-handkerchief. The Australians asked questions: "Is Sir Redvers Buller on board?" The answer "Yes" was signalled back, and immediately the Lancers gave three tremendous cheers, waving their broad-brimmed hats and gesticulating with energy while the steam siren emitted a frantic whoop of salutation. Then the speed of the larger vessel told, and we drew ahead of the transport until her continued cheers died away. She signalled again: "What won the Cesarewitch?" But the distance was now too great for us to learn whether the answer gave satisfaction or not.

We have a party of cinematographers on board, and when they found that we were going to speak the *Nineveh* they bustled about preparing their apparatus. But the cumbrous appliances took too long to set up, and, to the bitter disappointment of the artists, the chance of making a moving picture was lost for ever; and indeed it was a great pity, because the long green transport, pitching in the sea, now burying her bows in foam, now showing the red paint of her bottom, her decks crowded with the active brown figures of the soldiers, her halyards bright with signal flags, was a scene well worth recording even if it had not been the greeting given in mid-ocean to the commander of the army by the warlike contingent which the need or convenience of the Empire had drawn from the Antipodes.

South of the line the weather cools rapidly, and various theories are advanced to explain the swift change. According to some, it is due to the masses of ice at the Antarctic Pole; others contend that it is because we are further from the land. But whatever the cause may be, the fall in temperature produces a rise in spirits, and under greyer skies everyone develops activity. The consequence of this is the organisation of athletic sports. A committee is appointed. Sir Redvers Buller becomes President. A two days' meeting is arranged, and on successive afternoons the more energetic passengers race violently to and fro on the decks, belabour each other with bolsters, or tumble into unforeseen troughs of water to their huge contentment and the diversion of the rest.

Occasionally there are light gusts of controversy. It is Sunday. The parson proposes to read the service. The captain objects. He insists on the maintenance of naval supremacy. On board ship, "or at any rate on board this ship", no one but the captain reads the service. The minister, a worthy Irishman, abandons the dispute—not without regret. "Any other clergyman of the Church of England," he observes with warmth, "would have told the captain to go to Hell."

Then there is to be a fancy dress ball. Opinions are divided. On the one part it is urged that fancy dress balls are healthy and amusing. On the other, that they are exceedingly tiresome. The discussion is prolonged. In the end the objectors are overruled—still objecting. Such are the politics of the State.

Inoculation against enteric fever proceeds daily. The doctors lecture in the saloon. One injection of serum protects; a second secures the subject against attacks. Wonderful statistics are quoted in support of the experiment. Nearly everyone is convinced. The operations take place forthwith, and the next day sees haggard forms crawling about the deck in extreme discomfort and high fever. The day after, however, all have recovered and rise gloriously immune. Others, like myself, remembering that we still stand only on the threshold of pathology, remain unconvinced, resolved to trust to "health and the laws of health". But if they will invent a system of inoculation against bullet wounds I will hasten to submit myself.

Yesterday we passed a homeward-bound liner, who made great efforts to signal to us, but as she was a Union boat the captain refused to go near enough to read the flags, and we still remain ignorant of the state of the war. If the great lines of steamships to the Cape were to compete against each other, as do those of the Atlantic, by increasing their speeds, by lowering their rates, by improving the food and accommodation, no one would complain, but it is difficult to see how the public can be the gainers by the silly antagonism I have described. However, the end is drawing very near, and since we have had a safe and prosperous journey criticism may well waive the opportunity. Yet there are few among the travellers who will not experience a keen feeling of relief in exchanging the pettiness, the monotony, and the isolation of the voyage for the activity of great enterprise and the interest of real affairs: a relief which may, perhaps, be shared by the reader of these letters. Yet if he has found the account of a dull voyage dull, he should not complain; for is not that successful realism?

October 29

News at last! This morning we sighted a sail—a large homeward-bound steamer, spreading her canvas to catch the trades, and with who should say what tidings on board. We crowded the decks, and from every point of view telescopes, field glasses, and cameras were directed towards the stranger. She passed us at scarcely two hundred yards, and as she did so her crew and company, giving three hearty cheers, displayed a long black board, on which was written in white paint: "Boers defeated; three battles; Penn Symons killed." There was a little gasp of excitement. Everyone stepped back from the bulwarks. Those who had not seen ran eagerly up to ask what had happened. A dozen groups were formed, a hum of conversation arose, and meanwhile the vessels separated— for the pace of each was swift—and in a few moments the home- ward bound lay far in our wake.

What does it mean—this scrap of intelligence which tells so much and leaves so much untold? Tomorrow night we shall know all. This at least is certain: there has been fierce fighting in Natal, and, under Heaven, we have held our own: perhaps more. "Boers defeated." Let us thank God for that. The brave garrisons have repelled the invaders. The luck has turned at last. The crisis is over, and the army now on the seas may move with measured strides to effect a final settlement that is both wise and just. In that short message eighteen years of heartburnings are healed. The abandoned colonist, the shamed soldier, the "cowardly Englishman", the white flag, the "How about Majuba?"—all gone for ever. At last—"the Boers defeated". Hurrah! Hurrah! Hurrah!

So Sir Penn Symons is killed! Well, no one would have laid down his life more gladly in such a cause. Twenty years ago the merest chance saved him from the massacre at Isandhlwana, and Death promoted him in an afternoon from subaltern to senior captain. Thenceforward his rise was rapid. He commanded the First Division of the Tirah Expeditionary Force among the mountains with prudent skill. His brigades had no misfortunes: his rearguards came safely into camp. In the spring of 1898, when the army lay around Fort Jumrood, looking forward to a fresh campaign, I used often to meet him. Everyone talked of Symons, of his energy, of his jokes, of his enthusiasm. It was Symons who had built a racecourse on the stony plain; who had organised the Jumrood Spring Meeting; who won the principal event himself, to the delight of the private soldiers, with whom he was intensely popular; who, moreover, was to be first and foremost if the war with the tribes broke out again; and who was entrusted with much of the negotiations with their *jirgas*. Dinner with Symons in the mud tower of Jumrood Fort was an experience. The memory of many tales of sport and war remains. At the end the General would drink the old Peninsular toasts: "Our Men", "Our Women", "Our Religion", "Our Swords", "Ourselves", "Sweethearts and Wives", and "Absent Friends"—one for every night in the week. The night when I dined the toast was "Our Men". May the State in her necessities find others like him!

CHAPTER TWO

THE STATE OF THE GAME

Capetown: November 1, 1899

THE LONG-DRAWN voyage came to an end at last. On the afternoon of October 30 we sighted land, and looking westward I perceived what looked like a dark wave of water breaking the smooth rim of the horizon. A short time developed the wave into the rocks and slopes of Robben Island—a barren spot inhabited by lepers, poisonous serpents, and dogs undergoing quarantine. Then with the darkness we entered Table Bay, and, steaming slowly, reached the anchorage at ten o'clock. Another hour of waiting followed until the tugboat obeyed the signal; but at last she ran alongside, and there stepped on board a Man Who Knew. Others with despatches pushed roughly through the crowd of soldiers, officers, passengers, and war correspondents to the General's cabin. We caught the Man Who Knew, however, and, setting him half way up the ladder to the hurricane deck, required him forthwith to tell us of the war. Doubtless you have been well informed of all, or at any rate of much, that has passed. The man told his story quickly, with an odd quiver of excitement in his voice, and the audience—perhaps we were 300—listened breathless. Then for the first time we heard of Elandslaagte, of Glencoe, of Rietfontein, a tale of stubborn, well-fought fights with honour for both sides, triumph for neither. "Tell us about the losses—who are killed and wounded?" we asked this wonderful man. I think he was a passage agent or something like that.

So he told us—and among the group of officers gathered above him on the hurricane deck I saw now one, now another, turn away, and hurry out of the throng. A gentleman I had met on the voyage—Captain Weldon—asked questions. "Do you know any names of killed in the Leicesters?" The man reflected. He could not be sure:

he thought there was an officer named Weldon killed—oh, yes! he
remembered there were two Weldons—one killed, one wounded, but
he did not know which was in the Leicesters. "Tell us about
Mafeking," said someone else. Then we heard about Mafeking—the
armoured trains, the bombardment, the sorties, the dynamite
wagons—all, in fact, that is yet known of what may become an
historic defence. "And how many Boers are killed?" cried a private
soldier from the back. The man hesitated, but the desire to please
was strong within him. "More than two thousand," he said, and a
fierce shout of joy answered him. The crowd of brown uniforms
under the electric clusters broke up into loud-voiced groups; some
hastened to search for newspapers, some to repeat what they had
heard to others; only a few leaned against the bulwarks and looked
long and silently towards the land, where the lights of Capetown,
its streets, its quays, and its houses gleamed from the night like
diamonds on black velvet.

It is a long casualty list of officers—of the best officers in the
world. The brave and accomplished General of Glencoe; Colonel
Chisholme, who brought the 9th Lancers out of action in Afghanis-
tan; Sherston, who managed the Indian Polo Association; Haldane,
Sir William Lockhart's brilliant aide-de-camp; Barnes, adjutant of
the 4th Hussars, who played back of our team and went with me
to Cuba; Brooke, who had tempted fortune more often than anyone
else in the last four years—Chitral, Matabeleland, Samana, Tirah,
Atbara, and Omdurman—and fifty others who are only names to
me, but are dear and precious to many, all lying under the stony
soil or filling the hospitals at Pietermaritzburg and Durban. Two
thousand Boers killed! I wish I could believe there were.

Next morning Sir Redvers Buller landed in state. Sir F. Forestier-
Walker and his staff came to meet him. The ship was decked out in
bunting from end to end. A guard of honour of the Duke of Edin-
burgh's Volunteers lined the quay; a mounted escort attended the
carriage; an enormous crowd gathered outside the docks. At nine
o'clock precisely the General stepped on to the gangway. The crew
and stokers of the *Dunottar Castle* gave three hearty cheers; the
cinematograph buzzed loudly; forty cameras clicked; the guard
presented arms, and the harbour batteries thundered the salute.
Then the carriage drove briskly off into the town through streets
bright with waving flags and black with cheering people. So Sir
Redvers Buller came back again to South Africa, the land where his

first military reputation was made, where he won his Victoria Cross, and land which—let us pray—he will leave having successfully discharged the heavy task confided to him by the Imperial Government.

Now, what is the situation which confronts the General and the army? I will adventure an explanation, though the picture of war moves very swiftly. In their dealing with the military republics which had become so formidable a power throughout the Cape, the Ministers who were responsible for the security of our South African possessions were compelled to reckon with two volumes of public opinion—British and colonial. The colonial opinion was at its best (from our point of view) about three months ago. But the British opinion was still unformed. The delays and diplomatic disputes which have gradually roused the nation to a sense of its responsibilities and perils, and which were absolutely necessary if we were to embark on the struggle united, have had an opposite effect out here. The attempts to satisfy the conscientious public by giving the republics every possible opportunity to accept our terms and the delays in the despatch of troops which were an expensive tribute to the argument "Do not seek peace with a sword", have been misinterpreted in South Africa. The situation in the Cape Colony has become much graver. We have always been told of the wonderful loyalty of the Dutch. It is possible that had war broken out three months ago that loyalty would have been demonstrated for all time. War after three months of hesitation—for such it was considered—has proved too severe a test, and it is no exaggeration to say that a considerable part of the Colony trembles on the verge of rebellion. On such a state of public opinion the effect of any important military reverse would be lamentable.

Nor is the military position such as to exclude anxiety. The swift flame of war ran in a few days around the whole circle of the republican frontiers. Far away to the north there was a skirmish at Tuli. On the west Khama's territories are threatened with invasion. Mafeking is surrounded, isolated, and manfully defending itself against continual attack. Vryburg has been treacherously surrendered by its rebel inhabitants to the enemy. Kimberley offers a serene front to a hesitating attack, and even retaliates with armoured trains and other enterprises. The southern frontier is armed, and menaced, and the expectation of collision is strong. But it is on the eastern side that the Boers have concentrated their greatest energies. They have gone Nap on Natal. The configuration of the country favours an invader. The reader has scarcely to look at the map, with which he is already familiar, to realise how strategically powerful the Boer position was and is. The long tongue of plain running up into the mountains could be entered from both sides. The communications of the advanced garrisons would be assailed: their retreat imperilled. The Boers seemed bound to clear northern Natal of the troops. If, on the other hand, they were, or should now be, suddenly driven back on their own country, they have only to retire up the tongue of plain, with their exposed front narrowing every mile between the mountains, and await their pursuers on the almost inexpugnable position of Laing's Nek. Appreciating all this, their leaders have wisely resolved to put forth their main strength against the force in Natal, and by crushing it to rouse their sympathisers within the Cape Colony. Should they succeed either on this front or on any other to a serious extent, though the disaffection would not take a very violent form, for all the bravoes have already joined the enemy, the general insecurity would demand the employment of an army corps in addition to that already on the seas.

A democratic Government cannot go to war unless the country is behind it, and until it has general support must not place itself in a position whence, without fighting, there is no retreat. The difficulty of rallying public opinion in the face of the efforts of Mr. Morley, Mr. Courtney, Sir William Harcourt, and others has caused a most dangerous delay in the despatch of reinforcements. War has been aggravated by the Peace Party; and thus these humanitarian gentlemen are personally—for they occupy no official position—responsible for the great loss of life. They will find their several consolations: Mr. Morley will rejoice that he has faithfully pursued Mr. Gladstone's policy in South Africa; Mr. Courtney that he has been consistent at all costs; Sir William Harcourt that he has hampered the Government. But for those who lose their sons and brothers in a quarrel thus unnecessarily extended, there will only remain vain regrets, and to the eyewitness only a bitter anger.

For the last three months the Imperial Government has been in the unpleasant position of watching its adversaries grow continually stronger without being able to make adequate counter-preparations.

But when once this initial disability has been stated, it must also be admitted that the course of the military operations has been—apart from their success or failure—very lucky. The Boers had the advantage of drawing first blood, and the destruction of the armoured train near Mafeking was magnified by them, as by the sensational Press in Great Britain, into a serious disaster. A very bad effect was produced in the undecided districts—it is perhaps wiser not to specify them at this moment. But a few days later another armoured train ran out from Kimberley, and its Maxim guns killed five Boers without any loss to the troops. The magnifying process was also applied to this incident with equal though opposite results. Then came the news of the battle of Glencoe. The first accounts, which were very properly controlled—for we are at war with the pen as well as the sword—told only of the bravery of the troops, of the storming of the Boer position, and of the capture of prisoners. That the troops had suffered the heavier loss, that the Boers had retired to further positions in rear of the first, drawing their artillery with them, and that General Yule had retreated by forced marches to Ladysmith after the victory—for tactical victory it undoubtedly was—leaked into Cape Colony very gradually; nor was it until a week later that it was known that the wounded had been left behind, and that the camp with all stores and baggage, except ammunition, had fallen into the enemy's hands. Before that happened the news of Elandslaagte had arrived, and this brilliant action, which reflects no less credit on Generals French and Hamilton who fought it than on Sir George White who ordered it, dazzled all eyes, so that the sequel to Glencoe was unnoticed, or at any rate produced little effect on public opinion.

The Natal Field Force is now concentrated at Ladysmith, and confronts in daily opposition the bulk of the Boer army. Though the numbers of the enemy are superior and their courage claims the respect of their professional antagonists, it is difficult to believe that any serious reverse can take place in that quarter, and meanwhile many thousand soldiers are on the seas. But the fact is now abundantly plain to those who are acquainted with the local conditions and with the Boer character, that a fierce, certainly bloody, possibly prolonged struggle lies before the army of South Africa. The telegrams, however, which we receive from Great Britain of the national feeling, of the by-election, of Lord Rosebery's speech, are full of encouragement and confidence. "At last," says the British colonist, as he shoulders his rifle and marches out to fight, no less bravely than any soldier (witness the casualty lists), for the ties which bind South Africa to the Empire—"at last they have made up their minds at home."

CHAPTER THREE

ALONG THE SOUTHERN FRONTIER

East London: November 5, 1899

WE HAVE left Headquarters busy with matters that as yet concern no one but themselves in the Mount Nelson Hotel at Capetown—a most excellent and well-appointed establishment, which may be thoroughly appreciated after a sea voyage, and which, since many of the leading Uitlanders have taken up their abode there during the war, is nicknamed "The Helot's Rest". Last night I started by rail for East London, whence a small ship carries the weekly English mail to Natal, and so by this circuitous route I hope to reach Ladysmith on Sunday morning. We have thus gained three days on our friends who proceed by the *Dunottar Castle,* and who were mightily concerned when they heard —too late to follow—of our intentions. But though it is true in this case that the longest way round is the shortest way, there were possibilities of our journey being interrupted, because the line from De Aar Junction to Naauwpoort runs parallel to the southern frontier of the Free State, and though hostile enterprises have not yet been attempted against this section of the railways they must always be expected.

Railway travelling in South Africa is more expensive but just as comfortable as in India. Lying-down accommodation is provided for all, and meals can be obtained at convenient stopping places. The train, which is built on the corridor system, runs smoothly over the rails—so smoothly, indeed, that I found no difficulty in writing. The sun is warm, and the air keen and delicious. But the scenery would depress the most buoyant spirits. We climbed up the mountains during the night, and with the daylight the train was in the middle of the Great Karroo. Wherefore was this miserable land of stone and scrub created? Huge mounds of crumbling rock, fashioned by the rains into the most curious and unexpected shapes, rise from the gloomy desert of the plain. Yet, though the Karroo looks a hopeless wilderness, flocks of sheep at distant intervals—one sheep requires six hundred acres of this scrappy pasture for nourishment—manage to subsist; and in consequence, now and again the traveller sees some far-off farm.

We look about eagerly for signs of war. Little is as yet to be seen, and the Karroo remains unsympathetic. But all along the southern frontier of the Free State the expectation of early collision grows. The first sign after leaving Capetown is the Proclamation against treason published by Sir Alfred Milner. The notice-boards of the railway stations are freely placarded with the full text in English and Dutch, beginning with "Whereas a state of war exists between the Government of her Majesty and the Governments of the South African Republic and of the Orange Free State . . ." continuing to enjoin good and loyal behaviour on all, detailing the pains and penalties for disobedience, and ending with "God Save the Queen". Both races have recorded their opinions on their respective versions: the British by underlining the penalties, the Dutch by crossing out the first word of "God Save the Queen". It is signed "A. Milner", and below, in bitter irony, "W. P. Schreiner".

Beyond Matjesfontein every bridge, and even every culvert, is watched by a Kaffir with a flag, so that the train runs no risk of coming on unexpected demolitions. On the road to De Aar we passed the second half of the Brigade Division of Artillery, which sailed so long ago from the Mersey in the notorious transports *Zibengla* and *Zayathla*. The gunners were hurrying to the front in three long trains, each taking half a battery complete with guns, horses, and men. All were light-hearted and confident, as soldiers going off to the wars always are, and in this case their satisfaction at being on land after five weeks of uncomfortable voyage in antiquated ships was easily to be understood. But this is no time for reproaches.

At Beaufort West grave news awaited the mail, and we learned of the capitulation of twelve hundred soldiers near Ladysmith. It is generally believed that this will precipitate a rising of the Dutch throughout this part of the colony and an invasion by the commandos now gathered along the Orange River. The Dutch farmers talk loudly and confidently of "our victories", meaning those of the Boers, and the racial feeling runs high. But the British colonists

have an implicit faith—marvellous when the past is remembered—
in the resolve of the Imperial Government and of the nation never
to abandon them again.

At De Aar the stage of our journey which may be said to have
been uncertain began. Armoured trains patrol the line; small parties
of armed police guard the bridges; infantry and artillery detachments occupy the towns. De Aar, Colesberg, and Stormberg are
garrisoned as strongly as the present limited means allow, and all
the forces, regulars and volunteers alike, are full of enthusiasm.
But, on the other hand, the reports of Boer movements seem to
indicate that a hostile advance is imminent. The Colesberg bridge
across the Orange River has been seized by the enemy, the line
between Bethulie and Colesberg has just been cut, and each train
from De Aar to Stormberg is expected to be the last to pass un-
assailed. We, however, slept peacefully through the night, and,
passing Colesberg safely, arrived at Stormberg, beyond which all is
again secure.

Stormberg Junction stands at the southern end of a wide expanse
of rolling grass country, and though the numerous rocky hills, or
kopjes as they are called, which rise inconveniently on all sides,
make its defence by a small force difficult, a large force occupying an
extended position would be secure. Here we found the confirmation
of many rumours. The news of a Boer advance on Burghersdorp,
twenty-five miles away, is, it seems, well founded, and when our
train arrived the evacuation of Stormberg by its garrison, of a half-
battalion of the Berkshire Regiment, 350 men of the Naval Brigade,
a company of mounted infantry, and a few guns, was busily proceeding.

The sailors were already in their train, and only prevented from
starting by the want of an engine. The infantry and artillery were
to start in a few hours. It is rather an unsatisfactory business,
though the arrival of more powerful forces will soon restore the
situation. Stormberg is itself an important railway junction. For
more than a week the troops have been working night and day to
put it in a state of defence. Little redoubts have been built on the
kopjes, entrenchments have been dug, and the few houses near the
station are already strongly fortified. I was shown one of these by
the young officer in charge. The approaches were cleared of everything except wire fences and entanglements; the massive walls were
loopholed, the windows barricaded with sandbags, and the rooms

inside broken one into the other for convenience in moving about.

Its garrison of twenty-five men and its youthful commander surveyed the work with pride. They had laid in stores of all kinds for ten days, and none doubted that Fort Chabrol, as they called it, would stand a gallant siege. Then suddenly had come the message to evacuate and retreat. So it was with the others. The train with the naval detachment and its guns steamed off, and we gave it a feeble cheer. Another train awaited the Berkshires. The mounted infantry were already on the march. "Mayn't we even blow up this lot?" said a soldier, pointing to the house he had helped to fortify. But there was no such order, only this one which seemed to pervade the air: "The enemy are coming. Retreat—retreat—retreat!" The stationmaster—one of the best types of Englishmen to be found on a long journey—was calm and cheerful.

"No more traffic north of this," he said. "Yours was the last train through from De Aar. I shall send away all my men by the special tonight. And that's the end as far as Stormberg goes."

"And you?"

"Oh, I shall stay. I have lived here for twelve years, and am well known. Perhaps I may be able to protect the company's property."

While we waited the armoured train returned from patrolling—an engine between two carriages cloaked from end to end with thick plates and slabs of blue-grey iron. It had seen nothing of the advancing Boers, but, like us and like the troops, it had to retire southwards. There were fifty Uitlanders from Johannesburg on the platform. They had been employed entrenching; now they were bundled back again towards East London.

So we left Stormberg in much anger and some humiliation, and jolted away towards the open sea, where British supremacy is not yet contested by the Boer. At Molteno we picked up a hundred volunteers—fine-looking fellows all eager to encounter the enemy, but much surprised at the turn events had taken. They, too, were ordered to fall back. The Boers were advancing, and to despondent minds even the rattle of the train seemed to urge "Retreat, retreat, retreat".

I do not desire to invest this wise and prudent though discouraging move with more than its proper importance. Anything is better than to leave small garrisons to be overwhelmed. Until the Army

Corps comes the situation will continue to be unsatisfactory, and the ground to be recovered afterwards will increase in extent. But with the arrival of powerful and well-equipped forces the tide of war will surely turn.

CHAPTER FOUR

IN NATAL

Estcourt: November 6, 1899

THE READER may remember that we started post haste from Capetown, and, having the good fortune to pass along the southern frontier from De Aar to Stormberg by the last train before the interruption of traffic, had every hope of reaching Ladysmith while its investment was incomplete. I had looked forward to writing an account of our voyage from East London to Durban while on board the vessel; but the weather was so tempestuous, and the little steamer of scarcely 100 tons burthen so buffeted by the waves, that I lay prostrate in all the anguish of sea-sickness, and had no thought for anything else. Moreover, we were delayed some twenty hours by contrary winds; nor was it until we had passed St. John's that the gale, as if repenting, veered suddenly to the south-west and added as much to our speed as it had formerly delayed us. With the change of the wind the violence of the waves to some degree abated, and, though unable to then record them on paper, I had an opportunity of gaining some impressions of the general aspect of the coasts of Pondoland and Natal. These beautiful countries stretch down to the ocean in smooth slopes of the richest verdure, broken only at intervals by lofty bluffs crowned with forests. The many rivulets to which the pasture owes its life and the land its richness glide to the shore through deep-set creeks and chines, or plunge over the cliffs in cascades which the strong winds scatter into clouds of spray.

These are regions of possibility, and as we drove along before our now friendly wind I could not but speculate on the future. Here are wide tracts of fertile soil watered by abundant rains. The temperate sun warms the life within the soil. The cooling breeze refreshes the inhabitant. The delicious climate stimulates the vigour of the

European. The highway of the sea awaits the produce of his labour. All Nature smiles, and here at last is a land where white men may rule and prosper. As yet only the indolent Kaffir enjoys its bounty, and, according to the antiquated philosophy of Liberalism, it is to such that it should for ever belong. But while Englishmen choke and fester in crowded cities, while thousands of babies are born every month who are never to have a fair chance in life, there will be those who will dream another dream of a brave system of State-aided—almost State-compelled—emigration, a scheme of old age pensions that shall anticipate old age, and by preventing paupers terminate itself; a system that shall remove the excess of the old land to provide the deficiency of the new, and shall offer even to the most unfortunate citizen of the Empire fresh air and open opportunity. And as I pondered on all these things, the face of the country seemed changed. Thriving ports and townships rose up along the shore, and, upon the hillsides, inland towers, spires, and tall chimneys attested the wealth and industry of men. Here in front of us was New Brighton; the long shelving ledge of rock was a sea-wall already made, rows of stately buildings covered the grassy slopes; the shipping of many nations lay in the roadstead; above the whole scene waved The Flag, and in the foreground on the sandy beach the great-grandchildren of the crossing-sweeper and the sandwich-man sported by the waves that beat by the Southern Pole, or sang aloud for joy in the beauty of their home and the pride of their race. And then with a lurch—for the motion was still considerable—I came back from the land of dreams to reality and the hideous fact that Natal is invaded and assailed by the Boer.

The little steamer reached Durban safely at midnight on November 4, and we passed an impatient six hours in a sleeping town waiting for daylight and news. Both came in their turn. The sun rose, and we learned that Ladysmith was cut off. Still, "As far as you can as quickly as you can" must be the motto of the war correspondent, and seven o'clock found us speeding inland in the extra coach of a special train carrying the mails. The hours I passed in Durban were not without occupation. The hospital ship *Sumatra* lay close to our moorings, and as soon as it was light I visited her to look for friends, and found, alas! several in a sorry plight. All seemed to be as well as the tenderest care and the most lavish expenditure of money could make them. All told much the same tale—the pluck and spirit of the troops, the stubborn unpretentious valour of the Boer, the searching musketry. Everyone predicted a prolonged struggle.

"All these colonials tell you", said an officer severely wounded at Elandslaagte, "that the Boers only want one good thrashing to satisfy them. Don't you believe it. They mean going through with this to the end. What about our Government?"

And the answer that all were united at home, and that Boer constancy would be met with equal perseverance and greater resources, lighted the pain-drawn features with a hopeful smile.

"Well, I never felt quite safe with those politicians. I can't get about for two months" (he was shot through the thigh), "but I hope to be in at the death. It's our blood against theirs."

Pietermaritzburg is sixty miles from Durban, but as the railway zigzags up and down hill and contorts itself into curves that would horrify the domestic engineer, the journey occupies four hours. The town looks more like Ootacamund than any place I have seen. To those who do not know the delightful hill station of Southern India let me explain that Pietermaritzburg stands in a basin of smooth rolling downs, broken frequently by forests of fir and blue gum trees. It is a sleepy, dead-alive place. Even the fact that Colonel Knowle, the military engineer, was busily putting it into a state of defence, digging up its hills, piercing its walls, and encircling it with wire obstructions did not break its apathy. The *Times of Natal* struggled to rouse excitement, and placarded its office with the latest telegrams from the front, some of which had reached Pietermaritzburg *via* London. But the composure of the civil population is a useful factor in war, and I wish it were within the power of my poor pen to bring home to the people of England how excellently the colonists of Natal have deserved of the State.

There are several points to be remembered in this connection. First, the colonists have had many dealings with the Boers. They knew their strength, they feared their animosity. But they have never for one moment lost sight of their obligations as a British colony. Their loyalty has been splendid. From the very beginning they warned the Imperial Government that their territories would be invaded. Throughout the course of the long negotiations they knew that if war should come, on them would fall the first fury of the storm. Nevertheless, they courageously supported and acclaimed the action of the Ministry. Now at last there is war. It means a good deal to all of us, but more than to any it comes home

to the Natalian. He is invaded; his cattle have been seized by the
Boer; his towns are shelled or captured; the most powerful force on
which he relies for protection is isolated in Ladysmith; his capital
is being loopholed and entrenched; Newcastle has been abandoned,
Colenso has fallen, Estcourt is threatened; the possibility that the
whole province will be overrun stares him in the face. From the
beginning he asked for protection. From the beginning he was
promised complete protection; but scarcely a word of complaint is
heard. The townsfolk are calm and orderly, the Press dignified and
sober. The men capable of bearing arms have responded nobly.
Boys of sixteen march with men of fifty to war—to no light easy
war. All the volunteers are in the field bearing their full share of the
fighting like men. Nor are the Outlanders backward in their own
quarrel. The Imperial Light Infantry is eagerly filled. The Imperial
Light Horse can find no more vacancies, not even for those who will
serve without pay.

I talked with a wounded Gordon Highlander—one of those who
dashed across the famous causeway of Dargai and breasted the still
more glorious slope of Elandslaagte.

"We had the Imperial Horse with us," he said. "They're the best
I've ever seen."

The casualty lists tell the same tale. To storm the hill the regiment dismounted less than two hundred men. They reached the top
unchecked, their Colonel, their Adjutant, Lieutenant Barnes, seven
other officers, and upwards of sixty men killed or wounded—nearly
30 per cent. Many of this corps came from Johannesburg. After this
who will dare call Outlanders cowards? Not that it will ever matter
again.

Viewed in quieter days, the patient, trustful attitude of this
colony of Natal will impress the historian. The devotion of its people
to their Sovereign and to their motherland should endear them to
all good Englishmen, and win them general respect and sympathy;
and full indemnity to all individual colonists who have suffered loss
must stand as an Imperial debt of honour.

CHAPTER FIVE

A CRUISE IN THE ARMOURED TRAIN

Estcourt: November 9, 1899

HOW MANY more letters shall I write you from an unsatisfactory address? Sir George White's Headquarters are scarcely forty miles away, but between them and Estcourt stretches the hostile army. Whether it may be possible or wise to try to pass the lines of investment is a question which I cannot yet decide; and meanwhile I wait here at the nearest post collecting such information as dribbles through native channels, and hoping that early events may clear the road. To wait is often weary work— but even at this exciting time I come to a standstill at length with a distinct feeling of relief. The last month has been passed in continual travel. The fading, confused faces at Waterloo as the train swept along the platform; the cheering crowds at Southampton; the rolling decks of the *Dunottar Castle*; the suspense, the excitement of first news; a brief day's scurry at Capetown; the journey to East London by the last train to pass along the frontier; the tumultuous voyage in the *Umzimvubu* amid so great a gale that but for the Royal Mail the skipper would have put back to port; on without a check to Pietermaritzburg, and thence, since the need seemed urgent and the traffic slow, by special train here—all moving, restless pictures—and here at last—a pause.

Let us review the situation. On Wednesday last, on November 1, the Boer lines of investment drew round Ladysmith. On Thursday the last train passed down the railway under the fire of artillery. That night the line was cut about four miles north of Colenso. Telegraphic communication also ceased. On Friday Colenso was itself attacked. A heavy gun came into action from the hills which dominate the town, and the slender garrison of infantry volunteers and naval brigade evacuated in a hurry, and, covered to some extent by the armoured train, fell back on Estcourt.

Estcourt is a South African town—that is to say, it is a collection of about three hundred detached stone or corrugated iron houses, nearly all one-storied, arranged along two broad streets—for space is plentiful—or straggling away towards the country. The little place lies in a cup of the hills, which rise in green undulations on all sides. For this reason it will be a very difficult place to defend if the invaders should come upon it. It is, besides, of mean and insignificant aspect; but, like all these towns in Natal, it is the centre of a large agricultural district, at once the market and the storehouse of dozens of prosperous farms scattered about the country, and consequently it possesses more importance than the passing stranger would imagine. Indeed, it was a surprise to find on entering the shops how great a variety and quantity of goods these unpretentious shanties contained.

Estcourt now calls itself "The Front". There is another front forty miles away, but that is ringed about by the enemy, and since we live in expectation of attack, with no one but the Boers beyond the outpost line, Estcourt considers that its claim is just. Colonel Wolfe Murray, the officer who commands the lines of communication of the Natal Field Force, hastened up as soon as the news of the attack on Colenso was received to make preparation to check the enemy's advance.

The force at his disposal is not, however, large—two British battalions—the Dublin Fusiliers, who fought at Glencoe, and were hurried out of Ladysmith to strengthen the communications when it became evident that a blockade impended, and the Border Regiment from Malta, a squadron of the Imperial Light Horse, 300 Natal Volunteers with 25 cyclists, and a volunteer battery of nine-pounder guns—perhaps 2,000 men in all. With so few it would be quite impossible to hold the long line of hills necessary for the protection of the town, but a position has been selected and fortified, where the troops can maintain themselves—at any rate for several days. But the confidence of the military authorities in the strength of Estcourt may be gauged by the frantic efforts they are making to strengthen Pietermaritzburg, seventy-six miles, and even Durban, one hundred and thirty miles further back, by earthworks and naval guns. "The Boers invade Natal!" exclaims Mr. Labouchere in the number of *Truth* current out here. "As likely that the Chinese army should invade London." But he is not the only false prophet.

It seems, however, certain that a considerable force will be moved here soon to restore the situation and to relieve Ladysmith. Meanwhile we wait, not without anxiety or impatience. The Imperial Horse, a few mounted infantry, the volunteer cyclists, and the armoured train, patrol daily towards Colenso and the north, always expecting to see the approaching Boer commandos. Yesterday I travelled with the armoured train. This armoured train is a very puny specimen, having neither gun nor Maxims, with no roof to its trucks and no shutters to its loopholes, and being in every way inferior to the powerful machines I saw working along the southern frontier. Nevertheless it is a useful means of reconnaissance, nor is a journey in it devoid of interest. An armoured train! The very name sounds strange; a locomotive disguised as a knight-errant; the agent of civilisation in the habiliments of chivalry. Mr. Morley attired as Sir Lancelot would seem scarcely more incongruous. The possibilities of attack added to the keenness of the experience. We started at one o'clock. A company of the Dublin Fusiliers formed the garrison. Half were in the car in front of the engine, half in that behind. Three empty trucks, with a plate-laying gang and spare rails to mend the line, followed. The country between Estcourt and Colenso is open, undulating, and grassy. The stations, which occur every four or five miles, are hamlets consisting of half a dozen corrugated iron houses, and perhaps a score of blue gum trees. These little specks of habitation are almost the only marked feature of the landscape, which on all sides spreads in pleasant but monotonous slopes of green. The train maintained a good speed; and, though it stopped repeatedly to question Kaffirs or country folk, and to communicate with the cyclists and other patrols who were scouring the country on the flanks, reached Chieveley, five miles from Colenso, by about three o'clock; and from here the Ladysmith balloon, a brown speck floating above and beyond the distant hills, was plainly visible.

Beyond Chieveley it was necessary to observe more caution. The speed was reduced—the engine walked warily. The railway officials scanned the track, and often before a culvert or bridge was traversed we disembarked and examined it from the ground. At other times long halts were made while the officers swept the horizon and the distant hills with field glasses and telescopes. But the country was clear and the line undamaged, and we continued our slow advance. Presently Colenso came into view—a hundred tin-pot houses under the high hills to the northward. We inspected it deliberately. On a mound beyond the village rose the outline of the sandbag fort constructed by the Naval Brigade. The flagstaff, without the flag, still stood up boldly. But, so far as we could tell, the whole place was deserted.

There followed a discussion. Perhaps the Boers were lying in wait for the armoured train; perhaps they had trained a gun on some telegraph post, and would fire the moment the engine passed it; or perhaps, again, they were even now breaking the line behind us. Some Kaffirs approached respectfully, saluting. A Natal Volunteer —one of the cyclists—came forward to interrogate. He was an intelligent little man, with a Martini-Metford rifle, a large pair of field glasses, a dainty pair of grey skin cycling shoes, and a slouch hat. He questioned the natives, and reported their answers. The Kaffirs said that the Dutchmen were assuredly in the neighbourhood. They had been seen only that morning. "How many?" The reply was vague—twelve, or seventeen, or one thousand; also they had a gun—or five guns—mounted in the old fort, or on the platform of the station, or on the hill behind the town. At daylight they had shelled Colenso. "But why," we asked, "should they shell Colenso?" Evidently to make sure of the range of some telegraph post. "It only takes one shell to do the trick with the engine," said the captain who commanded. "Got to hit us first, though," he added. "Well, let's get a little bit nearer."

The electric bell rang three times, and we crept forward—halted —looked around, forward again—halt again—another look round; and so, yard by yard, we approached Colenso. Half a mile away we stopped finally. The officer, taking a sergeant with him, went on towards the village on foot. I followed. We soon reached the trenches that had been made by the British troops before they evacuated the place. "Awful rot giving this place up," said the officer. "These lines took us a week to dig." From here Colenso lay exposed about two hundred yards away—a silent, desolate village. The streets were littered with the belongings of the inhabitants. Two or three houses had been burned. A dead horse lay in the road, his four legs sticking stiffly up in the air, his belly swollen. The whole place had evidently been ransacked and plundered by the Boers and the Kaffirs. A few natives loitered near the far end of the street, and one, alarmed at the aspect of the train, waved a white rag on a stick steadily to and fro. But no Dutchmen were to be seen. We made our way back to the railway line and struck it at the spot where it was cut. Two lengths of rails had been lifted up, and, with the sleepers attached to them, flung over the embankment. The broken telegraph wires trailed untidily on the ground. Several of the posts were twisted. But the bridge across the Tugela was uninjured, and the damage to the lines was such as could be easily repaired. The Boers realise the advantage of the railway. At this moment, with their trains all labelled "To Durban", they are drawing supplies along it from Pretoria to within six miles of Ladysmith. They had resolved to use it in their further advance, and their confidence in the ultimate issue is shown by the care with which they avoid seriously damaging the permanent way. We had learned all that there was to learn—where the line was broken, that the village was deserted, that the bridge was safe, and we made haste to rejoin the train. Then the engine was reversed, and we withdrew out of range of the hills beyond Colenso at full speed—and some said that the Boers did not fire because they hoped to draw us nearer, and others that there were no Boers within ten miles.

On the way back I talked with the volunteer. He was friendly and communicative. "Durban Light Infantry," he said; "that's my corps. I'm a builder myself by trade—nine men under me. But I had to send them all away when I was called out. I don't know how I'm going on when I get back after it's over. Oh, I'm glad to come. I wish I was in Ladysmith. You see these Dutchmen have come quite far enough into our country. The Imperial Government promised us protection. You've seen what protection Colenso got; Dundee and Newcastle, just the same; I don't doubt they've tried their best, and I don't blame them; but we want help here badly. I don't hold with a man crying out for help unless he makes a start himself, so I came out. I'm a cyclist. I've got eight medals at home for cycling."

"How will you like a new one—with the Queen's head on it?"

His eye brightened.

"Ah," he said, "I should treasure that more than all the other eight—even more than the twenty-mile championship one."

So we rattled back to Estcourt through the twilight; and the long car, crowded with brown-clad soldiers who sprawled smoking on the floor or lounged against the sides, the rows of loopholes along the iron walls, the black smoke of the engine bulging overhead, the sense of headlong motion, and the atmosphere of war made the volunteer seem perhaps more than he was; and I thought him a true and valiant man, who had come forward in time of trouble quietly and soberly to bear his part in warfare, and who was ready, if necessary, to surrender his humble life in honourably sustaining the quarrel of the State. Nor do I care to correct the impression now.

CHAPTER SIX

DISTANT GUNS

Estcourt: November 10, 1899

WHEN I awoke yesterday morning there was a strange tremor in the air. A gang of platelayers and navvies were making a new siding by the station, and sounds of hammering also came from the engine shed. But this tremor made itself felt above these and all the other noises of a waking camp, a silent thudding, a vibration which scarcely seemed to constitute what is called sound, yet which left an intense impression on the ear. I went outside the tent to listen. Morning had just broken, and the air was still and clear. What little wind there was came from the northwards, from the direction of Ladysmith, and I knew that it carried to Estcourt the sound of distant cannon. When once the sounds had been localised it was possible to examine them more carefully. There were two kinds of reports: one almost a boom, the explosion evidently of some very heavy piece of ordnance; the other only a penetrating whisper, that of ordinary field guns. A heavy cannonade was proceeding. The smaller pieces fired at brief intervals, sometimes three or four shots followed in quick succession. Every few minutes the heavier gun or guns intervened. What was happening? We could only try to guess, nor do we yet know whether our guesses were right. It seems to me, however, that Sir George White must have made an attack at dawn on some persecuting Boer battery, and so brought on a general action.

Later in the day we rode out to find some nearer listening point. The whole force was making a reconnaissance towards Colenso, partly for reasons of security, partly to exercise the horses and men. Galloping over the beautiful grassy hills to the north of the town, I soon reached a spot whence the column could be seen. First of all came a cyclist—a Natal Volunteer pedalling leisurely along with his

rifle slung across his back—then two more, then about twenty.
Next, after an interval of a quarter of a mile, rode the cavalry—the
squadron of the Imperial Light Horse, sixty Natal Carabineers, a
company of mounted infantry, and about forty of the Natal
mounted police. That is the total cavalry force in Natal, all the rest
is bottled up in Ladysmith, and scarcely three hundred horsemen
are available for the defence of the colony against a hostile army
entirely composed of mounted men. Small were their numbers, but
the quality was good. The Imperial Light Horse have shown their
courage, and have only to display their discipline to equal advantage to be considered first-class soldiers. The Natal Carabineers are
excellent volunteer cavalry: the police an alert and reliable troop.
After the horse the foot: the Dublin Fusiliers wound up the hill like
a long brown snake. This is a fine regiment, which distinguished
itself at Glencoe, and has since impressed all who have been
brought in contact with it. The cheery faces of the Irishmen wore a
proud and confident expression. They had seen war. The other
battalion—the Border Regiment—had yet their spurs to win. The
volunteer battery was sandwiched between the two British battalions, and the rear of the column was brought up by the Durban
volunteers. The force, when it had thus passed in review, looked
painfully small, and this impression was aggravated by the knowledge of all that depended on it.

A high, flat-topped hill to the north-west promised a wide field
of vision and a nearer listening point for the Ladysmith cannonade,
which still throbbed and thudded dully. With my two companions
I rode towards it, and after an hour's climb reached the summit. The
land lay spread before us like a map. Estcourt, indeed, was hidden
by its engulfing hills, but Colenso was plainly visible, and the tin
roofs of the houses showed in squares and oblongs of pale blue
against the brown background of the mountain. Far away to the
east the dark serrated range of the Drakensberg rose in a mighty
wall. But it was not on these features that we turned our glasses.
To the right of Colenso the hills were lower and more broken, and
the country behind, though misty and indistinct, was exposed to
view. First there was a region of low rocky hills rising in strange
confusion and falling away on the further side to a hollow. Above
this extensive depression clouds of smoke from grass and other fires
hung and drifted, like steam over a cauldron. At the bottom—
invisible in spite of our great elevation—stood the town and camp

of Ladysmith. Westward rose the long, black, hog-backed outline of Bulwana Hill, and while we watched intently the ghost of a flash stabbed its side and a white patch sprang into existence, spread thinner, and vanished away. "Long Tom" was at his business.

The owner of the nearest farm joined us while we were thus engaged—a tall, red-bearded man of grave and intelligent mien. "They've had heavy fighting this morning," he said. "Not since Monday week" (the Black Monday of the war) "has there been such firing. But they are nearly finished now for the day." Absorbed by the distant drama, all the more thrilling since its meaning was doubtful and mysterious, we had shown ourselves against the skyline, and our conversation was now suddenly interrupted. Over the crest of the hill to the rear, two horsemen trotted swiftly into view. A hundred yards away to the left three or four more were dismounting among the rocks. Three other figures appeared on the other side. We were surrounded—but by the Natal Carabineers. "Got you, I think," said the sergeant, who now arrived. "Will you kindly tell us all about who you are?" We introduced ourselves as President Kruger and General Joubert, and presented the farmer as Mr. Schreiner, who had come to a secret conference, and having produced our passes, satisfied the patrol that we were not eligible for capture. The sergeant looked disappointed. "It took us half an hour to stalk you, but if you had only been Dutchmen we'd have had you fixed up properly." Indeed, the whole manoeuvre had been neatly and cleverly executed, and showed the smartness and efficiency of these irregular forces in all matters of scouting and reconnaissance. The patrol was then appeased by being photographed "for the London papers", and we hastened to accept the farmer's invitation to lunch. "Only plain fare," said he, "but perhaps you are used to roughing it."

The farm stood in a sheltered angle of the hill at no great distance from its summit. It was a good-sized house, with stone walls and a corrugated iron roof. A few sheds and outhouses surrounded it, four or five blue gums afforded a little shade from the sun and a little relief to the grassy smoothness of the landscape. Two women met us at the door, one the wife, the other, I think, the sister of our host. Neither was young, but their smiling faces showed the invigorating effects of this delicious air. "These are anxious times," said the older; "we hear the cannonading every morning at breakfast. What will come of it all?" Over a most excellent luncheon we discussed many things with these kind people, and spoke of how the nation was this time resolved to make an end of the long quarrel with the Boers, so that there should be no more uncertainty and alarm among loyal subjects of the Queen. "We have always known", said the farmer, "that it must end in war, and I cannot say I am sorry it has come at last. But it falls heavily on us. I am the only man for twenty miles who has not left his farm. Of course we are defenceless here. Any day the Dutchmen may come. They wouldn't kill us, but they would burn or plunder everything, and it's all I've got in the world. Fifteen years have I worked at this place, and I said to myself we may as well stay and face it out, whatever happens." Indeed, it was an anxious time for such a man. He had bought the ground, built the house, reclaimed waste tracts, enriched the land with corn and cattle, sunk all his capital in the enterprise, and backed it with the best energies of his life. Now everything might be wrecked in an hour by a wandering Boer patrol. And this was happening to a loyal and law-abiding British subject more than a hundred miles within the frontiers of Her Majesty's dominions! Now I felt the bitter need for soldiers—thousands of soldiers—so that such a man as this might be assured. With what pride and joy could one have said: "Work on, the fruits of your industry are safe. Under the strong arm of the Imperial Government your home shall be secure, and if perchance you suffer in the disputes of the Empire the public wealth shall restore your private losses." But when I recalled the scanty force which alone kept the field, and stood between the enemy and the rest of Natal, I knew the first would be an empty boast, and, remembering what had happened on other occasions, I thought the second might prove a barren promise.

We started on our long ride home, for the afternoon was wearing away and picket lines are dangerous at dusk. The military situation is without doubt at this moment most grave and critical. We have been at war three weeks. The army that was to have defended Natal, and was indeed expected to repulse the invaders with terrible loss, is blockaded and bombarded in its fortified camp. At nearly every point along the circle of the frontiers the Boers have advanced and the British retreated. Wherever we have stood we have been surrounded. The losses in the fighting have not been unequal— nor, considering the numbers engaged and the weapons employed, have they been very severe. But the Boers hold more than 1,200 unwounded British prisoners, a number that bears a disgraceful proportion to the casualty lists, and a very unsatisfactory relation to the number of Dutchmen that we have taken. All this is mainly the result of being unready. That we are unready is largely due to those in England who have endeavoured by every means in their power to hamper and obstruct the Government, who have scoffed at the possibility of the Boers becoming the aggressors, and who have represented every precaution for the defence of the colonies as a deliberate provocation to the Transvaal State. It is also due to an extraordinary under-estimation of the strength of the Boers. These military republics have been for ten years cherishing vast ambitions, and for five years, enriched by the gold mines, they have been arming and preparing for the struggle. They have neglected nothing, and it is a very remarkable fact that these ignorant peasant communities have had the wisdom and the enterprise to possess themselves of good advisers, and to utilise the best expert opinion in all matters of armament and war.

Their artillery is inferior in numbers, but in nothing else, to ours. Yesterday I visited Colenso in the armoured train. In one of the deserted British-built redoubts I found two boxes of shrapnel shells and charges. The Boers had not troubled to touch them. Their guns were of a later pattern, and fired powder and shell made up together like a great rifle cartridge. The combination, made for the first time in the history of war, of heavy artillery and swarms of mounted infantry is formidable and effective. The enduring courage and confident spirit of the enemy must also excite surprise. In short, we have grossly underrated their fighting powers. Most people in England—I, among them—thought that the Boer ultimatum was an act of despair, that the Dutch would make one fight for their honour, and, once defeated, would accept the inevitable. All I have heard and whatever I have seen out here contradict these false ideas. Anger, hatred, and the consciousness of military power impelled the Boers to war. They would rather have fought at their own time—a year or two later—when their preparations were still further advanced, and when the British were, perhaps, involved in other quarters. But, after all, the moment was ripe. Nearly everything was ready, and the whole people sprang to arms with alacrity, firmly believing that they would drive the British into the sea. To that opinion they still adhere. I do not myself share it; but it cannot be denied that it seems less absurd today than it did before a shot had been fired.

To return to Estcourt. Here we are passing through a most dangerous period. The garrison is utterly insufficient to resist the Boers; the position wholly indefensible. Indeed, we exist here on sufferance. If the enemy attack, the troops must fall back on Pietermaritzburg, if for no other reason because they are the only force available for the defence of the strong lines now being formed around the chief town. There are so few cavalry outside Ladysmith that the Boers could raid in all directions. All this will have been changed long before this letter reaches you, or I should not send it, but as I write the situation is saved only by what seems to me the over-confidence of the enemy. They are concentrating all their efforts on Ladysmith, and evidently hope to compel its surrender. It may, however, be said with absolute certainty that the place can hold out for a month at the least. How, then, could the Boers obtain the necessary time to reduce it? The reinforcements are on the seas. The railway works regularly with the coast. Even now sidings are being constructed and troop trains prepared. It is with all this that they should interfere, and they are perfectly competent to do so. They could compel us to retreat on Pietermaritzburg, they could tear up the railway, they could blow up the bridges; and by all these means they could delay the arrival of a relieving army, and so have a longer time to worry Ladysmith, and a better chance of making it a second Saratoga. Since Saturday last that has been our fear. Nearly a week has passed and nothing has happened. The chance of the Boers is fleeting; the transports approach the land; scarcely forty-eight hours remain. Yet, as I write, they have done nothing. Why? To some extent I think they have been influenced by the fear of the Tugela River rising behind their raiding parties, and cutting their line of retreat; to some extent by the serene and confident way in which General Wolfe Murray, placed in a most trying position, has handled his force and maintained by frequent reconnaissance and a determined attitude the appearance of actual strength; but when all has been said on these grounds, the fact will remain that the enemy have not destroyed the railway because they do not fear the reinforcements that are coming, because they do not believe that many will come, and because they are sure that, however many may come, they will defeat them. To this end they preserve the line, and watch the bridges as carefully as we do. It is by the railway that they are to be supplied in their march through Natal to the sea. After what they have accomplished it would be foolish to laugh at any of their ambitions, however wicked and extravagant these may be; but it appears to most military critics at this moment that they have committed a serious strategic error, and have thrown away the chance they had almost won. How much that error will cost them will depend on the operations of the relieving force, which I shall hope to chronicle as fully as possible in future letters.

CHAPTER SEVEN

THE FATE OF THE ARMOURED TRAIN

Pretoria: November 20, 1899

NOW I perceive that I was foolish to choose in advance a
definite title for these letters and to think that it could
continue to be appropriate for any length of time. In the
strong stream of war the swimmer is swirled helplessly about
hither and thither by the waves, and he can by no means tell where
he will come to land, or, indeed, that he may not be overwhelmed
in the flood. A week ago I described to you a reconnoitring expedition in the Estcourt armoured train, and I pointed out the many
defects in the construction and the great dangers in the employment of that forlorn military machine. So patent were these to all
who concerned themselves in the matter that the train was nicknamed in the camp "Wilson's death trap".

On Tuesday, the 14th, the mounted infantry patrols reported that
the Boers in small parties were approaching Estcourt from the
directions of Weenen and Colenso, and Colonel Long made a reconnaissance in force to ascertain what strength lay behind the
advanced scouts. The reconnaissance, which was marked only by
an exchange of shots between the patrols, revealed little, but it was
generally believed that a considerable portion of the army investing
Ladysmith was moving, or was about to move, southwards to
attack Estcourt, and endeavour to strike Pietermaritzburg. The
movement that we had awaited for ten days impended. Accordingly
certain military preparations, which I need not now specify, were
made to guard against all contingencies, and at daylight on
Wednesday morning another spray of patrols was flung out towards
the north and north-west, and the Estcourt armoured train was
ordered to reconnoitre towards Chieveley. The train was composed
as follows: an ordinary truck, in which was a 7-pounder muzzle-

loading gun, served by four sailors from the *Tartar*; an armoured car fitted with loopholes and held by three sections of a company of the Dublin Fusiliers; the engine and tender, two more armoured cars containing the fourth section of the Fusilier company, one company of the Durban Light Infantry (volunteers), and a small civilian breakdown gang; lastly, another ordinary truck with the tools and materials for repairing the road; in all five wagons, the locomotive, one small gun, and 120 men. Captain Haldane, D.S.O., whom I had formerly known on Sir William Lockhart's staff in the Tirah Expedition, and who was lately recovered from his wound at Elandslaagte, commanded.

We started at half-past five and, observing all the usual precautions, reached Frere Station in about an hour. Here a small patrol of the Natal police reported that there were no enemy within the next few miles, and that all seemed quiet in the neighbourhood. It was the silence before the storm. Captain Haldane decided to push on cautiously as far as Chieveley, near which place an extensive view of the country could be obtained. Not a sign of the Boers could be seen. The rolling grassy country looked as peaceful and deserted as on former occasions, and we little thought that behind the green undulations scarcely three miles away the leading commandos of a powerful force were riding swiftly forward on their invading path.

All was clear as far as Chieveley, but as the train reached the station I saw about a hundred Boer horsemen cantering southwards about a mile from the railway. Beyond Chieveley a long hill was lined with a row of black spots, showing that our further advance would be disputed. The telegraphist who accompanied the train wired back to Estcourt reporting our safe arrival, and that parties of Boers were to be seen at no great distance, and Colonel Long replied by ordering the train to return to Frere and remain there in observation during the day, watching its safe retreat at nightfall. We proceeded to obey, and were about a mile and three-quarters from Frere when on rounding a corner we saw that a hill which commanded the line at a distance of 600 yards was occupied by the enemy. So after all there would be a fight, for we could not pass this point without coming under fire. The four sailors loaded their gun— an antiquated toy—the soldiers charged their magazines, and the train, which was now in the reverse of the order in which it had started, moved slowly towards the hill.

The moment approached: but no one was much concerned, for the cars were proof against rifle fire, and this ridge could at the worst be occupied only by some daring patrol of perhaps a score of men. "Besides," we said to ourselves, "they little think we have a gun on board. That will be a nice surprise."

The Boers held their fire until the train reached that part of the track nearest to their position. Standing on a box in the rear armoured truck I had an excellent view through my glasses. The long brown rattling serpent with the rifles bristling from its spotted sides crawled closer to the rocky hillock on which the scattered black figures of the enemy showed clearly. Suddenly three wheeled things appeared on the crest, and within a second a bright flash of light—like a heliograph, but much yellower—opened and shut ten or twelve times. Then two much larger flashes; no smoke nor yet any sound, and a bustle and stir among the little figures. So much for the hill. Immediately over the rear truck of the train a huge white ball of smoke sprang into being and tore out into a cone like a comet. Then came the explosions of the near guns and the nearer shell. The iron sides of the truck tanged with a patter of bullets. There was a crash from the front of the train and half a dozen sharp reports. The Boers had opened fire on us at 600 yards with two large field guns, a Maxim firing small shells in a stream, and from riflemen lying on the ridge. I got down from my box into the cover of the armoured sides of the car without forming any clear thought. Equally involuntarily, it seems that the driver put on full steam, as the enemy had intended. The train leapt forward, ran the gauntlet of the guns, which now filled the air with explosions, swung round the curve of the hill, ran down a steep gradient, and dashed into a huge stone which awaited it on the line at a convenient spot.

To those who were in the rear truck there was only a tremendous shock, a tremendous crash, and a sudden full stop. What happened to the trucks in front of the engine is more interesting. The first, which contained the materials and tools of the break-down gang and the guard who was watching the line, was flung into the air and fell bottom upwards on the embankment. (I do not know what befell the guard, but it seems probable that he was killed.) The next, an armoured car crowded with the Durban Light Infantry, was carried on twenty yards and thrown over on its side, scattering its occupants in a shower on the ground. The third wedged itself across the track, half on and half off the rails. The rest of the train kept to the metals.

We were not long left in the comparative peace and safety of a railway accident. The Boer guns, swiftly changing their position, re-opened from a distance of 1,300 yards before anyone had got out of the stage of exclamations. The tapping rifle fire spread along the hillside, until it encircled the wreckage on three sides, and a third field gun came into action from some high ground on the opposite side of the line.

To all of this our own poor little gun endeavoured to reply, and the sailors, though exposed in an open truck, succeeded in letting off three rounds before the barrel was struck by a shell, and the trunnions, being smashed, fell altogether out of the carriage.

The armoured truck gave some protection from the bullets, but since any direct shell must pierce it like paper and kill everyone, it seemed almost safer outside, and, wishing to see the extent and nature of the damage, I clambered over the iron shield, and, dropping to the ground, ran along the line to the front of the train. As I passed the engine another shrapnel shell burst immediately, as it seemed, overhead, hurling its contents with a rasping rush through the air. The driver at once sprang out of the cab and ran to the shelter of the overturned trucks. His face was cut open by a splinter, and he complained in bitter futile indignation. He was a civilian. What did they think he was paid for? To be killed by bombshells? Not he. He would not stay another minute. It looked as if his excitement and misery—he was dazed by the blow on his head—would prevent him from working the engine further, and as only he understood the machinery all chances of escape seemed to be cut off. Yet when I told this man that if he continued to stay at his post he would be mentioned for distinguished gallantry in action, he pulled himself together, wiped the blood off his face, climbed back into the cab of his engine, and thereafter during the one-sided combat did his duty bravely and faithfully—so strong is the desire for honour and repute in the human breast.

I reached the overturned portion of the train uninjured. The volunteers who, though severely shaken, were mostly unhurt, were lying down under such cover as the damaged cars and the gutters of the railway line afforded. It was a very grievous sight to see these citizen soldiers, most of whom were the fathers of families, in such a perilous position. They bore themselves well, though greatly troubled, and their major, whose name I have not learned, directed their fire on the enemy; but since these, lying behind the crests of the surrounding hills, were almost invisible I did not expect that it would be very effective.

Having seen this much, I ran along the train to the rear armoured truck and told Captain Haldane that in my opinion the line might be cleared. We then agreed that he with musketry should keep the enemy's artillery from destroying us, and that I should try to throw the wreckage off the line, so that the engine and the two cars which still remained on the rails might escape.

I am convinced that this arrangement gave us the best possible chance of safety, though at the time it was made the position appeared quite hopeless.

Accordingly Haldane and his Fusiliers began to fire through their loopholes at the Boer artillery, and, as the enemy afterwards admitted, actually disturbed their aim considerably. During the time that these men were firing from the truck four shells passed through the armour, but luckily not one exploded until it had passed out on the further side. Many shells also struck and burst on the outside of their shields, and these knocked all the soldiers on their backs with the concussion. Nevertheless a well-directed fire was maintained without cessation.

The task of clearing the line would not, perhaps, in ordinary circumstances have been a very difficult one. But the breakdown gang and their tools were scattered to the winds, and several had fled along the track or across the fields. Moreover, the enemy's artillery fire was pitiless, continuous, and distracting. The affair had, however, to be carried through.

The first thing to be done was to detach the truck half off the rails from the one completely so. To do this the engine had to be moved to slacken the strain on the twisted couplings. When these had been released, the next step was to drag the partly derailed truck backwards along the line until it was clear of the other wreckage, and then to throw it bodily off the rails. This may seem very simple, but the dead weight of the iron truck half on the sleepers was enormous, and the engine wheels skidded vainly several times before any hauling power was obtained. At last the truck was drawn sufficiently far back, and I called for volunteers to overturn it from the side while the engine pushed it from the end. It was very evident that these men would be exposed to considerable danger. Twenty were called for, and there was an immediate response. But only nine, including the major of volunteers and four or five of the Dublin Fusiliers, actually stepped out into the open. The attempt was nevertheless successful. The truck heeled further over under their pushing, and, the engine giving a shove at the right moment, it fell off the line and the track was clear. Safety and success appeared in sight together, but disappointment overtook them.

The engine was about six inches wider than the tender, and the corner of its footplate would not pass the corner of the newly over-turned truck. It did not seem safe to push very hard, lest the engine should itself be derailed. So time after time the engine moved back a yard or two and shoved forward at the obstruction, and each time moved it a little. But soon it was evident that complications had set in. The newly-derailed truck became jammed with that originally off the line, and the more the engine pushed the greater became the block. Volunteers were again called on to assist, but though seven men, two of whom, I think, were wounded, did their best, the attempt was a failure.

Perseverance, however, is a virtue. If the trucks only jammed the tighter for the forward pushing, they might be loosened by pulling backwards. Now, however, a new difficulty arose. The coupling chains of the engine would not reach by five or six inches those of the overturned truck. Search was made for a spare link. By a solitary gleam of good luck one was found. The engine hauled at the wreck-age, and before the chains parted pulled it about a yard backwards. Now, certainly, the line was clear at last. But again the corner of the foot-plate jammed with the corner of the truck, and again we came to a jarring halt.

I have had, in the last four years, the advantage, if it be an advantage, of many strange and varied experiences, from which the student of realities might draw profit and instruction. But nothing was so thrilling as this: to wait and struggle among these clanging, rending iron boxes, with the repeated explosions of the shells and the artillery, the noise of the projectiles striking the cars, the hiss as they passed in the air, the grunting and puffing of the engine—poor, tortured thing, hammered by at least a dozen shells, any one of which, by penetrating the boiler, might have made an end of it all—the expectation of destruction as a matter of course, the realization of powerlessness, and the alternations of hope and despair—all this for seventy minutes by the clock with only four inches of twisted iron work to make the difference between danger, captivity, and shame on the one hand—safety, freedom, and triumph on the other.

Nothing remained but to continue pounding at the obstructing corner in the hopes that the iron work would gradually be twisted and torn, and thus give free passage. As we pounded so did the enemy. I adjured the driver to be patient and to push gently, for it did not seem right to imperil the slender chance of escape by running the risk of throwing the engine off the line. But after a dozen pushes had been given with apparently little result a shell struck the front of the engine, setting fire to the woodwork, and he thereupon turned on more steam, and with considerable momentum we struck the obstacle once more. There was a grinding crash; the engine staggered, checked, shore forward again, until with a clanging, tearing sound it broke past the point of interception, and nothing but the smooth line lay between us and home.

Brilliant success now seemed won, for I thought that the rear and gun trucks were following the locomotive, and that all might squeeze into them, and so make an honourable escape. But the longed-for cup was dashed aside. Looking backward, I saw that the couplings had parted or had been severed by a shell, and that the trucks still lay on the wrong side of the obstruction, separated by it from the engine. No one dared to risk imprisoning the engine again by making it go back for the trucks, so an attempt was made to drag the trucks up to the engine. Owing chiefly to the fire of the enemy this failed completely, and Captain Haldane determined to be content with saving the locomotive. He accordingly permitted the driver to retire along the line slowly, so that the infantry might get as much shelter from the ironwork of the engine as possible, and the further idea was to get into some houses near the station, about 800 yards away, and there hold out while the engine went for assistance.

As many wounded as possible were piled on to the engine, standing in the cab, lying on the tender, or clinging to the cowcatcher. And all this time the shells fell into the wet earth throwing up white clouds, burst with terrifying detonations overhead, or actually struck the engine and the iron wreckage. Besides the three field-guns, which proved to be 15-pounders, the shell-firing Maxim continued its work, and its little shells, discharged with an ugly thud, thud, thud, exploded with startling bangs on all sides. One I remember struck the foot-plate of the engine scarcely a yard from my face, lit up into a bright yellow flash, and left me wondering why I was still alive. Another hit the coals in the tender, hurling a black shower into the air. A third—this also I saw—struck the arm of a private in the Dublin Fusiliers. The whole arm was smashed to a horrid pulp—bones, muscle, blood, and uniform all mixed together. At the bottom hung the hand, unhurt, but swelled instantly to three times its ordinary size. The engine was soon crowded and began to steam homewards—a mournful, sorely battered locomotive—with the woodwork of the firebox in flames and the water spouting from its pierced tanks. The infantrymen straggled along beside it at the double.

Seeing the engine escaping the Boers increased their fire, and the troops, hitherto somewhat protected by the iron trucks, began to suffer. The major of volunteers fell, shot through the thigh. Here and there men dropped on the ground, several screamed—this is very rare in war—and cried for help. About a quarter of the force was very soon killed or wounded. The shells which pursued the retreating soldiers scattered them all along the track. Order and control vanished. The engine, increasing its pace, drew out from the thin crowd of fugitives and was soon in safety. The infantry continued to run down the line in the direction of the houses, and, in spite of their disorder, I honestly consider that they were capable of making a further resistance when some shelter should be reached. But at this moment one of those miserable incidents—much too frequent in this war—occurred.

A private soldier who was wounded, in direct disobedience of the positive orders that no surrender was to be made, took it on himself to wave a pocket-handkerchief. The Boers immediately ceased firing, and with equal daring and humanity a dozen horsemen galloped from the hills into the scattered fugitives, scarcely any of whom had seen the white flag, and several of whom were still firing, and called loudly on them to surrender. Most of the soldiers, uncertain what to do, then halted, gave up their arms, and became prisoners of war. Those further away from the horsemen continued to run and were shot or hunted down in twos and threes, and some made good their escape.

For my part I found myself on the engine when the obstruction was at last passed and remained there jammed in the cab next to the man with the shattered arm. In this way I travelled some 500 yards, and passed through the fugitives, noticing particularly a young officer, Lieutenant Frankland, who with a happy, confident smile on his face was endeavouring to rally his men. When I approached the houses where we had resolved to make a stand, I jumped on to the line, in order to collect the men as they arrived, and hence the address from which this letter is written, for scarcely had the locomotive left me than I found myself alone in a shallow cutting and none of our soldiers, who had all surrendered on the way, to be seen. Then suddenly there appeared on the line at the end of the cutting two men not in uniform. "Platelayers," I said to myself, and then, with a surge of realisation, "Boers." My mind retains a momentary impression of these tall figures, full of animated movement, clad in dark flapping clothes, with slouch, storm-driven hats poising on their rifles hardly a hundred yards away. I turned and ran between the rails of the track, and the only thought I achieved was this, "Boer marksmanship." Two bullets passed, both within a foot, one on either side. I flung myself against the banks of the cutting. But they gave no cover. Another glance at the figures; one was now kneeling to aim. Again I darted forward. Movement seemed the only chance. Again two soft kisses sucked in the air, but nothing struck me. This could not endure. I must get out of the cutting—that damnable corridor. I scrambled up the bank. The earth sprang up beside me, and something touched my hand, but outside the cutting was a tiny depression. I crouched in this, struggling to get my wind. On the other side of the railway a horseman galloped up, shouting to me and waving his hand. He was scarcely forty yards off. With a rifle I could have killed him easily. I knew nothing of white flags, and the bullets had made me savage. I reached down for my Mauser pistol. "This one at least," I said, and indeed it was a certainty; but alas! I had left the weapon in the cab of the engine in order to be free to work at the wreckage. What then? There was a wire fence between me and the horseman. Should I continue to fly? The idea of another shot at such a short range decided me. Death stood before me, grim sullen Death without his light-hearted companion, Chance. So I held up my hand, and like Mr. Jorrocks's foxes, cried "Capivy". Then I was herded with the other prisoners in a miserable group, and about the same time I noticed that my hand was bleeding, and it began to pour with rain.

Two days before I had written to an officer in high command at home, whose friendship I have the honour to enjoy: "There has been a great deal too much surrendering in this war, and I hope people who do so will not be encouraged." Fate had intervened, yet though her tone was full of irony she seemed to say, as I think Ruskin once said, "It matters very little whether your judgments of people are true or untrue, and very much whether they are kind or unkind," and repeating that I will make an end.

CHAPTER EIGHT

PRISONERS OF WAR

Pretoria: November 24, 1899

THE POSITION of a prisoner of war is painful and humiliating. A man tries his best to kill another, and finding that he cannot succeed asks his enemy for mercy. The laws of war demand that this should be accorded, but it is impossible not to feel a sense of humbling obligation to the captor from whose hand we take our lives. All military pride, all independence of spirit must be put aside. These may be carried to the grave, but not into captivity. We must prepare ourselves to submit, to obey, to endure. Certain things—sufficient food and water and protection during good behaviour—the victor must supply or be a savage, but beyond these all else is favour. Favours must be accepted from those with whom we have a long and bitter quarrel, from those who feel fiercely that we seek to do them cruel injustice. The dog who has been whipped must be thankful for the bone that is flung to him.

When the prisoners captured after the destruction of the armoured train had been disarmed and collected in a group we found that there were fifty-six unwounded or slightly wounded men, besides the more serious cases lying on the scene of the fight. The Boers crowded round, looking curiously at their prize, and we ate a little chocolate that by good fortune—for we had had no breakfast—was in our pockets, and sat down on the muddy ground to think. The rain streamed down from a dark leaden sky, and the coats of the horses steamed in the damp. "Voorwärts", said a voice, and, forming in a miserable procession, two wretched officers, a bare-headed, tattered Correspondent, four sailors with straw hats and "H.M.S. Tartar" in gold letters on the ribbons—ill-timed jauntiness—some fifty soldiers and volunteers, and two or three railwaymen, we started, surrounded by the active Boer horsemen.

Yet, as we climbed the low hills that surrounded the place of combat I looked back and saw the engine steaming swiftly away beyond Frere Station. Something at least was saved from the ruin; information would be carried to the troops at Estcourt, a good many of the troops and something of the wounded would escape, the locomotive was itself of value, and perhaps in saving all these things some little honour had been saved as well.

"You need not walk fast," said a Boer in excellent English; "take your time." Then another, seeing me hatless in the downpour, threw me a soldier's cap—one of the Irish Fusilier caps, taken, probably, near Ladysmith. So they were not cruel men, these enemy. That was a great surprise to me, for I had read much of the literature of this land of lies, and fully expected every hardship and indignity. At length we reached the guns which had played on us for so many minutes—two strangely long barrels sitting very low on carriages of four wheels, like a break in which horses are exercised. They looked offensively modern, and I wondered why our Army had not got field artillery with fixed ammunition and 8,000 yards' range. Some officers and men of the Staats Artillerie, dressed in a drab uniform with blue facings, approached us. The commander, Adjutant Roos—as he introduced himself—made a polite salute. He regretted the unfortunate circumstances of our meeting; he complimented the officers on their defence—of course it was hopeless from the first; he trusted his fire had not annoyed us; we should, he thought, understand the necessity for them to continue; above all he wanted to know how the engine had been able to get away, and how the line could have been cleared of wreckage under his guns. In fact, he behaved as a good professional soldier should, and his manner impressed me.

We waited here near the guns for half an hour, and meanwhile the Boers searched amid the wreckage for dead and wounded. A few of the wounded were brought to where we were, and laid on the ground, but most of them were placed in the shelter of one of the overturned trucks. As I write I do not know with any certainty what the total losses were, but the Boers say that they buried five dead, sent ten seriously wounded into Ladysmith, and kept three severely wounded in their field ambulances. Besides this, we are told that sixteen severely wounded escaped on the engine, and we have with the prisoners seven men, including myself, slightly wounded by splinters or injured in the derailment. If this be approximately correct, it seems that the casualties in the hour and a half of fighting were between thirty-five and forty: not many, perhaps, considering the fire, but out of 120 enough at least.

After a while we were ordered to march on, and looking over the crest of the hill a strange and impressive sight met the eye. Only about 300 men had attacked the train, and I had thought that this was the enterprise of a separate detachment, but as the view extended I saw that this was only a small part of a large, powerful force marching south, under the personal direction of General Joubert, to attack Estcourt. Behind every hill, thinly veiled by the driving rain, masses of mounted men, arranged in an orderly disorder, were halted, and from the rear long columns of horsemen rode steadily forward. Certainly I did not see less than 3,000, and I did not see nearly all. Evidently an important operation was in progress, and a collision either at Estcourt or Mooi River impended. This was the long expected advance: worse late than never.

Our captors conducted us to a rough tent which had been set up in a hollow in one of the hills, and which we concluded was General Joubert's headquarters. Here we were formed in a line, and soon surrounded by a bearded crowd of Boers cloaked in mackintosh. I explained that I was a Special Correspondent, and asked to see General Joubert. But in the throng it was impossible to tell who were the superiors. My credentials were taken from me by a man who said he was a field cornet; and who promised that they should be laid before the General forthwith. Meanwhile we waited in the rain, and the Boers questioned us. My certificate as a correspondent bore a name better known than liked in the Transvaal. Moreover, some of the private soldiers had been talking. "You are the son of Lord Randolph Churchill?" said a Scottish Boer, abruptly. I did not deny the fact. Immediately there was much talking, and all crowded round me, looking and pointing, while I heard my name repeated on every side. "I am a newspaper correspondent," I said, "and you ought not to hold me prisoner." The Scottish Boer laughed. "Oh," he said, "we do not catch lords' sons every day." Whereat they all chuckled, and began to explain that I should be allowed to play football at Pretoria.

All this time I was expecting to be brought before General Joubert, from whom I had some hopes I should obtain assurances that my character as a press correspondent would be respected. But suddenly a mounted man rode up and ordered the prisoners to

march away towards Colenso. The escort, twenty horsemen, closed
round us. I addressed their leader, and demanded either that I
should be taken before the General, or that my credentials should
be given back. But the so-called Field Cornet was not to be seen.
The only response was, "Voorwärts", and as it seemed useless,
undignified, and even dangerous to discuss the matter further with
these people, I turned and marched off with the rest.

We tramped for six hours across sloppy fields and along tracks
deep and slippery with mud, while the rain fell in a steady downpour and soaked everyone to the skin. The Boer escort told us
several times not to hurry and to go our own pace, and once they
allowed us to halt for a few moments. But we had had neither food
nor water, and it was with a feeling of utter weariness that I saw
the tin roofs of Colenso rise in the distance. We were put into a corrugated iron shed near the station, the floors of which were four
inches deep with torn railway forms and account books. Here we
flung ourselves down exhausted, and what with the shame, the
disappointment, the excitement of the morning, the misery of the
present, and physical weakness, it seemed that love of life was gone,
and I thought almost with envy of a soldier I had seen during the
fight lying quite still on the embankment, secure in the calm
philosophy of death from "the slings and arrows of outrageous
fortune".

After the Boers had lit two fires they opened one of the doors of
the shed and told us we might come forth and dry ourselves. A
newly-slaughtered ox lay on the ground, and strips of his flesh were
given to us. These we toasted on sticks over the fire and ate greedily,
though since the animal had been alive five minutes before one felt a
kind of cannibal. Other Boers not of our escort who were occupying
Colenso came to look at us. With two of these who were brothers,
English by race, Afrikanders by birth, Boers by choice, I had some
conversation. The war, they said, was going well. Of course, it was
a great matter to face the power and might of the British Empire,
still they were resolved. They would drive the English out of South
Africa for ever, or else fight to the last man. I said:

"You attempt the impossible. Pretoria will be taken by the
middle of March. What hope have you of withstanding a hundred
thousand soldiers?"

"If I thought", said the younger of the two brothers vehemently,
"that the Dutchmen would give in because Pretoria was taken, I

would smash my rifle on those metals this very moment. We will fight for ever." I could only reply:

"Wait and see how you feel when the tide is running the other way. It does not seem so easy to die when death is near." The man said, "I will wait."

Then we made friends. I told him that I hoped he would come safely through the war, and live to see a happier and a nobler South Africa under the flag which had been good enough for his fore-fathers; and he took off his blanket—which he was wearing with a hole in the middle like a cloak—and gave it to me to sleep in. So we parted, and presently, as night fell, the Field Cornet who had us in charge bade us carry a little forage into the shed to sleep on, and then locked us up in the dark, soldiers, sailors, officers, and Corres-pondent—a broken-spirited jumble.

I could not sleep. Vexation of spirit, a cold night, and wet clothes withheld sweet oblivion. The rights and wrongs of the quarrel, the fortunes and chances of the war, forced themselves on the mind. What men they were, these Boers! I thought of them as I had seen them in the morning riding forward through the rain—thousands of independent riflemen, thinking for themselves, possessed of beauti-ful weapons, led with skill, living as they rode without com-missariat or transport or ammunition column, moving like the wind, and supported by iron constitutions and a stern, hard Old Testament God who should surely smite the Amalekites hip and thigh. And then, above the rain storm that beat loudly on the corrugated iron, I heard the sound of a chaunt. The Boers were singing their evening psalm, and the menacing notes—more full of indignant war than love and mercy—struck a chill into my heart, so that I thought after all that the war was unjust, that the Boers were better men than we, that Heaven was against us, that Lady-smith, Mafeking, and Kimberley would fall, that the Estcourt garrison would perish, that foreign Powers would intervene, that we should lose South Africa, and that that would be the beginning of the end. So for the time I despaired of the Empire, nor was it till the morning sun—all the brighter after the rain storms, all the warmer after the chills—struck in through the windows that things reassumed their true colours and proportions.

CHAPTER NINE

THROUGH THE DUTCH CAMPS

Pretoria: November 30, 1899

THE BITTER wind of disappointment pierces even the cloak of sleep. Moreover, the night was cold and the wet clothes chilled and stiffened my limbs, provoking restless and satisfactory dreams. I was breakfasting with President Kruger and General Joubert. "Have some jam," said the President. "Thanks," I replied, "I would rather have marmalade." But there was none. Their evident embarrassment communicated itself to me. "Never mind," I said, "I'd just as soon have jam." But the President was deeply moved. "No, no," he cried; "we are not barbarians. Whatever you are entitled to you shall have, if I have to send to Johannesburg for it." So he got up to ring the bell, and with the clang I woke.

The first light of dawn was just peering in through the skylight of the corrugated iron shed. The soldiers lay in a brown litter about the floor, several snoring horribly. The meaning of it came home with a slap. Imprisoned; not able to come and go at will; about to be dragged off and put in some secluded place while others fought the great quarrel to the end; out of it all—like a pawn taken early in the game and flung aside into the box. I groaned with vexation, and, sitting up, aroused Frankland, who shared my blanket. Then the Boers unlocked the doors and ordered us to get ready to march at once.

The forage which we had spread on the floor rustled, and the first idea of escape crossed my mind. Why not lie buried underneath this litter until prisoners and escort had marched away together? Would they count? Would they notice? I did not think so. They would reason—we know they all went in; it is certain none could have escaped during the night: therefore all must be here this morning. Suppose they missed me? "Where is the 'reporter', with whom we talked last evening?" Haldane would reply that he must have slipped out of the door before it was shut. They might scour the country; but would they search the shed? It seemed most unlikely. The scheme pleased my fancy exceedingly, and I was just resolving to conceal myself, when one of the guards entered and ordered everyone to file out forthwith.

We chewed a little more of the ox, slain and toasted the night before, and drank some rainwater from a large puddle, and, after this frugal breakfast, intimated that we were ready. Then we set out—a sorry gang of dirty, tramping prisoners, but yesterday the soldiers of the Queen; while the fierce old farmers cantered their ponies about the veldt or closed around the column, looking at us from time to time with irritating disdain and still more irritating pity. We marched across the waggon bridge of the Tugela, and following the road, soon entered the hills. Among these we journeyed for several hours, wading across the gullies which the heavy rains had turned into considerable streams and persecuted by the slanting rays of the sun. Here and there parties of Boers met us, and much handshaking and patting on the back ensued between the new-comers and our escort. Once we halted at a little field hospital—a dozen tents and waggons with enormous red-cross flags, tucked away in a deep hollow.

We passed through Pieters without a check at the same toilsome plod and on to Nelthorpe. Here we began to approach the Dutch lines of investment round Ladysmith, and the advance of half an hour brought us to a very strong picket, where we were ordered to halt and rest. Nearly two hundred Boers swarmed round in a circle and began at once—for they are all keen politicians and as curious as children—to ask questions of every sort. What did we think of South Africa? Would we like to go in an armoured train again? How long would the English go on fighting? When would the war end? and the reply, "When you are beaten," was received with shouts of laughter.

"Oh no, old chappie, you can never beat us. Look at Mafeking. We have taken Mafeking. You will find Baden Powell waiting for you at Pretoria. Kimberley, too, will fall this week. Rhodes is trying to escape in a balloon, disguised as a woman—a fine woman." Great merriment at this. "What about Ladysmith?" "Ten days. Ten days more and then we shall have some whisky." Listen. There was the boom of a heavy gun, and, turning, I saw the white cloud of smoke hanging on the crest of Bulwana.

"That goes on always," said the Boer. "Can any soldiers bear that long? Oh, you will find all the English army at Pretoria. Indeed, if it were not for the sea-sickness we would take England. Besides, do you think the European Powers will allow you to bully us?"

I said, "Why bully if you are so strong?"

"Well, why should you come and invade our country?"

"Your country? I thought this was Natal."

"So it is: but Natal is ours. You stole it from us. Now we take it back again. That's all."

A hum of approval ran round the grinning circle. An old Boer came up. He did not understand what induced the soldiers to go in the armoured train. Frankland replied, "Ordered to. Don't you have to obey your orders?"

The old man shook his head in bewilderment, then he observed, "I fight to kill: I do not fight to be killed. If the Field Cornet was to order me to go in an armoured train, I would say to him, 'Field Cornet, go to hell.' "

"Ah, you are not soldiers."

"But we catch soldiers and kill soldiers and make soldiers run away."

There was a general chorus of "Yaw, yaw, yaw", and grunts of amusement.

"You English," said a well-dressed man, "die for your country: we Afrikanders live for ours."

I said, "Surely you don't think you will win this war?"

"Oh, yes; we will win all right this time, just the same as before."

"But it is not the same as before. Gladstone is dead, they are determined at home. If necessary they will send three hundred thousand men and spend a hundred millions."

"We are not afraid; no matter how many thousand penny soldiers you send," and an English Boer added, "Let 'em all come."

But there was one discordant note in the full chorus of confidence. It recurred again and again. "Where is Buller?" "When is Buller coming?" These merry fellows were not without their doubts.

"He will come when the army is ready."

"But we have beaten the army."

"No, the war has not begun yet."

"It's all over for you, old chappie, anyway."

It was a fair hit. I joined the general laughter, and, reviewing the incident by the light of subsequent events, feel I had some right to.

Very soon after this we were ordered to march again, and we began to move to the eastward in the direction of the Bulwana Hill, descending as we did so into the valley of the Klip River. The report of the intermittent guns engaged in the bombardment of Ladysmith seemed very loud and near, and the sound of the British artillery making occasional reply could be plainly distinguished. After we had crossed the railway line beyond Nelthorpe I caught sight of another evidence of the proximity of friends. High above the hills, to the left of the path, hung a speck of gold-beater's skin. It was the Ladysmith balloon. There, scarcely two miles away, were safety and honour. The soldiers noticed the balloon too. "Those are our blokes," they said. "We ain't all finished yet," and so they comforted themselves, and a young sergeant advanced a theory that the garrison would send out cavalry to rescue us.

We kept our eyes on the balloon till it was hidden by the hills, and I thought of all that lay at the bottom of its rope. Beleaguered Ladysmith, with its shells, its flies, its fever, and its filth seemed a glorious paradise to me.

We forded the Klip River breast high, and, still surrounded by our escort, trudged on towards the laagers behind Bulwana. But it was just three o'clock, after about ten hours' marching, that we reached the camp where we were to remain for the night. Having had no food—except the toasted ox, a disgusting form of nourishment—and being besides unused to walking far, I was so utterly worn out on arrival that at first I cared for nothing but to lie down under the shade of a bush. But after the Field Cornet had given us some tea and bully beef, and courteously bidden us to share the shelter of his tent, I felt equal to further argument.

The Boers were delighted and crowded into the small tent.

"Will you tell us why there is this war?"

I said that it was because they wanted to beat us out of South Africa and we did not like the idea.

"Oh no, that is not the reason." Now that the war had begun they would drive the British into the sea; but if we had been content with what we had they would not have interfered with us—except to get a port and have their full independence recognised.

"I will tell you what is the real cause of this war. It's all those damned capitalists. They want to steal our country, and they have bought Chamberlain, and now these three, Rhodes, Beit, and Chamberlain, think they will have the Rand to divide between them afterwards."

"Don't you know that the gold mines are the property of the shareholders, many of whom are foreigners—Frenchmen and Germans and others? After the war, whatever government rules, they will still belong to these people."

"What are we fighting for then?"

"Because you hate us bitterly, and have armed yourselves in order to attack us, and we naturally chose to fight when we are not occupied elsewhere. 'Agree with thine adversary whiles thou art in the way with him.' "

"Don't you think it wicked to try to steal our country?"

"We only want to protect ourselves and our own interests. We didn't want your country."

"No, but the damned capitalists do."

"If you had tried to keep on friendly terms with us there would have been no war. But you want to drive us out of South Africa. Think of a great Afrikander Republic—all South Africa speaking Dutch—a United States under your President and your Flag, sovereign and international."

Their eyes glittered. "That's what we want," said one. "Yaw, yaw," said the others, "and that's what we're going to have."

"Well, that's the reason of the war."

"No, no. You know it's those damned capitalists and Jews who have caused the war." And the argument recommenced its orbit.

So the afternoon wore away.

As the evening fell the Commandant required us to withdraw to some tents which had been pitched at the corner of the laager. A special tent was provided for the officers, and now, for the first time, they found themselves separated from their men. I had a moment in which to decide whether I would rank as officer or private, and chose the former, a choice I was soon to regret. Gradually it became night. The scene as the daylight faded was striking and the circumstances were impressive. The dark shadow of Bulwana mountain flung back over the Dutch camp, and the rugged, rock-strewn hills rose about it on all sides. The great waggons were arranged to enclosure a square, in the midst of which stood clusters of variously shaped tents and lines of munching oxen.

Within the laager and around it little fires began to glow, and by their light the figures of the Boers could be seen busy cooking and eating their suppers, or smoking in moody, muttering groups. All was framed by the triangular doorway of the tent, in which two ragged, bearded men sat nursing their rifles and gazing at their captives in silence. Nor was it till my companions prepared to sleep that the stolid guards summoned the energy and wit to ask, in struggling English (for these were real veldt Boers), the inevitable question, "And after all, what are we fighting for? Why is there this war?" But I was tired of arguing, so I said, "It is the will of God," and turned to rest with a more confident feeling than the night before, for I felt that these men were wearying of the struggle.

To rest but not to sleep, for the knowledge that the British lines at Ladysmith lay only five miles away filled my brain with hopes and plans of escape. I had heard it said that all Dutchmen slept between 12 and 2 o'clock, and I waited, trusting that our sentries would observe the national custom. But I soon saw that I should have been better situated with the soldiers. We three officers were twenty yards from the laager, and around our little tent, as I learned by peering through a rent in the canvas, no less than four men were posted. At intervals they were visited or relieved, at times they chatted together; but never for a minute was their vigilance relaxed, and the continual clicking of the Mauser breech bolts, as they played with their rifles, unpleasantly proclaimed their attention. The moon was full and bright, and it was obvious that no possible chance of success awaited an attempt.

With the soldiers the circumstances were more favourable. Their tent stood against the angle of the laager, and although the sentries watched the front and sides it seemed to me that a man might crawl through the back, and by walking boldly across the laager itself pass safely out into the night. It was certainly a road none would expect a fugitive to take; but whatever its chances it was closed to me, for the guard was changed at midnight and a new sentry stationed between our tent and those near the laager.

I examined him through the torn tent. He was quite a child—a boy of about fourteen—and needless to say appreciated the importance of his duties. He played this terrible game of soldiers with all his heart and soul; so at last I abandoned the idea of flight and fell asleep.

In the morning, before the sun was up, the Commandant Davel

came to rouse us. The prisoners were to march at once to Eland-slaagte Station. "How far?" we asked, anxiously, for all were very footsore. "Only a very little way—five hours' slow walking." We stood up—for we had slept in our clothes and cared nothing for washing—and said that we were ready. The Commandant then departed, to return in a few minutes bringing some tea and bully beef, which he presented to us with an apology for the plainness of the fare. He asked an English-speaking Boer to explain that they had nothing better themselves. After we had eaten and were about to set forth, Davel said, through his interpreter, that he would like to know from us that we were satisfied with the treatment we met with at his laager. We gladly gave him the assurance, and with much respect bade goodbye to this dignified and honourable enemy. Then we were marched away over the hills towards the north, skirting the picket line round Ladysmith to the left. Every half-mile or so the road led through or by some Boer laager, and the occupants—for it was a quiet day in the batteries—turned out in hundreds to look at us. I do not know how many men I saw, but certainly during this one march not less than 5,000. Of this great number two only offered insults to the gang of prisoners. One was a dirty, mean-looking little Hollander. He said, "Well, Tommy, you've got your franchise, anyhow." The other was an Irishman. He addressed himself to Frankland, whose badges proclaimed his regiment. What he said when disentangled from obscenity amounted to this: "I am glad to see you Dublin fellows in trouble." The Boers silenced him at once and we passed on. But that was all the taunting we received during the whole journey from Frere Station to Pretoria, and when one remembers that the burghers are only common men with hardly any real discipline, the fact seems very remarkable. But little and petty as it was it galled horribly. The soldiers felt the sting and scowled back; the officers looked straight before them. Yet it was a valuable lesson. Only a few days before I had read in the newspapers of how the Kaffirs had jeered at the Boer prisoners when they were marched into Pietermaritzburg, saying, "Where are your passes?" It had seemed a very harmless joke then, but now I understood how a prisoner feels these things.

It was about eleven o'clock when we reached Elandslaagte Station. A train awaited the prisoners. There were six or seven closed vans for the men and a first-class carriage for the officers. Into a compartment of this we were speedily bundled. Two Boers with rifles sat themselves between us, and the doors were locked. I was desperately hungry, and asked for both food and water. "Plenty is coming," they said, so we waited patiently, and sure enough, in a few minutes a railway official came along the platform, opened the door, and thrust before us in generous profusion two tins of preserved mutton, two tins of preserved fish, four or five loaves, half a dozen pots of jam, and a large can of tea. As far as I could see the soldiers fared no worse. The reader will believe that we did not stand on ceremony, but fell to at once and made the first satisfying meal for three days. While we ate a great crowd of Boers gathered around the train and peered curiously in at the windows. One of them was a doctor, who, noticing that my hand was bound up, inquired whether I were wounded. The cut caused by the splinter of bullet was insignificant, but since it was ragged and had received no attention for two days it had begun to fester. I therefore showed him my hand, and he immediately bustled off to get bandages and hot water and what not, with which, amid the approving grins of the rough fellows who thronged the platform, he soon bound me up very correctly.

The train whereby we were to travel was required for other business besides; and I noticed about a hundred Boers embarking with their horses in a dozen large cattle trucks behind the engine. At or about noon we steamed off, moving slowly along the line, and Captain Haldane pointed out to me the ridge of Elandslaagte, and gave me some further account of that successful action and of the great skill with which Hamilton had directed the infantry attack. The two Boers who were guarding us listened with great interest, but the single observation they made was that we had only to fight Germans and Hollanders at Elandslaagte. "If these had been veldt Boers in front of you——" My companion replied that even then the Gordon Highlanders might have made some progress. Whereat both Boers laughed softly and shook their heads with the air of a wiseacre, saying, "You will know better when you're as old as me," a remark I constantly endure from very worthy people.

Two stations beyond Elandslaagte the Boer commando, or portion of commando, left the train, and the care and thought that had been lavished on the military arrangements were very evident. All the stations on the line were fitted with special platforms three or four hundred yards long, consisting of earth embankments revetted with wood towards the line and sloping to the ground on the other side. The horsemen were thereby enabled to ride their horses out of the trucks, and in a few minutes all were cantering away across the plain. One of the Boer guards noticed the attention I paid to these arrangements. "It is in case we have to go back quickly to the Biggarsberg or Laing's Nek", he explained. As we travelled on I gradually fell into conversation with this man. His name, he told me, was Spaarwater, which he pronounced *Spare-water*. He was a farmer from the Ermolo district. In times of peace he paid little or no taxes. For the last four years he had escaped altogether. The Field Cornet, he remarked, was a friend of his. But for such advantages he lay under the obligation to serve without pay in war-time, providing horse, forage, and provisions. He was a polite, meek-mannered little man, very anxious in all the discussion to say nothing that could hurt the feelings of his prisoners, and I took a great liking to him. He had fought at Dundee. "That," he said, "was a terrible battle. Your artillery? *Bang! bang! bang!* came the shells all round us. And the bullets! *Whew*, don't tell me the soldiers can't shoot. They shoot jolly well, old chappie. I, too, can shoot. I can hit a bottle six times out of seven at a hundred yards, but when there is a battle then I do not shoot so well."

The other man, who understood a little English, grinned at this, and muttered something in Dutch.

"What does he say?" I inquired.

"He says 'He too'," replied Spaarwater. "Besides, we cannot see your soldiers. At Dundee I was looking down the hill and saw nothing except rows of black boots marching and the black belts of one of the regiments."

"But," I said, "you managed to hit some of them after all."

He smiled. "Ah, yes, we are lucky, and God is on our side. Why, after Dundee, when we were retiring, we had to cross a great open plain, never even an ant-hill, and you had put twelve great cannons —I counted them—and Maxims as well, to shoot us as we went; but not one fired a shot. Was it not God's hand that stopped them? After that we knew."

I said: "Of course the guns did not fire, because you had raised the white flag."

"Yes," he answered, "to ask for armistice, but not to give in. We are not going to give in yet. Besides, we have heard that your Lancers speared our wounded at Elandslaagte." We were getting on dangerous ground. He hastened to turn the subject. "It's all those lying newspapers that spread these reports on both sides, just like the capitalists made the war by lying."

A little further on the ticket collector came to join in the conversation. He was a Hollander, and very eloquent.

"Why should you English take this country away from us?" he asked, and the silent Boer chimed in in broken English. "Are not our farms our own? Why must we fight for them?"

I endeavoured to explain the ground of our quarrel. "After all British government is not a tyranny."

"It's no good for a working-man," said the ticket collector; "look at Kimberley. Kimberley was a good place to live in before the capitalists collared it. Look at it now. Look at me. What are my wages?"

I forget what he said they were, but they were extraordinary wages for a ticket collector.

"Do you suppose I should get such wages under the English Government?"

I said "No".

"There you are," he said. "No English Government for me," and added inconsequently, "We fight for our freedom."

Now I thought I had an argument that would tell. I turned to the farmer, who had been listening approvingly:

"Those are very good wages."

"Ah, yes."

"Where does the money come from?"

"Oh, from the taxes . . . and from the railroad."

"Well, now, you send a good deal of your produce by rail, I suppose?"

"Ya" (an occasional lapse into Dutch).

"Don't you find the rates very high?"

"Ya, ya," said both the Boers together; "very high."

"That is because he" (pointing to the ticket collector) "is getting such good wages. You are paying them." At this they both laughed heartily, and Spaarwater said that that was quite true, and that the rates were too high.

"Under the English Government," I said, "he will not get such high wages; you will not have to pay such high rates."

They received the conclusion in silence. Then Spaarwater said, "Yes, but we shall have to pay a tribute to your Queen."

"Does Cape Colony?" I asked.

"Well, what about that ironclad?"

"A present, a free-will offering because they are contented—as you will be some day—under our flag."

"No, no, old chappie, we don't want your flag; we want to be left alone. We are free, you are not free."

"How do you mean 'not free'?"

"Well, is it right that a dirty Kaffir should walk on the pavement —without a pass too? That's what they do in your British Colonies. Brother! Equal! Ugh! Free! Not a bit. We know how to treat Kaffirs."

Probing at random I had touched a very sensitive nerve. We had got down from underneath the political and reached the social. What is the true and original root of Dutch aversion to British rule? It is not Slagter's Nek, nor Broomplatz, nor Majuba, nor the Jameson Raid. Those incidents only fostered its growth. It is the abiding fear and hatred of the movement that seeks to place the native on a level with the white man. British government is associated in the Boer farmer's mind with violent social revolution. Black is to be proclaimed the same as white. The servant is to be raised against the master; the Kaffir is to be declared the brother of the European, to be constituted his legal equal, to be armed with political rights. The dominant race is to be deprived of their superiority; nor is a tigress robbed of her cubs more furious than is the Boer at this prospect.

I mused on the tangled skein of politics and party principles. This Boer farmer was a very typical character, and represented to my mind all that was best and noblest in the African Dutch character. Supposing he had been conducting Mr. Morley to Pretoria, not as a prisoner of war, but as an honoured guest, instead of me, what would their conversation have been? How excellently they would have agreed on the general question of the war! I could imagine the farmer purring with delight as his distinguished charge dilated in polished sentences upon liberty and the rights of nationalities. Both would together have bewailed the horrors of war and the crime of aggression; both would have condemned the tendencies of modern Imperialism and Capitalism; both would have been in complete accord whenever the names of Rhodes, Chamberlain, or Milner were mentioned. And the spectacle of this citizen soldier, called reluctant, yet not unwilling, from the quiet life of his farm to fight bravely in defence of the soil on which he lived, which his fathers had won by all manner of suffering and peril, and to preserve the independence which was his pride and joy, against great enemies of regulars—surely that would have drawn the most earnest sympathy of the eminent idealist. And then suddenly a change, a jarring note in the duet of agreement.

"*We* know how to treat Kaffirs in *this* country. Fancy letting the black filth walk on the pavement!"

And after that no more agreement: but argument growing keener and keener; gulf widening every moment.

"Educate a Kaffir! Ah, that's you English all over. No, no, old chappie. We educate 'em with a stick. Treat 'em with humanity and consideration—I like that. They were put here by the God Almighty to work for us. We'll stand no damned nonsense from them. We'll keep them in their proper places. What do you think? Insist on their proper treatment will you? Ah, that's what we're going to see about now. We'll settle whether you English are to interfere with us before this war is over."

The afternoon dragged away before the train passed near Dundee. Lieutenant Frankland had helped to storm Talana Hill, and was much excited to see the field of battle again under these new circumstances. "It would all have been different if Symons had lived. We should never have let them escape from under our guns. That commando would have been smashed up altogether."

"But what about the other commando that came up the next day?"

"Oh, the General would have managed them all right. He'd have soon found some way of turning them out." Nor do I doubt he would, if the fearless confidence with which he inspired his troops could have protected his life. But the bullet is brutally indiscriminating, and before it the brain of a hero or the quarters of a horse stand exactly the same chance to the vertical square inch.

After Talana Hill was lost to view we began to search for Majuba, and saw it just as night closed in—a great dark mountain with memories as sad and gloomy as its appearance. The Boer guards pointed out to us where they had mounted their big cannons to defend Laing's Nek, and remarked that the pass was now impregnable. I could not resist saying, "This is not the only road into the Transvaal." "Ah, but you English always come where we want you to come."

We now approached the frontier. I had indulged in hopes of

leaving the train while in the Volksrust Tunnel by climbing out of the window. The possibility had, however, presented itself to Spaarwater, for he shut both windows, and just before we reached the entrance opened the breech of his Mauser to show me that it was fully loaded. So prudence again imposed patience. It was quite dark when the train reached Volksrust, and we knew ourselves actually in the enemy's country. The platform was densely crowded with armed Boers. It appeared that two new commandos had been called out, and were waiting for trains to take them to the front. Moreover, a strong raiding party had just come back from British Swaziland. The windows were soon blocked with the bearded faces of men who gazed stolidly and commented freely to each other on our appearance. It was like being a wild beast in a cage. After some time a young woman pushed her way to the window and had a prolonged stare, at the end of which she observed in a loud voice (I must record it)—"Why, they're not so bad looking after all." At this there was general laughter, and Spaarwater, who was much concerned, said that they meant no harm, and that if we were annoyed he would have everyone cleared away. But I said: "Certainly not; let them feast their eyes." So they did, for forty minutes by the clock.

Their faces were plain and rough, but not unkindly. The little narrow-set pig eyes were the most displeasing feature. For the rest they looked what they were, honest ignorant peasants with wits sharpened by military training and the conditions of a new country. Presently I noticed at the window furthest from the platform one of quite a different type. A handsome boyish face without beard or moustache, and a very amiable expression. We looked at each other. There was no one else at that side of the carriage.

"Will you have some cigarettes?" he said, holding me out a packet. I took one, and we began to talk. "Is there going to be much more war?" he inquired anxiously.

"Yes, very much more; we have scarcely begun." He looked quite miserable.

I said, "You have not been at the front yet?"

"No, I am only just commandeered."

"How old are you?"

"Sixteen."

"That's very young to go and fight."

He shook his head sadly.

"What's your name?"

"Cameron."

"That's not a Dutch name?"

"No, I'm not a Dutchman. My father came from Scotland."

"Then why do you go and fight against the British?"

"How can I help it? I live here. You must go when you're commandeered. They wouldn't let me off. Mother tried her best. But it's 'come out and fight or leave the country' here, and we've got nothing but the farm."

"The Government would have paid you compensation afterwards."

"Ah! that's what they told father last time. He was loyal, and helped to defend the Pretoria laager. He lost everything, and he had to begin all over again."

"So now you fight against your country?"

"I can't help it," he repeated sullenly, "you must go when you're commandeered." And then he climbed down off the footboard, and I did not see him again—one piteous item of Gladstone's legacy—the ruined and abandoned loyalist in the second generation.

Before the train left Volksrust we changed our guards. The honest burghers who had captured us had to return to the front, and we were to be handed over to the police. The leader of the escort—a dear old gentleman—I am ignorant of his official rank—approached and explained through Spaarwater that it was he who had placed the stone and so caused our misfortunes. He said he hoped we bore no malice. We replied by no means, and that we would do the same for him with pleasure any day. Frankland asked him what rewards he would get for such distinguished service. In truth he might easily have been shot, had we turned the corner a minute earlier. The subaltern apparently contemplated some Republican V.C. or D.S.O. But the farmer was much puzzled by his question. After some explaining we learnt that he had been given fourteen days' furlough to go home to his farm and see his wife. His evident joy and delight were touching. I said "Surely this is a very critical time to leave the front. You may miss an important battle."

"Yes," he replied simply, "I hope so."

Then we said "good-bye", and I gave him, and also Spaarwater, a little slip of paper setting forth that they had shown kindness and courtesy to British prisoners of war, and personally requesting anyone into whose hands the papers might come to treat them well, should they themselves be taken by the Imperial forces.

We were then handed to a rather dilapidated policeman of a gendarme type, who spat copiously on the floor of the carriage and informed us that we should be shot if we attempted to escape. Having no desire to speak to this fellow, we let down the sleeping shelves of the compartment and, as the train steamed out of Volksrust, turned to sleep.

CHAPTER TEN

IN AFRIKANDER BONDS

Pretoria: December 8, 1899

IT WAS, as nearly as I can remember, midday when the train-load of prisoners reached Pretoria. We pulled up in a sort of siding with an earth platform on the right side which opened into the streets of the town. The day was fine, and the sun shone brightly. There was a considerable crowd of people to receive us; ugly women with bright parasols, loafers and ragamuffins, fat burghers too heavy to ride at the front, and a long line of untidy, white-helmeted policemen—"zarps" as they were called—who looked like broken-down constabulary. Someone opened—unlocked, that is the point—the door of the railway carriage and told us to come out; and out we came—a very ragged and tattered group of officers—and waited under the sun blaze and the gloating of many eyes. About a dozen cameras were clicking busily, establishing an im-perishable record of our shame. Then they loosed the men and bade them form in rank. The soldiers came out of the dark vans, in which they had been confined, with some eagerness, and began at once to chirp and joke, which seemed to me most ill-timed good humour. We waited altogether for about twenty minutes. Now for the first time since my capture I hated the enemy. The simple, valiant burghers at the front, fighting bravely as they had been told "for their farms", claimed respect, if not sympathy. But here in Pretoria all was petty and contemptible. Slimy, sleek officials of all nationali-ties—the red-faced, snub-nosed Hollander, the oily Portuguese half-caste—thrust or wormed their way through the crowd to look. I seemed to smell corruption in the air. Here were the creatures who had fattened on the spoils. There in the field were the heroes who won them. Tammany Hall was defended by the Ironsides.

From these reflections I was recalled by a hand on my shoulder.

A lanky, unshaven police sergeant grasped my arm. "You are not an officer," he said; "you go this way with the common soldiers," and he led me across the open space to where the men were formed in a column of fours. The crowd grinned: the cameras clicked again. I fell in with the soldiers and seized the opportunity to tell them not to laugh or smile, but to appear serious men who cared for the cause they fought for; and when I saw how readily they took the hint, and what influence I possessed with them, it seemed to me that perhaps with two thousand prisoners something some day might be done. But presently a superior official—superior in rank alone, for in other respects he looked a miserable creature—came up and led me back to the officers. At last, when the crowd had thoroughly satisfied their patriotic curiosity, we were marched off; the soldiers to the enclosed camp on the racecourse, the officers to the State Model Schools prison.

The distance was short, so far as we were concerned, and surrounded by an escort of three armed policemen to each officer, we swiftly traversed two sandy avenues with detached houses on either hand, and reached our destination. We turned a corner; on the other side of the road stood a long, low, red brick building with a slated verandah and a row of iron railings before it. The verandah was crowded with bearded men in *khaki* uniforms or brown suits of flannel—smoking, reading, or talking. They looked up as we arrived. The iron gate was opened, and passing in we joined sixty British officers "held by the enemy"; and the iron gate was then shut again.

"Hullo! How are you? Where did they catch you? What's the latest news of Buller's advance? Are we going to be exchanged?" and a dozen other questions were asked. It was the sort of reception accorded to a new boy at a private school, or, as it seemed to me, to a new arrival in hell. But after we had satisfied our friends in as much as we could, suggestions of baths, clothes, and luncheon were made which were very welcome. So we settled down to what promised to be a long and weary waiting.

The State Model Schools is a one-storied building of considerable size and solid structure, which occupies a corner formed by two roads through Pretoria. It consists of twelve large class-rooms, seven or eight of which were used by the British officers as dormitories and one as a dining-room; a large lecture-hall, which served as an improvised fives-court; and a well-fitted gymnasium. It stood in a quadrangular playground about one hundred and twenty yards square, in which were a dozen tents for the police guards, a cookhouse, two tents for the soldier servants, and a newly set-up bathshed. I do not know how the arrival of other prisoners may have modified these arrangements, but at the time of my coming into the prison, there was room enough for everyone.

The Transvaal Government provided a daily ration of bully beef and groceries, and the prisoners were allowed to purchase from the local storekeeper, a Mr. Boshof, practically everything they cared to order, except alcoholic liquors. During the first week of my detention we requested that this last prohibition might be withdrawn, and after profound reflection and much doubtings, the President consented to countenance the buying of bottled beer. Until this concession was obtained our liquid refreshment would have satisfied the most immoderate advocate of temperance, and the only relief was found when the Secretary of State for War, a kind-hearted Portuguese, would smuggle in a bottle of whisky hidden in his tail-coat pocket or amid a basket of fruit. A very energetic and clever young officer of the Dublin Fusiliers, Lieutenant Grimshaw, undertook the task of managing the mess, and when he was assisted by another subaltern—Lieutenant Southey, of the Royal Irish Fusiliers—this became an exceedingly well-conducted concern. In spite of the high prices prevailing in Pretoria prices which were certainly not lowered for our benefit—the somewhat meagre rations which the Government allowed were supplemented, until we lived, for three shillings a day, quite as well as any regiment on service

On arrival, every officer was given a new suit of clothes, bedding, towels, and toilet necessaries, and the indispensable Mr. Boshof was prepared to add to this wardrobe whatever might be required on payment either in money or by a cheque on Messrs. Cox & Co., whose accommodating fame had spread even to the distant hostile town. I took an early opportunity to buy a suit of tweeds of a dark neutral colour, and as unlike the suits of clothes issued by the Government as possible. I would also have purchased a hat, but another officer told me that he had asked for one and had been refused. After all, what use could I find for a hat, when there were plenty of helmets to spare if I wanted to walk in the courtyard? And yet my taste ran towards a slouch hat.

The case of the soldiers was less comfortable than ours. Their rations were very scanty: only one pound of bully beef once a week and two pounds of bread; the rest was made up with mealies, potatoes, and such-like—and not very much of them. Moreover, since they had no money of their own, and since prisoners of war received no pay, they were unable to buy even so much as a pound of tobacco. In consequence they complained a good deal, and were, I think, sufficiently discontented to require nothing but leading to make them rise against their guards.

The custody and regulating of the officers were entrusted to a board of management, four of whose members visited us frequently and listened to any complaints or requests. M. de Souza, the Secretary of War, was perhaps the most friendly and obliging of these, and I think we owed most of the indulgences to his representations. He was a far-seeing little man who had travelled to Europe, and had a very clear conception of the relative strengths of Britain and the Transvaal. He enjoyed a lucrative and influential position under the Government, and was therefore devoted to its interests, but he was nevertheless suspected by the Inner Ring of Hollanders and the Relations of the President of having some sympathy for the British. He had therefore to be very careful. Commandant Opperman, who was directly responsible for our safe custody, was in times of peace a Landrost or Justice. He was too fat to go and fight, but he was an honest and patriotic Boer, who would have gladly taken an active part in the war. He firmly believed that the Republics would win, and when, as sometimes happened, bad news reached Pretoria, Opperman looked a picture of misery, and would come to us and speak of his resolve to shoot his wife and children and perish in the defence of the capital. Dr. Gunning was an amiable little Hollander, fat, rubicund, and well educated. He was a keen politician, and much attached to the Boer Government, which paid him an excellent salary for looking after the State Museum. He had a wonderful collection of postage stamps, and was also engaged in forming a Zoological Garden. This last ambition had just before the war led him into most serious trouble, for he was unable to resist the lion which Mr. Rhodes had offered him. He confided to me that the President had spoken "most harshly" to him in consequence, and had peremptorily ordered the immediate return of the beast under threats of instant dismissal. Gunning said that he could not have borne such treatment, but that after all a man must live. My private impression is that he will acquiesce in any political settlement which leaves him to enlarge his museum undisturbed. But whether the Transvaal will be able to indulge in such luxuries, after blowing up many of other people's railway bridges, is a question which I cannot answer.

The fourth member of the Board, Mr. Malan, was a foul and objectionable brute. His personal courage was better suited to insulting the prisoners in Pretoria than to fighting the enemy at the front. He was closely related to the President, but not even this advantage could altogether protect him from taunts of cowardice, which were made even in the Executive Council, and somehow filtered down to us. On one occasion he favoured me with some of his impertinence; but I reminded him that in war either side may win, and asked whether he was wise to place himself in a separate category as regards behaviour to the prisoners. "Because", quoth I, "it might be so convenient to the British Government to be able to make one or two examples." He was a great gross man, and his colour came and went on a large over-fed face; so that his uneasiness was obvious. He never came near me again, but some days later the news of a Boer success arrived, and on the strength of this he came to the prison and abused a subaltern in the Dublin Fusiliers, telling him that he was no gentleman, and other things which it is not right to say to a prisoner. The subaltern happens to be exceedingly handy with his fists, so that after the war is over Mr. Malan is going to get his head punched quite independently of the general settlement.

Although, as I have frequently stated, there were no legitimate grounds of complaint against the treatment of British regular officers while prisoners of war, the days I passed at Pretoria were the most monotonous and among the most miserable of my life. Early in the sultry morning, for the heat at this season of the year was great, the soldier servants—prisoners like ourselves—would bring us a cup of coffee, and sitting up in bed we began to smoke the cigarettes and cigars of another idle, aimless day. Breakfast was at nine: a nasty uncomfortable meal. The room was stuffy, and there are more enlivening spectacles than seventy British officers caught by Dutch farmers and penned together in confinement. Then came the long morning, to be killed somehow by reading, chess, or cards— and perpetual cigarettes. Luncheon at one: the same as breakfast, only more so; and then a longer afternoon to follow a long morning. Often some of the officers used to play rounders in the small yard which we had for exercise. But the rest walked moodily up and down, or lounged over the railings and returned the stares of the occasional passers-by. Later would come the "Volksstem"—permitted by special indulgence—with its budget of lies.

Sometimes we get a little fillip of excitement. One evening, as I was leaning over the railings, more than forty yards from the nearest sentry, a short man with a red moustache walked quickly down the street, followed by two colley dogs. As he passed, but without altering his pace in the slightest, or even looking towards me, he said quite distinctly "Methuen beat the Boers to hell at Belmont." That night the air seemed cooler and the courtyard larger. Already we imagined the Republics collapsing and the bayonets of the Queen's Guards in the streets of Pretoria. Next day I talked to the War Secretary. I had made a large map upon the wall and followed the course of the war as far as possible by making squares of red and green paper to represent the various columns. I said: "What about Methuen? He has beaten you at Belmont. Now he should be across the Modder. In a few days he will relieve Kimberley." De Souza shrugged his shoulders. "Who can tell?" he replied; "but," he put his finger on the map, "there stands old Piet Cronje in a position called Scholz Nek, and we don't think Methuen will ever get past him." The event justified his words, and the battle which we call Magersfontein (and ought to call "Maasfontayne") the Boers call Scholz Nek.

Long, dull, and profitless were the days. I could not write, for the ink seemed to dry upon the pen. I could not read with any perseverance, and during the whole month I was locked up, I only completed Carlyle's *History of Frederick the Great* and Mill's *Essay on Liberty*, neither of which satisfied my peevish expectations. When at last the sun sank behind the fort upon the hill and twilight marked the end of another wretched day, I used to walk up and down the courtyard looking reflectively at the dirty, unkempt "zarps" who stood on guard, racking my brains to find some way, by force or fraud, by steel or gold, of regaining my freedom. Little did these Transvaal Policemen think, as they leaned on their rifles, smoking and watching the "tame officers", of the dark schemes of which they were the object, or of the peril in which they would stand but for the difficulties that lay *beyond* the wall. For we would have made short work of them and their weapons any misty night could we but have seen our way clear after that.

As the darkness thickened, the electric lamps were switched on and the whole courtyard turned blue-white with black velvet shadows. Then the bell clanged, and we crowded again into the stifling dining hall for the last tasteless meal of the barren day. The same miserable stories were told again and again—Colonel Moller's surrender after Talana Hill, and the white flag at Nicholson's Nek—until I knew how the others came to Pretoria as well as I knew my own story.

"We never realised what had happened until we were actually prisoners," said the officers of the Dublin Fusiliers Mounted Infantry, who had been captured with Colonel Moller on October 20. "The 'cease fire' sounded: no one knew what had happened. Then we were ordered to form up at the farmhouse, and there we found Boers, who told us to lay down our arms: we were delivered into their hands and never even allowed to have a gallop for freedom. But wait for the Court of Inquiry."

I used always to sit next to Colonel Carleton at dinner, and from him and from the others learned the story of Nicholson's Nek, which it is not necessary to repeat here, but which filled me with sympathy for the gallant commander and soldiers who were betrayed by the act of an irresponsible subordinate. The officers of the Irish Fusiliers told me of the amazement with which they had seen the white flag flying. "We had still some ammunition," they said; "it is true the position was indefensible—but we only wanted to fight it out."

"My company was scarcely engaged," said one poor captain, with tears of vexation in his eyes at the memory; and the Gloucesters told the same tale.

"We saw the hateful thing flying. The firing stopped. No one knew by whose orders the flag had been hoisted. While we doubted the Boers were all among us disarming the men."

I will write no more upon these painful subjects except to say this, that the hoisting of a white flag in token of surrender is an act which can be justified only by clear proof that there was no prospect of gaining the slightest military advantage by going on fighting; and that the raising of a white flag in any case by an unauthorised person—i.e. not the officer in chief command—in such a manner as to compromise the resistance of a force, deserves sentence of death, though in view of the high standard of discipline and honour prevailing in Her Majesty's army, it might not be necessary to carry the sentence into effect. I earnestly trust that in justice to gallant officers and soldiers, who have languished these weary months in Pretoria, there will be a strict inquiry into the circumstances under which they became prisoners of war. I have no doubt we shall be told that it is a foolish thing to wash dirty linen in public; but much better wash it in public than wear it foul.

One day shortly after I had arrived I had an interesting visit, for de Souza, wishing to have an argument brought Mr. Grobelaar to see me. This gentleman was the Under Secretary for Foreign Affairs, and had just returned from Mafeking, whither he had been conducting a 6-inch gun. He was a very well-educated person, and so far as I could tell, honest and capable besides. With him came Reuter's Agent, Mr. Mackay, and the odious Malan. I received them sitting on my bed in the dormitory, and when they had lighted cigars, of which I always kept a stock, we had a regular *durbar*. I began:

"Well, Mr. Grobelaar, you see how your Government treats representatives of the Press."

Grobelaar. "I hope you have nothing to complain of."

Self. "Look at the sentries with loaded rifles on every side. I might be a wild beast instead of a special correspondent."

Grobelaar. "Ah, but putting aside the sentries with loaded rifles, you do not, I trust, Mr. Churchill, make any complaint."

Self. "My chief objection to this place is that I am in it."

Grobelaar. "That of course is your misfortune, and Mr. Chamberlain's fault."

Self. "Not at all. We are a peace-loving people, but we had no choice but to fight or be—what was it your burghers told me in the camps?—'driven into the sea'. The responsibility of the war is upon you and your President."

Grobelaar. "Don't you believe that. We did not want to fight. We only wanted to be left alone."

Self. "You never wanted war?"

de Souza. "Ah, my God, no! Do you think we would fight Great Britain for amusement?"

Self. "Then why did you make every preparation—turn the Republics into armed camps—prepare deep-laid plans for the invasion of our Colonies?"

Grobelaar. "Why, what could we do after the Jameson Raid? We had to be ready to protect ourselves."

Self. "Surely less extensive armaments would have been sufficient to guard against another similar inroad."

Grobelaar. "But we knew your Government was behind the Raiders. Jameson was in front, but Rhodes and your Colonial Office were at his elbow."

Self. "As a matter of fact no two people were more disconcerted by the Raid than Chamberlain and Rhodes. Besides, the British Government disavowed the Raiders' action and punished the Raiders, who, I am quite prepared to admit, got no more than they deserved."

de Souza. "I don't complain about the British Government's action at the time of the Raid. Chamberlain behaved very honourably then. But it was afterwards, when Rhodes was not punished, that we knew it was all a farce, and that the British Government was bent on our destruction. When the burghers knew that Rhodes was not punished they lost all trust in England."

Malan. "Ya, ya. That Rhodes, he is the . . . at the bottom of it all. You wait and see what we will do to Rhodes when we take Kimberley."

Self. "Then you maintain, de Souza, that the distrust caused in this country by the fact that Rhodes was not punished—though how you can punish a man who breaks no law I cannot tell—was the sole cause of your Government making these gigantic military preparations, because it is certain that these preparations were the actual cause of war."

Grobelaar. "Why should they be a cause of war? We would never have attacked you."

Self. "But at this moment you are invading Cape Colony and Natal, while no British soldier has set foot on Republican soil. Moreover, it was you who declared war upon us."

Grobelaar. "Naturally we were not such fools as to wait till your army was here. As soon as you began to send your army, we were bound to declare war. If you had sent it earlier we should have fought earlier. Really, Mr. Churchill, you must see that that is only common sense."

Self. "I am not criticising your policy or tactics. You hated us bitterly—I dare say you had cause to. You made tremendous preparations—I don't say you were wrong—but look at it from our point of view. We saw a declared enemy armed and arming. Against us, and against us alone, could his preparations be directed. It was time we took some precautions: indeed, we were already too late. Surely what has happened at the front proves that we had no designs against you. You were ready. We were unready. It is the wolf and lamb if you like; but the wolf was asleep and never before was a lamb with such teeth and claws."

Grobelaar. "Do you really mean to say that we forced this war on you, that you did not want to fight us?"

Self. "The country did not wish for war with the Boers. Personally, I have always done so. I saw that you had six rifles to every burgher in the Republic. I knew what that meant. It meant that you were going to raise a great Afrikander revolt against us. One does not set extra places at table unless one expects company to dinner. On the other hand, we have affairs all over the world, and at any moment may become embroiled with a European power. At this time things are very quiet. The board is clear in other directions. We can give you our undivided attention. Armed and ambitious as you were, the war had to come sooner or later. I have always said 'sooner'. Therefore, I rejoiced when you sent your ultimatum and roused the whole nation."

Malan. "You don't rejoice quite so much now."

Self. 'My opinion is unaltered, except that the necessity for settling the matter has become more apparent. As for the result, that, as I think Mr. Grobelaar knows, is only a question of time and money expressed in terms of blood and tears."

Grobelaar. "No: our opinion is quite unchanged. We prepared for the war. We have always thought we could beat you. We do not doubt our calculations now. We have done better even than we expected. The President is extremely pleased."

Self. "There is no good arguing on that point. We shall have to fight it out. But if you had tried to keep on friendly terms with us, the war would not have come for a long time; and the delay was all on your side."

Grobelaar. "We have tried till we are sick of it. This Government was badgered out of its life with Chamberlain's despatches—such despatches. And then look how we have been lied about in your papers, and called barbarians and savages."

Self. "I think you have certainly been abused unjustly. Indeed, when I was taken prisoner the other day, I thought it quite possible I should be put to death, although I was a correspondent" (great laughter, "Fancy that!" etc.). "At the best I expected to be held in prison as a kind of hostage. See how I have been mistaken."

I pointed at the sentry who stood in the doorway, for even

members of the Government could not visit us alone. Grobelaar flushed. "Oh, well, we will hope that the captivity will not impair your spirits. Besides, it will not last long. The President expects peace before the New Year."

"I shall hope to be free by then."

And with this the interview came to an end, and my visitors withdrew. The actual conversation had lasted more than an hour, but the dialogue above is not an inaccurate summary.

About ten days after my arrival at Pretoria I received a visit from the American Consul, Mr. Macrum. It seems that some uncertainty prevailed at home as to whether I was alive, wounded or unwounded, and in what light I was regarded by the Transvaal authorities. Mr. Bourke Cockran, an American Senator who had long been a friend of mine, telegraphed from New York to the United States representative in Pretoria, hoping by this neutral channel to learn how the case stood. I had not, however, talked with Mr. Macrum for very long before I realised that neither I nor any other British prisoner was likely to be the better for any efforts which he might make on our behalf. His sympathies were plainly so much with the Transvaal Government that he even found it difficult to discharge his diplomatic duties. However, he so far sank his political opinions as to telegraph to Mr. Bourke Cockran, and the anxiety which my relations were suffering on my account was thereby terminated.

I had one other visitor in these dull days, whom I should like to notice. During the afternoon which I spent among the Boers in their camp behind Bulwana Hill I had exchanged a few words with an Englishman whose name is of no consequence, but who was the gunner entrusted with the aiming of the big 6-inch gun. He was a light-hearted jocular fellow outwardly, but I was not long in discovering that his anxieties among the Boers were grave and numerous. He had been drawn into the war, so far as I could make out, more by the desire of sticking to his own friends and neighbours than even of preserving his property. But besides this local spirit, which counterbalanced the racial and patriotic feelings, there was a very strong desire to be upon the winning side, and I think that he regarded the Boers with an aversion which increased in proportion as their successes fell short of their early anticipations. One afternoon he called at the State Model Schools prison and, being duly authorised to visit the prisoners, asked to see me. In the presence of Dr. Gunning, I had an interesting interview. At first our conversation was confined to generalities, but gradually, as the other officers in the room, with ready tact, drew the little Hollander Professor into an argument, my renegade and I were able to exchange confidences.

I was of course above all things anxious to get true news from the outer world, and whenever Dr. Gunning's attention was distracted by his discussion with the officers, I managed to get a little.

"Well, you know," said the gunner, "you English don't play fair at Ladysmith at all. We have allowed you to have a camp at Intombi Spruit for your wounded, and yet we see red cross flags flying in the town, and we have heard that in the Church there is a magazine of ammunition protected by the red cross flag. Major Erasmus, he says to me 'John, you smash up that building,' and so when I go back I am going to fire into the church." Gunning broke out into panegyrics on the virtues of the Afrikanders: my companion dropped his voice. "The Boers have had a terrible beating at Belmont; the Free Staters have lost more than 200 killed; much discouraged; if your people keep on like this the Free State will break up." He raised his voice, "Ladysmith hold out a month? Not possible; we shall give it a fortnight's more bombardment, and then you will just see how the burghers will scramble into their trenches. Plenty of whisky then, ha, ha, ha!" Then lower, "I wish to God I could get away from this, but I don't know what to do; they are always suspecting me and watching me, and I have to keep on pretending I want them to win. This is a terrible position for a man to be in: curse the filthy Dutchmen!"

I said, "Will Methuen get to Kimberley?"

"I don't know, but he gave them hell at Belmont and at Graspan, and they say they are fighting again today at Modder River. Major Erasmus is very down-hearted about it, but the ordinary burghers hear nothing but lies; all lies, I tell you. (*Crescendo*) Look at the lies that have been told about us! Barbarians! savages! every name your papers have called us, but you know better than that now; you know how well we have treated you since you have been a prisoner; and look at the way your people have treated our prisoners—put them on board ship to make them sea-sick! Don't you call that cruel?" Here Gunning broke in that it was time for visitors to leave the prison. And so my strange guest, a feather blown along by the wind, without character or stability, a renegade, a traitor to his blood and birthplace, a time-server, had to hurry away. I took his measure; nor did his protestations of alarm excite my sympathy, and yet somehow I did not feel unkindly towards him; a weak man is a pitiful object in times of trouble. Some of our countrymen who were living in the Transvaal and the Orange Free State at the outbreak of the war have been placed in such difficult positions and torn by so many conflicting emotions that they must be judged very tolerantly. How few men are strong enough to stand against the prevailing currents of opinion! Nor, after the desertion of the British residents in the Transvaal in 1881, have we the right to judge their successors harshly if they have failed us, for it was Great and Mighty Britain who was the renegade and traitor then.

No sooner had I reached Pretoria than I demanded my release from the Government, on the grounds that I was a Press correspondent and a non-combatant. So many people have found it difficult to reconcile this position with the accounts which have been published of what transpired during the defence of the armoured train, that I am compelled to explain. Besides the soldiers of the Dublin Fusiliers and Durban Light Infantry who had been captured, there were also eight or ten civilians, including a fireman, a telegraphist, and several men of the breakdown gang. Now it seems to me that according to international practice and the customs of war, the Transvaal Government were perfectly justified in regarding all persons connected with a military train as actual combatants; indeed, the fact that they were not soldiers was, if anything, an aggravation of their case. But the Boers were at that time overstocked with prisoners whom they had to feed and guard, and they therefore announced that the civilians would be released as soon as their identity was established, and only the military retained as prisoners.

In my case, however, an exception was to be made, and General Joubert, who had read the gushing accounts of my conduct which appeared in the Natal newspapers, directed that since I had taken part in the fighting I was to be treated as a combatant officer.

Now, as it happened, I had confined myself strictly to the business of clearing the line, which was entrusted to me, and although I do not pretend that I considered the matter in its legal aspect at the time, the fact remains that I did not give a shot, nor was I armed when captured. I therefore claimed to be included in the same category as the civilian railway officials and men of the breakdown gang, whose declared duty it was to clear the line, pointing out that though my action might differ in degree from theirs, it was of precisely the same character, and that if they were regarded as non-combatants I had a right to be considered a non-combatant too.

To this effect I wrote two letters, one to the Secretary of War and one to General Joubert; but, needless to say, I did not indulge in much hope of the result, for I was firmly convinced that the Boer authorities regarded me as a kind of hostage, who would make a pleasing addition to the collection of prisoners they were forming against a change of fortune. I therefore continued to search for a path of escape; and indeed it was just as well that I did so, for I never received any answer to either of my applications while I was a prisoner, although I have since heard that one arrived by a curious coincidence the very day *after* I had departed.

While I was looking about for means, and awaiting an opportunity to break out of the Model Schools, I made every preparation to make a graceful exit when the moment should arrive. I gave full instructions to my friends as to what was to be done with my clothes and the effects I had accumulated during my stay; I paid my account to date with the excellent Boshof; cashed a cheque on him for 20*l.*; changed some of the notes I had always concealed on my person since my capture into gold; and lastly, that there might be no unnecessary unpleasantness, I wrote the following letter to the Secretary of State:

State Model Schools Prison:
December 10, 1899

Sir,—I have the honour to inform you that as I do not consider that your Government have any right to detain me as a military prisoner, I have decided to escape from your custody. I have every confidence in the arrangements I have made with my friends outside, and I do not therefore expect to have another opportunity of seeing you. I therefore take this occasion to observe that I consider your treatment of prisoners is correct and humane, and that I see no grounds for complaint. When I return to the British lines I will make a public statement to this effect. I have also to thank you personally for your civility to me, and to express the hope that we may meet again at Pretoria before very long, and under different circumstances. Regretting that I am unable to bid you a more ceremonious or a personal farewell,

"I have the honour, to be, Sir,

"Your most obedient servant,

"WINSTON CHURCHILL."

To Mr. de Souza,
Secretary of War, South African Republic.

I arranged that this letter, which I took great pleasure in writing, should be left on my bed, and discovered so soon as my flight was known.

It only remained now to find a hat. Luckily for me Mr. Adrian Hofmeyr, a Dutch clergyman and pastor of Zeerust, had ventured before the war to express opinions contrary to those which the Boers thought befitting for a Dutchman to hold. They had therefore seized him on the outbreak of hostilities, and after much ill-treatment and many indignities on the Western border, brought him to the State Schools. He knew most of the officials, and could, I think, easily have obtained his liberty had he pretended to be in sympathy with the Republics. He was, however, a true man, and after the clergyman of the Church of England, who was rather a poor creature, omitted to read the prayer for the Queen one Sunday, it was to Hofmeyr's evening services alone that most of the officers would go. I borrowed his hat.

CHAPTER ELEVEN

I ESCAPE FROM THE BOERS

Lourenço Marques: December 22, 1899

HOW UNHAPPY is that poor man who loses his liberty! What can the wide world give him in exchange? No degree of material comfort, no consciousness of correct behaviour, can balance the hateful degradation of imprisonment. Before I had been an hour in captivity, as the previous pages evidence, I resolved to escape. Many plans suggested themselves, were examined, and rejected. For a month I thought of nothing else. But the peril and difficulty restrained action. I think that it was the report of the British defeat at Stormberg that clinched the matter. All the news we heard in Pretoria was derived from Boer sources, and was hideously exaggerated and distorted. Every day we read in the *Volksstem*—probably the most astounding tissue of lies ever presented to the public under the name of a newspaper—of Boer victories and of the huge slaughters and shameful flights of the British. However much one might doubt and discount these tales, they made a deep impression. A month's feeding on such literary garbage weakens the constitution of the mind. We wretched prisoners lost heart. Perhaps Great Britain would not persevere; perhaps Foreign Powers would intervene; perhaps there would be another disgraceful, cowardly peace. At the best the war and our confinement would be prolonged for many months. I do not pretend that impatience at being locked up was not the foundation of my determination; but I should never have screwed up my courage to make the attempt without the earnest desire to do something, however small, to help the British cause. Of course, I am a man of peace. I did not then contemplate becoming an officer of Irregular Horse. But swords are not the only weapons in the world. Something may be done with a pen. So I determined to take all hazards;

and, indeed, the affair was one of very great danger and difficulty.

The State Model Schools stand in the midst of a quadrangle, and are surrounded on two sides by an iron grille and on two by a corrugated iron fence about 10 ft. high. These boundaries offered little obstacle to anyone who possessed the activity of youth, but the fact that they were guarded on the inside by sentries, fifty yards apart, armed with rifle and revolver, made them a well-nigh insuperable barrier. No walls are so hard to pierce as living walls. I thought of the penetrating power of gold, and the sentries were sounded. They were incorruptible. I seek not to deprive them of the credit, but the truth is that the bribery market in the Transvaal has been spoiled by the millionaires. I could not afford with my slender resources to insult them heavily enough. So nothing remained but to break out in spite of them. With another officer who may for the present—since he is still a prisoner—remain nameless, I formed a scheme.

After anxious reflection and continual watching, it was discovered that when the sentries near the offices walked about on their beats they were at certain moments unable to see the top of a few yards of the wall. The electric lights in the middle of the quadrangle brilliantly lighted the whole place but cut off the sentries beyond them from looking at the eastern wall, for from behind the lights all seemed darkness by contrast. The first thing was therefore to pass the two sentries near the offices. It was necessary to hit off the exact moment when both their backs should be turned together. After the wall was scaled we should be in the garden of the villa next door. There our plan came to an end. Everything after this was vague and uncertain. How to get out of the garden, how to pass unnoticed through the streets, how to evade the patrols that surrounded the town, and above all how to cover the two hundred and eighty miles to the Portuguese frontiers, were questions which would arise at a later stage. All attempts to communicate with friends outside had failed. We cherished the hope that with chocolate, a little Kaffir knowledge, and a great deal of luck, we might march the distance in a fortnight, buying mealies at the native kraals and lying hidden by day. But it did not look a very promising prospect.

We determined to try on the night of the 11th of December, making up our minds quite suddenly in the morning, for these

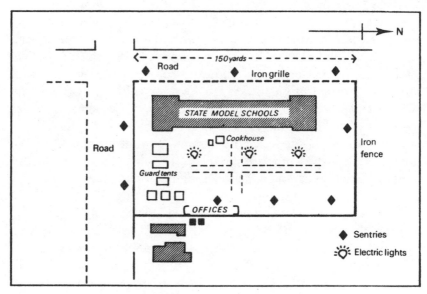

THE STATE MODEL SCHOOLS

things are best done on the spur of the moment. I passed the afternoon in positive terror. Nothing, since my schooldays, has ever disturbed me so much as this. There is something appalling in the idea of stealing secretly off in the night like a guilty thief. The fear of detection has a pang of its own. Besides, we knew quite well that on occasion, even on excuse, the sentries would fire. Fifteen yards is a short range. And beyond the immediate danger lay a prospect of severe hardship and suffering, only faint hopes of success, and the probability at the best of five months in Pretoria Gaol.

The afternoon dragged tediously away. I tried to read Mr. Lecky's *History of England*, but for the first time in my life that wise writer wearied me. I played chess and was hopelessly beaten. At last it grew dark. At seven o'clock the bell for dinner rang and the officers trooped off. Now was the time. But the sentries gave us no chance. They did not walk about. One of them stood exactly opposite the only practicable part of the wall. We waited for two hours, but the attempt was plainly impossible, and so with a most unsatisfactory feeling of relief to bed.

Tuesday, the 12th! Another day of fear, but fear crystallising more and more into desperation. Anything was better than further suspense. Night came again. Again the dinner bell sounded. Choosing my opportunity I strolled across the quadrangle and secreted myself in one of the offices. Through a chink I watched the sentries. For half an hour they remained stolid and obstructive. Then all of a sudden one turned and walked up to his comrade and they began to talk. Their backs were turned. Now or never. I darted out of my hiding place and ran to the wall, seized the top with my hands and drew myself up. Twice I let myself down again in sickly hesitation, and then with a third resolve scrambled up. The top was flat. Lying on it I had one parting glimpse of the sentries, still talking, still with their backs turned; but, I repeat, fifteen yards away. Then I lowered myself silently down into the adjoining garden and crouched among the shrubs. I was free. The first step had been taken, and it was irrevocable.

It now remained to await the arrival of my comrade. The bushes of the garden gave a good deal of cover, and in the moonlight their shadows lay black on the ground. Twenty yards away was the house, and I had not been five minutes in hiding before I perceived that it was full of people; the windows revealed brightly lighted rooms, and within I could see figures moving about. This was a fresh complication. We had always thought the house unoccupied. Presently—how long afterwards I do not know, for the ordinary measures of time, hours, minutes, and seconds are quite meaningless on such occasions—a man came out of the door and walked across the garden in my direction. Scarcely ten yards away he stopped and stood still, looking steadily towards me. I cannot describe the surge of panic which nearly overwhelmed me. I must be discovered. I dared not stir an inch. My heart beat so violently that I felt sick. But amid a tumult of emotion, reason, seated firmly on her throne, whispered, "Trust to the dark background." I remained absolutely motionless. For a long time the man and I remained opposite each other, and every instant I expected him to spring forward. A vague idea crossed my mind that I might silence him. "Hush, I am a detective. We expect that an officer will break out here tonight. I am waiting to catch him." Reason—scornful this time—replied: "Surely a Transvaal detective would speak Dutch. Trust to the shadow." So I trusted, and after a spell another man came out of the house, lighted a cigar, and both he and the other walked off together. No sooner had they turned than a cat pursued by a dog rushed into the bushes and collided with me. The startled animal uttered a "miaul" of alarm and darted back again, making a horrible rustling. Both men stopped at once. But it was only the cat, as they doubtless observed, and they passed out of the garden gate into the town.

I looked at my watch. An hour had passed since I climbed the wall. Where was my comrade? Suddenly I heard a voice from within the quadrangle say, quite loud, "All up." I crawled back to the wall. Two officers were walking up and down the other side jabbering Latin words, laughing and talking all manner of nonsense —amid which I caught my name. I risked a cough. One of the officers immediately began to chatter alone. The other said slowly and clearly, ". . . cannot get out. The sentry suspects. It's all up. Can you get back again?" But now all my fears fell from me at once. To go back was impossible. I could not hope to climb the wall unnoticed. Fate pointed onwards. Besides, I said to myself, "Of course, I shall be recaptured, but I will at least have a run for my money." I said to the officers, "I shall go on alone."

Now I was in the right mood for these undertakings—that is to say that, thinking failure almost certain, no odds against success affected me. All risks were less than the certainty. A glance at the plan (p. 82) will show that the gate which led into the road was only a few yards from another sentry. I said to myself, "Toujours de l'audace:" put my hat on my head, strode into the middle of the garden, walked past the windows of the house without any attempt at concealment, and so went through the gate and turned to the left. I passed the sentry at less than five yards. Most of them knew me by sight. Whether he looked at me or not I do not know, for I never turned my head. But after walking a hundred yards and hearing no challenge, I knew that the second obstacle had been surmounted. I was at large in Pretoria.

I walked on leisurely through the night humming a tune and choosing the middle of the road. The streets were full of Burghers, but they paid no attention to me. Gradually I reached the surburbs, and on a little bridge I sat down to reflect and consider. I was in the heart of the enemy's country. I knew no one to whom I could apply for succour. Nearly three hundred miles stretched between me and Delagoa Bay. My escape must be known at dawn. Pursuit would be immediate. Yet all exits were barred. The town was picketed, the country was patrolled, the trains were searched, the line was guarded. I had 75*l.* in my pocket and four slabs of chocolate, but the compass and the map which might have guided me, the opium tablets and meat lozenges which should have sustained me, were in my friend's pockets in the State Model Schools. Worst of all, I could not speak a word of Dutch or Kaffir, and how was I to get food or direction?

But when hope had departed, fear had gone as well. I formed a plan. I would find the Delagoa Bay Railway. Without map or compass I must follow that in spite of the pickets. I looked at the stars. Orion shone brightly. Scarcely a year ago he had guided me when lost in the desert to the banks of the Nile. He had given me water. Now he should lead to freedom. I could not endure the want of either.

After walking south for half a mile, I struck the railroad. Was it the line to Delagoa Bay or the Pietersburg branch? If it were the former it should run east. But so far as I could see this line ran northwards. Still, it might be only winding its way out among the hills. I resolved to follow it. The night was delicious. A cool breeze fanned my face and a wild feeling of exhilaration took hold of me. At any rate, I was free, if only for an hour. That was something. The fascination of the adventure grew. Unless the stars in their courses fought for me I could not escape. Where, then, was the need of caution? I marched briskly along the line. Here and there the lights of a picket fire gleamed. Every bridge had its watchers. But I passed them all, making very short détours at the dangerous places, and really taking scarcely any precautions. Perhaps that was the reason I succeeded.

As I walked I extended my plan. I could not march three hundred miles to the frontier. I would board a train in motion and hide under the seats, on the roof, on the couplings—anywhere. What train should I take? The first, of course. After walking for two hours I perceived the signal lights of a station. I left the line, and, circling round it, hid in the ditch by the track about 200 yards beyond it. I argued that the train would stop at the station and that it would not have got up too much speed by the time it reached me. An hour passed. I began to grow impatient. Suddenly I heard the whistle and the approaching rattle. Then the great yellow head lights of the engine flashed into view. The train waited five minutes at the station and started again with much noise and steaming. I crouched by the track. I rehearsed the act in my mind. I must wait until the engine had passed, otherwise I should be seen. Then I must make a dash for the carriages.

The train started slowly, but gathered speed sooner than I had expected. The flaring lights drew swiftly near. The rattle grew into a roar. The dark mass hung for a second above me. The engine-driver silhouetted against his furnace glow, the black profile of the engine, the clouds of steam rushed past. Then I hurled myself on the trucks, clutched at something, missed, clutched again, missed again, grasped some sort of hand-hold, was swung off my feet—my toes bumping on the line, and with a struggle seated myself on the couplings of the fifth truck from the front of the train. It was a goods train, and the trucks were full of sacks, soft sacks covered with coal dust. I crawled on top and burrowed in among them. In five minutes I was completely buried. The sacks were warm and comfortable. Perhaps the engine-driver had seen me rush up to the train and would give the alarm at the next station: on the other hand, perhaps not. Where was the train going to? Where would it be unloaded? Would it be searched? Was it on the Delagoa Bay line? What should I do in the morning? Ah, never mind that. Sufficient for the day was the luck thereof. Fresh plans for fresh contingencies. I resolved to sleep, nor can I imagine a more pleasing lullaby than the clatter of the train that carries you at twenty miles an hour away from the enemy's capital.

How long I slept I do not know, but I woke up suddenly with all feelings of exhilaration gone, and only the consciousness of oppressive difficulties heavy on me. I must leave the train before daybreak, so that I could drink at a pool and find some hiding-place while it was still dark. Another night I would board another train. I crawled from my cosy hiding-place among the sacks and sat again on the couplings. The train was running at a fair speed, but I felt it was time to leave it. I took hold of the iron handle at the back of the truck, pulled strongly with my left hand, and sprang. My feet struck the ground in two gigantic strides, and the next instant I was sprawling in the ditch, considerably shaken but unhurt. The train, my faithful ally of the night, hurried on its journey.

It was still dark. I was in the middle of a wide valley, surrounded by low hills, and carpeted with high grass drenched in dew. I searched for water in the nearest gully, and soon found a clear pool. I was very thirsty, but long after I had quenched my thirst I continued to drink, that I might have sufficient for the whole day.

Presently the dawn began to break, and the sky to the east grew yellow and red, slashed across with heavy black clouds. I saw with relief that the railway ran steadily towards the sunrise. I had taken the right line, after all.

Having drunk my fill, I set out for the hills, among which I hoped to find some hiding-place, and as it became broad daylight I entered a small grove of trees which grew on the side of a deep ravine. Here I resolved to wait till dusk. I had one consolation: no one in the world knew where I was—I did not know myself. It was now four o'clock. Fourteen hours lay between me and the night. My impatience to proceed, while I was still strong, doubled their length. At first it was terribly cold, but by degrees the sun gained power, and by ten o'clock the heat was oppressive. My sole companion was a gigantic vulture, who manifested an extravagant interest in my condition, and made hideous and ominous gurglings from time to time. From my lofty position I commanded a view of the whole valley. A little tin-roofed town lay three miles to the westward. Scattered farmsteads, each with a clump of trees, relieved the monotony of the undulating ground. At the foot of the hill stood a Kaffir kraal, and the figures of its inhabitants dotted the patches of cultivation or surrounded the droves of goats and cows which fed on the pasture. The railway ran through the middle of the valley, and I could watch the passage of the various trains. I counted four passing each way, and from this I drew the conclusion that the same number would run by night. I marked a steep gradient up which they climbed very slowly, and determined at nightfall to make another attempt to board one of these. During the day I ate one slab of chocolate, which, with the heat, produced a violent thirst. The pool was hardly half a mile away, but I dared not leave the shelter of the little wood, for I could see the figures of white men riding or walking occasionally across the valley, and once a Boer came and fired two shots at birds close to my hiding-place. But no one discovered me.

The elation and the excitement of the previous night had burnt away, and a chilling reaction followed. I was very hungry, for I had had no dinner before starting, and chocolate, though it sustains, does not satisfy. I had scarcely slept, but yet my heart beat so fiercely and I was so nervous and perplexed about the future that I could not rest. I thought of all the chances that lay against me; I dreaded and detested more than words can express the prospect of being caught and dragged back to Pretoria. I do not mean that I would rather have died than have been retaken, but I have often feared death for much less. I found no comfort in any of the philosophical ideas which some men parade in their hours of ease and strength and safety. They seemed only fair-weather friends. I realised with awful force that no exercise of my own feeble wit and strength could save me from my enemies, and that without the assistance of that High Power which interferes in the eternal sequence of causes and effects more often than we are always prone to admit, I could never succeed. I prayed long and earnestly for help and guidance. My prayer, as it seems to me, was swiftly and wonderfully answered. I cannot now relate the strange circumstances which followed, and which changed my nearly hopeless position into one of superior advantage. But after the war is over I shall hope to lengthen this account, and so remarkable will the addition be that I cannot believe the reader will complain.

The long day reached its close at last. The western clouds flushed into fire; the shadows of the hills stretched out across the valley. A ponderous Boer waggon, with its long team, crawled slowly along the track towards the town. The Kaffirs collected their herds and drew around their kraal. The daylight died, and soon it was quite dark. Then, and not till then, I set forth. I hurried to the railway line, pausing on my way to drink at a stream of sweet, cold water. I waited for some time at the top of the steep gradient in the hope of catching a train. But none came, and I gradually guessed, and I have since found that I guessed right, that the train I had already travelled in was the only one that ran at night. At last I resolved to walk on, and make, at any rate, twenty miles of my journey. I walked for about six hours. How far I travelled I do not know, but I do not think that it was very many miles in the direct line. Every bridge was guarded by armed men; every few miles were gangers' huts; at intervals there were stations with villages clustering round them. All the veldt was bathed in the bright rays of the full moon, and to avoid these dangerous places I had to make wide circuits and often to creep along the ground. Leaving the railroad I fell into bogs and swamps, and brushed through high grass dripping with dew, so that I was drenched to the waist. I had been able to take little exercise during my month's imprisonment, and I was soon tired out with walking, as well as from want of food and sleep. I felt very miserable when I looked around and saw here and there the lights of houses, and thought of the warmth and comfort within them, but knew that they only meant danger to me. After six or seven hours of walking I thought it unwise to go further lest I should exhaust myself, so I lay down in a ditch to sleep. I was nearly at the end of my tether. Nevertheless, by the will of God, I was enabled to sustain myself during the next few days, obtaining food at great risk here and there, resting in concealment by day and walking only at night. On the fifth day I was beyond Middelburg, so far as I could tell, for I dared not inquire nor as yet approach the stations near enough to read the names. In a secure hiding-place I waited for a suitable train, knowing that there is a through service between Middelburg and Lourenço Marques.

Meanwhile there had been excitement in the State Model Schools, temporarily converted into a military prison. Early on Wednesday morning—barely twelve hours after I had escaped—my absence was discovered—I think by Dr. Gunning. The alarm was given. Telegrams with my description at great length were despatched along all the railways. Three thousand photographs were printed. A warrant was issued for my immediate arrest. Every train was strictly searched. Everyone was on the watch. The worthy Boshof, who knew my face well, was hurried off to Komati Poort to

examine all and sundry people "with red hair" travelling towards
the frontier. The newspapers made so much of the affair that my
humble fortunes and my whereabouts were discussed in long
columns of print, and even in the crash of the war I became to the
Boers a topic all to myself. The rumours in part amused me. It was
certain, said the *Standard and Diggers' News*, that I had escaped
disguised as a woman. The next day I was reported captured at
Komati Poort dressed as a Transvaal policeman. There was great
delight at this, which was only changed to doubt when other
telegrams said that I had been arrested at Brugsbank, at Middelburg, and at Brokerspruit. But the captives proved to be harmless
people after all. Finally it was agreed that I had never left Pretoria.
I had—it appeared—changed clothes with a waiter, and was now
in hiding at the house of some British sympathiser in the capital.
On the strength of this all the houses of suspected persons were
searched from top to bottom, and these unfortunate people were, I
fear, put to a great deal of inconvenience. A special commission was
also appointed to investigate "stringently" (a most hateful adjec-
tive in such a connection) the causes "which had rendered it
possible for the War Correspondent of the *Morning Post* to escape".

The *Volksstem* noticed as a significant fact that I had recently
become a subscriber to the State Library, and had selected Mill's
essay "On Liberty". It apparently desired to gravely deprecate
prisoners having access to such inflammatory literature. The idea
will, perhaps, amuse those who have read the work in question.

I find it very difficult in the face of the extraordinary efforts
which were made to recapture me, to believe that the Transvaal
Government seriously contemplated my release *before* they knew I
had escaped them. Yet a telegram was swiftly despatched from
Pretoria to all the newspapers, setting forth the terms of a most
admirable letter, in which General Joubert explained the grounds
which prompted him generously to restore my liberty. I am inclined
to think that the Boers hate being beaten even in the smallest
things, and always fight on the win, tie, or wrangle principle; but in
my case I rejoice I am not beholden to them, and have not thus
been disqualified from fighting.

All these things may provoke a smile of indifference, perhaps
even of triumph, after the danger is past; but during the days when
I was lying up in holes and corners, waiting for a good chance to
board a train, the causes that had led to them preyed more than I

knew on my nerves. To be an outcast, to be hunted, to lie under a warrant for arrest, to fear every man, to have imprisonment—not necessarily military confinement either—hanging overhead, to fly the light, to doubt the shadows—all these things ate into my soul and have left an impression that will not perhaps be easily effaced.

On the sixth day the chance I had patiently waited for came. I found a convenient train duly labelled to Lourenço Marques standing in a siding. I withdrew to a suitable spot for boarding it—for I dared not make the attempt in the station—and, filling a bottle with water to drink on the way, I prepared for the last stage of my journey.

The truck in which I ensconced myself was laden with great sacks of some soft merchandise, and I found among them holes and crevices by means of which I managed to work my way to the inmost recess. The hard floor was littered with gritty coal dust, and made a most uncomfortable bed. The heat was almost stifling. I was resolved, however, that nothing should lure or compel me from my hiding-place until I reached Portuguese territory. I expected the journey to take thirty-six hours; it dragged out into two and a half days. I hardly dared sleep for fear of snoring.

I dreaded lest the trucks should be searched at Komati Poort, and my anxiety as the train approached this neighbourhood was very great. To prolong it we were shunted on to a siding for eighteen hours either at Komati Poort or the station beyond it. Once indeed they began to search my truck, and I heard the tarpaulin rustle as they pulled at it, but luckily they did not search deep enough, so that, providentially protected, I reached Delagoa Bay at last, and crawled forth from my place of refuge and of punishment, weary, dirty, hungry, but free once more.

Thereafter everything smiled. I found my way to the British Consul, Mr. Ross, who at first mistook me for a fireman off one of the ships in the harbour, but soon welcomed me with enthusiasm. I bought clothes, I washed, I sat down to dinner with a real table-cloth and real glasses; and fortune, determined not to overlook the smallest detail, had arranged that the steamer *Induna* should leave that very night for Durban. As soon as the news of my arrival spread about the town, I received many offers of assistance from the English residents, and lest any of the Boer agents with whom Lourenço Marques is infested should attempt to recapture me in neutral territory, nearly a dozen gentlemen escorted me to the steamer armed with revolvers. It is from the cabin of this little vessel, as she coasts along the sandy shores of Africa, that I write the concluding lines of this letter, and the reader who may persevere through this hurried account will perhaps understand why I write them with a feeling of triumph, and better than triumph, a feeling of pure joy.

CHAPTER TWELVE

BACK TO THE BRITISH LINES

Frere: December 24, 1899

THE VOYAGE of the *Induna* from Delagoa Bay to Durban was speedy and prosperous, and on the afternoon of the 23rd we approached our port, and saw the bold headland that shields it rising above the horizon to the southward. An hour's steaming brought us to the roads. More than twenty great transports and supply vessels lay at anchor, while three others, crowded from end to end with soldiery, circled impatiently as they waited for pilots to take them into the harbour. Our small vessel was not long in reaching the jetty, and I perceived that a very considerable crowd had gathered to receive us. But it was not until I stepped on shore that I realised that I was myself the object of this honourable welcome. I will not chronicle the details of what followed. It is sufficient to say that many hundreds of the people of Durban took occasion to express their joy at my tiny pinch of triumph over the Boers, and that their enthusiasm was another sincere demonstration of their devotion to the Imperial cause, and their resolve to carry the war to an indisputable conclusion.

After an hour of turmoil, which I frankly admit I enjoyed extremely, I escaped to the train, and the journey to Pietermaritzburg passed very quickly in the absorbing occupation of devouring a month's newspapers and clearing my palate from the evil taste of the exaggerations of Pretoria by a liberal antidote of our own versions. I rested a day at Government House, and enjoyed long conversations with Sir Walter Hely-Hutchinson—the Governor under whose wise administration Natal has become the most patriotic province of the Empire. Moreover, I was fortunate in meeting Colonel Hime, the Prime Minister of the Colony, a tall, grey, keen-eyed man, who talked only of the importance of fighting

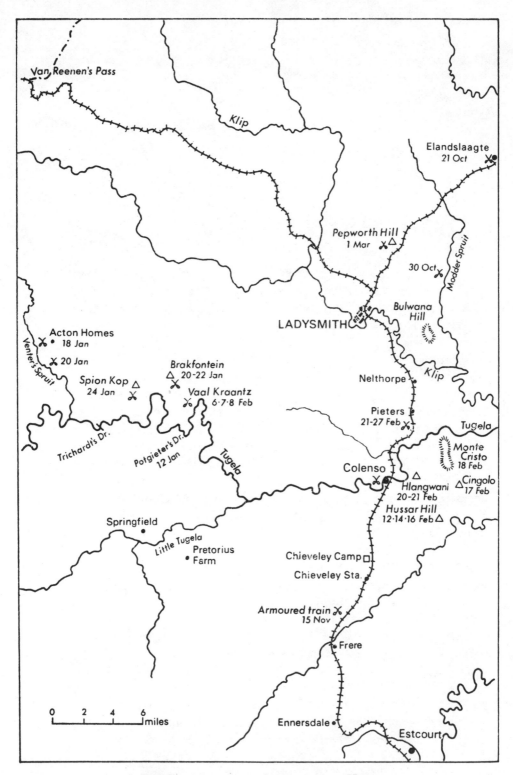

THE THEATRE OF THE OPERATIONS IN NATAL

this quarrel out to the end, and of the obstinate determination of the people he represented to stand by the Queen's Government through all the changing moods of fortune. I received then and have since been receiving a great number of telegrams and messages from all kinds of people and from all countries of the earth. One gentleman invited me to shoot with him in Central Asia. Another favoured me with a poem which he had written in my honour, and desired me to have it set to music and published. A third—an American— wanted me to plan a raid into Transvaal territory along the Delagoa Bay line to arm the prisoners and seize the President. Five Liberal Electors of the borough of Oldham wrote to say that they would give me their votes on a future occasion "irrespective of politics". Young ladies sent me woollen comforters. Old ladies forwarded their photographs; and hundreds of people wrote kind letters, many of which in the stir of events I have not yet been able to answer.

The correspondence varied vastly in tone as well as in character, and I cannot help quoting a couple of telegrams as specimens. The first was from a worthy gentleman who, besides being a substantial farmer, is also a member of the Natal Parliament. He wrote: "My heartiest congratulations on your wonderful and glorious deeds, which will send such a thrill of pride and enthusiasm through Great Britain and the United States of America, that the Anglo-Saxon race will be irresistible."

The intention of the other, although his message was shorter, was equally plain.

"*London, December 30th.* Best friends here hope you won't go making further ass of yourself.—M'Neill."

This shows, I think, how widely human judgement may differ even in regard to ascertained facts.

I found time to visit the hospitals—long barracks which before the war were full of healthy men, and are now crammed with sick and wounded. Everything seemed beautifully arranged, and what money could buy and care provide was at the service of those who had sustained hurt in the public contention. But for all that I left with a feeling of relief. Grim sights and grimmer suggestions were at every corner. Beneath a verandah a dozen wounded officers, profusely swathed in bandages, clustered in a silent brooding group. Nurses waited quietly by shut doors that none might disturb more serious cases. Doctors hurried with solemn faces from one building to another. Here and there men pushed stretchers on rubber-tyred wheels about the paths, stretchers on which motionless forms lay shrouded in blankets. One, concerning whom I asked, had just had part of his skull trepanned: another had suffered amputation. And all this pruning and patching up of broken men to win them a few more years of crippled life caught one's throat like the penetrating smell of the iodoform. Nor was I sorry to hasten away by the night mail northwards to the camps. It was still dark as we passed Estcourt, but morning had broken when the train reached Frere, and I got out and walked along the line inquiring for my tent, and found it pitched by the side of the very same cutting down which I had fled for my life from the Boer marksmen, and only fifty yards from the spot on which I had surrendered myself prisoner. So after much trouble and adventure I came safely home again to the wars. Six weeks had passed since the armoured train had been destroyed. Many changes had taken place. The hills which I had last seen black with the figures of the Boer riflemen were crowned with British pickets. The valley in which we had lain exposed to their artillery fire was crowded with the white tents of a numerous army. In the hollows and on the middle slopes canvas villages gleamed like patches of snowdrops. The iron bridge across the Blue Krantz River lay in a tangle of crimson-painted wreckage across the bottom of the ravine, and the railway ran over an unpretentious but substantial wooden structure. All along the line near the station fresh sidings had been built, and many trains concerned in the business of supply occupied them. When I had last looked on the landscape it meant fierce and overpowering danger, with the enemy on all sides. Now I was in the midst of a friendly host. But though much was altered some things remained the same. The Boers still held Colenso. Their forces still occupied the free soil of Natal. It was true that thousands of troops had arrived to make all efforts to change the situation. It was true that the British Army had even advanced ten miles. But Ladysmith was still locked in the strong grip of the invader, and as I listened I heard the distant booming of the same bombardment which I had heard two months before, and which all the time I was wandering had been remorselessly maintained and patiently borne.

Looking backward over the events of the last two months, it is impossible not to admire the Boer strategy. From the beginning they have aimed at two main objects: to exclude the war from their own territories, and to confine it to rocky and broken regions suited to their tactics. Up to the present time they have been entirely successful. Though the line of advance northwards through the Free State lay through flat open country, and they could spare few men to guard it, no British force has assailed this weak point. The "farmers" have selected their own ground and compelled the generals to fight them on it. No part of the earth's surface is better adapted to Boer tactics than Northern Natal, yet observe how we have been gradually but steadily drawn into it, until the mountains have swallowed up the greater part of the whole Army Corps. By degrees we have learned the power of our adversary. Before the war began men said: "Let them come into Natal and attack us if they dare. They would go back quicker than they would come." So the Boers came and fierce fighting took place, but it was the British who retired. Then it was said: "Never mind. The forces were not concentrated. Now that all the Natal Field Force is massed at Ladysmith, there will be no mistake." But still, in spite of Elandslaagte, concerning which the President remarked: "The foolhardy shall be punished," the Dutch advance continued. The concentrated Ladysmith force, twenty squadrons, six batteries, and eleven battalions, sallied out to meet them. The Staff said: "By tomorrow night there will not be a Boer within twenty miles of Ladysmith." But by the evening of October 30 the whole of Sir George White's command had been flung back into the town with three hundred men killed and wounded, and nearly a thousand prisoners. Then everyone said: "But now we have touched bottom. The Ladysmith position is the *ne plus ultra*. So far they have gone; but no further!" Then it appeared that the Boers were reaching out round the flanks. What was their design? To blockade Ladysmith? Ridiculous and impossible! However, send a battalion to Colenso to keep the communications open, and make assurance doubly sure. So the Dublin Fusiliers were railed southwards, and entrenched themselves at Colenso. Two days later the Boers cut the railway south of Ladysmith at Pieters, shelled the small garrison out of Colenso, shut and locked the gate on the Ladysmith force, and established themselves in the almost impregnable positions north of the Tugela. Still there was no realisation of the meaning of the investment. It would last a week, they said, and all the clever correspondents laughed at the veteran Bennet Burleigh for his hurry to get south before the door was shut. Only a week of isolation! Two months have passed. But all the time we have said: "Never mind; wait till our army comes. We will soon put a stop to the siege—for it soon became more than a blockade—of Ladysmith."

Then the army began to come. Its commander, knowing the disadvantageous nature of the country, would have preferred to strike northwards through the Free State and relieve Ladysmith at Bloemfontein. But the pressure from home was strong. First two brigades, then four, the artillery of two divisions, and a large mounted force were divered from the Cape Colony and drawn into Natal. Finally, Sir Redvers Buller had to follow the bulk of his army. Then the action of Colenso was fought, and in that unsatisfactory engagement the British leaders learned that the blockade of Ladysmith was no unstable curtain that could be brushed aside, but a solid wall. Another division is hurried to the mountains, battery follows battery, until at the present moment the South Natal Field Force numbers two cavalry and six infantry brigades, and nearly sixty guns. It is with this force that we hope to break through the lines of Boers who surround Ladysmith. The army is numerous, powerful, and high-spirited. But the task before it is one which no man can regard without serious misgivings.

Whoever selected Ladysmith as a military centre must sleep uneasily at nights. I remember hearing the question of a possible war with the Boers discussed by several officers of high rank. The general impression was that Ladysmith was a tremendous strategic position, which dominated the lines of approach both into the Transvaal and the Orange Free State, whereas of course it does nothing of the sort. The fact that it stands at the junction of the railways may have encouraged the belief, but both lines of advance are barred by a broken and tangled country abounding in positions of extraordinary strength. Tactically Ladysmith may be strongly defensible, politically it has become invested with much importance, but for strategic purposes it is absolutely worthless. It is worse. It is a regular trap. The town and cantonment stand in a huge circle of hills which enclasp it on all sides like the arms of a giant, and though so great is the circle that only guns of the heavier class can reach the town from the heights, once an enemy has established himself on these heights it is beyond the power of the garrison to dislodge him, or perhaps even to break out. Not only do the surrounding hills keep the garrison in, but they also form a formidable barrier to the advance of a relieving force. Thus it is that the ten thousand troops in Ladysmith are at this moment actually an encumbrance. To extricate them—I write advisedly, to endeavour to extricate them—brigades and divisions must be diverted from all the other easy lines of advance, and Sir Redvers Buller, who had always deprecated any attempt to hold Natal north of the Tugela, is compelled to attack the enemy on their own terms and their own ground.

What are those terms? The northern side of the Tugela River at nearly every point commands the southern bank. Ranges of high hills strewn with boulders and dotted with trees rise abruptly from the water, forming a mighty rampart for the enemy. Before this the river, a broad torrent with few and narrow fords and often precipitous banks, flows rapidly—a great moat. And before the river again, on our side stretches a smooth, undulating, grassy country—a regular glacis. To defend the rampart and sweep the glacis are gathered, according to my information derived in Pretoria, twelve thousand, according to the Intelligence Branch fifteen thousand, of the best riflemen in the world armed with beautiful magazine rifles, supplied with an inexhaustible store of ammunition, and supported by fifteen or twenty excellent quick-firing guns, all artfully entrenched and concealed. The drifts of the river across which our columns must force their way are all surrounded with trenches and rifle pits, from which a converging fire may be directed, and the actual bottom of the river is doubtless obstructed by entanglements of barbed wire and other devices. But when all these difficulties have been overcome the task is by no means finished. Nearly twenty miles of broken country, ridge rising beyond ridge, kopje above kopje, all probably already prepared for defence, intervene between the relieving army and the besieged garrison.

Such is the situation, and so serious are the dangers and difficulties that I have heard it said in the camp that on strict military grounds Ladysmith should be left to its fate; that a division should remain to hold this fine open country south of the Tugela and protect Natal; and that the rest should be hurried off to the true line of advance into the Free State from the south. Though I recognise all this, and do not deny its force, I rejoice that what is perhaps a strategically unwise decision has been taken. It is not possible to abandon a brave garrison without striking a blow to rescue them. The attempt will cost several thousand lives; and may even fail; but it must be made on the grounds of honour, if not on those of policy.

We are going to try almost immediately, for there is no time to to be lost. "The sands", to quote Mr. Chamberlain on another subject, "are running down in the glass." Ladysmith has stood two months' siege and bombardment. Food and ammunition stores are dwindling. Disease is daily increasing. The strain on the garrison has been, in spite of their pluck and stamina, a severe one. How long can they hold out? It is difficult to say precisely, because after the ordinary rations are exhausted determined men will eat horses and rats and beetles, and such like odds and ends, and so continue the defence. But another month must be the limit of their endurance, and then if no help comes Sir George White will have to fire off all his ammunition, blow up his heavy guns, burn waggons and equipment, and sally out with his whole force in a fierce endeavour to escape southwards. Perhaps half the garrison might succeed in reaching our lines, but the rest, less the killed and wounded, would be sent to occupy the new camp at Waterfall, which has been already laid out—such is the intelligent anticipation of the enemy— for their accommodation. So we are going to try to force the Tugela within the week, and I dare say my next letter will give you some account of our fortunes.

Meanwhile all is very quiet in the camps. From Chieveley, where there are two brigades of infantry, a thousand horse of sorts, including the 13th Hussars, and a dozen naval guns, it is quite possible to see the Boer positions, and the outposts live within range of each other's rifles. Yesterday I rode out to watch the evening bombardment which we make on their entrenchments with the naval 4·7 guns. From the low hill on which the battery is established the whole scene is laid bare. The Boer lines run in a great crescent along the hills. Tier above tier of trenches have been scored along their sides, and the brown streaks run across the grass of the open country south of the river. After tea in the captain's cabin—I should say tent—Commander Limpus of the *Terrible* kindly invited me to look through the telescope and mark the fall of the shots.

The glass was one of great power, and I could plainly see the figures of the Boers walking about in twos and threes, sitting on the embankments, or shovelling away to heighten them. We selected one particular group near a kraal, the range of which had been carefully noted, and the great guns were slowly brought to bear on the unsuspecting target. I looked through the spy-hole at the tiny picture—three dirty beehives for the kraal, a long breastwork of newly thrown up earth, six or seven miniature men gathered into a little bunch, two others skylarking on the grass behind the trench, apparently engaged in a boxing match. Then I turned to the guns. A naval officer craned along the seventeen-feet barrel, peering through the telescopic sights. Another was pencilling some calculations as to wind and light and other intricate details. The crew, attentive, stood around. At last all was done. I looked back to the enemy. The group was still intact. The boxers were still playing— one had pushed the other down. A solitary horseman had also come into the picture and was riding slowly across. The desire of murder rose in my heart. Now for a bag! Bang! I jumped at least a foot, disarranging the telescope, but there was plenty of time to reset it while the shell was hissing and roaring its way through nearly five miles of air. I found the kraal again and the group still there, but all motionless and alert, like startled rabbits. Then they began to bob into the earth, one after the other. Suddenly, in the middle of the kraal, there appeared a huge flash, a billowy ball of smoke, and clouds of dust. Bang! I jumped again; the second gun had fired. But before this shell could reach the trenches a dozen little figures scampered away, scattering in all directions. Evidently the first had not been without effect. Yet when I turned the glass to another part of the defences the Boers were working away stolidly, and only those near the explosion showed any signs of disturbance.

The bombardment continued for half an hour, the shells being flung sometimes into the trenches, sometimes among the houses of Colenso, and always directed with marvellous accuracy. At last the guns were covered up again in their tarpaulins, the crowd of military spectators broke up and dispersed amid the tents, and soon it became night.

CHAPTER THIRTEEN

CHRISTMAS AND NEW YEAR

Frere: January 4, 1900

DECEMBER 25.—Christmas Day! "Glory to God in the Highest, and on earth, peace and goodwill towards men." So no great shells were fired into the Boer entrenchments at dawn, and the hostile camps remained tranquil throughout the day. Even the pickets forbore to snipe each other, and both armies attended divine service in the morning and implored Heaven's blessing on their righteous causes. In the afternoon the British held athletic sports, an impromptu military tournament, and a gymkhana, all of which caused much merriment and diversion, and the Boers profited by the cessation of the shell fire to shovel away at their trenches. In the evening there were Christmas dinners in our camp—roast beef, plum pudding, a quart of beer for everyone, and various smoking concerts afterwards. I cannot describe the enemy's festivities.

But since that peaceful day we have had desultory picket firing, and the great guns in the naval battery have spoken whenever an opportunity presented itself. The opposing outpost lines are drawn so far apart that with the best intentions they can scarcely harm each other. But the long range of the small-bore rifles encourages fancy shooting, so that there is often a brisk fusillade and no one any the worse. On our side we have only had one infantry soldier wounded. We do not know what the fortunes of the Boers may have been, but it is probable that they lose a few men every day from the bombardment, and certain that on Monday last there were three burghers killed and several wounded and one horse. It happened in this wise: beyond the strong Infantry pickets which remain in position always, there is a more or less extended line of cavalry outposts, which are sprinkled all along the kopjes to the east and west of the camp, and are sometimes nearly three miles from it. On the Monday in question—New Year's Day to wit—200 Boers set forth and attacked our picket on the extreme right. The picket, which was composed of the South African Light Horse, fell back with discretion, and the Boers following without their usual caution did not observe that eight troopers had been dropped behind among the rocks and ledges of a donga; so that when twelve of them attempted to make their way up this natural zigzag approach in order to fire upon the retiring picket they were themselves received at 400 yards by a well-directed sputter of musketry, and were glad to make off with five riderless horses, two men upon one horse, and leaving three lying quite still on the ground. Thereafter the picket continued to retreat unmolested.

Indeed, the New Year opened well, and many little things seem to favour the hope that it is the turning point of the war. Besides our tiny skirmish on the right, Captain Gough, of the 16th Lancers, on the left, made his way along a convenient depression, almost to the river bank, and discovered Boers having tea in their camp at scarcely 1,800 yards. Forthwith he opened fire, causing great commotion; hurried upsetting of the tea, scrambling into tents for rifles, "confounded impudence of these cursed rooineks! Come quickly Hans, Pieter, O'Brien, and John Smith, and let us mend their manners. What do they mean by harassing us?" And in a very few minutes there was a wrathful rattle of firing all along the trenches on the hillside, which spread far away to the right and left as other Boers heard it. What the deuce is this? Another attack! Till at last the Maxim shell gun caught the infection, and began pom, pom, pom! pom, pom, pom! and so on at intervals. Evidently much angry passion was aroused in the Boer camp, and all because Captain Gough had been trying his luck at long range volleys. The situation might have become serious; the event was, however, fortunate. No smoke betrayed the position of the scouting party; no bullets found them. A heavy shower of metal sang and whistled at random in the air. The donga afforded an excellent line of retreat, and when the adventurous patrol had retired safely into the camp they were amused to hear the Boers still busy with the supposed chastisement of their audacious assailants.

But these are small incidents which, though they break the monotony of the camp, do not alter nor, each by itself, greatly accelerate the course of the war. Good news came in on New Year's

Day from other quarters. Near Belmont the Canadians and Queenslanders fell on a raiding or reckless commando, took them on at their own game, hunted them and shot them among the rocks until the white flag was upon the right side for once and hoisted in honest surrender. Forty prisoners and twenty dead and wounded; excellent news to all of us; but causing amazing joy in Natal, where every colonist goes into an ecstasy over every crumb of British success.

Moreover, we have good news from East London. General Gatacre is stolidly and patiently repairing the opening misfortune of his campaign: has learned by experience much of the new conditions of the war. Strange that the Boers did not advance after their victory; stranger still that they retired from Dordrecht. Never mind whether their stillness be due to national cautiousness or good defensive arrangements. Since they don't want Dordrecht, let us go there; and there we go accordingly. Out of this there arises on New Year's Day a successful skirmish, in the account of which the name of De Montmorency is mentioned. In Egypt the name was associated with madcap courage. Here they talk of prudent skill. The double reputation should be valuable.

And, perhaps, the best news of all comes from Arundel, near Colesberg, where Generals French and Brabazon with the cavalry column—for it is nearly all mounted—are gradually sidling and coaxing the Boers back out of the Colony. They are a powerful combination: French's distinguished military talents, and Brabazon's long and deep experience of war. So, with this column there are no frontal attacks—perhaps they are luckier than we in respect of ground—no glorious victories (which the enemy call victories, too); very few people hurt and a steady advance, as we hear on the first day of the year, right up to Colesberg.

Perhaps the tide of war has really begun to turn. Perhaps 1900 is to mark the beginning of a century of good luck and good sense in British policy in Africa. When I was a prisoner at Pretoria the Boers showed me a large green pamphlet Mr. Reitz had written. It was intended to be an account of the Dutch grounds of quarrel with the English, and was called "A Century of Wrong". Much was distortion and exaggeration, but a considerable part dealt with acknowledged facts. Wrong in plenty there has been on both sides, but latterly more on theirs than on ours; and the result is war— bitter, bloody war tearing the land in twain; dividing brother from brother, friend from friend, and opening a terrible chasm between the two white races who must live side by side as long as South Africa stands above the ocean, and by whose friendly co-operation alone it can enjoy the fullest measure of prosperity. "A century of wrong!" British ignorance of South Africa, Boer ignorance of civilisation, British intolerance, Boer brutality, British interference, Boer independence, clash, clash, clash, all along the line! and then fanatical, truth-scorning missionaries, experimental philanthropists, high-handed jingo administrators, colonial ministers who disliked all colonies on the glorious principles of theoretic liberalism, bad generals thinking of their own reputations, not of their country's success, and a series of miserable events recalled sufficiently well by their names—Slagter's Nek, Kimberley, Moshesh, Majuba, Jameson, all these arousing first resentment, then loathing, then contempt, and, finally, a Great Desire, crystallising into a Great Conspiracy for a United Dutch South Africa, free from the flag that has elsewhere been regarded as the flag of freedom. And so inevitably to war—war with peculiar sadness and horror, in which the line of cleavage springs between all sorts of well-meaning people that used to know one another in friendship; but war which, whatever its fortunes, certainly sweeps the past into obscurity. We have done with "a century of wrong". God send us now "a century of right".

CHAPTER FOURTEEN

A MILITARY DEMONSTRATION AND SOME GOOD NEWS

Chieveley: January 8, 1900

BOOM. THUD, thud. Boom. Boom. Thud—thud thud—thud thud thud thud—boom. A long succession of queer moaning vibrations broke the stillness of the sleeping camp. I became suddenly awake. It was two o'clock on the morning of January 6. The full significance of the sounds came with consciousness. We had all heard them before—heavy cannonading at Ladysmith. They were at it again. How much longer would the heroic garrison be persecuted?

I turned to rest once more. But the distant guns forbade sleep. The reports grew momentarily more frequent, until at last they merged into one general roar. This was new. Never before had we heard such bombarding. Louder and louder swelled the cannonade, and presently the deep note of the heavy artillery could scarcely be distinguished above the incessant discharges of field pieces. So I lay and listened. What was happening eighteen miles away over the hills? Another bayonet attack by the garrison? Or perhaps a general sortie: or perhaps, but this seemed scarcely conceivable, the Boers had hardened their hearts and were delivering the long expected, long threatened assault.

An officer came to my tent with the daylight. Something big happening at Ladysmith—hell of a cannonade—never heard anything like it—worse than Colenso—what do you think of it? But I was without opinion; nor did I find anyone anxious to pronounce. Meanwhile the firing was maintained, and we breakfasted to its accompaniment. Until half-past ten there was not the slightest diminution or intermission. As the day advanced, however, it gradually died away, showing either that the fight was over, or, as it afterwards turned out, that it had passed into the hands of riflemen.

We all spent an anxious morning speculating on the reason and result of the engagement. About noon there arrived an unofficial message by heliograph, which the young officer at the signal station confided to his friends. It was brief. "General attack all sides by Boers—everywhere repulsed—but fight still going on."

At one o'clock, just as we were sitting down to luncheon, came an orderly at full gallop with the order for the whole force in Chieveley to turn out at once. Whereat the camp, till then dormant under the midday sun, sprang to life like a disturbed ant-hill. Some said we were about to make a regular attack on Colenso, while many of the covering army of Boers were busy at Ladysmith. Others suggested a night assault—with the bayonet. The idea was very pleasant to the hearts of the infantry. But I soon learned that no serious operation was in contemplation, and that the force was merely to make a demonstration before Colenso with the object of bringing some of the Boers back from Ladysmith, and of so relieving the pressure on Sir George White.

The demonstration was, however, a very imposing affair. First of all the mounted forces threw out a long fringe of patrols all along the front. Behind this the squadrons made a line of black bars. The mounted infantry, Bethune's Horse, and the Natal Caribineers formed the left, the South African Light Horse the centre, and the 13th Hussars and Thorneycroft's Mounted Infantry twisted back to watch the right. Behind this curtain marched the infantry, Hild-yard's Brigade on the right, Barton's on the left, line after line of brown men ten yards apart, two hundred yards between the lines, spreading in this open formation over a wide expanse of country, and looking a mighty swarm. Behind these again dark blocks of artillery and waggons moved slowly forward. Behind, and above all, the naval battery began to throw its shells into the village.

The cavalry soon cleared the front, the squadrons wheeled about, the patrols retreated. The South African Light Horse, with whom I now have the honour to serve, were stationed in rear of Gun Hill, a rocky eminence so called because a heavy battery was placed there in the last engagement. From this feature an excellent view of the operation was afforded, and thence we watched the whole develop-ment.

Sir Francis Clery, General Hildyard, and their respective Staffs had also taken their position on Gun Hill, so that its crest was thickly crowded with figures peering exhaustively through field glasses and telescopes. The infantry, who were now moving steadily forward, were literally sprinkled all over the country.

In the text-books compiled from the results of past experience the military student reads that armies divide to march and concentrate to fight. "Nous avons changé tout cela." Here we concentrate to march and disperse to fight. I asked General Hildyard what formation his brigade was in. He replied, "Formation for taking advantage of ant-heaps." This is a valuable addition to the infantry drill.

Meanwhile the demonstration was in progress, and not without effect. Only the well-informed realised that it was a demonstration, and the privates, as they walked phlegmatically on, did not know that they were not about to be plunged into another deluge of fire.

"You watch it, Bill," I heard one man remark, "we'll have that —— laughing hyena" (the Vickers-Maxim gun) "let off at us in a minute."

The Boers, too, seemed to be deceived, or, at any rate, doubtful, for we could see them in twos and threes, and presently in fives and sixes, galloping into their trenches, which were evidently deep enough to shelter horse and man. It was most probable that larger bodies had already begun their countermarch from Ladysmith. We were not wasting our time or our trouble.

The infantry halted about three thousand yards from the enemy's position, and the artillery, which numbered fourteen guns, trotted forward and came into action. All these movements, which had been very deliberately made, had taken a long time, and it was now nearly five o'clock. Dark thunder-clouds and a drizzle of rain descended on the silent Boer position, and the range of hills along which it stretched lay in deep shadow as if under the frown of Heaven. Our batteries also were ranged in this gloomy zone, but with the reserves and on the hill whence we were watching there was bright sunlight.

The bombardment and the storm broke over the Boer entrenchments simultaneously. A swift succession of fierce red flashes stabbed out from the patches of gunners, teams, and waggons, and with yellow gleams soft white balls of smoke appeared among the houses of Colenso and above the belts of scrub which extend on either side. The noise of explosions of gun and projectile came back to us on the hill in regular order, and above them rang the startling discharges of the 4·7 naval guns, whose shells in bursting raised huge brown dust clouds from houses, trench, or hillside. At the same time the thunder began to rumble, and vivid streaks of blue light scarred the sombre hills. We watched the impressive spectacle in safety and the sunlight.

Besides creating a diversion in favour of Ladysmith the object of our demonstration was to make the enemy reveal his position and especially the positions of his guns. In this latter respect, however, we were defeated. Though they must have suffered some loss and more annoyance from the bombardment, and though much of the infantry was well within the range of their guns, the Boers declined to be drawn, and during two hours' shelling they did not condescend to give a single shot in reply. It needs a patient man to beat a Dutchman at waiting. So about seven o'clock we gave up trying.

It had been intended to leave the troops on the enemy's front until night and withdraw them after dark, the idea being to make him anxious lest a night attack should be designed. But as some of the battalions had turned out without having their dinners, Sir Francis Clery decided not to keep them under arms longer, and the whole force withdrew gracefully and solemnly to camp.

Here we found news from Ladysmith. "Enemy everywhere repulsed for the present." For the present! Hold on only a little longer, gallant garrison, and if it be in the power of 25,000 British soldiers to help you, your troubles and privations shall soon be ended—and what a dinner we will have together then!

That night we tried to congratulate or encourage Ladysmith, and the searchlight perseveringly flashed the Morse code on the clouds. But before it had been working half an hour the Boer searchlight saw it and hurried to interfere, flickering, blinking, and crossing to try to confuse the dots and dashes, and appeared to us who watched this curious aerial battle—Briton and Boer fighting each other in the sky with vibrations of ether—to confuse them more effectually.

Next morning, however, the sun came out for uncertain periods, and Ladysmith was able to tell her own story briefly and jerkily, but still a very satisfactory account.

At two o'clock, according to Sir George White, the Boers in great numbers, evidently reinforced from Colenso, surprised the pickets and began a general attack on the outpost line round the town, particularly directing their efforts on Cæsar's Camp and Waggon

Hill. The fighting became very close, and the enemy, who had after all hardened their hearts, pushed the attack with extraordinary daring and vigour. Some of the trenches on Waggon Hill were actually taken three times by the assailants. But every time General Hamilton—the skilful Hamilton as he has been called—flung them out again by counter-attacks. At one place, indeed, they succeeded in holding on all day, nor was it until the dusk of the evening, when the rain and thunderstorm which we saw hanging over Colenso broke on Ladysmith, that Colonel Park led forth the Devon Regiment—who, having had half their officers killed or wounded by a shell some days before, were probably spiteful—and drove the Dutchmen helter skelter at the point of the bayonet. So that by night the Boers were repulsed at every point, with necessarily great slaughter, greater at any rate than on our side. Their first experience of assaulting! Encore!

Battles now-a-days are fought mainly with firearms, but no troops, however brave, however well directed, can enjoy the full advantage of their successes if they exclude the possibilities of cold steel and are not prepared to maintain what they have won, if necessary with their fists. The moral strength of an army which welcomes the closest personal encounter must exceed that of an army which depends for its victories only on being able to kill its foes at a distance. The bayonet is the most powerful weapon we possess out here. Firearms kill many of the enemy, but it is the white weapon that makes them run away. Rifles can inflict the loss, but victory depends, for us at least, on the bayonets.

Of the losses we as yet know nothing, except that Lord Ava is seriously wounded, a sad item for which the only consolation is that the Empire is worth the blood of its noblest citizens. But for the general result we rejoice. Ladysmith, too, is proud and happy. Only ten thousand of us, and look what we do! A little reproach-fully, perhaps; for it is dull work fighting week after week without alcohol or green vegetables.

Well, it looks as if their trials were very nearly over. Sir Charles Warren's Division marches to Frere today. All the hospitals have been cleared ready for those who may need them. If all's well we shall have removed the grounds of reproach by this day week. The long interval between the acts has come to an end. The warning bell has rung. Take your seats, ladies and gentlemen. The curtain is about to rise.

"High time, too," say the impatient audience, and with this I must agree; for, looking from my tent as I write, I can see the smoke-puff bulging on Bulwana Hill as "Long Tom" toils through his seventy-second day of bombardment, and the white wisp seems to beckon the relieving army onward.

CHAPTER FIFTEEN

THE DASH FOR POTGIETER'S FERRY

Spearman's Hill: January 13, 1900

SECRETS USUALLY leak out in a camp, no matter how many people are employed to keep them. For two days before January 10 rumours of an impending move circulated freely. There are, moreover, certain signs by which anyone who is acquainted with the under machinery of an army can tell when operations are imminent. On the 6th we heard that orders had been given to clear the Pietermaritzburg hospitals of all patients, evidently because new inmates were expected. On the 7th it was reported that the hospitals were all clear. On the 8th an ambulance train emptied the field hospitals at Frere, and that same evening there arrived seven hundred civilian stretcher-bearers—brave men who had volunteered to carry wounded under fire, and whom the army somewhat ungratefully nicknames the "Body-snatchers". Nor were these grim preparations the only indications of approaching activity. The commissariat told tales of accumulations of supplies— twenty-one days' packed in waggons—of the collection of transport oxen and other details, meaningless by themselves, but full of significance when viewed side by side with other circumstances. Accordingly I was scarcely surprised when, chancing to ride from Chieveley to Frere on the afternoon of the 10th, I discovered the whole of Sir Charles Warren's Division added to the already extensive camp.

This was the first move of the complicated operations by which Sir Redvers Buller designed to seize the passage of the Tugela at Potgieter's Ferry: Warren (seven battalions, comprising Coke's and Woodgate's Brigades and five batteries) from Estcourt to Frere. When I got back to Chieveley all was bustle in the camp. Orders to march at dawn had arrived. At last the long pause was finished; waiting was over; action had begun.

So far as Chieveley was concerned, the following was the programme: Barton's Brigade to entrench itself strongly and to remain before Colenso, covering the head of the line of communications, and demonstrating against the position; Hildyard's Brigade to move westward at daylight on the 11th to Pretorius's Farm; cavalry, guns, and baggage (miles of it) to take a more circuitous route to the same place. Thither also Hart was to move from Frere, joining Hildyard and forming Clery's Division. Warren was to rest until the next day. The force for the relief of Ladysmith, exclusive of Barton's Brigade and communication troops, was organised as follows:

Commander-in-Chief: SIR REDVERS BULLER

CLERY'S DIVISION consisting of	WARREN'S DIVISION consisting of
Hildyard's Brigade,	Lyttelton's Brigade,
Hart's Brigade,	Woodgate's Brigade,
1 squad. 13th Hussars,	1 squad. 15th Hussars,
3 batteries,	3 batteries,
R.E.	R.E.

CORPS TROOPS

Coke's Brigade (3 battalions),
1 field battery R.A.,
1 howitzer battery R.A.,
2 4·7 naval guns and Naval Brigade,
8 long-range naval 12-pounder guns,
1 squadron 13th Hussars,
R.E., &c.

CAVALRY (DUNDONALD)

1st Royal Dragoons,
14th Hussars.
4 squadrons South African Light Horse.
1 squadron Imperial Light Horse.
Bethune's Mounted Infantry.
Thorneycroft's Mounted Infantry.
1 squadron Natal Carabineers.
1 squadron Natal Police.
1 company K.R.R. Mounted Infantry.
6 machine guns.

Or, to sum the whole up briefly, 19,000 infantry, 3,000 cavalry, and 60 guns.

All were busy with their various tasks—Barton's Brigade entrenching, making redoubts and shelter pits, or block-houses of railway iron; the other brigades packing up ready for the march as night closed in. In the morning we started. The cavalry were responsible for the safety of the baggage convoy, and with Colonel Byng, who commanded the column, I waited and watched the almost interminable procession defile. Ox waggons piled high with all kinds of packages, and drawn sometimes by ten or twelve pairs of oxen, mule waggons, Scotch carts, ambulance waggons, with huge red-cross flags, ammunition carts, artillery, slaughter cattle, and, last of all, the naval battery, with its two enormous 4·7 pieces, dragged by long strings of animals, and guarded by straw-hatted khaki-clad blue-jackets, passed in imposing array, with here and there a troop of cavalry to protect them or to prevent straggling. And here let me make an unpleasant digression. The vast amount of baggage this army takes with it on the march hampers its movements and utterly precludes all possibility of surprising the enemy. I have never before seen even officers accommodated with tents on service, though both the Indian frontier and the Soudan lie under a hotter sun than South Africa. But here today, within striking distance of a mobile enemy whom we wish to circumvent, every private soldier has canvas shelter, and the other arrangements are on an equally elaborate scale. The consequence is that roads are crowded, drifts are blocked, marching troops are delayed, and all rapidity of movement is out of the question. Meanwhile, the enemy completes the fortification of his positions, and the cost of capturing them rises. It is a poor economy to let a soldier live well for three days at the price of killing him on the fourth.*

We marched off with the rearguard at last, and the column twisted away among the hills towards the west. After marching about three miles we reached the point where the track from Frere joined the track from Chieveley, and here two streams of waggons flowed into one another like the confluence of rivers. Shortly after this all the mounted forces with the baggage were directed to concentrate at the head of the column, and, leaving the tardy waggons to toil along at their own pace, we trotted swiftly forward. Pretorius's Farm was reached at noon—a tin-roofed house, a few sheds, a dozen trees, and an artificial pond filled to the brim by the recent rains. Here drawn up in the spacious plain were the Royal

---

* This complaint was not in one respect justified by what followed, for after we left Spearman's we only saw our tents for a day or two, and at rare intervals, until Ladysmith was relieved.

Dragoons—distinguished from the Colonial Corps by the bristle of lances bare of pennons above their ranks and by their great horses— one squadron of the already famous Imperial Light Horse, and Bethune's Mounted Infantry. The Dragoons remained at the farm, which was that night to be the camping place of Clery's division. But all the rest of the mounted forces, about a thousand men, and a battery of artillery were hurried forward to seize the bridge across the Little Tugela at Springfield.

So on we ride, "trot and walk", lightly and easily over the good turf, and winding in scattered practical formations among the beautiful verdant hills of Natal. Presently we topped a ridge and entered a very extensive basin of country—a huge circular valley of green grass with sloping hills apparently on all sides and towards the west, bluffs, rising range above range, to the bright purple wall of the Drakensberg. Other valleys opened out from this, some half veiled in thin mist, others into which the sun was shining, filled with a curious blue light, so that one seemed to be looking down into depths of clear water, and everyone rejoiced in the splendours of the delightful landscape.

But now we approached Springfield, and perhaps at Springfield we should find the enemy. Surely if they did not oppose the passage they would blow up the bridge. Tiny patrols—beetles on a green baize carpet—scoured the plain, and before we reached the crease— scarcely perceptible at a mile's distance, in which the Little Tugela flows—word was brought that no Dutchmen were anywhere to be seen. Captain Gough, it appeared, with one man had ridden over the bridge in safety; more than that, had actually explored three miles on the further side: did not believe there was a Boer this side of the Tugela: would like to push on to Potgieter's and make certain: "Perhaps we can seize Potgieter's tonight. They don't like having a flooded river behind them." So we come safely to Springfield— three houses, a long wooden bridge "erected by public subscription, at a cost of 4,300*l*."—half a dozen farms with their tin roofs and tree clumps seen in the neighbourhood—and no Boers. Orders were to seize the bridge: seized accordingly; and after all had crossed and watered in the Little Tugela—swollen by the rains to quite a considerable Tugela, eighty yards wide—we looked about for something else to do.

Meanwhile more patrols came in; all told the same tale: no Boers anywhere. Well, then, let us push on. Why not seize the heights above Potgieter's? If held, they would cost a thousand men to storm; now, perhaps, they might be had for nothing. Again, why not? Orders said, "Go to Springfield"; nothing about Potgieter's at all. Never mind—if cavalry had never done more than obey their orders how different English history would have been! Captain Birdwood, 11th Bengal Lancers, glorious regiment of the Indian frontier, now on Lord Dundonald's staff, was for pushing on. All and sundry were eager to get on. "Have a dash for it." It is very easy to see what to do in the field of war until you put on the thick blue goggles of responsibility. Dundonald reflected, reflected again, and finally resolved. *Voorwärts!* So on we went accordingly. Three hundred men and two guns were left to hold the Springfield bridge, seven hundred men and four guns hurried on through the afternoon to Potgieter's Ferry, or, more properly speaking, the heights commanding it, and reached them safely at six o'clock, finding a strong position strengthened by loopholed stone walls, unguarded and unoccupied. The whole force climbed to the top of the hills, and with great labour succeeded in dragging the guns with them before night. Then we sent back to announce what we had done and to ask for reinforcements.

The necessity for reinforcements seemed very real to me, for I have a wholesome respect for Boer military enterprise; and after the security of a great camp the dangers of our lonely unsupported perch on the hills came home with extra force. "No Boers this side of the Tugela." How did we know? We had not seen any, but the deep valleys along the river might easily conceal two thousand horsemen. I said to myself, the Boer has always a reason for everything he does. He left the Springfield bridge standing. It would have cost him nothing to blow it up. Why, then, had he neglected this obvious precaution? Again, the position we had seized had actually been fortified by the enemy. Why, then, had they abandoned it to a parcel of horsemen without a shot fired? I could quite understand that the flooded Tugela was not a satisfactory feature to fight in front of, but it seemed certain that they had some devilry prepared for us somewhere. The uninjured bridge appeared to me a trap: the unguarded position a bait. Suppose they were, we should be attacked at daylight. Nothing more than a soldier should always expect; but what of the position? The line we had to hold to cover the approaches to our hill-top was far greater than seven hundred men could occupy. Had we been only cavalry and mounted men we could have fallen back after the position became untenable, but we were encumbered with four field-guns—a source of anxiety, not of strength. So I began to long for infantry. Two thousand good infantry would make everything absolutely secure. And ten miles away were infantry by thousands, all delighted to march every mile nearer the front.

We passed a wet and watchful night without food or sleep, and were glad to find the break of day unbroken by the musketry of a heavy attack. From our lofty position on the heights the whole country beyond the Tugela was spread like a map. I sat on a great rock which overhung the valley, and searched the landscape inch by inch with field glasses. After an hour's study my feeling of insecurity departed. I learned the answer to the questions which had perplexed the mind. Before us lay the "devilry" the Boers had prepared, and it was no longer difficult to understand why the Springfield bridge had been spared and the heights abandoned.*

The ground fell almost sheer six hundred feet to the flat bottom of the valley. Beneath, the Tugela curled along like a brown and very sinuous serpent. Never have I seen such violent twists and bends in a river. At times the waters seemed to loop back on themselves. One great loop bent towards us, and at the arch of this the little ferry of Potgieter's floated, moored to ropes which looked through the field glasses like a spider's web. The ford, approached by roads cut down through the steep bank, was beside it, but closed for the time being by the flood. The loop of river enclosed a great tongue of land which jutted from the hills on the enemy's side almost to our feet. A thousand yards from the tip of this tongue rose a line of low kopjes crowned with reddish stones. The whole tongue was virtually ours. Our guns on the heights or on the bank could sweep it from flank to flank, enfilade and cross fire. Therefore the passage of the river was assured. We had obtained what amounted to a practical bridgehead, and could cross whenever we thought fit. But the explanation of many things lay beyond. At the base of the tongue, where it sprang from the Boer side of the valley, the ground rose in a series of gentle grassy slopes to a long horseshoe of hills, and along this, both flanks resting securely on unfordable reaches of the river, out of range from our heights of any but the heaviest guns, approachable by a smooth grass glacis, which was exposed to

---

* *Vide* map on p. 164, which will be found to illustrate the subsequent letters.

two or three tiers of cross fire and converging fire, ran the enemy's position. Please look at the sketch below, which shows nothing but what it is meant to.

It will be seen that there is no difficulty in shelling the Boers out of the little kopjes, of fortifying them, and of passing the army on to the tip of the tongue; but to get off the tongue on to the smooth plateau that runs to Ladysmith it was necessary to force the tremendous Boer position enclosing the tongue. In technical language the possession of the heights virtually gave us a bridgehead on the Tugela, but the debouches from that bridgehead were barred by an exterior line of hills fortified and occupied by the enemy.

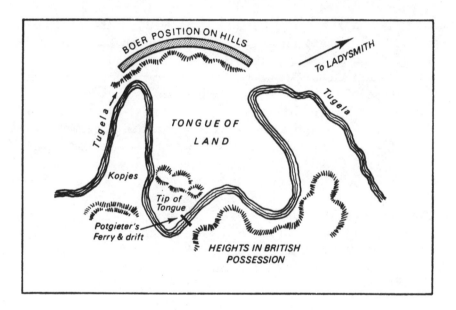

What will Sir Redvers Buller do? In a few hours we shall know. To cross and deliver a frontal attack will cost at least three thousand men. Is a flank attack possible? Can the position be turned? Fords few and far between, steep banks, mighty positions on the further banks: such are some of the difficulties. But everyone has confidence in the general. An officer who had been serving on the Kimberley side came here. "I don't understand," he said, "how it is you are all so cheerful here after Colenso. You should hear the troops at Modder River." But it is a poor army that cannot take a repulse

and come up smiling, and when the private soldiers put their faith
in any man they are very constant. Besides, Buller's personality
impresses everyone with the idea of some great reserve of force.
Certainly he has something up his sleeve. The move to Potgieter's
has been talked of for a month and executed with the greatest
ostentation and deliberation. Surely something lies behind it all. So
at least we all believe, and in the meanwhile trust wholeheartedly.

But some part of the army will certainly cross at Potgieter's; and
as I looked down on the smooth smiling landscape it seemed very
strange to think that in a few days it would blaze into a veritable
hell. Yet the dark lines of shelter trenches, the redoubts crowning
the hills, the bristle of tiny black figures busily entrenching against
the sky line, hundreds of horses grazing in the plain, all promised a
fierce and stubborn defence. I turned about. The country to the
southward was also visible. What looked to the naked eye like an
endless thin rope lay streaked across the spacious veldt, and when I
looked through the glass I saw that it was ten or twelve miles of
marching men and baggage. The armies were approaching. The
collision impended.

Nothing happened during the day except the capture of the
ferry, which daring enterprise was carried out by volunteers from
the South African Light Horse. Six swimmers, protected by a
covering party of twenty men, swam the flooded Tugela and began
to haul the punt back, whereat the Boers concealed in the kopjes
opened a brisk fire at long range on the naked figures, but did not
hit anyone nor prevent them all from bringing the punt safely to
our side: a dashing exploit, of which their regiment—the "Cockyoli-
birds", as the army, with its customary irreverence, calls us on
account of the cock's feather cockades we wear in our hats (miserable jealousy!)—are immensely proud.

The falling of the Tugela increased the danger of our position, and
I was delighted when I woke up the next morning, the second of our
adventurous occupation, to find Colonel Sandbach, to whom I had
confided my doubts, outside my tent, saying "I suppose you'll be
happy now. Two battalions have arrived." And, sure enough, when
I looked southwards, I saw a steady rivulet of infantry trickling
through the gorge, and forming a comfortable brown inundation in
the hollow where our camp lay. A few minutes later Sir Redvers
Buller and his staff rode up to see things for themselves, and then
we knew that all was well.

The General made his way to the great stone we call the observatory, and lying down on his back peered through a telescope in silence for the best part of an hour. Then he went off to breakfast with the Cavalry Brigade staff. A few officers remained behind to take a still more exhaustive view. "There'll be some wigs on that green before long." "What a wonderful sight it will be from here!" "What a place to see a battle from!" Two artillerymen were loitering near. Said one: "We ought to have the Queen up here, in her little donkey carriage." "Ah, we'd do it all right then," replied his comrade. But when I looked at the peaceful plain and reflected on the storm and tumult presently to burst upon it, I could not help being glad that no gentle eye would view that bloody panorama.

CHAPTER SIXTEEN

TRICHARDT'S DRIFT AND
THE AFFAIR OF ACTON HOMES

Venter's Spruit: January 22, 1900

O N THURSDAY, January 11, Sir Redvers Buller began his operations for forcing the Tugela and relieving Ladysmith. Barton's Brigade entrenched itself at Chieveley, guarding the line of railway communication. Hildyard's Brigade marched westward six miles to Pretorius's Farm, where they were joined by the cavalry, the naval guns, three batteries Field Artillery, and Hart's Brigade from Frere. The infantry and two batteries remained and encamped, making Clery's Division, while the mounted forces under Dundonald moved forward to take the bridge across the Little Tugela at Springfield, and, finding this unoccupied, pushed on and seized the heights overlooking Potgieter's Drift on the Tugela. On the 12th Warren's Division, comprising the brigades of Lyttelton and Woodgate, with three batteries, marched to Springfield, where they camped. On the 13th the mounted troops, holding the heights above Potgieter's Drift, were strengthened by the arrival of two battalions of Lyttelton's Brigade from Springfield. Sir Redvers Buller established his headquarters in this camp. On the 14th the rest of the brigade followed, and the same day the corps troops, consisting of Coke's Brigade, one howitzer, and one field battery, reached Springfield. On the 15th Coke moved to the position before Potgieter's, and the naval guns were established on the heights commanding the ford. All this while the Boers contented themselves with fortifying their horseshoe position which enclosed the debouches from Potgieter's Drift, and only picket firing disturbed the general peace.

Such was the situation when I wrote my last letter. It was soon to develop, though in a most leisurely and deliberate manner. The

mounted forces, which had arrived at Spearman's Hill, as the
position before Potgieter's was called, on the 11th, passed nearly a
week of expectation. Daily we watched the enemy fortifying his
position, and observed the long lines of trenches which grew and
spread along the face of the opposite hills. Daily we made reconnoitring expeditions both east and west along the Tugela, expeditions always attended with incident, sometimes with adventure.
One day Colonel Byng crawled with two squadrons to the summit of
a high hill which overlooked the road from Colenso to Potgieter's,
and a long and patient vigil was rewarded by the arrival of five
Boer ox waggons toiling sluggishly along with supplies, on which
we directed a rapid and effective fire till they found some refuge in
a cutting. Another day we strengthened ourselves with two guns,
and, marching nearly to the junction of the Tugelas, gave the Boers
camped there an honest hour's shelling, and extricated a patrol of
Bethune's Mounted Infantry from a rather disagreeable position, so
that they were able to bring off a wounded trooper. Nightly the
cavalry camp went to sleep in the belief that a general attack would
open on the enemy's position at dawn. Day after day the expected
did not happen. Buller had other resources than to butt his head
against the tremendous entrenchments which were springing up
before him. Everyone discussed every conceivable alternative, and
in the meanwhile it was always "battle tomorrow", but never
"battle today". And so it has continued until this moment, and the
great event—the main trial of strength—still impends.

But though there has been but little powder burned the situation
has materially altered, and its alteration has been entirely to our
advantage. We have crossed the Tugela. The river which for two
months has barred the advance of the relieving army lies behind us
now. The enemy entrenched and entrenching in a strong position
still confronts us, but the British forces are across the Tugela, and
have deployed on the northern bank. With hardly any loss Sir
Redvers Buller has gained a splendid advantage. The old inequality
of ground has been swept away, and the strongest army yet moved
under one hand in South Africa stands face to face with the Boers
on the ordinary terms of attack and defence. Let me describe the
steps by which this result has been obtained.

On the afternoon of the 16th, as we were sitting down to luncheon,
we noticed a change in the appearance of the infantry camps on the
reverse slopes of Spearman's Hill. There was a busy bustling of men;

the tents began to look baggy, then they all subsided together; the white disappeared, and the camping grounds became simply brown patches of moving soldiery. Lyttelton's Brigade had received orders to march at once. Whither? It was another hour before this part of the secret transpired. They were to cross the river and seize the near kopjes beyond Potgieter's Drift. Orders for cavalry and guns to move arrived in quick succession; the entire cavalry force, excepting only Bethune's Mounted Infantry, to march at 5.30 p.m., with five days' rations, 150 rounds per man, and what they stood up in—tents, blankets, waterproof sheets, picketing gear, all to be left behind. Our camp was to remain standing. The infantry had struck theirs. I puzzled over this for some time, in fact until an officer pointed out that our camp was in full view of the Boer outposts on Spion Kop, while the infantry camps were hidden by a turn of the hill. Evidently a complex and deeply laid scheme was in progress.

In the interval, while the South African Light Horse were preparing for the march, I rode up to Gun Hill to watch the operation of seizing the near kopjes, which stood on the tongue of land across the river, and as nearly as possible in the centre of the horseshoe position of the enemy. The sailors were hauling their two great guns to the crest of the hill ready to come into action to support the infantry attack. Far below, the four battalions crept through the scrub at the foot of the hills towards the ferry. As they arrived at the edge of the open ground the long winding columns dissolved into sprays of skirmishers, line behind line of tiny dashes, visible only as shadows on the smooth face of the veldt, strange formations, the result of bitter practical experience. Presently the first line—a very thin line—men twenty paces apart—reached the ferry punt and the approaches to the Waggon Drift, and scrambled down to the brim of the river. A single man began to wade and swim across, carrying a line. Two or three others followed. Then a long chain of men, with arms locked—a sort of human caterpillar—entered the water, struggled slowly across, and formed up under the shelter of the further bank. All the time the Boers, manning their trenches and guns, remained silent. The infantry of the two leading battalions were thus filtering uneventfully across when the time for the cavalry column to start arrived.

There was a subdued flutter of excitement as we paraded, for though both our destination and object were unknown, it was clearly understood that the hour of action had arrived. Everything was moving. A long cloud of dust rose up in the direction of Springfield. A column of infantry—Coke's Brigade—curled out of its camp near Spearman's Hill, and wound down towards the ferry at Potgieter's. Eight curiously proportioned guns (naval 12-pounders), with tiny wheels and thin elongated barrels, were passed in a string, each tied to the tail of a waggon drawn by twenty oxen. The howitzer battery hurried to follow; its short and squat pieces, suggesting a row of venomous toads, made a striking contrast. As the darkness fell the cavalry column started. On all sides men were marching through the night: much important business was toward, which the reader may easily understand by studying the map, but cannot without such attention.

Having placed his army within striking distance of the various passages across the Tugela, Sir Redvers Buller's next object was to cross and debouch. To this end his plan appears to have been—for information is scarcely yet properly codified—something as follows: Lyttelton's Brigade, the corps troops forming Coke's Brigade, the ten naval guns, the battery of howitzers, one field battery, and Bethune's Mounted Infantry to demonstrate in front of the Potgieter position, keeping the Boers holding the horseshoe in expectation of a frontal attack, and masking their main position; Sir Charles Warren to march by night from Springfield with the brigades of Hart, Woodgate, and Hildyard, the Royal Dragoons, six batteries of artillery, and the pontoon train to a point about five miles west of Spearman's Hill, and opposite Trichardt's Drift on the Tugela. Here he was to meet the mounted forces from Spearman's Hill, and with these troops he was next day, the 17th, to throw bridges, force the passage of the river, and operate at leisure and discretion against the right flank of the enemy's horseshoe before Potgieter's, resting on Spion Kop, a commanding mountain, ultimately joining hands with the frontal force from Spearman's Hill at a point on the Acton Homes–Ladysmith road. To sum up briefly, seven battalions, twenty-two guns, and three hundred horse under Lyttelton to mask the Potgieter position; twelve battalions, thirty-six guns, and sixteen hundred horse to cross five miles to the westward, and make a turning movement against the enemy's right. The Boer covering army was to be swept back on Ladysmith by a powerful left arm, the pivoting shoulder of which was at Potgieter's, the elbow at Trichardt's Drift, and the enveloping hand—the cavalry under Lord Dundonald—stretching out towards Acton Homes.

So much for the plan; now for its execution or modifications. One main feature has characterised the whole undertaking—its amazing deliberation. There was to be absolutely no hurry of any kind whatever. Let the enemy entrench and fortify. If necessary, we were prepared to sap up to his positions. Let him discover where the attack impended. Even then all his resistance should be overborne. And it seems now that this same deliberation which was so punctiliously observed, when speed appeared an essential to success, baffled the enemy almost as much as it mystified the troops. However, the event is not yet decided.

After about two hours' easy marching the cavalry reached the point of rendezvous among the hills opposite Trichardt's Drift, and here we halted and awaited developments in the blackness. An hour passed. Then there arrived Sir Charles Warren and staff. "Move the cavalry out of the way—fifteen thousand men marching along this road tonight." So we moved accordingly and waited again. Presently the army began to come. I remember that it poured with rain, and there was very little to look at in the gloom, but, nevertheless, it was not possible to stand unmoved and watch the ceaseless living stream—miles of stern-looking men marching in fours so quickly that they often had to run to keep up, of artillery, ammunition columns, supply columns, baggage, slaughter cattle, thirty great pontoons, white-hooded, red-crossed ambulance waggons, all the accessories of an army hurrying forward under the cover of night—and before them a guiding star, the red gleam of war.

We all made quite sure that the bridges would be built during the night, so that with the dawn the infantry could begin to cross and make an immediate onfall. But when morning broke the whole force was revealed spread about the hills overlooking the drift and no sound of artillery proclaimed the beginning of an action. Of course, since a lightning blow had been expected, we all wondered what was the cause of the delay. Some said folly, others incapacity, others even actual laziness. But so far as the operations have proceeded I am not inclined to think that we have lost anything by not hurrying on this occasion. As I write all is going well, and it would have been a terrible demand to make of infantry that they should attack, after a long night march, such a position as lay and still lies in part before us. In fact it was utterly impossible to do anything worth doing that day beyond the transportation; so that, though the Boers were preparing redoubts and entrenchments with frantic energy, we might just as well take our time.

At about eight o'clock a patrol of the Imperial Light Horse, under Captain Bridges, having ascertained that only a few Dutch scouts were moving within range on the further bank, the passage of the river began. Two battalions of Hildyard's Brigade, the West Yorkshires and the Devons, moved towards the drift in the usual open formation, occupied the houses, and began to entrench themselves in the fields. Six batteries came into action from the wooded heights commanding the passage. The pontoons advanced. Two were launched, and in them the West Yorkshire Regiment began to cross, accumulating gradually in the shelter of the further bank. Then the sappers began to build the bridges. Half a dozen Boers fired a few shots at long range, and one unfortunate soldier in the Devons was killed. The batteries opened on the farms, woods, and kopjes beyond the river, shelling them assiduously, though there was not an enemy to be seen, and searching out the ground with great thoroughness. I watched this proceeding of making "sicker" from the heights. The drift was approached from the ground where we had bivouacked by a long, steep, descending valley. At nine o'clock the whole of Hart's Brigade poured down this great gutter and extended near the water. The bridge was growing fast—span after span of pontoons sprang out at the ends as it lay along the bank. Very soon it would be long enough to tow into position across the flood. Moreover, the infantry of the West Yorks and Devons had mostly been ferried across, and were already occupying the lately well-shelled farms and woods. At eleven o'clock the bridge was finished, the transported infantry were spreading up the hills, and Woodgate's Brigade moved forward down the valley.

It soon became time for the cavalry to cross, but they were not accommodated, as were the infantry, with a convenient bridge. About a quarter of a mile downstream from Trichardt's Drift there is a deep and rather dangerous ford, called the Waggon Drift. Across this at noon the mounted men began to make their way, and what with the uneven bottom and the strong current there were a good many duckings. The Royal Dragoons mounted on their great horses, indeed, passed without much difficulty, but the ponies of the Light Horse and Mounted Infantry were often swept off their feet, and the ridiculous spectacle of officers and men floundering in the torrent or rising indignantly from the shallows provided a large crowd of spectators—who had crossed by the bridge—with a comedy. Tragedy was not, however, altogether excluded, for a trooper of the 13th Hussars was drowned, and Captain Tremayne, of the same regiment, who made a gallant attempt to rescue him, was taken from the water insensible.

During the afternoon the busy Engineers built a second bridge across the river, and by this and the first the artillery, the ammunition columns, and the rest of the mass of wheeled transport defiled. All that day and through the night this monotonous business of passing the waggons across continued. The cavalry had bivouacked —all tents and even waterproofs were now left behind—within the infantry picket lines, and we awoke at the break of day expecting to hear the boom of the first gun. "Quite right to wait until there was a whole day to make the attack in. Suppose that was the reason we did not hurry yesterday." But no guns fired near Trichardt's Drift, and only the frontal force at Potgieter's began its usual bombardment. Sir Charles Warren, moreover, said that his artillery had not finished crossing—one battery still to cross—and that there was no hurry. Deliberation was the order of the day. So again everyone was puzzled, and not a few were critical, for in modern times everyone thinks, and even a native camp follower has his views on tactics and strategy.

A very complete consolation awaited the cavalry. All that Warren did with his infantry on this day, the 18th, was to creep cautiously forward about two miles towards the Boer position, which with its left resting on Spion Kop stretched along the edge and crest of a lofty plateau, from which long gently sloping spurs and *arêtes* ran down to the river. For us, however, there was more diverting employment. "The mounted brigade will guard the left flank of the infantry." Such was the order; and is not offence the surest defence? Accordingly all the irregular cavalry moved in a considerable column westward across the front of the Boer position, endeavouring to find where its flank rested, and prying with inquisitive patrols at every object of interest. The order of march was as follows: First, the composite regiment (one squadron of Imperial Light Horse, the 60th Rifles, Mounted Infantry, and one squadron of Natal Carabineers), 350 of the very best; next, four squadrons of the South African Light Horse, good shooting high-class colonial Volunteers with officers of experience; then Thorneycroft's

Mounted Infantry. "Lived in Natal all our lives! Know every inch of it, sir!" And behind these alert mounted riflemen moved the ponderous and terrible regulars, 13th Hussars and Royals, with the dreaded *arme blanche*, "Wait till we get among them." Altogether a formidable brigade.

There were many halts, and no one hurried, so that at two o'clock the whole cavalry formed a line of observation along the lower kopjes by the river about five miles long. The composite regiment was not, however, to be seen. Major Graham, who commanded it, had been observed trotting swiftly off to the westward. Two hundred Boers had also been reported moving in that direction. Presently came the sound of distant musketry—not so very distant either. Everyone pricked up his ears. Two miles away to the left was a green hill broken by rocky kopjes. Looking through my glasses I could see ten or twelve riderless horses grazing. A mile further on a group of Boers sheltering behind a kopje from the continual fire was visible. Suddenly one galloped away madly, and even at the distance it was possible to see the cloud of dust from pursuing bullets. A straggling column of Boers was trekking away across the plain back to their main position. Then came reports and rumours. "Ambuscaded the Dutchmen—shot 'em to bits—some of them cut off—come and bag the lot." Behind the rumours Barnes, adjutant of the Imperial Light Horse, joyful, with a breathless horse; he explained how they had seen two hundred Boers moving towards distant hills, to make sure of their line of retreat by the Acton Homes road into the Free State; galloped to cut them off; reached the hills first, with just five minutes to spare; dismounted, commanding the road, and waited.

The Boers admitted afterwards that they thought that the squadrons visible on the other hills two miles back were the head of our column, and they also blamed their scouts, particularly one, an Austrian. "It all comes of trusting these cursed foreigners! If we had only had a *veldt* Boer out we should never have been caught." Caught, however, they undoubtedly were. The Carabineers and the Imperial Light Horse held their fire until the scouts walked into their midst, and then let drive at the main body, 300 yards range, mounted men, smooth open grass plain. There was a sudden furious, snapping fusilade. The Boer column stopped paralysed; then they broke and rushed for cover. The greater number galloped fast from the field; some remained on the ground dead or wounded. Others took refuge among the rocks of the kopjes and apparently proposed to hold out until dark, and hence the arrival of Lieutenant Barnes demanding reinforcements, 60th Rifles, Mounted Infantry, and anything else, so as to attack these fellows in flank and "bag the lot". Meanwhile Lord Dundonald had arrived on our hill. "Certainly, every man we can spare." Off gallops the Mounted Infantry and one squadron of the South African Light Horse, and later on some of Thorneycroft's, and later still the Brigadier himself. I arrived in time to see the end. The Boers—how many we could not tell—were tenaciously holding the black rocks of a kopje and were quite invisible. The British riflemen curved round them in a half-moon, firing continually at the rocks. The squadron of South African Light Horse had worked almost behind the enemy, and every Dutchman who dared make a dash for liberty ran a terrible gauntlet. Still the surrender did not come. The white flag flickered for a moment above the rocks, but neither side stopped firing. Evidently a difference of opinion among the enemy. What do we care for that? Night is coming on. Let us rush them with the bayonet and settle the matter. This from the Rifles—nobody else had bayonets. So a section pushes forward against the rocks, crawling along the ground. Anxious to see the surrender, I followed on my pony, but on the instant there broke out a savage fire from the kopje, and with difficulty I found shelter in a donga. Here were two of the Natal Carabineers—one a bearded man of the well-to-do farmer class, the other a young fair-haired gentleman—both privates, both as cool as ice. "Vewy astonishing outburst of fire," said the younger man in a delicate voice. "I would recommend your remaining here with your horse for the present." Accordingly we lay still on the grass slope and awaited developments. The young gentleman put his helmet over the crest on the end of his rifle, and was much diverted to hear the bullets whistle round it. At intervals he substituted his head for the helmet and reported the state of the game. "Bai Jove, the Rifles are in a hot place." I peered cautiously. A hundred yards away the Mounted Infantry section were extended. The dust spurts rose around the men, who remained pinned to the earth, scarcely able to raise their heads to fire. Whatever passed over them came whizzing in our direction. The Natal Volunteer, however, was too much interested in the proceedings to forego his view. "Deah, deah, they've fixed bayonets! Why, they're coming back. They've had someone hurt." I looked again for a

moment. The line of riflemen was certainly retiring, wriggling back-
wars slowly on their bellies. Two brown forms lay still and hunched
in the abandoned position. Then suddenly the retiring riflemen
sprang up and ran for shelter in our donga. One lad jumped right in
among us laughing and panting, and the whole party turned at once
and lined the bank. First-class infantry can afford to retire at the
double, sure that they will stop at a word. "We got to within fifty
yards of the Dutchmen," they said; "but it was too hot to go
further. They've shot two fellows through the head." Eventually we
all retired to the main position on the ridge above us. Lord Dundonald and his staff had just arrived.

"There! there's the white flag again. Shoot the devils!" cried a
soldier, and the musketry crashed out fiercely. "What's to be done,
sir?" said the Captain, turning to the Brigadier; "the white flag has
been up off and on for the last half-hour, but they don't stop firing,
and they've just killed two of my men."

"Give them one more chance." "Cease fire—cease fire there, will
you?" for the men were very angry, and so at last the musketry died
away, and there was silence. Then from among the rocks three dark
figures stood up holding up their hands, and at this tangible
evidence of surrender we got on our horses and galloped towards
them waving pocket handkerchiefs and signalling flags to show
them that their surrender was accepted. Altogether there were
twenty-four prisoners—all Boers of the most formidable type—a
splendid haul, and I thought with delight of my poor friends the
prisoners at Pretoria. This might redeem a few. Then we searched
the ground, finding ten dead or dying and twenty loose horses, ten
dead and eight badly wounded men. The soldiers crowded round
these last, covering them up with blankets or mackintoshes, prop-
ing their heads with saddles for pillows, and giving them water and
biscuits from their bottles and haversacks. Anger had turned to pity
in an instant. The desire to kill was gone. The desire to comfort
replaced it. A little alert officer—Hubert Gough, now a captain,
soon to command a regiment—came up to me. Two minutes before
his eyes were bright and joyous with the excitement of the man
hunt. He had galloped a mile—mostly under fire—to bring the
reinforcements to surround the Boers. "Bag the lot, you know."
Now he was very sad. "There's a poor boy dying up there—only a
boy, and so cold—who's got a blanket?"

So the soldiers succoured the Boer wounded, and we told the

prisoners that they would be shown courtesy and kindness worthy of brave men and a famous quarrel. The Boer dead were collected and a flag of truce was sent to the enemy's lines to invite a burying and identification party at dawn. I have often seen dead men, killed in war—thousands at Omdurman—scores elsewhere, black and white, but the Boer dead aroused the most painful emotions. Here by the rock under which he had fought lay the Field Cornet of Heilbronn, Mr. de Mentz—a grey-haired man of over sixty years, with firm aquiline features and a short beard. The stony face was grimly calm, but it bore the stamp of unalterable resolve; the look of a man who had thought it all out, and was quite certain that his cause was just, and such as a sober citizen might give his life for. Nor was I surprised when the Boer prisoners told me that Mentz had refused all suggestions of surrender, and that when his left leg was smashed by a bullet he had continued to load and fire until he bled to death; and they found him, pale and bloodless, holding his wife's letter in his hand. Beside him was a boy of about seventeen shot through the heart. Further on lay our own two poor riflemen with their heads smashed like eggshells; and I suppose they had mothers or wives far away at the end of the deep-sea cables. Ah, horrible war, amazing medley of the glorious and the squalid, the pitiful and the sublime, if modern men of light and leading saw your face closer, simple folk would see it hardly ever.

It could not be denied that the cavalry had scored a brilliant success. We had captured twenty-four, killed ten, and wounded eight—total, forty-two. Moreover, we had seen the retreating Boers dragging and supporting their injured friends from the field, and might fairly claim fifteen knocked out of time, besides those in our hands, total fifty-seven; a fine bag, for which we had had to pay scarcely anything. Two soldiers of the Mounted Infantry killed; one trooper of the Imperial Light Horse slightly, and one officer, Captain Shore—the twenty-third officer of this regiment hit during the last three months—severely wounded.

CHAPTER SEVENTEEN

THE BATTLE OF SPION KOP

Venter's Spruit: January 25, 1900

IT IS the remarkable characteristic of strong races, as of honourable men, to keep their tempers in the face of disappointment, and never to lose a just sense of proportion; and it is, moreover, the duty of every citizen in times of trouble to do or say or even to think nothing that can weaken or discourage the energies of the State. Sir Redvers Buller's army has met with another serious check in the attempt to relieve Ladysmith. We have approached, tested, and assailed the Boer positions beyond the Tugela, fighting more or less continuously for five days, and the result is that we find they cannot be pierced from the direction of Trichardt's Drift any more than at Colenso. With the loss of more than two thousand men out of a small army, we find it necessary to recross the river and seek for some other line of attack; and meanwhile the long and brave resistance of Ladysmith must be drawing to a close. Indeed, it is the opinion of many good judges that further efforts to relieve the town will only be attended with further loss. As to this I do not pronounce, but I am certain of one thing—that further efforts must be made without regard to the loss of life which will attend them.

I have seen and heard a good deal of what has passed here. I have often been blamed for the freedom with which I have written of other operations and criticised their commanders. I respectfully submit that I am as venomous an amateur strategist as exists at this time. It is very easy—and much more easy than profitable—when freed from all responsibility to make daring suggestions and express decided opinions. I assert that I would not hesitate to criticise mercilessly if I was not myself sobered by the full appreciation of the extraordinary difficulties which the relief of Ladysmith presents; and if there be anyone who has any confidence in my desire to write the truth I appeal to him to be patient and calm, to recognise that perhaps the task before Sir Redvers Buller and his subordinates is an actual impossibility, that if these generals are not capable men—among the best that our times produce—it is difficult to know where and how others may be obtained, and finally to brutally face the fact that Sir George White and his heroic garrison may be forced to become the prisoners of the Boers, remembering always that nothing that happens, either victory or defeat, in northern Natal can affect the ultimate result of the war. In a word, let no one despair of the Empire because a few thousand soldiers are killed, wounded, or captured. Now for the story as plainly and briefly as possible.

When Buller had arrived at Potgieter's he found himself confronted by a horseshoe position of great strength, enclosing and closing the debouches from the ford where he had secured a practical bridgehead. He therefore masked Potgieter's with seven battalions and twenty-four guns, and sent Warren with twelve battalions and thirty-six guns to turn the right, which rested on the lofty hill—almost mountain—of Spion Kop. The Boers, to meet this turning movement, extended their line westwards along the heights of the Tugela valley almost as far as Acton Homes. Their whole position was, therefore, shaped like a note of interrogation laid on its side, —⌒, the curve in front of General Lyttelton, the straight line before Sir Charles Warren. At the angle formed by the junction of the curve and the line stands Spion Kop—"look-out hill". The curved position in front of General Lyttelton has been already described in a previous letter. The straight position in front of Sir Charles Warren ran in two lines along the edge and crest of a plateau which rises steeply two miles from the river, but is approachable by numerous long *arêtes* and dongas. These letters have completed the chronicle down to the evening of the 18th, when the successful cavalry action was fought on the extreme left.

I do not know why nothing was done on the 19th, but it does not appear that anything was lost by the delay. The enemy's entrenchments were already complete, and neither his numbers nor the strength of his positions could increase.

On the 20th Warren, having crept up the *arêtes* and dongas, began his attack. The brigades of Generals Woodgate and Hart pushed forward on the right, and the Lancashire and Irish regiments,

fighting with the usual gallantry of Her Majesty's troops, succeeded, in spite of a heavy fire of rifles and artillery, in effecting
lodgments at various points along the edge of the plateau, capturing
some portions of the enemy's first line of entrenchments. On the
extreme left the cavalry under Lord Dundonald demonstrated
effectively, and the South African Light Horse under Colonel Byng
actually took and held without artillery support of any kind a high
hill, called henceforward "Bastion Hill", between the Dutch right
and centre. Major Childe, the officer whose squadron performed this
daring exploit, was killed on the summit by the shell fire to which
the successful assailants were subjected by the Boers. In the evening
infantry reinforcements of Hildyard's Brigade arrived, and at dawn
the cavalry handed over the hill to their charge. The losses during
the day did not exceed three hundred and fifty officers and men
wounded—with fortunately, a small proportion of killed—and fell
mainly on the Lancashire Fusiliers, the Dublin Fusiliers (always in
the front), and the Royal Lancaster Regiment. They were not disproportioned to the apparent advantage gained.

On the 21st the action was renewed. Hart's and Woodgate's
brigades on the right made good and extended their lodgments,
capturing all the Boer trenches of their first defensive line along the
edge of the plateau. To the east of "Bastion Hill" there runs a deep
re-entrant, which appeared to open a cleft between the right and
centre of the Boer position. The tendency of General Hildyard's
action, with five battalions and two batteries, on the British left
this day was to drive a wedge of infantry into this cleft and so split
the Boer position in two. But as the action developed, the great
strength of the second line of defence gradually revealed itself. It
ran along the crest of the plateau, which rises about a thousand
yards from the edge in a series of beautiful smooth grassy slopes of
concave surface, forming veritable glacis for the musketry of the
defence to sweep; and it consisted of a line of low rock and earth
redoubts and shelter trenches, apparently provided with overhead
cover, and cleverly arranged to command all approaches with fire—
often with cross-fire, sometimes with converging fire. Throughout
the 21st, as during the 20th, the British artillery, consisting of six
field batteries and four howitzers, the latter apparently of tremendous power, bombarded the whole Boer position ceaselessly,
firing on each occasion nearly three thousand shells. They claim to
have inflicted considerable loss on the enemy, and must have

inflicted some, but failed utterly and painfully to silence the musketry, to clear the trenches, or reach and overpower the Dutch artillery, which did not number more than seven or eight guns and two Maxim shell-guns, but which were better served and manœuvred and of superior quality. The losses in the action of the 20th were about one hundred and thirty officers and men killed and wounded, but this must be regarded as severe in the face of the fact that no serious collision or even contact took place.

During the 22nd and 23rd the troops held the positions they had won, and the infantry were subjected to a harassing shell fire from the Boer guns, which, playing from either flank, searched the re-entrants in which the battalions sheltered, and which, though they did not cause a greater loss than forty men on the 22nd and twenty-five on the 23rd, nevertheless made their position extremely un-comfortable. It was quite evident that the troops could not be fairly required to endure this bombardment, against which there was no protection, indefinitely. Nor was any good object, but rather the contrary, to be gained by waiting.

Three alternatives presented themselves to the council of war held on the 22nd. First, to attack the second Boer position frontally along the crest by moonlight. This would involve a great slaughter and a terrible risk. Secondly, to withdraw again, beyond the Tugela, and look elsewhere for a passage: a moral defeat and a further delay in the relief of Ladysmith; and thirdly, to attack by night the mountain of Spion Kop, and thence to enfilade and command the Boer entrenchments. Sir Redvers Buller, who has always disdained effect, was for the second course—unpalatable as it must have been to a fearless man; miserable as it is to call off infantry after they have made sacrifices and won positions, and to call them off a second time. The discussion was an informal one, and no votes were taken, but the General yielded to the advice of his subordinate, rightly, I hold, because now at least we know the strength of the enemy's position, whereas before we only dreaded it; and knowledge is a better reason for action than apprehension.

It was therefore decided to attack Spion Kop by night, rush the Boer trenches with the bayonet, entrench as far as possible before dawn, hold on during the day, drag guns up at night, and thus dominate the Boer lines. There is, of course, no possible doubt that Spion Kop is the key of the whole position, and the reader has only to think of the horizontal note of interrogation, and remember that the mountain at the angle divides, commands, and enfilades the enemy's lines, to appreciate this fact. The questions to be proved were whether the troops could hold out during the day, and whether the place could be converted into a fort proof against shell fire and armed with guns during the following night. Fate has now decided both.

General Woodgate was entrusted with the command, and Colonel Thorneycroft with much of the arrangement and direction of the night attack. It does not seem that anything but good resulted from this too soon broken co-operation. Thorneycroft declined to attack on the night of the 22nd because the ground had not been reconnoitred, and he wanted to be sure of his way. The infantry therefore had another day's shelling on the 23rd. Good reconnaissances were, however, made, Lyttelton was strengthened by two Fusilier battalions from Chieveley, Warren was reinforced by Talbot Coke's Brigade and the Imperial Light Infantry, and at one o'clock on the morning of January 24 General Woodgate started from his camp with the Lancashire Fusiliers, the Royal Lancaster Regiment, two companies of the South Lancashires, and Thorneycroft's Mounted Infantry. Guided by Colonel Thorneycroft the force made its way successfully up the southern spur of the mountain, over most difficult and dangerous ground, and surprised the Boers guarding the entrenchments on the summit. At three o'clock those listening in the plain heard the sudden outburst of musketry, followed by the loud cheers of the troops, and knew that the position had been carried. Ten soldiers were killed and wounded in the firing. Six Boers perished by the bayonet. The force then proceeded to fortify itself, but the surface of the hill was extremely unsuited to defence. The rocks which covered the summit made digging an impossibility, and were themselves mostly too large to be built into sangars. Such cover, however, as had been made by the Boers was utilised and improved.

Morning broke, and with it the attack. The enemy, realising the vital importance of the position, concentrated every man and gun at his disposal for its recapture. A fierce and furious shell fire was opened forthwith on the summit, causing immediate and continual loss. General Woodgate was wounded, and the command devolved on a regimental officer, who, at half-past six, applied for reinforcements in a letter which scarcely displayed that composure and determination necessary in such a bloody debate.

Sir Redvers Buller then took the extreme step of appointing Major Thorneycroft—already only a local lieutenant-colonel—local Brigadier-General commanding on the summit of Spion Kop. The Imperial Light Infantry, the Middlesex Regiment, and a little later the Somersets, from General Talbot Coke's Brigade, were ordered to reinforce the defence, but General Coke was directed to remain below the summit of the hill, so that the fight might still be conducted by the best fighting man.

The Boers followed, and accompanied their shells by a vigorous rifle attack on the hill, and about half-past eight the position became most critical. The troops were driven almost entirely off the main plateau and the Boers succeeded in reoccupying some of their trenches. A frightful disaster was narrowly averted. About twenty men in one of the captured trenches abandoned their resistance, threw up their hands, and called out that they would surrender. Colonel Thorneycroft, whose great stature made him everywhere conspicuous, and who was from dawn till dusk in the first firing line, rushed to the spot. The Boers advancing to take the prisoners—as at Nicholson's Nek—were scarcely thirty yards away. Thorneycroft shouted to the Boer leader: "You may go to hell. I command on this hill and allow no surrender. Go on with your firing." Which latter they did with terrible effect, killing many. The survivors, with the rest of the firing line, fled two hundred yards, were rallied by their indomitable commander, and, being reinforced by two brave companies of the Middlesex Regiment, charged back, recovering all lost ground, and the position was maintained until nightfall. No words in these days of extravagant expression can do justice to the glorious endurance which the English regiments—for they were all English—displayed throughout the long dragging hours of hell fire. Between three and four o'clock the shells were falling on the hill from both sides, as I counted, at the rate of seven a minute, and the strange discharges of the Maxim shell guns—the "pom-poms" as these terrible engines are called for want of a correct name—lacerated the hillsides with dotted chains of smoke and dust. A thick and continual stream of wounded flowed rearwards. A village of ambulance waggons grew up at the foot of the mountain. The dead and injured, smashed and broken by the shells, littered the summit till it was a bloody, reeking shambles. Thirst tormented the soldiers, for though water was at hand the fight was too close and furious to give even a moment's breathing space. But nothing could weaken the stubborn vigour of the defence. The Dorset Regiment—the last of Talbot Coke's Brigade—was ordered to support the struggling troops. The gallant Lyttelton of his own accord sent the Scottish Rifles and the 3rd King's Royal Rifles from Potgieter's to aid them. But though their splendid attack did not help the main action; though the British artillery, unable to find or reach the enemy's guns, could only tear up the ground in impotent fury; though the shell fire and rifle fire never ceased for an instant—the magnificent infantry maintained the defence, and night closed in with the British still in possession of the hill.

I find it convenient, and perhaps the reader will allow me, to break into a more personal account of what followed. It drove us all mad to watch idly in camp the horrible shelling that was directed on the captured position, and at about four o'clock I rode with Captain R. Brooke, 7th Hussars, to Spion Kop, to find out what the true situation was. We passed through the ambulance village, and leaving our horses climbed up the spur. Streams of wounded met us and obstructed the path. Men were staggering along alone, or supported by comrades, or crawling on hands and knees, or carried on stretchers. Corpses lay here and there. Many of the wounds were of a horrible nature. The splinters and fragments of the shell had torn and mutilated in the most ghastly manner. I passed about two hundred while I was climbing up. There was, moreover, a small but steady leakage of unwounded men of all corps. Some of these cursed and swore. Others were utterly exhausted and fell on the hillside in stupor. Others again seemed drunk, though they had had no liquor. Scores were sleeping heavily. Fighting was still proceeding, and stray bullets struck all over the ground, while the Maxim shell guns scourged the flanks of the hill and the sheltering infantry at regular intervals of a minute. The 3rd King's Royal Rifles were out of reach. The Dorset Regiment was the only battalion not thrown into the fight, and intact as an effective unit.

I had seen some service and Captain Brooke has been through more fighting than any other officer of late years. We were so profoundly impressed by the spectacle and situation that we resolved to go and tell Sir Charles Warren what we had seen. The fight had been so close that no proper reports had been sent to the General, so he listened with great patience and attention. One thing was quite clear—unless good and efficient cover could be made during

the night, and unless guns could be dragged to the summit of the
hill to match the Boer artillery, the infantry could not, perhaps
would not, endure another day. The human machine will not stand
certain strains for long.

The questions were, could guns be brought up the hill; and, if so,
could the troops maintain themselves? The artillery officers had
examined the track. They said "No", and that even if they could
reach the top of the hill they would only be shot out of action. Two
long-range naval 12-pounders, much heavier than the field-guns,
had arrived. The naval lieutenant in charge said he could go anywhere, or would have a try any way. He was quite sure that if he
could get on the top of the hill he would knock out the Boer guns or
be knocked out by them, and that was what he wanted to find out.
I do not believe that the attempt would have succeeded, or that the
guns could have been in position by daylight, but the contrast in
spirit was very refreshing.

Another informal council of war was called. Sir Charles Warren
wanted to know Colonel Thorneycroft's views. I was sent to obtain
them. The darkness was intense. The track stony and uneven. It
was hopelessly congested with ambulances, stragglers, and wounded
men. I soon had to leave my horse, and then toiled upwards, finding
everywhere streams of men winding about the almost precipitous
sides of the mountain, and an intermittent crackle of musketry at
the top. Only one solid battalion remained—the Dorsets. All the
others were intermingled. Officers had collected little parties, companies and half-companies; here and there larger bodies had
formed, but there was no possibility, in the darkness, of gripping
anybody or anything. Yet it must not be imagined that the infantry
were demoralised. Stragglers and weaklings there were in plenty.
But the mass of the soldiers were determined men. One man I
found dragging down a box of ammunition quite by himself. "To
do something," he said. A sergeant with twenty men formed up was
inquiring what troops were to hold the position. Regimental
officers everywhere cool and cheery, each with a little group of men
around him, all full of fight and energy. But the darkness and the
broken ground paralysed everyone.

I found Colonel Thorneycroft at the top of the mountain. Everyone seemed to know, even in the confusion, where he was. He was
sitting on the ground surrounded by the remnants of the regiment
he had raised, who had fought for him like lions and followed him

like dogs. I explained the situation as I had been told and as I thought. Naval guns were prepared to try, sappers and working parties were already on the road with thousands of sandbags. What did he think? But the decision had already been taken. He had never received any messages from the General, had not had time to write any. Messages had been sent him, he had wanted to send others himself. The fight had been too hot, too close, too interlaced for him to attend to anything, but to support this company, clear those rocks, or line that trench. So, having heard nothing and expecting no guns, he had decided to retire. As he put it tersely: "Better six good battalions safely down the hill than a mop up in the morning." Then we came home, drawing down our rearguard after us very slowly and carefully, and as the ground grew more level the regiments began to form again into their old solid blocks.

Such was the fifth of the series of actions called the Battle of Spion Kop. It is an event which the British people may regard with feelings of equal pride and sadness. It redounds to the honour of the soldiers, though not greatly to that of the generals. But when all that will be written about this has been written, and all the bitter words have been said by the people who never do anything themselves, the wise and just citizen will remember that these same generals are, after all, brave, capable, noble English gentlemen, trying their best to carry through a task which may prove to be impossible, and is certainly the hardest ever set to men.

The Lancashire Fusiliers, the Imperial Light Infantry—whose baptism of fire it was—Thorneycroft's, and the Middlesex Regiment sustained the greater part of the losses.

We will have another try, and, if it pleases God, do better next time.

CHAPTER EIGHTEEN

THROUGH THE FIVE DAYS' ACTION

Venter's Spruit: January 25, 1900

THE IMPORTANCE of giving a general and comprehensive account of the late actions around and on Spion Kop prevented me from describing its scenes and incidents. Events, like gentlemen at a levee, in these exciting days tread so closely on each other's heels that many pass unnoticed, and most can only claim the scantiest attention. But I will pick from the hurrying procession a few—distinguished for no other reason than that they have caught my eye—and from their quality the reader may judge of the rest.

The morning of the 20th discovered the cavalry still encamped behind the hills near the Acton Homes road, on which they had surprised the Boers two days before. The loud and repeated discharge of the artillery advised us that the long-expected general action had begun. What part were the cavalry to play? No orders had been sent to Lord Dundonald except that he was to cover the left flank of the infantry. But the cavalry commander, no less than his brigade, proposed to interpret these Instructions freely. Accordingly, at about half-past nine, the South African Light Horse, two squadrons of the 13th Hussars, and a battery of four machine guns moved forward towards the line of heights along the edge and crest of which ran the Boer position with the intention of demonstrating against them, and the daring idea—somewhere in the background— of attacking and seizing one prominent feature which jutted out into the plain, and which, from its boldness and shape, we had christened "Bastion Hill". The composite regiment, who watched the extreme left, were directed to support us if all was clear in their front at one o'clock, and Thorneycroft's Mounted Infantry, who kept touch between the main cavalry force and the infantry left flank, had similar orders to co-operate.

At ten o'clock Lord Dundonald ordered the South African Light
Horse to advance against Bastion Hill. If the resistance was severe
they were not to press the attack, but to content themselves with a
musketry demonstration. If, however, they found it convenient to
get on they were to do so as far as they liked. Colonel Byng thereon
sent two squadrons under Major Childe to advance, dismounted
frontally on the hill, and proposed to cover their movements by the
fire of the other two squadrons, who were to gallop to the shelter of
a wood and creep thence up the various dongas to within effective
range.

Major Childe accepted his orders with alacrity, and started forth
on what seemed, as I watched from a grassy ride, a most desperate
enterprise. The dark brown mass of Bastion Hill appeared to
dominate the plain. On its crest the figures of the Boers could be
seen frequently moving about. Other spurs to either flanks looked
as if they afforded facilities for cross fire. And to capture this formidable position we could dismount only about a hundred and fifty
men; and had, moreover, no artillery support of any kind. Yet as
one examined the hill it became evident that its strength was
apparent rather than real. Its slopes were so steep that they presented no good field of fire. Its crest was a convex curve, over and
down which the defenders must advance before they could command the approaches, and when so advanced they would be exposed
without shelter of any kind to the fire of the covering troops. The
salient was so prominent and jutted out so far from the general line
of hills, and was besides shaped so like a blunted redan, that its
front face was secure from flanking fire. In fact there was plenty of
dead ground in its approaches, and, moreover, dongas—which are
the same as nullahs in India or gullies in Australia—ran agreeably
to our wishes towards the hill in all directions. When first we had
seen the hill three days before we had selected it as a weak point in
the Dutch line. It afterwards proved that the Boers had no illusions
as to its strength and had made their arrangements accordingly.

So soon as the dismounted squadrons had begun their advance,
Colonel Byng led the two who were to cover it forward. The wood
we were to reach and find shelter in was about a thousand yards
distant, and had been reported unoccupied by the Boers, who
indeed confined themselves strictly to the hills after their rough
handling on the 18th by the cavalry. We moved off at a walk.
spreading into a wide open order, as wise colonial cavalry always do,

And it was fortunate that our formation was a dispersed one, for no sooner had we moved into the open ground than there was the flash of a gun far away among the hills to the westward. I had had some experience of artillery fire in the armoured train episode, but there the guns were firing at such close quarters that the report of the discharge and the explosion of the shell were almost simultaneous. Nor had I ever heard the menacing hissing roar which heralds the approach of a long-range projectile. It came swiftly, passed overhead with a sound like the rending of thin sheets of iron, and burst with a rather dull explosion in the ground a hundred yards behind the squadrons, throwing up smoke and clods of earth. We broke into a gallop, and moved in curving course towards the wood. I suppose we were a target a hundred yards broad by a hundred and fifty deep. The range was not less than seven thousand yards, and we were at the gallop. Think of this, Inspector-General of Artillery: the Boer gunners fired ten or eleven shells, every one of which fell among or within a hundred yards of our ranks. Between us and the wood ran a deep donga with a river only fordable in places flowing through it. Some confusion occurred in crossing this, but at last the whole regiment was across, and found shelter from the terrible gun—perhaps there were two—on the further bank. Thanks to our dispersed formation only two horses had been killed, and it was possible to admire without having to deplore the skill of the artillerists who could make such beautiful practice at such a range.

Colonel Byng thought it advisable to leave the horses in the cover of the protecting river bank, and we therefore pushed on, dismounted, and, straggling through the high maize crop without presenting any target to the guns, reached the wood safely. Through this we hurried as far as its further edge. Here the riflemen on the hill opened with long-range fire. It was only a hundred yards into the donga, and the troopers immediately began running across in twos and threes. In the irregular corps all appearances are sacrificed to the main object of getting where you want to without being hurt. No one was hurt.

Colonel Byng made his way along the donga to within about twelve or fourteen hundred yards, and from excellent cover opened fire on the Boers holding the summit of the hill. A long musketry duel ensued without any loss to our side, and with probably no more to the enemy. The colonial troopers, as wary as the Dutch, showed very little to shoot at, so that, though there were plenty of

bullets, there was no bloodshed. Regular infantry would probably
have lost thirty or forty men.

I went back for machine guns, and about half an hour later they
were brought into action at the edge of the wood. Boers on the sky-
line at two thousand yards—tat-tat-tat-tat-tat half a dozen times
repeated; Boers galloping to cover; one—yes, by Jupiter!—one on
his back on the grass; after that no more targets to shoot at; continuous searching of the sky-line, however, on the chance of killing
someone, and, in any case, to support the frontal attack. We had
altogether three guns—the 13th Hussars' Maxim under Lieutenant
Clutterbuck, detached from the 4th Hussars; one of Lord Dundonald's battery of Colts under Mr. Hill, who is a Member of
Parliament, and guides the majestic course of Empire besides
managing machine guns; and our own Maxim, all under Major
Villiers.

These three machines set up a most exhilarating splutter, flaring
and crackling all along the edge of the wood, and even attracted the
attention of the Boers. All of a sudden there was a furious rush and
roar overhead; two or three little casuarina trees and a shower of
branches fell to the ground. What on earth could this be? The main
action was crashing away on the right. Evidently a shell had passed
a few feet over our heads, but was it from our guns shelling the hills
in front, or from the enemy? In another minute the question was
answered by another shell. It was our old friend the gun to the
westward, who, irritated by the noisy Maxims, had resolved to put
his foot down. Whizz! Bang! came a third shot, exploding among
the branches just behind the Colt gun, to the great delight of Mr.
Hill, who secured a large fragment, which I have advised him to lay
on the table in the smoking-room of the House for the gratification,
instruction, and diversion of other honourable members. The next
shell smashed through the roof of a farmhouse which stood at the
corner of the wood, and near which two troops of the 13th Hussars,
who were escorting the Maxims and watching the flanks, had left
their led horses. The next, in quick succession, fell right among
them, killing one, but luckily, very luckily, failed to burst. The
officer then decided to move the horses to a safer place. The two
troops mounted and galloped off. They were a tiny target, only a
moving speck across the plain. But the Boer gunners threw a shell
within a yard of the first troop leader. All this at seven thousand
yards! English artillery experts, please note and if possible copy.

While these things were passing the advancing squadrons had begun to climb the hill, and found to their astonishment that they were scarcely fired at. It was of great importance, however, that the Boers should be cleared from the summit by the Maxim fire, and lest this should be diverted on our own men by mistake I left the wood for the purpose of signalling back how far the advance had proceeded and up to what point the guns could safely fire. The ground was broken; the distance considerable. Before I reached the hill the situation had changed. The enemy's artillery had persuaded the Maxims that they would do better to be quiet—at any rate until they could see something to shoot at. Major Childe had reached the top of the hill, one man of his squadron, ten minutes in front of anyone else, waving his hat on his rifle at the summit to the admiration of thousands of the infantry, all of whom saw this act of conspicuous recklessness and rejoiced. Lord Dundonald had galloped up to support the attack with Thorneycroft's Mounted Infantry and the rest of the 13th Hussars. We, the South African Light Horse, had taken Bastion Hill.

To advance further forward, however, proved quite impossible. The Boers had withdrawn to a second position a thousand yards in rear of the top of the hill. From this they directed a most accurate and damnable fire on all who showed themselves on the plateau. Beneath the crest one sat in safety and listened to the swish of bullets passing overhead. Above, the men were content to lie quite still underneath the rocks and wait for darkness. I had a message for Major Childe and found him sitting on this dangerous ground, partly sheltered by a large rock—a serene old gentleman, exhausted with his climb, justly proud of its brilliant success.

I found no reason to remain very long on the plateau, and had just returned to the Brigadier when the Boer guns began to shell the tip of the hill. The first two or three projectiles skimmed over the surface, and roared harmlessly away. But the Boers were not long in striking their mark. Two percussion shells burst on the exposed side of the hill, and then a well-exploded shrapnel searched its summit, searched and found what it sought. Major Childe was instantly killed by a fragment that entered his brain, and half a dozen troopers were more or less seriously wounded. After that, as if satisfied, the enemy's gun turned its attention elsewhere.

I think this death of Major Childe was a very sad event even among the inevitable incidents of war. He had served many years ago in the Blues, and since then a connection with the Turf had made him not unknown and well liked in sporting circles. Old and grey as he was, the call to arms had drawn him from home, and wife, and comfort, as it is drawing many of all ages and fortunes now. And so he was killed in his first fight against the Boers after he had performed an exploit—his first and last in war—which would most certainly have brought him honourable distinction. He had a queer presentiment of impending fate, for he had spoken a good deal to us of the chances of death, and had even selected his own epitaph, so that on the little wooden cross which stands at the foot of Bastion Hill—the hill he himself took and held—there is written: "Is it well with the child? It is well!"

The coign of vantage which I found on the side of the hill was not only to a great extent sheltered from the bullets, but afforded an extensive view of the general action, and for the rest of the day I remained with Lord Dundonald watching its development. But a modern action is very disappointing as a spectacle. There is no smoke except that of the bursting shells. The combatants are scattered, spread over a great expanse of ground, concealed wherever possible, clad in neutral tint.

All the pomp and magnificence of Omdurman, the solid lines of infantry, the mighty Dervish array, bright with flashing spears and waving flags, were excluded. Rows of tiny dots hurried forward a few yards and vanished into the brown of the earth. Bunches and clusters of brown things huddled among the rocks or in sheltered spots. The six batteries of artillery unlimbered, and the horses, hidden in some safe place, were scarcely visible.

Once I saw in miniature through glasses a great wave of infantry surge forward along a spur and disappear beyond a crest line. The patter of the Mauser rifles swelled into a continuous rumbling like a train of waggons passing over a pontoon bridge, and presently the wave recoiled; the minute figures that composed it squeezed themselves into cover among some rocks, a great many groups of men began carrying away black objects. A trickle of independent dots dispersed itself. Then we groaned. There had been a check. The distant drama continued. The huddling figures began to move again —lithe, active forms moving about rearranging things—officers, we knew, even at the distance. Then the whole wave started again full of impetus—started—went forward, and never came back. And at this we were all delighted, and praised the valour of our unequalled infantry, and wished we were near enough to give them a cheer.

So we watched until nightfall, when some companies of the Queen's, from General Hildyard's Brigade, arrived, and took over the charge of our hill from us, and we descended to get our horses, and perhaps some food, finding, by good luck, all we wanted, and lay down on the ground to sleep, quite contented with ourselves and the general progress of the army.

The action of the 21st had begun before I awoke, and a brisk fusillade was going on all along the line. This day the right attack stood still, or nearly so, and the activity was confined to the left, where General Hildyard, with five battalions and two batteries, skilfully felt and tested the enemy's positions and found them most unpleasantly strong. The main difficulty was that our guns could not come into action to smash the enemy in his trenches without coming under his rifle fire, because the edge of the plateau was only a thousand yards from the second and main Boer position, and unless the guns were on the edge of the plateau they could see very little and do less. The cavalry guarded the left flank passively, and I remember no particular incident except that our own artillery flung the fragments of two premature shells among us and wounded a soldier in the Devonshire Regiment. The following fact, however, is instructive. Captain Stewart's squadron of the South African Light Horse dismounted, held an advanced kopje all day long under a heavy fire, and never lost a man. Two hundred yards further back was another kopje held by two companies of regular infantry under equal fire. The infantry had more than twenty men hit.

On the 22nd the action languished and the generals consulted. The infantry had made themselves masters of all the edge of the plateau, and the regiments clustered in the steep re-entrants like flies on the side of a wall. The Boers endeavoured to reach them with shells, and a desultory musketry duel also proceeded.

During the afternoon I went with Captain Brooke to visit some of the battalions of General Hart's Brigade and see what sort of punishment they were receiving. As we rode up the watercourse which marks the bottom of the valley a shrapnel shell cleared the western crest line and exploded among one of the battalions. At first it seemed to have done no harm, but as we climbed higher and nearer we met a stretcher carried by six soldiers. On it lay a body with a handkerchief thrown across the face. The soldiers bearing the stretcher were all covered with blood.

We proceeded and soon reached the battalions. A company of the Dublin Fusiliers were among those captured in the armoured train, and I have the pleasure of knowing most of the officers of this regiment. So we visited them first—a dozen gentlemen—begrimed, unwashed, unshaven, sitting on the hillside behind a two-foot wall of rough stones and near a wooden box, which they called the "Officers' Mess". They were in capital spirits in spite of every abominable circumstance.

"What did you lose in the action?"

"Oh, about fifty. Poor Hensley was killed, you know; that was the worst of it."

Captain Hensley was one of the smallest and bravest men in the army, and the Dublin Fusiliers, who should be good judges, regarded him as their very best officer for all military affairs, whether attack, retreat, or reconnaissance. Each had lost a friend, but collectively as a regiment they had lost a powerful weapon.

"Very few of us left now," said the colonel, surveying his regiment with pride.

"How many?"

"About four hundred and fifty."

"Out of a thousand?"

"Well, out of about nine hundred."

This war has fallen heavily on some regiments. Scarcely any has suffered more severely, none has won greater distinction, than the Dublin Fusiliers—everywhere at the front—Dundee, Lombard's Kop, Colenso, Chieveley, Colenso again and even here at Spion Kop. Half the regiment, more than half the officers killed or wounded or prisoners.

But the survivors were as cheery as ever.

"Do these shells catch anyone?"

"Only two or three an hour. They don't come always: every half-hour we get half a dozen. That last one killed an officer in the next regiment. Rather bad luck, picking an officer out of all these men—only one killed today so far, a dozen wounded."

I inquired how much more time remained before the next consignment of shells was due. They said about ten minutes. I thought that would just suit me, and bade them good morning, for I have a horror of being killed when not on duty; but Captain Brooke was anxious to climb to the top and examine the Boer position, and since we had come so far it was perhaps worth while going on. So we did, and with great punctuality the shells arrived.

We were talking to the officers of another regiment when they began. Two came in quick succession over the eastern wall of the valley and then one over the western. All three burst—two on impact, one in the air. A fourth ripped along a stone shelter behind which skirmishers were firing. A fifth missed the valley altogether and screeched away into the plain clear of the hills. The officers and men were quite callous. They scarcely troubled to look up. The soldiers went on smoking or playing cards or sleeping as if nothing had happened. Personally I felt no inclination to any of these pursuits, and I thought to sit and wait indefinitely, for the caprice of one of these shrieking iron devils would be most trying to anyone. But apparently you can get accustomed to anything. The regiment where the officer had been killed a few minutes before was less cheerful and callous. The little group of officers crouching in the scanty shelter had seen one of their number plucked out of their midst and slain—uselessly as it seemed. They advised us to take cover, which we would gladly have done had there been any worth speaking of; for at this moment the Boers discharged their Vickers-Maxim gun—the "pom-pom"—and I have never heard such an extraordinary noise. Seven or eight bangs, a rattle, an amazing cluttering and whistling overhead, then the explosions of the little shells, which scarred the opposite hillside in a long row of puffs of brown dust and blue-white smoke, suggesting a lash from a knotted scourge.

"Look out!" we were told, "they always follow that with a shell." And so they did, but it passed overhead without harming anyone. Again the Vickers-Maxim flung its covey of projectiles. Again we crouched for the following shell; but this time it did not come—immediately. I had seen quite enough, however, so we bade our friends good luck—never good-bye on active service—and hurried, slowly, on account of appearances, from this unhealthy valley. As we reached our horses I saw another shell burst among the infantry. After that there was another interval. Further on we met a group of soldiers returning to their regiment. One lad of about nineteen was munching a biscuit. His right trouser leg was soaked with blood. I asked whether he was wounded. "No, sir; it's only blood from an officer's head," he answered, and went on—eating his biscuit. Such were the fortunes for four days of the two brigades forming Warren's left attack.

I have already written a general account of the final action of Spion Kop on January 24, and have little to add. As soon as the news spread through the camps that the British troops were occupying the top of the mountain I hurried to Gun Hill, where the batteries were arrayed, and watched the fight from a flank. The spectacle was inconsiderable but significant. It was like a shadow peep-show. Along the mighty profile of the hill a fringe of little black crotchets advanced. Then there were brown and red smudges of dust from shells striking the ground and white puffs from shrapnel bursting in the air—variations from the black and white. Presently a stretcher borne by five tiny figures jerks slowly forward, silhouetted on the sky-line; more shells; back goes the stretcher laden, a thicker horizontal line than before. Then—a rush of crotchets rearwards—one leading two mules, mules terrified, jibbing, hanging back—all in silhouette one moment, the next all smudged with dust cloud; God help the driver; shadows clear again; driver still dragging mules—no, only one mule now; other figures still running rearwards. Suddenly reinforcements arrive, hundreds of them; the whole sky-line bristles with crotchets moving swiftly along it, bending forward almost double, as if driving through a hailstorm. Thank heaven for that—only just in time too —and then more smudges on the shadow screen.

Sir Charles Warren was standing near me with his staff. One of his officers came up and told me that they had been disturbed at breakfast by a Boer shell, which had crashed through their waggon, killing a servant and a horse. Presently the General himself saw me. I inquired about the situation, and learned for the first time of General Woodgate's wound—death it was then reported—and that Thorneycroft had been appointed brigadier-general. "We have put what we think is the best fighting man in command regardless of seniority. We shall support him as he may request. We can do no more."

I will only relate one other incident—a miserable one. The day before the attack on Spion Kop I had chanced to ride across the pontoon bridge. I heard my name called, and saw the cheery face of a boy I had known at Harrow—a smart, clean-looking young gentleman—quite the rough material for Irregular Horse. He had just arrived and pushed his way to the front; hoped, so he said, "to get a job". This morning they told me that an unauthorised Press correspondent had been found among the killed on the summit. At least they thought at first it was a Press correspondent, for no one seemed to know him. A man had been found leaning forward on his rifle, dead. A broken pair of field glasses, shattered by the same shell that had killed their owner, bore the name "M'Corquodale". The name and the face flew together in my mind. It was the last joined subaltern of Thorneycroft's Mounted Infantry—joined in the evening, shot at dawn.

Poor gallant young Englishman! he had soon "got his job". The great sacrifice had been required of the Queen's latest recruit.

CHAPTER NINETEEN

A FRESH EFFORT AND
AN ARMY CHAPLAIN

Spearman's Hill: February 4, 1900

T HE FIRST gleams of daylight crept underneath the waggon, and the sleepers, closely packed for shelter from the rain showers, awoke. Those who live under the conditions of a civilised city, who lie abed till nine and ten of the clock in artificially darkened rooms, gain luxury at the expense of joy. But the soldier, who fares simply, sleeps soundly, and rises with the morning star, wakes in an elation of body and spirit without an effort and with scarcely a yawn. There is no more delicious moment in the day than this, when we light the fire and, while the kettle boils, watch the dark shadows of the hills take form, perspective, and finally colour, knowing that there is another whole day begun, bright with chance and interest, and free from all cares. All cares—for who can be worried about the little matters of humdrum life when he may be dead before the night? Such a one was with us yesterday—see, there is a spare mug for coffee in the mess—but now gone for ever. And so it may be with us tomorrow. What does it matter that this or that is misunderstood or perverted; that So-and-so is envious and spiteful; that heavy difficulties obstruct the larger schemes of life, clogging nimble aspiration with the mud of matters of fact? Here life itself, life at its best and healthiest, awaits the caprice of the bullet. Let us see the development of the day. All else may stand over, perhaps for ever. Existence is never so sweet as when it is at hazard. The bright butterfly flutters in the sunshine, the expression of the philosophy of Omar Khayyám, without the potations.

But we awoke on the morning of the 25th in most gloomy spirits. I had seen the evacuation of Spion Kop during the night, and I did not doubt that it would be followed by the abandonment of all efforts to turn the Boer left from the passages of the Tugela at and near Trichardt's Drift. Nor were these forebodings wrong. Before the sun was fairly risen orders arrived, "All baggage to move east of Venter's Spruit immediately. Troops to be ready to turn out at thirty minutes' notice." General retreat, that was their meaning. Buller was withdrawing his train as a preliminary to disengaging, if he could, the fighting brigades, and retiring across the river. Buller! So it was no longer Warren! The Commander-in-Chief had arrived, in the hour of misfortune, to take all responsibility for what had befallen the army, to extricate it, if possible, from its position of peril, to encourage the soldiers, now a second time defeated without being beaten, to bear the disappointment. Everyone knows how all this, that looked so difficult, was successfully accomplished.

The army was irritated by the feeling that it had made sacrifices for nothing. It was puzzled and disappointed by failure which it did not admit nor understand. The enemy were flushed with success. The opposing lines in many places were scarcely a thousand yards apart. As the infantry retired the enemy would have commanding ground from which to assail them at every point. Behind flowed the Tugela, a deep, rapid, only occasionally fordable river, eighty-five yards broad, with precipitous banks. We all prepared ourselves for a bloody and even disastrous rearguard action. But now, I repeat, when things had come to this pass, Buller took personal command. He arrived on the field calm, cheerful, inscrutable as ever, rode hither and thither with a weary staff and a huge notebook, gripped the whole business in his strong hands, and so shook it into shape that we crossed the river in safety, comfort, and good order, with most remarkable mechanical precision, and without the loss of a single man or a pound of stores.

The fighting troops stood fast for two days, while the train of waggons streamed back over the bridges and parked in huge black squares on the southern bank. Then, on the night of the 26th, the retreat began. It was pitch dark, and a driving rain veiled all lights. The ground was broken. The enemy near. It is scarcely possible to imagine a more difficult operation. But it was performed with amazing ease. Buller himself—not Buller by proxy or Buller at the end of a heliograph—Buller himself managed it. He was the man who gave orders, the man whom the soldiers looked to. He had

already transported his train. At dusk he passed the Royals over
the ford. By ten o'clock all his cavalry and guns were across the
pontoon bridges. At ten he began disengaging his infantry, and by
daylight the army stood in order on the southern bank. While the
sappers began to take the pontoon bridges to pieces the Boers, who
must have been astonished by the unusual rapidity of the movement, fired their first shell at the crossing. We were over the river
none too soon.

A successful retreat is a poor thing for a relieving army to boast
of when their gallant friends are hard pressed and worn out. But
this withdrawal showed that this force possesses both a leader and
machinery of organisation, and it is this, and this alone, that has
preserved our confidence. We believe that Buller gauged the
capacity of one subordinate at Colenso, of another at Spion Kop,
and that now he will do things himself, as he was meant to do. I
know not why he has waited so long. Probably some pedantic
principle of military etiquette: "Commander-in-Chief should occupy
a central position; turning movements should be directed by
subordinates." But the army believes that this is all over now, and
that for the future Buller will trust no one but himself in great
matters; and it is because they believe this that the soldiers are
looking forward with confidence and eagerness to the third and last
attempt—for the sands at Ladysmith have run down very low—to
shatter the Boer lines.

We have waited a week in the camp behind Spearman's Hill. The
General has addressed the troops himself. He has promised that we
shall be in Ladysmith soon. To replace the sixteen hundred killed
and wounded in the late actions, drafts of twenty-four hundred men
have arrived. A mountain battery, A Battery R.H.A., and two
great fortress guns have strengthened the artillery. Two squadrons
of the 14th Hussars have been added to the cavalry, so that we are
actually today numerically stronger by more than a thousand men
than when we fought at Spion Kop, while the Boers are at least
five hundred weaker—attrition *versus* recuperation. Everyone has
been well fed, reinforced and inspirited, and all are prepared for a
supreme effort, in which we shall either reach Ladysmith or be flung
back truly beaten with a loss of six or seven thousand men.

I will not try to foreshadow the line of attack, though certain
movements appear to indicate where it will be directed. But it is
generally believed that we fight tomorrow at dawn, and as I write

this letter seventy guns are drawing up in line on the hills to open the preparatory bombardment.

It is a solemn Sunday, and the camp, with its white tents looking snug and peaceful in the sunlight, holds its breath that the beating of its heart may not be heard. On such a day as this the services of religion would appeal with passionate force to thousands. I attended a church parade this morning. What a chance this was for a man of great soul who feared God! On every side were drawn up deep masses of soldiery, rank behind rank—perhaps, in all, five thousand. In the hollow square stood the General, the man on whom everything depended. All around were men who within the week had been face to face with Death, and were going to face him again in a few hours. Life seemed very precarious, in spite of the sunlit landscape. What was it all for? What was the good of human effort? How should it befall a man who died in a quarrel he did not understand? All the anxious questionings of weak spirits. It was one of those occasions when a fine preacher might have given comfort and strength where both were sorely needed, and have printed on many minds a permanent impression. The bridegroom Opportunity had come. But the Church had her lamp untrimmed. A chaplain with a raucous voice discoursed on the details of "The siege and surrender of Jericho." The soldiers froze into apathy, and after a while the formal perfunctory service reached its welcome conclusion.

As I marched home an officer said to me: "Why is it, when the Church spends so much on missionary work among heathens, she does not take the trouble to send good men to preach in time of war? The medical profession is represented by some of its greatest exponents. Why are men's wounded souls left to the care of a village practitioner?" Nor could I answer; but I remembered the venerable figure and noble character of Father Brindle in the River War, and wondered whether Rome was again seizing the opportunity which Canterbury disdained—the opportunity of telling the glad tidings to soldiers about to die.

CHAPTER TWENTY

THE COMBAT OF VAAL KRANTZ

General Buller's Headquarters: February 9, 1900

DURING THE ten days that passed peacefully after the British retreat from the positions beyond Trichardt's Drift, Sir Redvers Buller's force was strengthened by the arrival of a battery of Horse Artillery, two powerful siege guns, two squadrons of the 14th Hussars, and drafts for the Infantry battalions, amounting to 2,400 men. Thus not only was the loss of 1,600 men in the five days' fighting round Spion Kop made good, but the army was actually a thousand stronger than before its repulse. Good and plentiful rations of meat and vegetables were given to the troops, and their spirits were restored by the General's public declaration that he had discovered the key to the enemy's position, and the promise that within a week from the beginning of the impending operation Ladysmith should be relieved. The account of the straits to which the gallant garrison was now reduced by famine, disease, and war increased the earnest desire of officers and men to engage the enemy and, even at the greatest price, to break his lines. In spite of the various inexplicable features which the actions of Colenso and Spion Kop presented, the confidence of the army in Sir Redvers Buller was still firm, and the knowledge that he himself would personally direct the operations, instead of leaving their conduct to a divisional commander, gave general satisfaction and relief.

On the afternoon of February 4 the superior officers were made acquainted with the outlines of the plan of action to be followed. The reader will, perhaps, remember the description in a former letter of the Boer position before Potgieter's and Trichardt's Drift as a horizontal note of interrogation, of which Spion Kop formed the centre angle —⌒. The fighting of the previous week had been directed towards the straight line, and on the angle. The new operation was aimed at the curve. The general scheme was to seize the hills which formed the left of the enemy's position and roll him up from left to right. It was known that the Boers were massed mainly in their central camp behind Spion Kop, and that, as no demonstration was intended against the position in front of Trichardt's Drift, their whole force would be occupying the curve and guarding its right flank. The details of the plan were well conceived.

The battle would begin by a demonstration against the Brakfontein position, which the Boers had fortified by four tiers of trenches, with bombproof casemates, barbed-wire entanglements, and a line of redoubts, so that it was obviously too strong to be carried frontally. This demonstration would be made by Wynne's Brigade (formerly Woodgate's), supported by six batteries of Artillery, the Howitzer Battery, and the two 4·7 naval guns. These troops crossed the river by the pontoon bridge at Potgieter's on the 3rd and 4th, relieving Lyttelton's Brigade which had been in occupation of the advanced position on the low kopjes.

A new pontoon bridge was thrown at the angle of the river a mile below Potgieter's, the purpose of which seemed to be to enable the frontal attack to be fully supported. While the artillery preparation of the advance against Brakfontein and Wynne's advance was going on, Clery's Division (consisting of Hart's Brigade and Hildyard's) and Lyttelton's Brigade were to mass near the new pontoon bridge (No. 2), as if about to support the frontal movement. When the bombardment had been in progress for two hours these three brigades were to move, not towards the Brakfontein position, but eastwards to Munger's Drift, throw a pontoon bridge covered first by one battery of Field Artillery withdrawn from the demonstration, secondly by the fire of guns which had been dragged to the summit of Swartkop, and which formed a powerful battery of fourteen pieces, viz., six 12-pounder long range naval guns, two 15-pounder guns of the 64th Field Battery, six 9-pounder mountain guns, and lastly by the two 50-pounder siege guns. As soon as the bridge was complete Lyttelton's Brigade would cross, and, ignoring the fire from the Boer left, extended along the Doornkloof heights, attack the Vaal Krantz ridge, which formed the left of the horseshoe curve around the debouches of Potgieter's. This attack was to be covered on its right by the guns already specified on Swartkop and the 64th Field Battery, and prepared by the six artillery batteries employed in the demonstration, which were to withdraw one by one at intervals of ten minutes, cross No. 2 pontoon bridge, and take up new positions opposite to the Vaal Krantz ridge.

If and when Vaal Krantz was captured all six batteries were to move across No. 3 bridge and take up positions on the hill, whence they could prepare and support the further advance of Clery's Division, which, having crossed, was to move past Vaal Krantz, pivot to the left on it, and attack the Brakfontein position from its left flank. The 1st Cavalry Brigade under Burn-Murdoch (Royals, 13th and 14th Hussars, and A Battery R.H.A.) would also cross and run the gauntlet of Doornkloof and break out on to the plateau beyond Clery's Division. The 2nd Cavalry Brigade (South African Light Horse, Composite Regiment, Thorneycroft's, and Bethune's Mounted Infantry, and the Colt Battery) were to guard the right and rear of the attacking troops from any attack coming from Doornkloof. Wynne was to co-operate as opportunity offered. Talbot Coke was to remain in reserve. Such was the plan, and it seemed to all who heard it good and clear. It gave scope to the whole force, and seemed to offer all the conditions for a decisive trial of strength between the two armies.

On Sunday afternoon the infantry brigades began to move to their respective positions, and at daylight on the 5th the Cavalry Division broke its camp behind Spearman's. At nine minutes past seven the bombardment of the Brakfontein position began, and by half-past seven all the artillery except the Swartkop guns were firing in a leisurely fashion at the Boer redoubts and entrenchments. At the same time Wynne's Brigade moved forward in dispersed formation towards the enemy, and the cavalry began to defile across the front and to mass near the three infantry brigades collected near No. 2 pontoon bridge. For some time the Boers made no reply, but at about ten o'clock their Vickers-Maxim opened on the batteries firing from the Potgieter's plain, and the fire gradually increased as other guns, some of great range, joined in, until the artillery was sharply engaged in an unsatisfactory duel—fifty guns exposed in the open against six or seven guns concealed and impossible to find. The Boer shells struck all along the advanced batteries, bursting between the guns, throwing up huge fountains of dust and smoke, and covering the gunners at times completely from view. Shrapnel shells were also flung from both flanks and ripped the dusty plain with their scattering bullets. But the artillery stood to their work like men, and though they apparently produced no impression on the Boer guns, did not suffer as severely as might have been expected, losing no more than fifteen officers and men altogether. At intervals of ten minutes the batteries withdrew in beautiful order and ceremony and defiled across the second pontoon bridge. Meanwhile Wynne's Brigade had advanced to within twelve hundred yards of the Brakfontein position and retired, drawing the enemy's heavy fire; the three brigades under Clery had moved to the right near Munger's Drift; the cavalry were massed in the hollows at the foot of Swartkop; and the engineers had constructed the third pontoon bridge, performing their business with excellent method and despatch under a sharp fire from Boer skirmishers and a Maxim.

The six batteries and the howitzers now took up positions opposite Vaal Krantz, and seventy guns began to shell this ridge in regular preparation and to reply to three Boer guns which had now opened from Doornkloof and our extreme right. A loud and crashing cannonade developed. At midday the Durham Light Infantry of Lyttelton's Brigade crossed the third pontoon bridge and advanced briskly along the opposite bank on the Vaal Krantz ridge. They were supported by the 3rd King's Royal Rifles, and behind these the other two battalions of the Brigade strengthened the attack. The troops moved across the open in fine style, paying no attention to the enemy's guns on Doornkloof, which burst their shrapnel at seven thousand yards (shrapnel at seven thousand yards!) with remarkable accuracy. In an hour the leading companies had reached the foot of the ridge, and the active riflemen could be seen clambering swiftly up. As the advance continued one of the Boer Vickers-Maxim guns which was posted in rear of Vaal Krantz found it wise to retire and galloped off unscathed through a tremendous fire from our artillery: a most wonderful escape.

The Durham Light Infantry carried the hill at the point of the bayonet, losing seven officers and sixty or seventy men, and capturing five Boer prisoners, besides ten horses and some wounded. Most of the enemy, however, had retired before the attack, unable to endure the appalling concentration of artillery which had prepared it. Among those who remained to fight to the last were five or six armed Kaffirs, one of whom shot an officer of the Durhams. To these no quarter was given. Their employment by the Dutch in this war shows that while they furiously complain of Khama's defence of his territory against their raiding parties on the ground that white men must be killed by white men, they have themselves no such scruples. There is no possible doubt about the facts set forth above, and the incident should be carefully noted by the public.

By nightfall the whole of General Lyttelton's Brigade had occupied Vaal Krantz, and were entrenching themselves. The losses in the day's fighting were not severe, and though no detailed statement has yet been compiled, I do not think they exceeded one hundred and fifty. Part of Sir Redvers Buller's plan had been successfully executed. The fact that the action had not been opened until 7 a.m. and had been conducted in a most leisurely manner left the programme only half completed. It remained to pass Clery's Division across the third bridge, to plant the batteries in their new position on Vaal Krantz, to set free the 1st Cavalry Brigade in the plain beyond, and to begin the main attack on Brafokntein. It remained and it still remains.

During the night of the 5th Lyttelton's Brigade made shelters and traverses of stones, and secured the possession of the hill; but it was now reported that field guns could not occupy the ridge because, first, it was too steep and rocky—though this condition does not apparently prevent the Boers dragging their heaviest guns to the tops of the highest hills—and, secondly, because the enemy's long-range rifle fire was too heavy. The hill, therefore, which had been successfully captured, proved of no value whatever. Beyond it was a second position which was of great strength, and which if it was ever to be taken must be taken by the infantry without artillery support. This was considered impossible or at any rate too costly and too dangerous to attempt.

During the next day the Boers continued to bombard the captured ridge, and also maintained a harassing long-range musketry fire. A great gun firing a hundred-pound 6-in. shell came into action from the top of Doornkloof, throwing its huge projectiles on Vaal Krantz and about the bivouacs generally; one of them exploded within a few yards of Sir Redvers Buller. Two Vickers-Maxims from either side of the Boer position fired at brief intervals, and other guns burst shrapnel effectively from very long range on the solitary brigade which held Vaal Krantz. To this bombardment the Field Artillery and the naval guns—seventy-two pieces in all, both big and little—made a noisy but futile response. The infantry of

Lyttelton's Brigade, however, endured patiently throughout the day, in spite of the galling cross-fire and severe losses. At about four in the afternoon the Boers made a sudden attack on the hill, creeping to within short range, and then opened a quick fire. The Vickers-Maxim guns supported this vigorously. The pickets at the western end of the hill were driven back with loss, and for a few minutes it appeared that the hill would be retaken. But General Lyttelton ordered half a battalion of the Durham Light Infantry, supported by the King's Royal Rifles, to clear the hill, and these fine troops, led by Colonel Fitzgerald, rose up from their shelters and, giving three rousing cheers—the thin, distant sound of which came back to the anxious, watching army—swept the Boers back at the point of the bayonet. Colonel Fitzgerald was, however, severely wounded.

While these things were passing a new pontoon bridge was being constructed at a bend of the Tugela immediately under the Vaal Krantz ridge, and by five o'clock this was finished. Nothing else was done during the day, but at nightfall Lyttelton's Brigade was relieved by Hildyard's, which marched across the new pontoon (No. 4) under a desultory shell fire from an extreme range. Lyttelton's Brigade returned under cover of darkness to a bivouac underneath the Swartkop guns. Their losses in the two days' operations had been 225 officers and men.

General Hildyard, with whom was Prince Christian Victor, spent the night in improving the defences of the hill and in building new traverses and head cover. At midnight the Boers made a fresh effort to regain the position, and the sudden roar of musketry awakened the sleeping army. The attack, however, was easily repulsed. At daybreak the shelling began again, only now the Boers had brought up several new guns, and the bombardment was much heavier. Owing, however, to the excellent cover which had been arranged the casualties during the day did not exceed forty. The cavalry and transport, who were sheltering in the hollows underneath Swartkop, were also shelled, and it was thought desirable to move them back to a safer position.

In the evening Sir Redvers Buller, who throughout these two days had been sitting under a tree in a somewhat exposed position, and who had bivouacked with the troops, consulted with his generals. Many plans were suggested, but there was a general consensus of opinion that it was impossible to advance further

along this line. At eleven at night Hildyard's Brigade was withdrawn from Vaal Krantz, evacuating the position in good order,
and carrying with them their wounded, whom till dark it had been
impossible to collect. Orders were issued for the general retirement
of the army to Springfield and Spearman's, and by ten o'clock on the
8th this operation was in full progress.

With feelings of bitter disappointment at not having been permitted to fight the matter out, the infantry, only two brigades of
which had been sharply engaged, marched by various routes to
their former camping grounds, and only their perfect discipline
enabled them to control their grief and anger. The cavalry and
artillery followed in due course, and thus the fourth attempt to
relieve Ladysmith, which had been begun with such hopes and
enthusiasm, fizzled out into failure. It must not, however, be
imagined that the enemy conducted his defence without pro-
portionate loss.

What I have written is a plain record of facts, and I am so deeply
conscious of their significance that I shall attempt some explanation.

The Boer covering army numbers at least 12,000 men, with
perhaps a dozen excellent guns. They hold along the line of the
Tugela what is practically a continuous position of vast strength.
Their superior mobility, and the fact that they occupy the chord,
while we must move along the arc of the circle, enables them to
forefront us with nearly their whole force wherever an attack is
aimed, however it may be disguised. Therefore there is no way of
avoiding a direct assault. Now, according to Continental experience
the attacking force should outnumber the defence by three to one.
Therefore Sir Redvers Buller should have 36,000 men. Instead of
this he has only 22,000. Moreover, behind the first row of positions,
which practically runs along the edge of an unbroken line of steep
flat-topped hills, there is a second row standing back from the edge
at no great distance. Any attack on this second row the artillery
cannot support, because from the plain below they are too far off
to find the Boer guns, and from the edge they are too close to the
enemy's riflemen. The ground is too broken, in the opinion of many
generals, for night operations. Therefore the attacking infantry of
insufficient strength must face unaided the fire of cool, entrenched
riflemen, armed with magazine weapons and using smokeless
powder.

Nevertheless, so excellent is the quality of the infantry that if the whole force were launched in attack it is not impossible that they would carry everything before them. But after this first victory it will be necessary to push on and attack the Boers investing Ladysmith. The line of communications must be kept open behind the relieving army or it will be itself in the most terrible danger. Already the Boers' position beyond Potgieter's laps around us on three sides. What if we should break through, only to have the door shut behind us? At least two brigades would have to be left to hold the line of communications. The rest, weakened by several fierce and bloody engagements, would not be strong enough to effect the relief.

The idea of setting all on the turn of the battle is very grateful and pleasant to the mind of the army, which only asks for a decisive trial of strength, but Sir Redvers Buller has to remember that his army, besides being the Ladysmith Relief Column, is also the only force which can be spared to protect South Natal. Is he, therefore, justified in running the greater risks? On the other hand, how can we let Ladysmith and all its gallant defenders fall into the hands of the enemy? It is agonising to contemplate such a conclusion to all the efforts and sacrifices that have been made. I believe and trust we shall try again. As long as there is fighting one does not reflect on this horrible situation. I have tried to explain some of the difficulties which confront the General. I am not now concerned with the attempts that have been made to overcome them. A great deal is incomprehensible, but it may be safely said that if Sir Redvers Buller cannot relieve Ladysmith with his present force we do not know of any other officer in the British Service who would be likely to succeed.

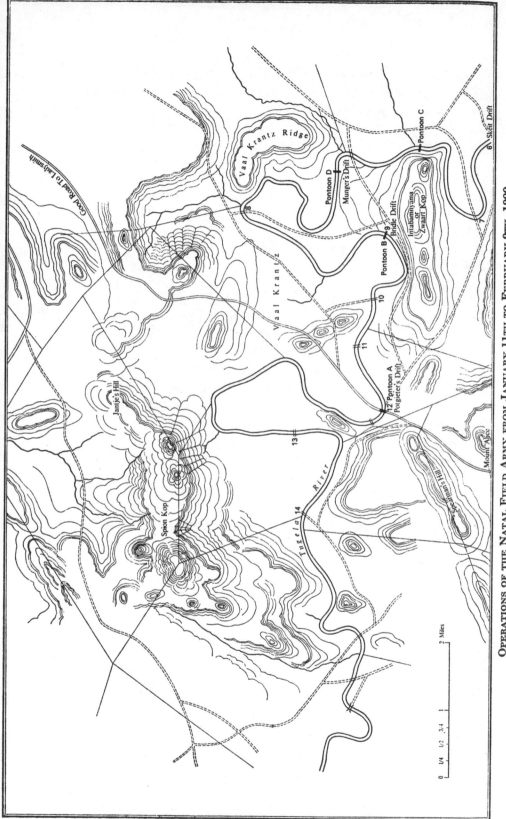

Operations of the Natal Field Army from January 11th to February 9th, 1900

CHAPTER TWENTY-ONE

HUSSAR HILL

General Buller's Headquarters: February 15, 1900

WHEN SIR REDVERS BULLER broke off the combat of Vaal Krantz, and for the third time ordered his unbeaten troops to retreat, it was clearly understood that another attempt to penetrate the Boer lines was to be made without delay.

The army has moved from Spearman's and Springfield to Chieveley, General Lyttelton, who had succeeded Sir Francis Clery, in command of the 2nd Division and 4th Brigade, marching via Pretorius's Farm on the 9th and 10th, Sir Charles Warren covering the withdrawal of the supplies and transport and following on the 10th and 11th. The regular Cavalry Brigade, under Burn-Murdoch, was left with two battalions to hold the bridge at Spring-field, beyond which place the Boers, who had crossed the Tugela in some strength at Potgieter's, were reported to be showing consider-able activity. The left flank of the marching infantry columns was covered by Dundonald's Brigade of Light Horse, and the operations were performed without interruption from the enemy.

On the 12th orders were issued to reconnoitre Hussar Hill, a grassy and wooded eminence four miles to the east of Chieveley, and the direction of the next attack was revealed. The reader of the accounts of this war is probably familiar with the Colenso position and understands its great strength. The proper left of this position rests on the rocky, scrub-covered hill of Hlangwani, which rises on the British side of the Tugela. If this hill can be captured and artillery placed on it, and if it can be secured from cross-fire, then all the trenches of Fort Wylie and along the river bank will be com-pletely enfiladed, and the Colenso position will become untenable, so that Hlangwani is the key of the Colenso position. In order, however, to guard this key carefully the Boers have extended

their left—as at Trichardt's Drift they extended their right—
until it occupies a very lofty range of mountains four or five miles
to the east of Hlangwani, and along all this front works have been
constructed on a judicious system of defence. The long delays have
given ample time to the enemy to complete his fortifications, and
the trenches here are more like forts than field works, being provided with overhead cover against shells and carefully made loopholes. In front of them stretches a bare slope, on either side rise
formidable hills from which long-range guns can make a continual
cross-fire. Behind this position, again, are others of great strength.

But there are also encouraging considerations. We are to make—
at least in spite of disappointments we hope and believe we are to
make—a supreme effort to relieve Ladysmith. At the same time
we are the army for the defence of South Natal. If we had put the
matter to the test at Potgieter's and failed, our line of communications might have been cut behind us, and the whole army, weakened
by the inevitable heavy losses of attacking these great positions,
might have been captured or dispersed. Here we have the railway
behind us. We are not as we were at Potgieter's "formed to a flank".
We derive an accession of strength from the fact that the troops
holding Railhead are now available for the general action.

Besides these inducements this road is the shortest way. Buller,
therefore, has elected to lose his men and risk defeat—without
which risk no victory can be won—on this line. Whether he will
succeed or not were foolish to prophesy, but it is the common belief
that this line offers as good a chance as any other and that at last
the army will be given a fair run, and permitted to begin a general
engagement and fight it out to the end. If Buller goes in and wins he
will have accomplished a wonderful feat of arms, and will gain the
lasting honour and gratitude of his country. If he is beaten he will
deserve the respect and sympathy of all true soldiers as a man who
has tried to the best of his ability to perform a task for which his
resources were inadequate. I hasten to return to the chronicle.
Hussar Hill—so-called because a small post of the 13th Hussars was
surprised on it six weeks ago and lost two men killed—is the high
ground opposite Hlangwani and the mountainous ridges called
Monte Cristo and Cingolo, on which the artillery must be posted to
prepare the attack. Hence the reconnaissance of the 12th.

At eight o'clock—we never get up early in this war—Lord
Dundonald started from the cavalry camp near Stuart's Farm with

the South African Light Horse, the Composite Regiment, Thorney-croft's Mounted Infantry, the Colt Battery, one battalion of infantry, the Royal Welsh Fusiliers, and a battery of Field Artillery. The Irregular Horse were familiar with the ground, and we soon occupied Hussar Hill, driving back a small Boer patrol which was watching it, and wounding two of the enemy. A strong picket line was thrown out all round the captured ground and a dropping musketry fire began at long range with the Boers, who lay hidden in the surrounding dongas. At noon Sir Redvers Buller arrived, and made a prolonged reconnaissance of the ground with his telescope. At one o'clock we were ordered to withdraw, and the difficult task of extricating the advanced pickets from close contact with the enemy was performed under a sharp fire, fortunately without the loss of a man.

After you leave Hussar Hill on the way back to Chieveley camp it is necessary to cross a wide dip of ground. We had withdrawn several miles in careful rearguard fashion, the guns and the bat-talion had gone back, and the last two squadrons were walking across this dip towards the ridge on the homeward side. Perhaps we had not curled in our tail quite quick enough, or perhaps the enemy has grown more enterprising of late, in any case just as we were reaching the ridge a single shot was fired from Hussar Hill, and then without more ado a loud crackle of musketry burst forth. The distance was nearly two thousand yards, but the squadrons in close formation were a good target. Everybody walked for about twenty yards, and then without the necessity of an order broke into a brisk canter, opening the ranks to a dispersed formation at the same time. It was very dry weather, and the bullets striking between the horsemen raised large spurts of dust, so that it seemed that many men must surely be hit. Moreover, the fire had swelled to a menac-ing roar. I chanced to be riding with Colonel Byng in rear, and looking round saw that we had good luck. For though bullets fell among the troopers quite thickly enough, the ground two hundred yards further back was all alive with jumping dust. The Boers were shooting short.

We reached the ridge and cover in a minute, and it was very pretty to see these irregular soldiers stop their horses and dismount with their carbines at once without any hesitation. Along the ridge Captain Hill's Colt Battery was drawn up in line, and as soon as the front was clear the four little pink guns began spluttering furiously.

The whole of the South African Light Horse dismounted and, lining the ridge, opened fire with their rifles. Thorneycroft's Mounted Infantry came into line on our left flank, and brought two tripod Maxims into action with them. Lord Dundonald sent back word to the battery to halt and fire over our heads, and Major Gough's Regiment and the Royal Welsh Fusiliers, who had almost reached cover, turned round of their own accord and hurried eagerly in the direction of the firing, which had become very loud on both sides.

There now ensued a strange little skirmish, which would have been a bloody rifle duel but for the great distance which separated the combatants and for the cleverness with which friends and foes concealed and sheltered themselves. Not less than four hundred men on either side were firing as fast as modern rifles will allow. Between us stretched the smooth green dip of ground. Beyond there rose the sharper outlines of Hussar Hill, two or three sheds, and a few trees. That was where the Boers were. But they were quite invisible to the naked eye, and no smoke betrayed their positions. With a telescope they could be seen—a long row of heads above the grass. We were equally hidden. Still their bullets—a proportion of their bullets— found us, and I earnestly trust that some of ours found them. Indeed there was a very hot fire, in spite of the range. Yet no one was hit. Ah, yes, there was one, a tall trooper turned sharply on his side, and two of his comrades carried him quickly back behind a little house, shot through the thigh. A little further along the firing line another was being helped to the rear. The Colt Battery drew the cream of the fire, and Mr. Garrett, one of the experts sent out by the firm, was shot through the ankle, but he continued to work his gun. Captain Hill walked up and down his battery exposing himself with great delight, and showing that he was a very worthy representative of an Irish constituency.

I happened to pass along the line on some duty or other when I noticed my younger brother, whose keen desire to take some part in the public quarrel had led me, in spite of misgivings, to procure him a lieutenancy, lying on the ground, with his troop. As I approached I saw him start in the quick, peculiar manner of a stricken man. I asked him at once whether he was hurt, and he said something—he thought it must be a bullet—had hit him on the gaiter and numbed his leg. He was quite sure it had not gone in, but when we had carried him away we found—as I expected—that he was shot through the leg. The wound was not serious, but the doctors declared he would be a month in hospital. It was his baptism of fire, and I have since wondered at the strange caprice which strikes down one man in his first skirmish and protects another time after time. But I suppose all pitchers will get broken in the end. Outwardly I sympathised with my brother in his misfortune, which he mourned bitterly, since it prevented him taking part in the impending battle, but secretly I confess myself well content that this young gentleman should be honourably out of harm's way for a month.

It was neither our business nor our pleasure to remain and continue this long-range duel with the Boers. Our work for the day was over, and all were anxious to get home to luncheon. Accordingly, as soon as the battery had come into action to cover our withdrawal we commenced withdrawing squadron by squadron and finally broke off the engagement, for the Boers were not inclined to follow further. At about three o'clock our loss in this interesting affair was one officer, Lieutenant John Churchill, and seven men of the South African Light Horse wounded and a few horses. Thorneycroft's Mounted Infantry also had two casualties, and there were two more in the Colt detachments. The Boers were throughout invisible, but two days later when the ground was revisited we found one dead burgher—so that at any rate they lost more heavily than we. The Colt guns worked very well, and the effect of the fire of a whole battery of these weapons was a marked diminution in the enemy's musketry. They were mounted on the light carriages patented by Lord Dundonald, and the advantage of these in enabling the guns to be run back by hand, so as to avoid exposing the horses, was very obvious.

I shall leave the great operation which, as I write, has already begun, to another letter, but since gaiety has its value in these troublous times let the reader pay attention to the story of General Hart and the third-class shot. Major-General Hart, who commands the Irish Brigade, is a man of intrepid personal courage—indeed, to his complete contempt for danger the heavy losses among his battalions, and particularly in the Dublin Fusiliers, must be to some extent attributed. After Colenso there were bitter things said on this account. But the reckless courage of the General was so remarkable in subsequent actions that, being brave men themselves, they forgave him everything for the sake of his daring.

During the first day at Spion Kop General Hart discovered a soldier sitting safely behind a rock and a long way behind the firing line.

"Good afternoon, my man," he said in his most nervous, apologetic voice; "what are you doing here?"

"Sir," replied the soldier, "an officer told me to stop here, sir."

"Oh! Why?"

"I'm a third-class shot, sir."

"Dear me," said the General after some reflection, "that's an awful pity, because you see you'll have to get quite close to the Boers to do any good. Come along with me and I'll find you a nice place," and a mournful procession trailed off towards the most advanced skirmishers.*

* The map at the end of Chapter Twenty-five illustrates this and succeeding chapters.

CHAPTER TWENTY-TWO

THE ENGAGEMENT OF MONTE CRISTO

Cingolo Nek: February 19, 1900

NOT SINCE I wrote the tale of my escape from Pretoria have I taken up my pen with such feelings of satisfaction and contentment as I do tonight. The period of doubt and hesitation is over. We have grasped the nettle firmly, and as shrewdly as firmly, and have taken no hurt. It remains only to pluck it. For heaven's sake no over-confidence or premature elation; but there is really good hope that Sir Redvers Buller has solved the Riddle of the Tugela—at last. At last! I expect there will be some who will inquire—"Why not 'at first'?" All I can answer is this: There is certainly no more capable soldier of high rank in all the army in Natal than Sir Redvers Buller. For three months he has been trying his best to pierce the Boer lines and the barrier of mountain and river which separates Ladysmith from food and friends; trying with an army—magnificent in everything but numbers and not inconsiderable even in that respect—trying at a heavy price of blood in Africa, of anxiety at home. Now, for the first time, it seems that he may succeed. Knowing the General and the difficulties, I am inclined to ask, not whether he might have succeeded sooner, but rather whether anyone else would have succeeded at all. But to the chronicle!

Anyone who stands on Gun Hill near Chieveley can see the whole of the Boer position about Colenso sweeping before him in a wide curve. The mountain wall looks perfectly unbroken. The river lies everywhere buried in its gorge, and is quite invisible. To the observer there is only a smooth green bay of land sloping gently downward, and embraced by the rocky, scrub-covered hills. Along this crescent of high ground runs—or rather, by God's grace, ran—the Boer line, strong in its natural features, and entrenched from end to end.

When the map is consulted, however, it is seen that the Tugela does not flow uniformly along the foot of the hills as might be expected, but that after passing Colenso village, which is about the centre of the position, it plunges into the mountainous country, and bends sharply northward; so that, though the left of the Boer line might appear as strong as the right, there was this difference, that the Boer right had the river on its front, the Boer left had it in its rear.

The attack of the 15th of December had been directed against the Boer right, because after reconnaissance Sir Redvers Buller deemed that, in spite of the river advantage, the right was actually the weaker of the two flanks. The attack of the 15th was repulsed with heavy loss. It might, therefore, seem that little promise of success attended an attack on the Boer left. The situation, however, was entirely altered by the great reinforcements in heavy artillery which had reached the army, and a position which formerly appeared unassailable now looked less formidable.

Let us now consider the Boer left by itself. It ran in a chain of sangars, trenches, and rifle pits, from Colenso village, through the scrub by the river, over the rugged hill of Hlangwani, along a smooth grass ridge we called "The Green Hill", and was extended to guard against a turning movement on to the lofty wooded ridges of Monte Cristo and Cingolo and the neck joining these two features. Sir Redvers Buller's determination was to turn this widely extended position on its extreme left, and to endeavour to crumple it from left to right. As it were, a gigantic right arm was to reach out to the eastward, its shoulder at Gun Hill, its elbow on Hussar Hill, its hand on Cingolo, its fingers, the Irregular Cavalry Brigade, actually behind Cingolo.

On February 12th a reconnaissance in force of Hussar Hill was made by Lord Dundonald. On the 14th the army moved east from Chieveley to occupy this ground. General Hart with one brigade held Gun Hill and Railhead. The First Cavalry Brigade watched the left flank at Springfield, but with these exceptions the whole force marched for Hussar Hill. The Irregular Cavalry covered the front, and the South African Light Horse, thrown out far in advance, secured the position by half-past eight, just in time to forestall a force of Boers which had been despatched, so soon as the general movement of the British was evident, to resist the capture of the hill. A short sharp skirmish followed, in which we lost a few horses and men, and claim to have killed six Boers, and which was terminated after half an hour by the arrival of the leading infantry battalion—the Royal Welsh Fusiliers. During the day the occupation was completed, and the brigades of Generals Wynne, Coke, and Barton, then joining Warren's Division with the artillery, entrenched themselves strongly and bivouacked on the hill. Meanwhile Lyttelton's Division marched from its camp in the Blue Krantz Valley, east of Chieveley, along the valley to a position short of the eastern spurs of Hussar Hill. These spurs are more thickly wooded and broken than the rest of the hill, and about four o'clock in the afternoon some hundred Boers established themselves among the rocks and opened a sharp fire. They were, however, expelled from their position by the artillery and by the fire of the advanced battalions of Lyttelton's Division operating from the Blue Krantz Valley.

During the 15th and 16th a desultory artillery duel proceeded on both sides with slight loss to us. The water question presented some difficulty, as the Blue Krantz River was several miles from Hussar Hill and the hill itself was waterless. A system of iron tanks mounted on ox waggons was arranged, and a sufficient though small supply maintained. The heavy artillery was also brought into action and strongly entrenched. The formidable nature of the enemy's position and the evident care with which he had fortified it may well have added to the delay by giving cause for the gravest reflection.

On the afternoon of the 16th Sir Redvers Buller resolved to plunge, and orders were issues for a general advance at dawn. Colonel Sandbach, under whose supervision the Intelligence Department has attained a new and a refreshing standard of efficiency, made comprehensive and, as was afterwards proved, accurate reports of the enemy's strength and spirit, and strongly recommended the attack on the left flank. Two hours before dawn the army was on the move. Hart's Brigade, the 6-inch and other great guns at Chieveley, guarded Railhead. Hlangwani Hill, and the long line of entrenchments rimming the Green Hill, were masked and fronted by the display of the field and siege batteries, whose strength in guns was as follows:

	Guns
Four 5-inch siege guns	4
Six naval twelve-pounder long-range guns . .	6
Two 4·7 naval guns	2

One battery howitzers 6
One battery corps artillery (R.F.A.) . . . 6
Two brigade divisions R.F.A. 36
One mountain battery 6
                                                ——
                                                66

and which were also able to prepare and support the attack on
Cingolo Nek and Monte Cristo Ridge. Cingolo Ridge itself, however,
was almost beyond their reach. Lyttelton's Division with Wynne's
Fusilier Brigade was to stretch out to the eastward and, by a wide
turning movement pivoting on the guns and Barton's Brigade,
attack the Cingolo Ridge. Dundonald's Cavalry Brigade was to
make a far wider detour and climb up the end of the ridge, thus
making absolutely certain of finding the enemy's left flank at
last.

By daybreak all were moving, and as the Irregular Cavalry
forded the Blue Krantz stream on their enveloping march we heard
the boom of the first gun. The usual leisurely bombardment had
begun, and I counted only thirty shells in the first ten minutes,
which was not very hard work for the gunners considering that
nearly seventy guns were in action. But the artillery never hurry
themselves, and indeed I do not remember to have heard in this war
a really good cannonade, such as we had at Omdurman, except for
a few minutes at Vaal Krantz.

The Cavalry Brigade marched ten miles eastward through most
broken and difficult country, all rock, high grass, and dense
thickets, which made it imperative to move in single file, and the
sound of the general action grew fainter and fainter. Gradually,
however, we began to turn again towards it. The slope of the
ground rose against us. The scrub became more dense. To ride
further was impossible. We dismounted and led our horses, who
scrambled and blundered painfully among the trees and boulders.
So scattered was our formation that I did not care to imagine what
would have happened had the enemy put in an appearance. But
our safety lay in these same natural difficulties. The Boers doubtless
reflected, "No one will ever try to go through such ground as that"
—besides which war cannot be made without running risks. The
soldier must chance his life.

The general must not be afraid to brave disaster. But how
tolerant the arm-chair critics should be of men who try daring

coups and fail! You must put your head into the lion's mouth if the performance is to be a success. And then I remembered the attacks on the brave and capable General Gatacre after Stormberg, and wondered what would be said of us if we were caught "dismounted and scattered in a wood".

At length we reached the foot of the hill and halted to reconnoitre the slopes as far as was possible. After half an hour, since nothing could be seen, the advance was resumed up the side of a precipice and through a jungle so thick that we had to cut our road. It was eleven o'clock before we reached the summit of the ridge and emerged on to a more or less open plateau, diversified with patches of wood and heaps of great boulders. Two squadrons had re-formed on the top and had deployed to cover the others. The troopers of the remaining seven squadrons were working their way up about four to the minute. It would take at least two hours before the command was complete: and meanwhile! Suddenly there was a rifle shot. Then another, then a regular splutter of musketry. Bullets began to whizz overhead. The Boers had discovered us.

Now came the crisis. There might be a hundred Boers on the hill, in which case all was well. On the other hand there might be a thousand, in which case——! and retreat down the precipice was, of course, quite out of the question. Luckily there were only about a hundred, and after a skirmish, in which one of the Natal Carabineers was unhappily killed, they fell back and we completed our deployment on the top of the hill.

The squadron of Imperial Light Horse and the Natal Carabineers now advanced slowly along the ridge, clearing it of the enemy, slaying and retrieving one field cornet and two burghers, and capturing ten horses. Half-way along the Queen's, the right battalion of Hildyard's attack, which, having made a small detour, had now rushed the top, came into line and supported the dismounted men. The rest of the cavalry descended into the plain on the other side of the ridge, outflanking and even threatening the retreat of its defenders, so that in the end the Boers, who were very weak in numbers, were hunted off the ridge altogether, and Cingolo was ours. Cingolo and Monte Cristo are joined together by a neck of ground from which both heights rise steeply. On either side of Monte Cristo and Cingolo long spurs run at right angles to the main hill.

By the operations of the 17th the Boer line had been twisted off Cingolo, and turned back along the subsidiary spurs of Monte

Cristo, and the British forces had placed themselves diagonally across the left of the Boer position thus:

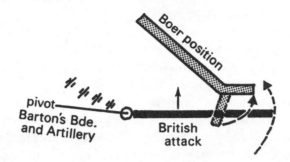

The advantages of this situation were to be enjoyed on the morrow.

Finding our further advance barred by the turned-back position the enemy had adopted, and which we could only attack frontally, the cavalry threw out a line of outposts which were soon engaged in a long-range rifle duel, and prepared to bivouac for the night. Cingolo Ridge was meanwhile strongly occupied by the infantry, whose line ran from its highest peak slantwise across the valley of the Gomba Stream to Hussar Hill, where it found its pivot in Barton's Brigade and the artillery. The Boers, who were much disconcerted by the change in the situation, showed themselves ostentatiously on the turned-back ridge of their position as if to make themselves appear in great strength, and derisively hoisted white flags on their guns. The Colonial and American troops (for in the South African Light Horse we have a great many Americans, and even one who served under Sheridan) made some exceedingly good practice at the extreme ranges. So the afternoon passed, and the night came in comparative quiet.

At dawn the artillery began on both sides, and we were ourselves awakened by Creusot shells bursting in our bivouac. The enemy's fire was chiefly directed on the company of the Queen's which was holding the top of Cingolo, and only the good cover which the great rocks afforded prevented serious losses. As it was several men were injured. But we knew that we held the best cards; and so did the Boers. At eight o'clock Hildyard's Brigade advanced against the peak of the Monte Cristo ridge which lay beyond the neck. The

West Yorks led, the Queen's and East Surrey supported. The musketry swelled into a constant crackle like the noise of a good fire roaring up the chimney, but, in spite of more than a hundred casualties, the advance never checked for an instant, and by half-past ten o'clock the bayonets of the attacking infantry began to glitter among the trees of the summit. The Boers, who were lining a hastily-dug trench half-way along the ridge, threatened in front with an overwhelming force and assailed in flank by the long-range fire of the cavalry, began to fall back. By eleven o'clock the fight on the part of the enemy resolved itself into a rearguard action.

Under the pressure of the advancing and enveloping army this degenerated very rapidly. When the Dutchman makes up his mind to go he throws all dignity to the winds, and I have never seen an enemy leave the field in such a hurry as did these valiant Boers who found their flank turned, and remembered for the first time that there was a deep river behind them. Shortly after twelve o'clock the summit of the ridge of Monte Cristo was in our hands. The spurs which started at right angles from it were, of course, now enfiladed and commanded. The Boers evacuated both in great haste. The eastern spur was what I have called the "turned-back" position. The cavalry under Dundonald galloped forward and seized it as soon as the enemy were seen in motion, and from this advantageous standpoint we fired heavily into their line of retreat. They scarcely waited to fire back, and we had only two men and a few horses wounded.

The spur on the Colenso or western side was none other than the Green Hill itself, and judging rightly that its frowning entrenchments were now empty of defenders Sir Redvers Buller ordered a general advance frontally against it. Two miles of trenches were taken with scarcely any loss. The enemy fled in disorder across the river. A few prisoners, some wounded, several cartloads of ammunition and stores, five camps with all kinds of Boer material, and last of all, and compared to which all else was insignificant, the dominating Monte Cristo ridge stretching northward to within an easy spring of Bulwana Hill, were the prize of victory. The soldiers, delighted at the change of fortune, slept in the Boer tents—or would have done had these not been disgustingly foul and stinking.

From the captured ridge we could look right down into Ladysmith, and at the first opportunity I climbed up to see it for myself. Only eight miles away stood the poor little persecuted town, with whose fate there is wrapt up the honour of the Empire, and for whose sake so many hundred good soldiers have given life or limb— a twenty-acre patch of tin houses and blue gum trees, but famous to the uttermost ends of the earth.

The victory of Monte Cristo has revolutionised the situation in Natal. It has laid open a practicable road to Ladysmith. Great difficulties and heavy opposition have yet to be encountered and overcome, but the word "impossible" must no longer be—should, perhaps, never have been used. The success was won at the cost of less than two hundred men killed and wounded, and surely no army more than the Army of Natal deserves a cheaply bought triumph.

CHAPTER TWENTY-THREE

THE PASSAGE OF THE TUGELA

Hospital ship Maine: March 4, 1900

SINCE I finished my last letter, on February the 21st, I have found no time to sit down to write until now, because we have passed through a period of ceaseless struggle and emotion, and I have been seeing so many things that I could not pause to record anything. It has been as if a painter prepared himself to paint some portrait, but was so fascinated by the beauty of his model that he could not turn his eyes from her face to the canvas; only that the spectacles which have held me have not always been beautiful. Now the great event is over, the long and bloody conflict around Ladysmith has been gloriously decided, and I take a few days' leisure on the good ship *Maine*, where everyone is busy getting well, to think about it all and set down some things on paper.

First and foremost there was the Monte Cristo ridge, that we had captured on the 18th, which gave us the Green Hill, Hlangwani Hill, and, when we chose to take it, the whole of the Hlangwani plateau. The Monte Cristo ridge is the centrepiece to the whole of this battle. As soon as we had won it I telegraphed to the *Morning Post* that now at last success was a distinct possibility. With this important feature in our possession it was certain that we held the key to Ladysmith, and though we might fumble a little with the lock, sooner or later, barring the accidents of war, we should open the door.

As Monte Cristo had given Sir Redvers Buller Hlangwani, so Hlangwani rendered the whole of the western section (the eastern section was already in our hands) of the Colenso position untenable by the enemy, and they, finding themselves commanded and enfiladed, forthwith evacuated it. On the 19th General Buller made good his position on Green Hill, occupied Hlangwani with Barton's Brigade, built or improved his roads and communications from

Hussar Hill across the Gomba Valley, and brought up his heavy guns. The Boers, who were mostly on the other side of the river, resisted stubbornly with artillery, with their Vickers-Maxim guns and the fire of skirmishers, so that we suffered some slight loss, but could not be said to have wasted the day. On the 20th the south side of the Tugela was entirely cleared of the enemy, who retired across the bridge they had built, and, moreover, a heavy battery was established on the spurs of Hlangwani to drive them out of Colenso. In the afternoon Hart's Brigade advanced from Chieveley, and his leading battalion, under Major Stuart-Wortley, occupied Colenso village without any resistance.

The question now arose—Where should the river be crossed? Sir Redvers Buller possessed the whole of the Hlangwani plateau, which, as the reader may perceive by looking at the map opposite p. 202, fills up the re-entrant angle made opposite Pieters by the Tugela after it leaves Colenso. From this Hlangwani plateau he could either cross the river where it ran north and south or where it ran east and west. Sir Redvers Buller determined to cross the former reach beyond Colenso village. To do this he had to let go his hold on the Monte Cristo ridge and resign all the advantages which its possession had given him, and had besides to descend into the low ground, where his army must be cramped between the high hills on its left and the river on its right.

There was, of course, something to be said for the other plan, which was advocated strongly by Sir Charles Warren. The crossing, it was urged, was absolutely safe, being commanded on all sides by our guns, and the enemy could make no opposition except with artillery. Moreover, the army would get on its line of railway and could "advance along the railroad". This last was a purely imaginary advantage, to be sure, because the railway had no rolling-stock, and was disconnected from the rest of the line by the destruction of the Tugela bridge. But what weighed with the Commander-in-Chief much more than the representations of his lieutenant was the accumulating evidence that the enemy were in full retreat. The Intelligence reports all pointed to this situation. Boers had ridden off in all directions. Waggons were seen trekking along every road to the north and west. The camps between us and Ladysmith began to break up. Everyone said, "This is the result of Lord Roberts's advance: the Boers find themselves now too weak to hold us off. They have raised the siege."

But this conclusion proved false in the sense that it was premature. Undoubtedly the Boers had been reduced in strength by about 5,000 men, who had been sent into the Free State for its defence. Until the Monte Cristo ridge was lost to them they deemed themselves quite strong enough to maintain the siege. When, however, this position was captured, the situation was revolutionised. They saw that we had found their flank, and thoroughly appreciated the significance and value of the long high wedge of ground, which cut right across the left of their positions, and seemed to stretch away almost to Bulwana Mountain. They knew perfectly well that if we advanced by our right along the line of this ridge, which they called "the Bush Kop", supporting ourselves by it as a man might rest his hand on a balustrade, we could turn their Pieters position just as we had already turned their entrenchments at Colenso.

Therein lay the true reason of their retirement, and in attributing it either to Lord Roberts's operations or to the beating we had given them on the 18th we made a mistake, which was not repaired until much blood had been shed.

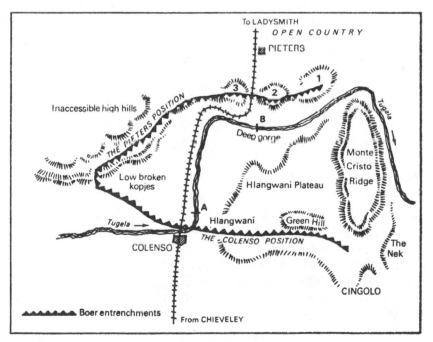

THE COLENSO POSITION

I draw a rough diagram to assist the reader who will take the trouble to study the map. It is only drawn from memory, and its object is to show how completely the Monte Cristo ridge turned both the line of entrenchments through Colenso and that before Pieters. But no diagrams, however exaggerated, would convince so well as would the actual ground.

In the belief, however, that the enemy were in retreat the General resolved to cross the river at A by a pontoon bridge and follow the railway line. On the 21st, therefore, he moved his army westward across the Hlangwani plateau, threw his bridge, and during the afternoon passed his two leading infantry brigades over it. As soon as the Boers perceived that he had chosen this line of advance their hopes revived. "Oh," we may imagine them saying, "if you propose to go that way, things are not so bad after all." So they returned to the number of about nine thousand burghers, and manned the trenches of the Pieters position, with the result that Wynne's Lancashire Brigade, which was the first to cross, soon found itself engaged in a sharp action among the low kopjes, and suffered a hundred and fifty casualties, including its General, before dark. Musketry fire was continuous throughout the night. The 1st Cavalry Brigade had been brought in from Springfield on the 20th, and on the morning of the 22nd both the regular and irregular cavalry were to have crossed the river. We accordingly marched from our camp at the neck between Cingolo and Monte Cristo and met the 1st Cavalry Brigade, which had come from Chieveley, at the pontoon bridge. A brisk action was crackling away beyond the river, and it looked as if the ground scarcely admitted of our intervention. Indeed, we had hardly arrived when a staff officer came up, and brought us orders to camp near Hlangwani Hill, as we should not cross that day.

Presently I talked to the Staff Officer, who chanced to be a friend of mine, and chanced, besides, to be a man with a capacity for sustained thought, an eye for country, and some imagination. He said: "I don't like the situation; there are more of them than we expected. We have come down off our high ground. We have taken all the big guns off the big hills. We are getting ourselves cramped up among these kopjes in the valley of the Tugela. It will be like being in the Coliseum and shot at by every row of seats."

Sir Redvers Buller, however, still believing he had only a rearguard in front of him, was determined to persevere. It is, perhaps, his strongest characteristic obstinately to pursue his plan in spite of all advice, in spite, too, of his horror of bloodshed, until himself convinced that it is impracticable. The moment he is satisfied that this is the case no considerations of sentiment or effect prevent him from coming back and starting afresh. No modern General ever cared less for what the world might say. However unpalatable and humiliating a retreat might be, he would make one so soon as he was persuaded that adverse chances lay before him. "To get there in the end," was his guiding principle. Nor would the General consent to imperil the ultimate success by asking his soldiers to make a supreme effort to redress a false tactical move. It was a principle which led us to much blood and bitter disappointment, but in the end to victory.

Not yet convinced, General Buller, pressing forward, moved the whole of his infantry, with the exception of Barton's Brigade, and nearly all the artillery, heavy and field, across the river, and in the afternoon sent two battalions from Norcott's Brigade and the Lancashire Brigade—to the vacant command of which Colonel Kitchener had been appointed—forward against the low kopjes. By nightfall a good deal of this low, rolling ground was in our possession, though at some cost in men and officers.

At dusk the Boers made a fierce and furious counter-attack. I was watching the operations from Illangwani Hill through a powerful telescope. As the light died my companions climbed down the rocks to the cavalry camp and left me alone staring at the bright flashes of the guns which stabbed the obscurity on all sides. Suddently, above the booming of the cannon, there arose the harsh rattling roar of a tremendous fusillade. Without a single intermission this continued for several hours. The Howitzer Battery, in spite of the darkness, evidently considered the situation demanded its efforts, and fired salvoes of lyddite shells, which, bursting in the direction of the Boer positions, lit up the whole scene with flaring explosions. I went anxiously to bed that night, wondering what was passing beyond the river, and the last thing I can remember was the musketry drumming away with unabated vigour.

There was still a steady splutter at dawn on the 23rd, and before the light was full grown the guns joined in the din. We eagerly sought for news of what had passed. Apparently the result was not unfavourable to the army. "Push for Ladysmith today, horse, foot, and artillery" was the order, "Both cavalry brigades to cross the river at once." Details were scarce and doubtful. Indeed, I cannot yet give any accurate description of the fighting on the night of the 22nd, for it was of a confused and desperate nature, and many men must tell their tale before any general account can be written.

What happened, briefly described, was that the Boers attacked heavily at nightfall with rifle fire all along the line, and, in their eagerness to dislodge the troops, came to close quarters on several occasions at various points. At least two bayonet charges are recorded. Sixteen men of Stuart-Wortley's Composite Battalion of Reservists of the Rifle Brigade and King's Royal Rifles showed blood on their bayonets in the morning. About three hundred officers and men were killed or wounded. The Boers also suffered heavily, leaving dead on the ground, among others a grandson of President Kruger. Prisoners were made and lost, taken and rescued by both sides; but the daylight showed that victory rested with the British, for the infantry were revealed still tenaciously holding all their positions.

At eight o'clock the cavalry crossed the river under shell fire directed on the bridge, and were massed at Fort Wylie, near Colenso. I rode along the railway line to watch the action from one of the low kopjes. A capricious shell fire annoyed the whole army as it sheltered behind the rocky hills, and an unceasing stream of stretchers from the front bore true witness to the serious nature of the conflict, for this was the third and bloodiest day of the seven days' fighting called the battle of Pieters.

I found Sir Redvers Buller and his staff in a somewhat exposed position, whence an excellent view could be obtained. The General displayed his customary composure, asked me how my brother's wound was getting on, and told me that he had just ordered Hart's Brigade, supported by two battalions from Lyttelton's Division, to assault the hill marked "3" on my diagram, and hereinafter called Inniskilling Hill. "I have told Hart to follow the railway. I think he can get round to their left flank under cover of the river bank," he said, "but we must be prepared for a counter-attack on our left as soon as they see what I'm up to;" and he then made certain dispositions of his cavalry, which brought the South African Light Horse close up to the wooded kopje on which we stood. I must now describe the main Pieters position, one hill of which was about to be attacked.

It ran, as the diagram shows, from the high and, so far as we were concerned, inaccessible hills on the west to the angle of the river, and then along the three hills marked 3, 2, and 1. I use this inverted sequence of numbers because we were now attacking them in the wrong order.

Sir Redvers Buller's plan was as follows: On the 22nd he had taken the low kopjes, and his powerful artillery gave him complete command of the river gorge. Behind the kopjes, which acted as a kind of shield, and along the river gorge he proposed to advance his infantry until the angle of the river was passed and there was room to stretch out his, till then, cramped right arm and reach round the enemy's left on Inniskilling Hill, and so crumple it.

This perilous and difficult task was entrusted to the Irish Brigade, which comprised the Dublin Fusiliers, the Inniskilling Fusiliers, the Connaught Rangers, and the Imperial Light Infantry, who had temporarily replaced the Border Regiment—in all about three thousand men, supported by two thousand more. Their commander, General Hart, was one of the bravest officers in the army, and it was generally felt that such a leader and such troops could carry the business through if success lay within the scope of human efforts.

The account of the ensuing operation is so tragic and full of mournful interest that I must leave it to another letter.

CHAPTER TWENTY-FOUR

THE BATTLE OF PIETERS:
THE THIRD DAY

Hospital ship *Maine*: March 5, 1900

AT HALF PAST twelve on the 23rd General Hart ordered his brigade to advance. The battalions, which were sheltering among stone walls and other hastily constructed cover on the reverse slope of the kopje immediately in front of that on which we stood, rose up one by one and formed in rank. They then moved off in single file along the railroad, the Inniskilling Fusiliers leading, the Connaught Rangers, Dublin Fusiliers, and the Imperial Light Infantry following in succession. At the same time the Durham Light Infantry and the 2nd Rifle Brigade began to march to take the place of the assaulting brigade on the advanced kopje.

Wishing to have a nearer view of the attack, I descended the wooded hill, cantered along the railway—down which the procession of laden stretchers, now hardly interrupted for three days, was still moving—and, dismounting, climbed the rocky sides of the advanced kopje. On the top, in a little half-circle of stones, I found General Lyttelton, who received me kindly, and together we watched the development of the operation. Nearly a mile of the railway line was visible, and along it the stream of Infantry flowed steadily. The telescope showed the soldiers walking quite slowly, with their rifles at the slope. Thus far, at least, they were not under fire. The low kopjes which were held by the other brigades shielded the movement. A mile away the river and railway turned sharply to the right; the river plunged into a steep gorge, and the railway was lost in a cutting. There was certainly plenty of cover; but just before the cutting was reached the iron bridge across the Onderbrook Spruit had to be crossed, and this was evidently commanded by the enemy's riflemen. Beyond the railway and the moving trickle of men the brown dark face of Inniskilling Hill, crowned with sangars and entrenchments, rose up gloomy and, as yet, silent.

The patter of musketry along the left of the army, which reached back from the advanced kopjes to Colenso village, the boom of the heavy guns across the river, and the ceaseless thudding of the field artillery making a leisurely preparation, were an almost unnoticed accompaniment to the scene. Before us the infantry were moving steadily nearer to the hill and the open ground by the railway bridge, and we listened amid the comparatively peaceful din for the impending fire storm.

The head of the column reached the exposed ground, and the soldiers began to walk across it. Then at once above the average fusillade and cannonade rose the extraordinary rattling roll of Mauser musketry in great volume. If the reader wishes to know exactly what this is like he must drum the fingers of both his hands on a wooden table, one after the other as quickly and as hard as he can. I turned my telescope on the Dutch defences. They were no longer deserted. All along the rim of the trenches, clear cut and jet black, against the sky stood a crowded line of slouch-hatted men, visible as far as their shoulders, and wielding what looked like thin sticks.

Far below by the red ironwork of the railway bridge—2,000 yards, at least, from the trenches—the surface of the ground was blurred and dusty. Across the bridge the infantry were still moving, but no longer slowly—they were running for their lives. Man after man emerged from the sheltered railroad, which ran like a covered way across the enemy's front, into the open and the driving hail of bullets, ran the gauntlet and dropped down the embankment on the further side of the bridge into safety again. The range was great, but a good many soldiers were hit and lay scattered about the iron-work of the bridge. "Pom-pom-pom", "pom-pom-pom", and so on, twenty times went the Boer automatic gun, and the flights of little shells spotted the bridge with puffs of white smoke. But the advancing infantry never hesitated for a moment, and continued to scamper across the dangerous ground, paying their toll accordingly. More than sixty men were shot in this short space. Yet this was not the attack. This was only the preliminary movement across the enemy's front.

The enemy's shells, which occasionally burst on the advanced kopje, and a whistle of stray bullets from the left, advised us to change our position, and we moved a little further down the slope towards the river. Here the bridge was no longer visible. I looked towards the hill-top, whence the roar of musketry was ceaselessly proceeding. The artillery had seen the slouch hats, too, and for-getting their usual apathy in the joy of a live target, concentrated a most hellish and terrible fire on the trenches.

Meanwhile the afternoon had been passing. The infantry had filed steadily across the front, and the two leading battalions had already accumulated on the eastern spurs of Inniskilling Hill. At four o'clock General Hart ordered the attack, and the troops forth-with began to climb the slopes. The broken ground delayed their progress, and it was nearly sunset by the time they had reached the furthest position which could be gained under cover. The Boer entrenchments were about four hundred yards away. The *arête* by which the Inniskillings had advanced was bare, and swept by a dreadful frontal fire from the works on the summit and a still more terrible flanking fire from the other hills. It was so narrow that, though only four companies were arranged in the firing line, there was scarcely room for two to deploy. There was not, however, the slightest hesitation, and as we watched with straining eyes we could see the leading companies rise up together and run swiftly forward on the enemy's works with inspiring dash and enthusiasm.

But if the attack was superb, the defence was magnificent; nor could the devoted heroism of the Irish soldiers surpass the stout endurance of the Dutch. The artillery redoubled their efforts. The whole summit of the hill was alive with shell. Shrapnel flashed into being above the crests, and the ground sprang up into dust whipped by the showers of bullets and splinters. Again and again whole sections of the entrenchments vanished in an awful uprush of black earth and smoke, smothering the fierce blaze of the lyddite shells from the howitzers and heavy artillery. The cannonade grew to a tremendous thundering hum. Not less than sixty guns were firing continuously on the Boer trenches. But the musketry was never subdued for an instant. Amid the smoke and the dust the slouch hats could still be seen. The Dutch, firm and undaunted, stood to their parapets and plied their rifles with deadly effect.

The terrible power of the Mauser rifle was displayed. As the charging companies met the storm of bullets they were swept away. Officers and men fell by scores on the narrow ridge. Though assailed in front and flank by the hideous whispering Death, the survivors hurried obstinately onward, until their own artillery were forced to cease firing, and it seemed that, in spite of bullets, flesh and blood would prevail. But at the last supreme moment the weakness of the attack was shown. The Inniskillings had almost reached their goal. They were too few to effect their purpose; and when the Boers saw that the attack had withered they shot all the straighter, and several of the boldest leapt out from their trenches and, running forward to meet the soldiers, discharged their magazines at the closest range. It was a frantic scene of blood and fury.

Thus confronted, the Irish perished rather than retire. A few men indeed ran back down the slope to the nearest cover, and there savagely turned to bay, but the greater part of the front line was shot down. Other companies, some from the Connaught Rangers, some headed by the brave Colonel Sitwell, from the Dublin Fusiliers, advanced to renew—it was already too late to support—the attack, and as the light faded another fierce and bloody assault was delivered and was repulsed. Yet the Irish soldiers would not leave the hill, and, persuaded at length that they could not advance further, they lay down on the ground they had won, and began to build walls and shelters, from behind which they opened a revengeful fire on the exulting Boers. In the two attacks both colonels, three majors, twenty officers, and six hundred men had fallen out of an engaged force of scarcely one thousand two hundred. Then darkness pulled down the curtain, and the tragedy came to an end for the day.

All through the night of the 23rd a heavy rifle fire was maintained by both sides. Stray bullets whistled about the bivouacs, and the South African Light Horse, who had selected a most sheltered spot to sleep in, had a trooper hit. There were a certain number of casualties along the whole front. As soon as it was daylight I rode out with Captain Brooke to learn what had happened in the night. We knew that the hill had not been carried before dusk, but hoped, since the combatants were so close together, that in the darkness the bayonet would have settled the matter.

We had just reached the hollow behind the advanced kopje from which I had watched the attack on the previous evening, when suddenly a shrapnel shell burst in the air above our heads with a sharp, startling bang. The hollow and slope of the hill were crowded with Infantry battalions lying down in quarter column. The bullets and splinters of the shell smote the ground on all sides. We were both mounted and in the centre of the cone of dispersion. I was immediately conscious that nothing had happened to me, though the dust around my horse was flicked up, and I concluded that everyone had enjoyed equally good fortune. Indeed, I turned to Brooke, and was about to elaborate my theory that shrapnel is comparatively harmless, when I saw some stir and turmoil and no less than eight men were picked up killed or wounded by this explosion. I have only once before seen in war such a successful shell, and on that occasion I was studying the effect from the other side.

My respect for modern artillery was mightily increased by this example of its power. Two more shells followed in quick succession. The first struck down four men, and broke in two the leg of an infantry officer's charger, so that the poor beast galloped about in a circle, preventing his rider from dismounting for some time; the second shore along the howitzer battery, killing one soldier and wounding an officer, five soldiers, and three horses. All this occurred in a space of about two minutes, and the three shells between them accounted for nineteen men and four horses. Then the gun, which was firing "on spec", and could not see the effect of its fire, turned its attention elsewhere; but the thought forced itself on me, "Fancy if there had been a battery". The crowded infantry waiting in sup- port would certainly have been driven out of the re-entrant with frightful slaughter. Yet in a European war there would have been not one, but three or four batteries. I do not see how troops can be handled in masses under such conditions, even when in support and on reverse slopes. Future warfare must depend on the individual.

We climbed on to the top of the kopje, which was sprinkled with staff officers and others—all much interested in the exhibition of shell fire, which they discussed as a purely scientific question. Inniskilling Hill was still crowned with the enemy, though they no longer showed above their trenches. Its slopes were scored with numerous brown lines, the stone walls built by the attacking brigade during the night, and behind these the telescope showed the infantry clustering thickly. The Boers on their part had made some new trenches in advance of those on the crest of the hill, so that the opposing firing lines were scarcely three hundred yards apart, which meant that everyone in them must lie still or run grave risks. Thus they remained all day, firing at each other continually, while on the bare ground between them the dead and wounded lay thickly scattered, the dead mixed with the living, the wounded untended, without dressings, food, or water, and harassed by the fire from both sides and from our artillery. It was a very painful thing to watch these poor fellows moving about feebly and trying to wriggle themselves into some position of safety, and it reminded me of the wounded Dervishes after Omdurman—only these were our own countrymen.

It seems that a misunderstanding, of the rights and wrongs of which the reader shall be himself a judge, arose with the enemy. When day broke, the Boers, who were much nearer to the wounded than were our troops, came out of their trenches with a Red Cross flag, and the firing thereupon ceased locally. Our people ought then to have been ready to come forward with another Red Cross flag, and an informal truce might easily have been arranged for an hour or two. Unfortunately, however, there was some delay on our part. The Boers therefore picked up their own wounded, of whom there were a few, gave some of our men a little water, and took away their rifles. All this was quite correct; but the Boers then proceeded to strip and despoil the dead and wounded, taking off their boots and turning out their pockets, and this so infuriated the watching soldiers behind the wall that they forthwith fired on the Boers, Red Cross flag notwithstanding. This, of course, was the signal for fighting to recommence fiercely, and during the day neither side would hear of parley. The Boers behaved cruelly in various instances, and several wounded men who tried to crawl away were deliberately destroyed by being shot at close quarters with many bullets.

During the 24th there was heavy firing on both sides, but no movement of infantry on either. The army suffered some loss from the Boer artillery, particularly the automatic guns, which were well served, and which enfiladed many of our positions on the slopes of the low kopjes. In this way Colonel Thorold, of the Royal Welsh Fusiliers, and other officers, met their deaths. The casualties were principally in Hildyard's English and Kitchener's Lancashire Brigades. Hart's six battalions found good cover in the gorge of the Tugela.

Sir Redvers Buller now saw that his plan of filing his army round the angle of the river and across the enemy's front would, in any case, be very costly, and was perhaps impossible. He, therefore, determined to get back to the Hlangwani plateau, and try the extreme left of the enemy's position. He had the strategic advantage of being on interior lines, and was consequently able to move his troops with great ease from one flank to the other. His new plan was to pass the brigades of his left and centre across the pontoon bridge from the left to the right, so that Hart, who was formerly the extreme right, would now become almost the extreme left, and, having thus extended his right arm, to cross the river where it flowed east and west, and make a still wider swoop on the enemy's flank.

The first thing to do was to move the heavy guns, and this, with certain redistributions of the cavalry, occupied the whole day. A long-range four-gun naval battery was established on the western slopes of the Monte Cristo ridge. Another similar battery was placed on the spurs of Hlangwani. The 4·7 naval guns and the 5 in. fortress battery were brought into line in the centre of the Hlangwani plateau. All this was good. The big guns were getting back on to the big hills. The firing, which continued all day, swelled into a roar towards night as the Boers made vigorous attempts to drive Hart's Brigade from its lodgments. They were, however, foiled in their endeavour to squeeze in between the troops and the river.

The battalions, who were attacked frontally, lay down with fixed bayonets and prayed that the Boers might be encouraged by their silence to make an assault. The latter, however, were fully aware of the eagerness of the soldiers for personal collision, and kept their distance. The firing on both sides was unaimed, and very little harm was done. No one, however, had much sleep. The condition of the wounded, still lying sore and thirsty on the bare hillside, was now so shocking that Sir Redvers Buller was forced, much against his inclination, at dawn on the 25th, to send in a flag of truce to the Boer commander and ask for an armistice. This the Boers formally refused, but agreed that if we would not fire on their positions during the day they would not prevent our bearer companies from removing the wounded and burying the dead.

The arrangement worked well; the enemy were polite to our medical officers, and by noon all the wounded had been brought down and the dead buried. The neglect and exposure for forty-eight hours had much aggravated the case of the former, and the bodies of the dead, swollen, blackened, and torn by the terrible wounds of the expansive bullets, now so generally used by the enemy, were ugly things to see. The fact that no regular armistice was agreed on was an advantage, as we were not thereby debarred from making military movements. The Boers improved their entrenchments, and Sir Redvers Buller employed the day in withdrawing his train across the river. This movement, seeming to foreshadow another retreat, sorely disquieted the troops, who were only reassured by the promise of a general onslaught from the other flank at no distant time.

The strange quiet of this Sunday, the first day since the 14th of the month unbroken by musketry and cannonade, was terminated at nine o'clock at night.

The Boers had seen the waggons passing back over the bridge, and were anxious to find out whether or not the infantry were following, and if the low kopjes were evacuated. They therefore opened a tremendous magazine fire at long range on the brigades holding the line from Colenso village to the angle of the river. The fusillade was returned, and for ten minutes the musketry was louder than at any other time in this campaign. Very few casualties occurred, however, and after a while the Boers, having learned that the positions were still occupied, ceased firing, and the British soon imitated them, so that, except for the ceaseless "sniping", silence was restored.

At dawn on the 26th the artillery reopened on both sides, and during the day a constant bombardment was maintained, in which we, having more guns, fired the greater number of shells, and the Dutch, having larger targets, hit a greater number of men. The losses were not, however, severe, except in view of the fact that they had to be endured by the infantry idly and passively.

Considerable movements of troops were made. Colenso and the kopjes about Fort Wylie were converted into a bridge-head, garrisoned by Talbot Coke's Brigade. A new line of communications was opened around the foot of Hlangwani. A pontoon bridge (B) was arranged ready to be thrown below the falls of the river, not far from the still intact Boer bridge. Hildyard's English Brigade stood fast on the advanced low kopjes forming the extreme left of the line. Hart's command held its position about the slopes of Inniskilling Hill and in the gorge of the river. Barton's Fusilier Brigade, Kitchener's Lancashire Brigade, and the two remaining battalions of Norcott's (formerly Lyttelton's) Brigade crossed the old bridge to the Hlangwani plateau.

All was now ready for the final attack on the left of the Pieters position, and in spite of the high quality of the Infantry it was generally recognised throughout the army that the fate of Lady-smith must depend on the success of the next day's operations. The spirit of the army was still undaunted, but they had suffered much from losses, exposure, and disappointment.

Since January 11, a period of more than six weeks, the troops had been continuously fighting and bivouacking. The peaceful intervals of a few days had merely been in order to replenish stores and ammunition. During this time the only reinforcements to reach the army had been a few drafts, a cavalry regiment, a horse battery, and some heavy guns. Exclusive of the 1,100 casualties suffered at Colenso in December, the force, rarely more than 20,000 men, had had over 3,500 killed and wounded, had never had a single gleam of success, and had hardly seen the enemy who hit them so hard.

Colenso, Spion Kop, Vaal Krantz, and the third day at Pieters were not inspiring memories, and though everyone was cheered by the good news of the entanglement of Cronje's army on the western side, yet it was felt that the attempt to be made on the morrow would be the last effort the Natal Field Army would be asked or allowed to make. And oppressed by these reflections we went anxiously to rest on the eve of Majuba Day.

CHAPTER TWENTY-FIVE

UPON MAJUBA DAY

Commandant's Office, Durban: March 6, 1900

DAY BROKE behind a cloudy sky, and the bang of an early gun reminded us that a great business was on hand. The bivouac of the Irregular Cavalry, which, since they had re-crossed the river, had been set at the neck between Monte Cristo and Cingolo, was soon astir. We arose—all had slept in their boots and had no need to dress—drank some coffee and rejoiced that the day promised to be cool. It would help the infantry, and on the infantry all depended.

At half-past six Dundonald's Brigade marched towards the northern end of the Hlangwani plateau, where we were to take up positions on the spurs of Monte Cristo and along the bluffs of the south bank of the Tugela, from which we might assist the infantry attack, and particularly the attack of Barton's Brigade, by long-range rifle fire, and by our Colt battery and Maxim guns. While we marched the artillery fire grew more rapid, as battery after battery joined in the bombardment; and when we reached the high wooded ridge which we were ordered to line, I could see our shells bursting merrily in the enemy's trenches.

The position which had been assigned to the South African Light Horse afforded a close yet extensive view of the whole scene. Deep in its gorge below our feet flowed the Tugela, with the new pontoon bridge visible to the left, just below a fine waterfall. Behind us, on a rounded spur of Monte Cristo, one of the long-range batteries was firing away busily. Before us, across the river, there rose from the water's edge first a yellow strip of sandy foreshore, then steep, scrub-covered banks, and then smooth, brown slopes, terminating in the three hills which were to be successively assaulted, and which were surmounted by the dark lines of the Boer forts and trenches.

It was like a stage scene viewed from the dress circle. Moreover, we were very comfortable. There were large convenient rocks to sit behind in case of bullets, or to rest a telescope on, and the small trees which sparsely covered the ridge gave a partial shade from the sun. Opposite our front a considerable valley, thickly wooded, ran back from the river, and it was our easy and pleasant task to "fan" this, as an American officer would say, by scattering a ceaseless shower of rifle and machine-gun bullets throughout its length. Under these satisfactory circumstances I watched the battle.

It developed very slowly, and with the deliberation which characterises all our manœuvres. The guns gradually worked themselves into a state of excitement, and what with our musketry, supplemented by that of the Border Regiment and the Composite Battalion, whose duties were the same as ours, and the machine-guns puffing like steam engines, we soon had a capital loud noise, which I think is a most invigorating element in an attack. Besides this, the enemy's sharpshooters were curiously subdued. They found an unexpected amount of random bullets flying about, and, as they confessed afterwards, it puzzled and disturbed them.

The spectacle of two thousand men firing for half a day at nothing may provoke the comment "shocking waste of ammunition". Very likely there was waste. But all war is waste, and cartridges are the cheapest item in the bill. At any rate, we made it too hot for the "snipers" to show their heads, which was certainly worth fifty men to the assaulting brigades. This method of preparing an attack by a great volume of unaimed—not undirected—rifle fire is worthy of the closest attention. I have only once before noticed its employment, and that was when Sir Bindon Blood attacked and took the Tanga Pass. Then, as now, it was most effective.

While we were thus occupied the Infantry of Barton's Brigade were marching across the pontoon bridge, turning to their right and filing along the sandy foreshore. The plan of attack to which Sir Redvers Buller had finally committed himself was as follows: Hildyard's Brigade to hold its position on the low kopjes; Barton's Brigade to cross the new pontoon bridge opposite to the left of the enemy's position, and assault the hill marked "8" on my diagram, and hereinafter called Barton's Hill. Next Kitchener's Brigade was

to cross, covered by Barton's fire, to assault the centre hill marked
"2", and called Railway Hill. Lastly, Norcott's two untouched
battalions were to join the rest of their brigade, and, supported by
General Hart's Brigade, to attack Inniskilling Hill.

In brief, we were to stretch out our right arm, reach round the
enemy's flank, and pivoting on Hildyard's Brigade crumple him
from (his) left to right. It was the same plan as before, only that we
now had our right hand on the Monte Cristo ridge, from which commanding position our long-range guns could enfilade and even take
in reverse some of the enemy's trenches.

The leading brigade was across the river by nine o'clock, and by
ten had reached its position ready for attacking at the foot of
Barton's Hill. The advance began forthwith and the figures of the
Infantry could be seen swarming up the steep slopes of the river
gorge. The Boers did very little to stop the attack. They knew their
weakness. One side of Barton's Hill was swept and commanded by
the guns on Monte Cristo. The other side, at the back of which was
the donga we were "fanning", was raked by the heavy artillery
on the Hlangwani spur and by the field batteries arranged along the
south side of the river. Observe the influence of the Monte Cristo
ridge! It made Barton's Hill untenable by the Boers; and Barton's
Hill prepared the way for an attack on Railway Hill, and Railway
Hill—but I must not anticipate. Indeed, next to Monte Cristo,
Barton's Hill was the key of the Boer position, and so unfortunate
was the enemy's situation that he could not hold this all-important
feature once he had lost the Monte Cristo ridge.

What was tactically possible and safe—for the Boer is a cautious
warrior—was done. Knowing that his left would be turned he
extended a sort of false left in the air beyond the end of the Monte
Cristo ridge, and here he brought a gun into action, which worried
us among other people but did not, of course, prevent any military
movement.

By noon the whole of Barton's Hill was in the possession of his
brigade, without, as it seemed to us, any serious opposition. The
artillery then turned its attention to the other objectives of the
attack. The Boer detached left was, however, of considerable
strength, and as soon as Barton had occupied this hill (which proved,
moreover, far more extensive than had been expected), he was
heavily attacked by rifle fire from its under features and from a
network of dongas to the eastward, and as the artillery were busy

preparing the attack on Railway Hill, the brigade, particularly the Scots and Irish Fusiliers, soon became severely engaged and suffered grievous loss.

The fact that Barton's Hill was in our possession made the Boers on Railway and Inniskilling Hills very insecure. A powerful infantry force was holding the left of their position, and though it was itself being actively attacked on the eastern face, it could spare at least a battalion to assail their flank and threaten their rear. Covered by this flanking fire, by the long-range musketry, and by a tremendous bombardment, in which every gun, from the lumbering 5 in. siege guns to the little 9-pounder mountain battery, joined, the main attack was now launched. It proceeded simultaneously against Railway Hill, Inniskilling Hill, and the neck between them, but as the general line was placed obliquely across the Boer front, the attack fell first on Railway Hill and the neck.

The right battalions drew up in many long lines on the sides of the river gorge. Then men began gradually to work their way upwards, until all the dead patches of ground and every scrap of cover sheltered a fierce little group. Behind the railway embankment, among the rocks, in the scrub, in a cutting, near a ruined house, clusters of men eagerly awaited the decisive moment: and all this time more than seventy guns concentrated their fire on the entrenchments, scattering the stones and earth high in the air. Then, suddenly, shortly after four o'clock, all further attempts at advancing under cover were abandoned, and the Lancashire Brigade marched proudly into the open ground and on the enemy's works. The Mauser musketry burst forth at once, and the bullets, humming through the assaulting waves of infantry, reached us on our hillside and wounded a trooper in spite of the distance. But, bullets or no bullets, we could not take our eyes off the scene.

The Lancashire Brigade advanced on a wide front. Norcott's Riflemen were already prolonging their line to the right. The Boer fire was dispersed along the whole front of attack, instead of converging on one narrow column. The assault was going to succeed. We stood up on our rocks. Bayonets began to glitter on the distant slope. The moving lines increased their pace. The heads of the Boers bobbing up and down in their trenches grew fewer and fewer. They knew the tide was running too strongly. Death and flight were thinning their ranks. Then the sky-line of Railway Hill bristled with men, who dropped on their knees forthwith and fired in particular haste at something that was running away down the other side. There was the sound of cheering. Railway Hill was ours. I looked to the left.

The neck between the hills was lined with trenches. The South Lancashire Regiment had halted, pinned to the ground by the Boer fire. Were they going to lose the day for us when it was already won? The question was soon answered. In an instant there appeared on the left of the Boer trench a dozen—only a dozen—violent forms rushing forward. A small party had worked their way to the flank, and were at close quarters with cold steel. And then—by contrast to their former courage—the valiant burghers fled in all directions, and others held out their rifles and bandoliers and begged for mercy, which was sometimes generously given, so that by the time the whole attack had charged forward into the trenches there was a nice string of thirty-two prisoners winding down the hill: at which token of certain victory we shouted loudly.

Inniskilling Hill alone remained, and that was almost in our hands. Its slopes were on three sides alive with the active figures of the Light Brigade, and the bayonets sparkled. The hill ran into a peak. Many of the trenches were already deserted, but the stone breastwork at the summit still contained defenders. There, painted against the evening sky, were the slouch hats and moving rifles. Shell after shell exploded among them: overhead, in their faces, in the trench itself, behind them, before them, around them. Sometimes five and six shells were bursting on the very apex at the same instant. Showers of rock and splinters fell on all sides.

Yet they held their ground and stayed in greater peril than was ever mortal man before. But the infantry were drawing very near. At last the Dutchmen fled. One, a huge fellow in a brown jersey, tarried to spring on the parapet and empty his magazine once more into the approaching ranks, and while he did so a 50 lb. lyddite shell burst, as it seemed, in the midst of him, and the last defender of Inniskilling Hill vanished.

Then the artillery put up their sights and began to throw their shells over the crest of hill and ridge, so that they might overtake fugitives. The valleys behind fumed and stewed. Wreaths of dust and smoke curled upward. The infantry crowned the trenches all along the line, some firing their rifles at the flying enemy, others beckoning to nearer folk to surrender, and they all cheered in the triumph of successful attack till the glorious sound came down to us who watched, so that the whole army took up the shout, and all men knew that the battle of Pieters was won.

Forthwith came orders for the cavalry to cross the river, and we mounted in high expectation, knowing that behind the captured hill lay an open plain stretching almost to the foot of Bulwana. We galloped swiftly down to the pontoon bridge, and were about to pass over it, when the General-in-Chief met us. He had ridden to the other bank to see for himself and us. The Boer artillery were firing heavily to cover the retreat of their riflemen. He would not allow us to go across that night lest we should lose heavily in horses. So the brigade returned disappointed to its former position, watered horses, and selected a bivouac. I was sent to warn the Naval Battery that a heavy counter-stroke would probably be made on the right of Barton's Brigade during the night, and, climbing the spur of Monte Cristo, on which the guns were placed, had a commanding view of the field.

In the gathering darkness the Boer artillery, invisible all day, was betrayed by its flashes. Two "pom-poms" flickered away steadily from the direction of Doorn Kloof, making a regular succession of small bright flame points. Two more guns were firing from the hills to our left. Another was in action far away on our right. There may have been more, but even so it was not much artillery to oppose our eleven batteries. But it is almost an open question whether it is better to have many guns to shoot at very little, or few guns to shoot at a great deal; hundreds of shells tearing up the ground or a dozen plunging into masses of men. Personally, I am convinced that future warfare will be to the few, by which I mean that to escape annihilation soldiers will have to fight in widely dispersed formations, when they will have to think for themselves, and when each must be to a great extent his own general; and with regard to artillery, it appears that the advantages of defensive action, range, concealment, and individual initiative may easily counterbalance numbers and discipline. The night fell upon these reflections, and I hastened to rejoin the cavalry.

On the way I passed through Sir Charles Warren's camp, and there found a gang of prisoners—forty-eight of them—all in a row, almost the same number that the Boers had taken in the armoured train. Looking at these very ordinary people, who grinned and chattered without dignity, and who might, from their appearance, have been a knot of loafers round a public-house, it was difficult to understand what qualities made them such a terrible foe.

"Only forty-eight, sir," said a private soldier, who was guarding them, "and there wouldn't have been so many as that if the officers hadn't stopped us from giving them the bayonet. I never saw such cowards in my life; shoot at you till you come up to them, and then beg for mercy. I'd teach 'em." With which remark he turned to the prisoners, who had just been issued rations of beef and biscuit, but who were also very thirsty, and began giving them water to drink from his own canteen, and so left me wondering at the opposite and contradictory sides of human nature as shown by Briton as well as Boer.

We got neither food nor blankets that night, and slept in our waterproofs on the ground; but we had at last that which was better than feast or couch, for which we had hungered and longed through many weary weeks, which had been thrice forbidden us, and which was all the more splendid since it had been so long delayed—Victory.

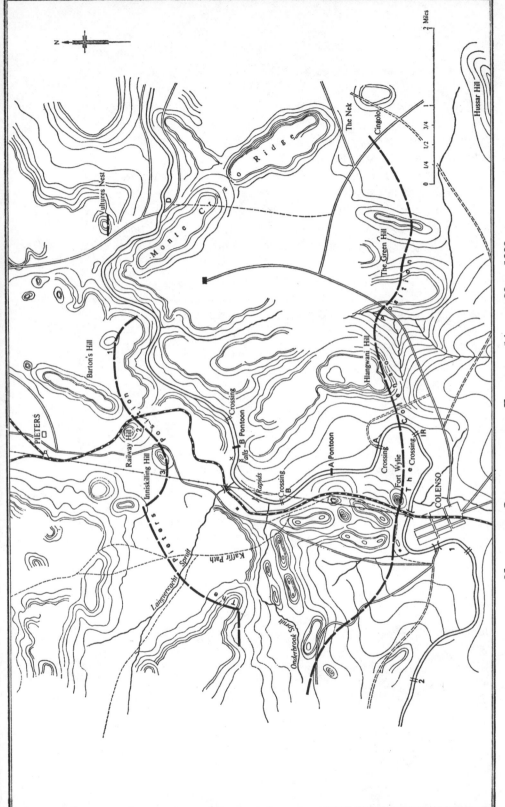

MAP OF THE OPERATIONS FROM FEBRUARY 14TH TO 28TH, 1900

CHAPTER TWENTY-SIX

THE RELIEF OF LADYSMITH

Commandant's Office, Durban: March 9, 1900

THE SUCCESSFUL action of the 27th had given Sir Redvers Buller possession of the whole of the left and centre of the Pieters position, and in consequence of these large sections of their entrenchments having fallen into British hands, the Boers evacuated the remainder and retreated westward on to the high hills and northward towards Bulwana Mountain.

About ninety prisoners were captured in the assault, and more than a hundred bodies were counted in the trenches. After making allowances for the fact that these men were for the most part killed by shell fire, and that therefore the proportion of killed to wounded would necessarily be higher than if the loss were caused by bullets, it seems probable that no less than three hundred wounded were removed. Forty were collected by British ambulance parties. Of the Boers who were killed in the retreat no accurate estimate can be formed, but the dongas and kopjes beyond the position were strewn with occasional corpses. Undoubtedly the enemy was hard hit in personnel, and the fact that we had taken two miles of entrenchments as well as considerable stores of ammunition proved that a very definite and substantial success had been won.

But we were not prepared for the complete results that followed the operations of the 27th. Neither the General nor his army expected to enter Ladysmith without another action. Before us a smooth plain, apparently unobstructed, ran to the foot of Bulwana, but from this forbidding eminence a line of ridges and kopjes was drawn to the high hills of Doorn Kloof, and seemed to interpose another serious barrier. It was true that this last position was within range, or almost within range, of Sir George White's guns, so that its defenders might be caught between two fires, but we knew, and thought the Boers knew, that the Ladysmith garrison was too feeble from want of food and other privations to count for very much. So Sir Redvers Buller, facing the least satisfactory assumption, determined to rest his army on the 28th, and attack Bulwana Hill on March 1.

He accordingly sent a message by heliograph into Ladysmith to say that he had beaten the enemy thoroughly, and was sending on his cavalry to reconnoitre. Ladysmith had informed herself, however, of the state of the game. Captain Tilney, from his balloon, observed all that passed in the enemy's lines on the morning of the 28th. At first, when he heard no artillery fire, he was depressed, and feared lest the relieving army had retreated again. Then, as it became day, he was sure that this was not so, for the infantry in crowds were occupying the Boer position, and the mounted patrols pricked forward into the plain. Presently he saw the Boers rounding up their cattle and driving them off to the north. Next they caught and began to saddle their horses. The great white tilted waggons of the various laagers filed along the road around the eastern end of Bulwana. Lastly, up went a pair of shears over "Long Tom", and at this he descended to the earth with the good news that the enemy were off at last.

The garrison, however, had been mocked by false hopes before, and all steeled themselves to wait "at least another ten days".

Meanwhile, since there was no fire from the enemy's side, our cavalry and artillery were rapidly and safely crossing the river. There was a considerable block at the bridge when the South African Light Horse arrived, and we had full leisure to examine the traffic. Guns, men, horses, and mules were hurrying across to the northern bank, and an opposing stream of wounded flowed steadily back to the south. I watched these with interest.

First came a young officer riding a pony and smoking a cigarette, but very pale and with his left arm covered with bloody bandages. Brooke greeted him and asked, "Bone?" "Yes," replied the subaltern laconically, "shoulder smashed up." We expressed our sympathy. "Oh, that's all right; good show, wasn't it? The men are awfully pleased;" and he rode slowly on up the hill—the type of an unyielding race—and stoical besides; for wounds, especially shattered bones, grow painful after twelve or fourteen hours. A string of wounded passed by on stretchers, some lying quite still, others sitting up and looking about them; one, also an officer, a dark.

black-moustached captain, whose eyes were covered with a bandage, kept his bearers busy with continual impatient questions. "Yes, but what I want to know is this, did they get into them with the bayonet?" The volunteer stretcher-bearers could make no satisfactory reply, but said, "Yes, they give 'em 'ell, sir." "Where, on the left of Railway Hill?" "Oh, everywhere, sir." The group passed by, and the last thing I heard was, "How much of the artillery has crossed? Are they sending the cavalry over? What the. . . ."

Presently came stretchers with wounded Boers. Most of these poor creatures were fearfully shattered. One tall man with a great fierce beard and fine features had a fragment of rock or iron driven through his liver. He was, moreover, stained bright yellow with lyddite, but did not seem in much pain, for he looked very calm and stolid. The less seriously injured among the soldiers hobbled back alone or assisted by their comrades.

I asked a smart-looking sergeant of the Dublin Fusiliers, who was limping along with a broken foot, whether the regiment had been again heavily engaged. Of course they had.

"Sure, we're always in the thick of it, sorr. Mr. —— was hit; no, not badly; only his wrist, but there's not many of the officers left; only two now who were at Talana."

At last the time came for the cavalry to cross the bridge, and as we filed on to the floating roadway we were amused to see a large fingerpost at the entrance, on which the engineers had neatly painted, "To Ladysmith". The brigade passed over the neck between Railway and Inniskilling Hills, and we massed in a suitable place on the descending slopes beyond. We looked at the country before us, and saw that it was good. Here at last was ground cavalry could work on at some speed. Ladysmith was still hidden by the remaining ridges, but we thought that somehow, and with a little luck, we might have a look at it before night.

Under Bulwana the waggons of the Boers and several hundred horsemen could be seen hurrying away. It was clearly our business to try to intercept them unless they had made good covering dispositions. Patrols were sent out in all directions, and a squadron of Thorneycroft's Mounted Infantry proceeded to Pieters Station, where a complete train of about twenty trucks had been abandoned by the enemy. While this reconnaissance was going on I climbed up Inniskilling Hill to examine the trenches. It was occupied by the

East Surrey Regiment, and the soldiers were very eager to do the
honours. They had several things to show: "Come along here, sir;
there's a bloke here without a head; took clean off, sir"; and were
mightily disappointed that I would not let them remove the
blanket which covered the grisly shape.

The trench was cut deep in the ground, and, unlike our trenches,
there was scarcely any parapet. A few great stones had been laid in
front, but evidently the Boer believed in getting well into the
ground. The bottom was knee deep in cartridge cases, and every
few yards there was an enormous heap of Mauser ammunition,
thousands of rounds, all fastened neatly, five at a time, in clips. A
large proportion were covered with bright green slime, which the
soldiers declared was poison, but which on analysis may prove to be
wax, used to preserve the bullet.

The Boers, however, were not so guiltless of other charges. A
field officer of the East Surreys, recognising me, came up and
showed me an expansive bullet of a particularly cruel pattern. The
tip had been cut off, exposing the soft core, and four slits were
scored down the side. Whole boxes of this ammunition had been
found. An officer who had been making calculations told me that
the proportion of illegal bullets was nearly one in five. I should not
myself have thought it was so large, but certainly the improper
bullets were very numerous. I have a specimen of this particular
kind by me as I write, and I am informed by people who shoot big
game that it is the most severe bullet of its kind yet invented. Five
other sorts have been collected by the medical officers, who have
also tried to classify the wounds they respectively produce.

I cannot be accused of having written unfairly about the enemy;
indeed, I have only cared to write what I thought was the truth
about everybody. I have tried to do justice to the patriotic virtues
of the Boers, and it is now necessary to observe that the character
of these people reveals, in stress, a dark and spiteful underside. A
man—I use the word in its fullest sense—does not wish to lacerate
his foe, however earnestly he may desire his life.

The popping of musketry made me hasten to rejoin my regiment.
The squadron of mounted infantry had reached Pieters Railway
Station, only to be heavily fired on from a low hill to the westward;
and they now came scampering back with half a dozen riderless
horses. Happily, the riders mostly arrived on foot after a few
minutes. But it was evidently necessary to push forward very care-

fully. Indeed, it is hard to imagine how pursuits will occur in future war. A hundred bold men with magazine rifles on a ridge can delay a whole army. The cavalry must reconnoitre and retire. Infantry and guns must push forward. Meanwhile the beaten troops are moving steadily to safety.

In a little while—to revert to the narrative—the horse artillery battery came up, and the offending hill was conscientiously shelled for an hour. Then the patrols crept forward again, but progress was necessarily slow. We were still six miles from Ladysmith at three o'clock.

At this hour the Boer ambulances had been invited to come for such of their wounded as could be moved, for since the enemy returned our wounded from Spion Kop we have followed the practice of sending back theirs on all occasions should they prefer it.

Anxious to find out the impression produced on the Boers by the late actions, I hastened to meet the ambulances, which, preceded by three horsemen carrying a large white flag, were now coming from the direction of Bulwana. They were stopped at our cavalry picket line, and a report of their arrival was sent back to the nearest brigadier. Their leader was a fine old fellow of the genuine veldt Boer type. He spoke English fluently, and we were soon in conversation.

Cronje's surrender had been officially announced to us on the previous day, and I inquired whether he had heard of it. He replied that he knew Cronje was in difficulties, but understood he had managed to escape with his army. As for the surrender, it might be true or it might be false. "We are told so many lies that we believe nothing."

But his next remark showed that he realised that the tide had begun to turn. "I don't know what we poor Afrikanders have done that England won't let us be a nation." I would have replied that I remembered having heard something about "driving the English into the sea", but I have been over this ground before in every sense, and knew the futility of any discussion. Indeed, when the debate is being conducted with shells, bullets, and bayonets, words are feeble weapons. So I said with an irony which was quite lost on him, "It must be all those damned capitalists," and this, of course, won his complete agreement, so that he confided that losing the position we had taken on the 27th was "a sore and bitter blow".

It happened that two squadrons of the 13th Hussars had ridden forward beyond us towards Bulwana, and at this moment the Boer artillery began to shell them rather heavily. We watched the proceedings for a few minutes, and the Boer was much astonished to see soldiers riding leisurely forward in regular though open order without paying the slightest attention to the shrapnel. Then several more squadrons were ordered to support the reconnaissance. A great company of horsemen jingled past the halted ambulances and cantered off in the direction of the firing. My companion regarded these steadfastly, then he said:

"Why do they all look so pleased?"

"Because they think they are going to fight; but they will not be allowed to. It is only desired to draw your fire and reconnoitre."

The whole plain was now occupied by cavalry, both brigades being on the move.

"Little did we think a week ago", said the Boer, "that we should see such a sight as this, here in this plain."

"Didn't you think we should get through?"

"No, we didn't believe it possible."

"And you find the soldiers brave?"

"They do not care for life."

"And Ladysmith?"

"Ah," his eye brightened, "there's pluck, if you like. Wonderful!"

Then we agreed that it was a sad and terrible war, and whoever won we would make the gold mines pay, so that "the damned capitalists" should not think they had scored, and thus we parted.

I afterwards learned that the Boer ambulances removed twenty-seven of their wounded. The condition of the others was too serious to allow of their being moved, and in spite of every attention they all died while in our hands.

When I rejoined the South African Light Horse the Irregular Brigade had begun to advance again. Major Gough's Composite Regiment had scouted the distant ridge and found it unoccupied. Now Dundonald moved his whole command thither, and with his staff climbed to the top. But to our disappointment Ladysmith was not to be seen. Two or three other ridges hung like curtains before us. The afternoon had passed, and it was already after six o'clock. The Boer artillery was still firing, and it seemed rash to attempt to reconnoitre further when the ground was broken and the light fading.

The order was given to retire and the movement had actually

begun when a messenger came back from Gough with the news that the last ridge between us and the town was unoccupied by the enemy, that he could see Ladysmith, and that there was, for the moment, a clear run in. Dundonald immediately determined to go on himself into the town with the two squadrons who were scouting in front, and to send the rest of the brigade back to camp. He invited me to accompany him, and without delay we started at a gallop.

Never shall I forget that ride. The evening was deliciously cool. My horse was strong and fresh, for I had changed him at midday. The ground was rough with many stones, but we cared little for that. Beyond the next ridge, or the rise beyond that, or around the corner of the hill, was Ladysmith—the goal of all our hopes and ambitions during weeks of almost ceaseless fighting. Ladysmith— the centre of the world's attention, the scene of famous deeds, the cause of mighty efforts—Ladysmith was within our reach at last. We were going to be inside the town within an hour. The excitement of the moment was increased by the exhilaration of the gallop. Onward wildly, recklessly, up and down hill, over the boulders, through the scrub, Hubert Gough with his two squadrons, Macken- zie's Natal Carabineers and the Imperial Light Horse, were clear of the ridges already. We turned the shoulder of a hill, and there before us lay the tin houses and dark trees we had come so far to see and save.

The British guns on Cæsar's Camp were firing steadily in spite of the twilight. What was happening? Never mind, we were nearly through the dangerous ground. Now we were all on the flat. Brigadier, staff, and troops let their horses go. We raced through the thorn bushes by Intombi Spruit.

Suddenly there was a challenge. "Halt, who goes there?" "The Ladysmith Relief Column," and thereat from out of trenches and rifle pits artfully concealed in the scrub a score of tattered men came running, cheering feebly, and some were crying. In the half light they looked ghastly pale and thin. A poor, white-faced officer waved his helmet to and fro, and laughed foolishly, and the tall, strong colonial horsemen, standing up in their stirrups, raised a loud resounding cheer, for then we knew we had reached the Lady- smith picket line.

Presently we arranged ourselves in military order, Natal Cara- bineers and Imperial Light Horse riding two and two abreast so that there might be no question about precedence, and with Gough, the youngest regimental commander in the army, and one of the best, at the head of the column, we forded the Klip River and rode into the town.

That night I dined with Sir George White, who had held the town for four months against all comers, and was placed next to Hamilton, who won the fight at Elandslaagte and beat the Boers off Waggon Hill, and next but one to Hunter, whom everyone said was the finest man in the world. Never before had I sat in such brave company nor stood so close to a great event. As the war drives slowly to its close more substantial triumphs, larger battles, wherein the enemy suffers heavier loss, the capture of towns, and the surrender of armies may mark its progress. But whatever victories the future may have in store, the defence and relief of Ladysmith, because they afford, perhaps, the most remarkable examples of national tenacity and perseverance which our later history contains, will not be soon forgotten by the British people, whether at home or in the Colonies.

CHAPTER TWENTY-SEVEN

AFTER THE SIEGE

Durban: March 10, 1900

SINCE THE road by which Dundonald's squadrons had entered the town was never again closed by the enemy, the siege of Ladysmith may be said to have ended on the last day of February. During the night the heavy guns fired at intervals, using up the carefully husbanded ammunition in order to prevent the Boers from removing their artillery.

On March 1 the garrison reverted to a full half-ration of biscuits and horseflesh, and an attempt was made to harass the Boers, who were in full retreat towards the Biggarsberg. Sir George White had made careful inquiries among the regiments for men who would undertake to walk five miles and fight at the end of the march. But so reduced were the soldiers through want of food that, though many volunteered, only two thousand men were considered fit out of the whole garrison. These were, however, formed into a column, under Colonel Knox, consisting of two batteries of artillery, two squadrons of the 19th Hussars and 5th Lancers, "all that was left of them", with horses, and detachments, each about two hundred and fifty strong, from the Manchester, Liverpool, and Devon Regiments, the 60th Rifles, and the Gordon Highlanders, and this force moved out of Ladysmith at dawn on the 1st to attack the Boers on Pepworth's Hill, in the hope of interfering with their entrainment at Modderspruit Station.

The Dutch, however, had left a rearguard sufficient to hold in check so small a force, and it was two o'clock before Pepworth's Hill was occupied. The batteries then shelled Modderspruit Station, and very nearly caught three crowded trains, which just managed to steam out of range in time. The whole force of men and horses was by this time quite exhausted. The men could scarcely carry their

rifles. In the squadron of 19th Hussars nine horses out of sixty fell
down and died, and Colonel Knox therefore ordered the withdrawal
into the town.

Only about a dozen men were killed or wounded in this affair, but
the fact that the garrison was capable of making any offensive
movement after their privations is a manifest proof of their soldierly
spirit and excellent discipline.

On the same morning Sir Redvers Buller advanced on Bulwana
Hill. Down from the commanding positions which they had won
by their courage and endurance marched the incomparable infantry, and by 2 o'clock the plain of Pieters was thickly occupied
by successive lines of men in extended order, with long columns of
guns and transport trailing behind them. Shortly before noon it was
ascertained that Bulwana Hill was abandoned by the enemy, and
the army was thereon ordered to camp in the plain, no further
fighting being necessary.

The failure to pursue the retreating Boers when two fine cavalry
brigades were standing idle and eager must be noticed. It is probable that the Boer rearguard would have been sufficiently strong to
require both infantry and guns to drive it back. It is certain that
sharp fighting must have attended the effort. Nevertheless the
opinion generally expressed was that it should have been made. My
personal impression is that Sir Redvers Buller was deeply moved by
the heavy losses the troops had suffered, and was reluctant to
demand further sacrifices from them at this time. Indeed, the price
of victory had been a high one.

In the fortnight's fighting, from February 14 to February 28, two
generals, six colonels commanding regiments, a hundred and five
other officers, and one thousand five hundred and eleven soldiers
had been killed or wounded out of an engaged force of about
eighteen thousand men; a proportion of slightly under 10 per cent.

In the whole series of operations for the relief of Ladysmith the
losses amounted to three hundred officers and more than five
thousand men, out of a total engaged force of about twenty-three
thousand, a proportion of rather more than 20 per cent. Nor had
this loss been inflicted in a single day's victorious battle, but was
spread over twenty-five days of general action in a period of ten
weeks; and until the last week no decided success had cheered the
troops.

The stress of the campaign, moreover, had fallen with peculiar force on certain regiments: the Lancashire Fusiliers sustained losses of over 35 per cent, the Inniskillings of 40 per cent, and the Dublin Fusiliers of over 60 per cent. It was very remarkable that the fighting efficiency of these regiments was in no way impaired by such serious reductions. The casualties among the officers maintained their usual glorious disproportion, six or seven regiments in the army having less than eight officers left alive and unwounded. Among the cavalry the heaviest losses occurred in Dundonald's Brigade, the South African Light Horse, Thorneycroft's Mounted Infantry, and the squadron of Imperial Light Horse, each losing a little less than a quarter of their strength.

The ceaseless marching and fighting had worn out the clothes and boots of the army, and a certain number of the guns of the field artillery were unserviceable through constant firing. The troops, besides clothes, needed fresh meat, an exclusive diet of tinned food being unwholesome if unduly prolonged. Sir Redvers Buller's estimate that a week's rest was needed does not seem excessive by the light of such facts, but still one more effort might have saved much trouble later on. On March 3 the relieving army made its triumphal entry into Ladysmith, and passing through the town camped on the plain beyond. The scene was solemn and stirring, and only the most phlegmatic were able to conceal their emotions. The streets were lined with the brave defenders, looking very smart and clean in their best clothes, but pale, thin, and wasp-waisted—their belts several holes tighter than was satisfactory.

Before the little Town Hall, the tower of which, sorely battered, yet unyielding, seemed to symbolise the spirit of the garrison, Sir George White and his staff sat on their skeleton horses. Opposite to them were drawn up the pipers of the Gordon Highlanders. The townsfolk, hollow-eyed but jubilant, crowded the pavement and the windows of the houses. Everyone who could find a flag had hung it out, but we needed no bright colours to raise our spirits.

At eleven o'clock precisely the relieving army began to march into the town. First of all rode Sir Redvers Buller with his headquarters staff and an escort of the Royal Dragoons. The infantry and artillery followed by brigades, but in front of all, as a special recognition of their devoted valour, marched the Dublin Fusiliers, few, but proud.

Many of the soldiers, remembering their emerald island, had fastened sprigs of green to their helmets, and all marched with a swing that was wonderful to watch. Their Colonel and their four officers looked as happy as kings are thought to be. As the regiments passed Sir George White, the men recognised their former general, and, disdaining the rules of the service, waved their helmets and rifles, and cheered him with intense enthusiasm. Some even broke from the ranks. Seeing this the Gordon Highlanders began to cheer the Dublins, and after that the noise of cheering was continual, every regiment as it passed giving and receiving fresh ovations.

All through the morning and on into the afternoon the long stream of men and guns flowed through the streets of Ladysmith, and all marvelled to see what manner of men these were—dirty, war-worn, travel-stained, tanned, their uniforms in tatters, their boots falling to pieces, their helmets dinted and broken, but nevertheless magnificent soldiers, striding along, deep-chested and broad-shouldered, with the light of triumph in their eyes and the blood of fighting ancestors in their veins. It was a procession of lions. And presently, when the two battalions of Devons met—both full of honours—and old friends breaking from the ranks gripped each other's hands and shouted, everyone was carried away, and I waved my feathered hat, and cheered and cheered until I could cheer no longer for joy that I had lived to see the day.

At length all was over. The last dust-brown battalion had passed away and the roadway was again clear. Yet the ceremony was incomplete. Before the staff could ride away the Mayor of Ladysmith advanced and requested Sir George White to receive an address which the townspeople had prepared and were anxious to present to him. The General dismounted from his horse, and standing on the steps of the Town Hall, in the midst of the inhabitants whom he had ruled so rigorously during the hard months of the siege, listened while their Town Clerk read their earnest grateful thanks to him for saving their town from the hands of the enemy. The General replied briefly, complimented them on their behaviour during the siege, thanked them for the way in which they had borne their many hardships and submitted to the severe restrictions which the circumstances of war had brought on them, and rejoiced with them that they had been enabled by their devotion and by the bravery of the soldiers to keep the Queen's flag flying over Ladysmith. And then everybody cheered everybody else, and so, very tired and very happy, we all went home to our belated luncheons.

Walking through the streets it was difficult to see many signs of the bombardment. The tower of the Town Hall was smashed and chipped, several houses showed large holes in their walls, and heaps of broken brickwork lay here and there. But on the whole the impression produced was one of surprise that the Boers had done so little damage with the sixteen thousand shells they had fired during the siege.

On entering the houses, however, the effect was more apparent. In one the floor was ripped up, in another the daylight gleamed through the corrugated iron roof, and in some houses the inner walls had been completely destroyed, and only heaps of rubbish lay on the floor.

The fortifications which the troops had built, though of a very strong and effective character, were neither imposing nor conspicuous; indeed, being composed of heaps of stone they were visible only as dark lines on the rugged kopjes, and if the fame of the town were to depend on relics of the war it would not long survive the siege.

But memories dwell among the tin houses and on the stony hills that will keep the name of Ladysmith fresh and full of meaning in the hearts of our countrymen. Every trench, every mound has its own tale to tell, some of them sad, but not one shameful. Here and there, scattered through the scrub by the river or on the hills of red stones almost red hot in the sun blaze, rise the wooden crosses which mark the graves of British soldiers. Near the iron bridge a considerable granite pyramid records the spot where Dick-Cunyngham, Colonel of the Gordons—what prouder office could a man hold?—fell mortally wounded on the 6th of January. Another monument is being built on Waggon Hill to commemorate the brave men of the Imperial Light Horse who lost their lives but saved the day. The place is also marked where the noble Ava fell.

But there was one who found, to use his own words, "a strange sideway out of Ladysmith", whose memory many English-speaking people will preserve. I do not write of Steevens as a journalist, nor as the master of a popular and pleasing style, but as a man. I knew him, though I had met him rarely. A dinner up the Nile, a chance meeting at an Indian junction, five days on a Mediterranean steamer, two in a Continental express, and a long Sunday at his house near Merton—it was a scanty acquaintance, but sufficient to be quite certain that in all the varied circumstances and conditions to which men are subjected Steevens rang true. Modest yet proud, wise as well as witty, cynical but above all things sincere, he combined the characters of a charming companion and a good comrade.

His conversation and his private letters sparkled like his books and articles. Original expressions, just similitudes, striking phrases, quaint or droll ideas welled in his mind without the slightest effort. He was always at his best. I have never met a man who talked so well, so easily. His wit was the genuine article—absolutely natural and spontaneous.

I once heard him describe an incident in the Nile campaign, and the description amused me so much that I was impatient to hear it again, and when a suitable occasion offered I asked him to tell his tale to the others. But he told it quite differently, and left me wondering which version was the better. He could not repeat himself if he tried, whereas most of the renowned talkers I have met will go over the old impression with the certainty of a phonograph.

But enough of his words. He was not a soldier, but he walked into the Atbara zareba with the leading company of the Seaforth Highlanders. He wrote a vivid account of the attack, but there was nothing in it about himself.

When the investment of Ladysmith shut the doors on soldiers, townspeople, and War Correspondents alike, Steevens set to work to do his share of keeping up the good spirits of the garrison and of relieving the monotony of the long days. Through the first three months of the siege no local event was awaited with more interest than the publication of a *Ladysmith Lyre*, and the weary defenders had many a good laugh at its witticisms.

Sun, stink, and sickness harassed the beleaguered. The bombardment was perpetual, the relief always delayed; hope again and again deferred. But nothing daunted Steevens, depressed his courage, or curbed his wit. What such a man is worth in gloomy days those may appreciate who have seen the effect of public misfortunes on a modern community.

At last he was himself stricken down by enteric fever. When it seemed that the worst was over there came a fatal relapse, and the brightest intellect yet sacrificed by this war perished; nor among all the stubborn garrison of Ladysmith was there a stouter heart or a more enduring spirit.

Dismal scenes were to be found at the hospital camp by Intombi Spruit. Here, in a town of white tents, under the shadow of Bulwana, were collected upwards of two thousand sick and wounded—

a fifth of the entire garrison. They were spared the shells, but exposed to all the privations of the siege.

Officers and men, doctors and patients, presented alike a most melancholy and even ghastly appearance. Men had been wounded, had been cured of their wounds, and had died simply because there was no nourishing food to restore their strength. Others had become convalescent from fever, but had succumbed from depression and lack of medical comforts. Hundreds required milk and brandy, but there was only water to give them. The weak died: at one time the death rate averaged fifteen a day. Nearly a tenth of the whole garrison died of disease. A forest of crosses, marking the graves of six hundred men, sprang up behind the camp.

It was a painful thing to watch the hungry patients, so haggard and worn that their friends could scarcely recognise them; and after a visit to Intombi I sat and gloated for an hour at the long train of waggons filled with all kinds of necessary comforts which crawled along the roads, and the relief of Ladysmith seemed more than ever worth the heavy price we had paid.

On the evening after Buller's victorious army had entered the town I went to see Sir George White, and was so fortunate as to find him alone and disengaged. The General received me in a room the windows of which gave a wide view of the defences. Bulwana, Cæsar's Camp, Waggon Hill lay before us, and beneath—for the house stood on high ground—spread the blue roofs of Ladysmith. From the conversation that followed, and from my own knowledge of events, I shall endeavour to explain so far as is at present possible the course of the campaign in Natal; and I will ask the reader to observe that only the remarks actually quoted should be attributed to the various officers.

Sir George White told me how he had reached Natal less than a week before the declaration of war. He found certain arrangements in progress to meet a swiftly approaching emergency, and he had to choose between upsetting all these plans and entirely reconstructing the scheme of defence, or of accepting what was already done as the groundwork of his operations.

Sir Penn Symons, who had been commanding in the Colony, and who was presumably best qualified to form an opinion on the military necessities, extravagantly under-rated the Boer fighting power. Some of his calculations of the force necessary to hold various places seem incredible in the light of recent events. But everyone was wrong about the Boers, and the more they knew the worse they erred. Symons laughed at the Boer military strength, and laboured to impress his opinions on Sir George White, who having Hamilton's South African experience to fall back on, however, took a much more serious view of the situation, and was particularly disturbed at the advanced position of the troops at Dundee. He wanted to withdraw them. Symons urged the opposite considerations vehemently. He was a man of great personal force, and his manner carried people with him. "Besides," said the General, with a kindling eye and extraordinary emphasis, "he was a good, brave fighting man, and you know how much that is worth in war."

In spite of Symons's confidence and enthusiasm White hated to leave troops at Dundee, and Sir Archibald Hunter, his chief of staff, agreed with him. But not to occupy a place is one thing: to abandon it after it has been occupied another.

They decided to ask Sir Walter Hely-Hutchinson what consequences would in his opinion follow a withdrawal. They visited him at ten o'clock at night, and put the question straightly. Thus appealed to, the Governor declared that in that event "loyalists would be disgusted and discouraged; the results as regards the Dutch would be grave, many, if not most, would very likely rise, believing us to be afraid . . . and the effect on the natives, of whom there are some 750,000 in Natal and Zululand, might be disastrous."

On hearing the opinion expressed by a man of the Governor's ability and local knowledge, Sir Archibald Hunter said that it was a question "of balancing drawbacks", and advised that the troops be retained at Glencoe. So the matter was clinched, "and", said Sir George, "when I made up my mind to let Symons stay I shared and shared alike with him in the matter of troops, giving him three batteries, a regiment, and an infantry brigade, and keeping the same myself."

For his share in this discussion the Governor was at one time subjected to a considerable volume of abuse in the public Press, it being charged against him that he had "interfered" with the military arrangements.

Sir Walter Hely-Hutchinson, with whom I have had many pleasant talks, makes this invariable reply: "I never said a word to Sir George White until I was asked. When my opinion was called for I gave it according to the best of my judgment."

In the actual event Dundee had to be abandoned, nor was this a deliberate evacuation arising out of any regular military policy, but a swift retreat without stores or wounded, compelled by the force of the enemy.

It is, therefore, worth while considering how far the Governor's judgement had been vindicated by events. Undoubtedly loyalists throughout the Colony were disgusted, and that they were not discouraged was mainly due to the fact that with the Anglo-Saxon peoples anger at the injury usually overcomes dismay. The effect on the Dutch was grave, but was considerably modified by the electrical influence of the victory of Elandslaagte, and the spectacle of Boer prisoners marching southward.

The whole of the Klip River country, however, rose, and many prominent Natal Dutch farmers joined the enemy. The loyalty of the natives alone exceeded the Governor's anticipations, and their belief in the British power and preference for British rule was found to stand more knocking about than those best able to judge expected. We have reaped a rich reward in this dark season for having consistently pursued a kindly and humane policy towards the Bantu races; and the Boers have paid a heavy penalty for their cruelty and harshness.

On the subject of holding Ladysmith Sir George White was quite clear. "I never wanted to abandon Ladysmith; I considered it a place of primary importance to hold. It was on Ladysmith that both Republics concentrated their first efforts. Here, where the railways join, the armies of the Free State and the Transvaal were to unite, and the capture of the town was to seal their union."

It is now certain that Ladysmith was an essential to the carefully thought out Boer plan of campaign. To make quite sure of victory they directed twenty-five thousand of their best men on it under the Commandant-General himself. Flushed with the spirit of invasion, they scarcely reckoned on a fortnight's resistance; nor in their wildest nightmares did they conceive a four months' siege terminating in the furious inroad of a relieving army.

Exasperated at unexpected opposition—for they underrated us even more than we underrated them—they sacrificed around Ladysmith their chances of taking Pietermaritzburg and raiding all Natal; and it is moreover incontestable that in their resolve to take the town, on which they had set their hearts, they were provoked into close fighting with Sir Redvers Buller's army, and even to make an actual assault on the defences of Ladysmith, and so suffered far heavier losses than could otherwise have been inflicted on so elusive an enemy in such broken country.

"Besides," said the General, "I had no choice in the matter. I did not want to leave Ladysmith, but even if I had wanted, it would have been impossible."

He then explained how not only the moral value, the political significance of Ladysmith, and the great magazines accumulated there rendered it desirable to hold the town, but that the shortness of time, the necessity of evacuating the civil population, and of helping in the Dundee garrison, made its retention actually obligatory.

Passing to the actual siege of the town, Sir George White said that he had decided to make an active defence in order to keep the enemy's attention fixed on his force, and so prevent them from invading South Natal before the reinforcements could arrive. With that object he had fought the action of October 30, which had turned out so disastrously. After that he fell back on his entrenchments, and the blockade began.

"The experience we had gained of the long-range guns possessed by the enemy", said Sir George, "made it necessary for me to occupy a very large area of ground, and I had to extend my lines accordingly. My lines are now nearly fourteen miles in circumference. If I had taken up a smaller position we should have been pounded to death."

He said that the fact that they had plenty of room alone enabled them to live, for the shell fire was thus spread over a large area, and, as it were, diluted. Besides this the cattle were enabled to find grazing, but these extended lines were also a source of weakness. At one time on several sections of the defences the garrison could only provide two hundred men to the mile.

"That is scarcely the prescribed proportion. I would like to have occupied Bulwana, in which case we should have been quite comfortable, but I did not dare extend my lines any further. It was better to endure the bombardment than to run the risk of being stormed. Because my lines were so extended I was compelled to keep all the cavalry in Ladysmith."

Until they began to eat instead of feed the horses this powerful mounted force, upwards of three thousand strong, had been his mobile, almost his only reserve. Used in conjunction with an elaborate system of telephones the cavalry from their central position could powerfully reinforce any threatened section.

The value of this was proved on January 6. The General thought that the fierce assault delivered by the enemy on that day vindicated his policy in not occupying Bulwana and in keeping his cavalry within the town, on both of which points he had been much criticised.

He spoke with some bitterness of the attacks which had been made on him in the newspapers. He had always begged that the relieving operations should not be compromised by any hurry on his account, and he said, with earnestness, "It is not fair to charge me with all the loss of life they have involved." He concluded by saying, deliberately: "I regret Nicholson's Nek; perhaps I was rash then, but it was my only chance of striking a heavy blow. I regret nothing else. It may be that I am an obstinate man to say so, but if I had the last five months to live over again I would not—with that exception—do otherwise than I have done."

And then I came away and thought of the cheers of the relieving troops. Never before had I heard soldiers cheer like that. There was not much doubt about the verdict of the army on Sir George White's conduct of the defence, and it is one which the nation may gracefully accept.

But I am anxious also to discuss the Ladysmith episode from Sir Redvers Buller's point of view. This officer reached Cape Town on the very day that White was driven back on Ladysmith. His army, which would not arrive for several weeks, was calculated to be strong enough to overcome the utmost resistance the Boer Republics could offer.

To what extent he was responsible for the estimates of the number of troops necessary is not known. It is certain, however, that everyone—Ministers, generals, colonists, and intelligence officers—concurred in making a most remarkable miscalculation.

It reminds me of Jules Verne's story of the men who planned to shift the axis of the earth by the discharge of a great cannon. Everything was arranged. The calculations were exact to the most minute fraction. The world stood aghast at the impending explosion. But the men of science, whose figures were otherwise so accurate, had left out a nought, and their whole plan came to nothing. So it was with the British. Their original design of a containing division in Natal, and an invading army of three divisions in the Free State, would have been excellent if only they had written "army corps" instead of "division".

Buller found himself confronted with an alarming and critical situation in Natal. Practically the whole force which had been deemed sufficient to protect the Colony was locked up in Lady-smith, and only a few lines of communication troops stood between the enemy and the capital or even the seaport. Plainly, therefore, strong reinforcements—at least a division—must be hurried to Natal without an hour's unnecessary delay.

When these troops were subtracted from the forces in the Cape Colony all prospect of pursuing the original plan of invading the Free State was destroyed. It was evident that the war would assume dimensions which no one had ever contemplated.

The first thing to be done therefore was to grapple with the immediate emergencies, and await the arrival of the necessary troops to carry on the war on an altogether larger scale. Natal was the most acute situation. But there were others scarcely less serious and critical. The Cape Colony was quivering with rebellion. The Republican forces were everywhere advancing. Kimberley and Mafeking were isolated. A small British garrison held a dangerous position at Orange River bridge. Nearly all the other bridges had been seized or destroyed by rebels or invaders.

From every quarter came clamourings for troops. Soldiers were wanted with vital need at Stormberg, at Rosemead Junction, at Colesberg, at De Aar, but most of all they were wanted in Natal— Natal, which had been promised protection "with the whole force of the Empire", and which was already half overrun and the rest almost defenceless. So the army corps, which was to have marched irresistibly to Bloemfontein and Pretoria, had to be hurled into the country—each unit as it arrived—wherever the need was greatest where all were great.

Sir Redvers Buller, thus assailed by the unforeseen and pressed on every side, had to make up his mind quickly. He looked to Natal. It was there that the fiercest fighting was in progress and that the strength and vigour of the enemy was apparently most formidable. He had always regarded the line of the Tugela as the only defensive line which British forces would be strong enough to hold, and had recorded his opinion against placing any troops north of that river.

In spite of this warning Ladysmith had been made a great military depot, and had consequently come to be considered a place of primary importance. It was again a question of balancing drawbacks. Buller therefore telegraphed to White asking him whether he could entrench and maintain himself pending the arrival of reinforcements. White replied that he was prepared to make a prolonged defence of Ladysmith. To this proposal the General-in-Chief assented, observing only "but the line of the Tugela is very tempting".

General Buller's plan now seems to have been briefly as follows: First, to establish a *modus vivendi* in the Cape Colony, with sufficient troops to stand strictly on the defensive; secondly, to send a strong force to Natal, and either restore the situation there, or, failing that, extricate Sir George White so that his troops would be again available for the defence of the Southern portion of the Colony; thirdly, with what was left of the army corps—no longer strong enough to invade the Free State—to relieve Kimberley; fourthly, after settling Natal to return with such troops as could be spared and form with reinforcements from home a fresh army to carry out the original scheme of invading the Free State.

The defect in this plan was that there were not enough troops to carry it out. As we had underestimated the offensive vigour which the enemy was able to develop before the army could reach South Africa, so now we altogether miscalculated his extraordinary strength on the defensive. But it is impossible to see what else could have been done, and at any rate no one appreciated the magnitude of the difficulties more correctly than Sir Redvers Buller. He knew Northern Natal and understood the advantages that the Boers enjoyed among its mountains and kopjes.

On one occasion he even went so far as to describe the operation he had proposed as a "forlorn hope", so dark and gloomy was the situation in South Africa during the first fortnight in November. It was stated that the General was ordered by the War Office to go to Natal, and went there against his own will and judgement. This, however, was not true; and when I asked him he replied: "It was the most difficult business of all. I knew what it meant, and that it was doubtful whether we should get through to Ladysmith. I had not the nerve to order a subordinate to do it. I was the big man. I had to go myself."

What followed, with the exception of the battle of Colenso, our first experience of the Boer behind entrenchments, has been to some extent described in these letters. Viewed in the light of after knowledge it does not appear that the holding of Ladysmith was an unfortunate act.

The flower of the Boer army was occupied and exhausted in futile efforts to take the town and stave off the relieving forces. Four precious months were wasted by the enemy in a vain enterprise. Fierce and bloody fighting raged for several weeks with heavy loss to both sides, but without shame to either. In the end the British were completely victorious. Not only did their garrison endure famine, disease, and bombardment with constancy and composure and repel all assaults, but the soldiers of the relief column sustained undismayed repeated disappointments and reverses, and finally triumphed because through thick and thin they were loyal to their commander and more stubborn even than the stubborn Dutch.

In spite of, perhaps because of, some mistakes and many misfortunes the defence and relief of Ladysmith will not make a bad page in British history. Indeed it seems to me very likely that in future times our countrymen will think that we were most fortunate to find after a prolonged peace leaders of quality and courage, who were moreover honourable gentlemen, to carry our military affairs through all kinds of difficulties to a prosperous issue; and whatever may be said of the generals it is certain that all will praise the enduring courage of the regimental officer and the private soldier.

IAN
HAMILTON'S
MARCH

THIS COLLECTION OF LETTERS IS INSCRIBED

TO

LIEUT.-GENERAL IAN HAMILTON,

C.B., D.S.O.

WITH WHOSE MILITARY ACHIEVEMENTS

IT IS LARGELY CONCERNED

CONTENTS

MAPS AND PLANS

PREFACE

THIS BOOK is a continuation of those letters to the *Morning Post* newspaper on the South African War, which have been lately published under the title "London to Ladysmith *via* Pretoria". Although the letters had been read to some extent in their serial form, their reproduction in a book has been indulgently regarded by the public; and I am encouraged to repeat the experiment.

The principal event with which the second series deals is the march of Lieutenant-General Ian Hamilton's column on the flank of Lord Roberts's main army from Bloemfontein to Pretoria. This force, which encountered and overcame the brunt of the Boer resistance, which, far from the railway, marched more than 400 miles through the most fertile parts of the enemy's country, which fought ten general actions and fourteen smaller affairs, and captured five towns, was, owing to the difficulties of telegraphing, scarcely attended by a single newspaper correspondent, and accompanied continuously by none. Little has therefore been heard of its fortunes, nor do I know of anyone who is likely to write an account.

The letters now submitted to the public find in these facts their chief claim to be reprinted. While written in the style of personal narrative I have hitherto found it convenient to follow, they form a complete record of the operations of the flank column from the day when Ian Hamilton left Bloemfontein to attack the Waterworks position, until he returned to Pretoria after the successful engagement of Diamond Hill.

Although in an account written mainly in the field, and immediately after the actual events, there must be mistakes, no care has been spared in the work. The whole book has been diligently revised. Four letters, which our long marches did not allow me to finish while with the troops, have been added and are now published for the first time. The rest have been lengthened or corrected by the light of after-knowledge and reflection, and although the epistolary

form remains, I hope the narrative will be found to be fairly con-
secutive.

I do not want the reader to think that the personal incidents and
adventures described in this book are extraordinary, and beyond
the common lot of those who move unrestricted about the field of
war. They are included in the narrative, not on account of any
peculiar or historic interest, but because this method is the easiest,
and, so far as my wit serves me, the best way of telling the story
with due regard at once to detail and proportion.

In conclusion I must express my obligations to the proprietors
of the *Morning Post* newspaper for the assistance they have given
my publishers in allowing them to set up the copy as each letter
arrived from the war; to the DUKE OF MARLBOROUGH, to whom I
am indebted for the details of the strength and composition of the
force which will be found in the Appendix, and for much assistance
in the attempt to attain accuracy; and thirdly, to MR. FRANKLAND,
whose manly record of the heavy days he passed as a prisoner in
Pretoria may help to make this book acceptable to the public.

                                   WINSTON S. CHURCHILL

LONDON
September 10, 1900

CHAPTER ONE

A ROVING COMMISSION

In the train near Pieters, Natal: March 31, 1900

LADYSMITH, HER garrison and her rescuers, were still recovering, the one from the effects of long confinement, the other from over-exertion. All was quiet along the Tugela except for the plashing of the waters, and from Hunger's Poort to Weenen no sound of rifle or cannon shot disturbed the echoes.

The war had rolled northward: the floods of invasion that had isolated—almost overwhelmed—Ladysmith and threatened to submerge the whole country had abated and receded, so that the Army of Natal might spread itself out to feed and strengthen at its leisure and convenience on the re-conquered territory.

Knox's (Ladysmith) Brigade went into camp at Arcadia, five miles west of the town. Howard's (Ladysmith) Brigade retired to the breezy plains south of Colenso. Clery's Division—for the gallant Clery, recovered from his sickness, had displaced the gallant and successful Lyttelton—moved north and encamped beyond Elandslaagte along the banks of Sunday's River. Hunter's Division was disposed with one brigade at Elandslaagte and one at Tinta Inyoni. Warren, whom it was no longer necessary to send to the Cape Colony, established himself and his two brigades north of Ladysmith, along the railway line to the Orange Free State. Brocklehurst, with the remnants of what had once been almost a Cavalry Division, and now could scarcely mount three squadrons, occupied a neighbouring plain, sending his regiments one by one to Colenso, or even Mooi River, to be re-horsed; and around all this great Army, resting after its labours and preparing for fresh efforts, the Cavalry brigades of Dundonald and Burn-Murdoch drew an immense curtain of pickets and patrols which extended from Acton Homes in the east, through Bester's Station right round to

Wessel's Nek and further still, and which enabled the protected soldiers within to close their eyes by night and stretch their legs by day.

Meanwhile, the burghers had all retreated to the Drakensberg and the Biggarsberg and other refuges, from which elevated positions they defied intrusion or attack, and their scattered line stretched in a vast crescent even around our widely extended front from the Tintwa Pass, through Waschbank to Pomeroy.

But with the exception of outpost skirmishes, wholly unimportant to those not engaged in them, a strange peace brooded over Natal, and tranquillity was intensified by the recollection of the struggle that was over and the anticipation of the struggle that impended. It was a lull in the storm.

All this might be war, but it was not journalism. The tempest for the moment had passed, and above the army in Natal the sky was monotonously blue. It was true that dark clouds hung near the northern horizon, but who should say when they would break? Not, at any rate, for three weeks, I thought, and so resolved to fill the interval by trying to catch a little of the tempest elsewhere.

After the relief of Ladysmith four courses offered themselves to Sir Redvers Buller. To stand strictly on the defensive in Natal and to send Lord Roberts every man and gun who could be spared; to break into the Free State by forcing Van Reenen's Pass or the Tintwa; to attack the twelve thousand Boers in the Biggarsberg, clear Natal, and invade the Transvaal through the Vryheid district; and, lastly, to unite and reorganise and co-operate with Lord Roberts's main advance either by striking west or north.

Which course would be adopted? I made inquiries. Staff officers, bland and inscrutable—it is wonderful how well men can keep secrets they have not been told—continued to smile and smile. Brigadiers frankly confessed their ignorance. The general-in-chief observed pleasantly that he would "go for" the enemy as soon as he was ready, but was scarcely precise about when and where.

It was necessary to go to more humble sources for truth, and after diligent search I learned from a railway porter, or somebody like that, that all attempts to repair the bridge across the Sunday's River had been postponed indefinitely. This, on further inquiry, proved to be true.

Now, what does this mean? It means, I take it, that no direct advance against the Biggarsberg is intended for some time; and as the idea of reducing the Natal Army to reinforce the Cape Colony forces has been definitely abandoned the western line of advance suggests itself.

It would be absurd to force Van Reenen's Pass with heavy loss of life, when by waiting until the main army has reached, let us say, Kroonstad, we could walk through without opposition; so that it looks very likely that the Natal troops will do nothing until Lord Roberts's advance is more developed, and that then they will enter the Free State and operate in conjunction with him, all of which is strategy and common sense besides. At any rate there will be a long delay.

Therefore, I said to myself, I will go to Bloemfontein, see all that may be seen there and on the way, and rejoin the Natal Army when it comes through the passes. Such was the plan, and the reader shall be a witness of its abandonment.

I left the camp of Dundonald's Brigade early in the morning of the 29th of March, and riding through Ladysmith, round the hill on which stands the battered convent, now serving as headquarters, and down the main street, along which the relieving Army had entered the city, reached the railway station and caught the 10 a.m. down train.

We were delayed for a few minutes by the departure for Elands-laagte of a train load of Volunteers, the first to reach the Natal Army, and the officers hastened to look at these citizen soldiers. There were five companies in all, making nearly a thousand men, fine-looking fellows, with bright intelligent eyes, which they turned inquiringly on every object in turn, pointing and laughing at the numerous shell holes in the corrugated iron engine sheds and other buildings of the station.

A few regulars—sunburnt men, who had fought their way in with Buller—sauntered up to the trucks, and began a conversation with the reinforcement. I caught a fragment: "Cattle trucks, are they? Well, they didn't give us no blooming cattle trucks. No, no! We came into Ladysmith in a first-class doubly extry Pullman car. 'Oo sent 'em? Why, President —— Kruger, of course," whereat there was much laughter.

I must explain that the epithet which the average soldier uses so often as to make it perfectly meaningless, and which we conveniently express by a ——, is always placed immediately before the noun it is intended to qualify. For instance, no soldier would

under any circumstances say " —— Mr. Kruger has pursued a ——
reactionary policy," but "Mr. —— Kruger has pursued a reactionary —— policy." Having once voyaged for five days down the
Nile in a sailing boat with a company of Grenadiers, I have had
the best opportunities for being acquainted with these idiomatic
constructions, and I insert this little note in case it may be useful
to some of our national poets and minstrels.

The train started across the well-known ground, and how fast
and easily it ran. Already we were bounding through the scrub
in which a month before Dundonald's leading squadrons, galloping
in with beating hearts, had met the hungry picket line.

Intombi Spruit hospital camp was reached in a quarter of an
hour. Hospital camp no longer, thank goodness! Since the bridge
had been repaired the trains had been busy, and two days before I
left the town the last of the 2,500 sick had been moved down to
the great hospital and convalescent camps at Mooi River and High-
lands, or on to the ships in the Durban Harbour. Nothing remained
behind but 100 tents and marquees, a stack of iron cots, the cook
houses, the drinking-water tanks, and 600 graves. Ghastly Intombi
had faded into the past, as a nightmare flies at the dawn of day.

We sped swiftly across the plain of Pieters, and I remembered
how I had toiled across it, some five months before, a miserable
captive, casting longing eyes at the Ladysmith balloon, and
vigilantly guarded by the Boer mounted escort. Then the train ran
into the deep ravine between Barton's Hill and Railway Hill,
the ravine the cavalry had "fanned" on the day of the battle, and,
increasing its pace as we descended towards the Tugela, carried us
along the whole front of the Boer position. Signs of the fighting
appeared on every side. Biscuit tins flashed brightly on the hillside like heliographs. In places the slopes were honeycombed with
little stone walls and traverses, masking the sheltering refuges of
the infantry battalions during the week they had lain in the sun-
blaze exposed to the cross-fire of gun and rifle. White wooden
crosses gleamed here and there among the thorn bushes. The
dark lines of the Boer trenches crowned the hills. The train swept
by—and that was all.

I knew every slope, every hillock and accident of ground, as one
knows men and women in the world. Here was good cover. There
was a dangerous space. Here it was wise to stoop, and there to
run. Behind that steep kopje a man might scorn the shrapnel.

Those rocks gave sure protection from the flanking rifle fire. Only a month ago how much these things had meant. If we could carry that ridge it would command those trenches, and that might mean the hill itself, and perhaps the hill would lead to Ladysmith. Only a month ago these things meant honour or shame, victory or defeat, life or death. An anxious Empire and a waiting world wanted to know about every one of them—and now they were precisely what I have said, dark jumbled mounds of stone and scrub, with a few holes and crevices scratched in them, and a litter of tin pots, paper, and cartridge-cases strewn about.

The train steamed cautiously over the temporary wooden bridge at Colenso and ran into the open country beyond. On we hurried past the green slope where poor Long's artillery had been shot to bits, past Gun Hill, whence the great naval guns had fired so often, through Chieveley Camp, or rather through the site of Chieveley Camp, past the wreck of the armoured train—still lying where we had dragged it with such labour and peril, just clear of the line—through Frere and Estcourt, and so, after seven hours' journey, we came to Pietermaritzburg.

An officer who was travelling down with me pointed out the trenches on the signal hill above the town.

"Seems queer," he said, "to think that the Boers might so easily have taken this town. When we dug those trenches they were expected every day, and the Governor, who refused to leave the capital and was going to stick it out with us, had his kit packed ready to come up into the entrenchments at an hour's notice."

It was very pleasant to know that those dark and critical days were gone, and that the armies in the field were strong enough to maintain the Queen's dominions against any further invasion; yet one could not but recall with annoyance that the northern part of Natal was still in the hands of the enemy. Not for long, however, shall this endure.

After waiting in Pietermaritzburg long enough only to dine, I proceeded by the night train to Durban, and was here so fortunate as to find a Union boat, the *Guelph*, leaving almost immediately for East London. The weather was fine, the sea comparatively smooth, and the passengers few and unobtrusive, so that the voyage, being short, might almost be considered pleasant.

The captain took the greatest interest in the war, which he had followed with attention, and with the details and incidents of which he was extraordinarily familiar. He had brought out a ship full of volunteers, new drafts, and had much to say concerning the British soldier and his comrades in arms.

The good news which had delighted and relieved everyone had reached him in the most dramatic and striking manner. When they left England Roberts had just begun his welcome advance, and the public anxiety was at its height. At Madeira there was an English cable to say that he was engaging Cronje, and that no news had arrived for three days. This was supplied, however, by the Spanish wire, which asserted with circumstantial details that the British had been heavily defeated and had fled south beyond the Orange River. With this to reflect on, they had to sail. Imagine the doubts and fears that flourished in ten days of ignorance, idleness, and speculation. Imagine with what feelings they approached St. Helena. He told me that when the tug boat came off no man dared hail them for news. Nor was it until the launch was alongside that a soldier cried out nervously, "The war, the war: what's happened there!" and when they heard the answer, "Cronje surrendered; Ladysmith relieved," he said that such a shout went up as he had never heard before, and I believed him.

After twenty-four hours of breeze and tossing the good ship found herself in the roads at East London, and having by this time had quite enough of the sea I resolved to disembark forthwith.

CHAPTER TWO

EXIT GENERAL GATACRE

Bethany: April 13, 1900

I F Y O U go to sleep when the train leaves East London, you should wake, all being well, to find yourself at Queenstown.

Queenstown lies just beyond the high-water mark of war. The tide had flowed strong after Stormberg, and it looked as if Queenstown would be engulfed, at any rate for a time. But Fortune and General Gatacre protected it. Sterkstroom entrenched itself, and prepared for daily attacks. Molteno was actually shelled. Queenstown suffered none of the horrors of war except martial law, which it bore patiently rather than cheerfully.

Nothing in the town impresses the traveller, but at the dining-room of the railway station there is a very little boy, about twelve years old, who, unaided, manages to serve, with extraordinary despatch and a grand air, a whole score of passengers during the brief interval allowed for refreshments.

Five months earlier I had passed along this line, hoping to get into Ladysmith before the door was shut, and had been struck by this busy child, who seemed a product of America rather than of Africa. Much had happened in the meantime, not so far from where he lived. But here he was still—the war had not interfered with him, Queenstown was beyond the limit.

At Sterkstroom a line of empty trenches, the Red Cross flag over a hospital, and an extension to the cemetery enclosure filled with brown mounds which the grass had not yet had time to cover, showed that we had crossed the line between peace and war. Passing through Molteno, the last resting-place of the heroic de Montmorency, the train reached Stormberg. Scarcely any traces of the Boer occupation were to be seen; the marks of their encampments behind the ridge where they had laagered—a litter of meat

tins, straw, paper, and the like, the grave of Commandant Swane-
poole and several nameless heaps, a large stone (in the stationmaster's possession) with the words engraved on it: "In memory of
the Transvaal commando, Stormberg, December 1899", and that
was all. The floods had abated and receded. This was the only
jetsam that remained.

At Stormberg I changed my mind, or, rather—for it comes to
the same thing and sounds better—I made it up.

I heard that no immediate advance from Bloemfontein was
likely or even possible for a fortnight. Therefore, I said, I will go
to Capetown, and shelter for a week at "The Helot's Rest". After
all, what is the use of a roving commission if one cannot rove at
random or caprice?

So to Capetown I went accordingly—seven hundred miles in
forty-eight hours of bad trains over sections of the line only newly
reopened. But to Capetown I will not take the reader. Indeed, I
strongly recommend him to stick to the war and keep his attention
at the front, for Capetown at this present time is not an edifying
place. Yet, since he may be curious to know some reason for such
advice, let me explain.

Capetown, which stands, as some writers have observed, beneath
the shadow of Table Mountain, has been—and may be again in
times of peace—a pleasant place in which to pursue business or
health; but now it is simply a centre of intrigue, scandal, falsehood,
and rumour.

The visitor stays at the Mount Nelson Hotel, if he can be so
fortunate as to secure a room. At this establishment he finds all
the luxuries of a first-class European hotel without the resulting
comfort. There is a good dinner, but it is cold before it reaches him;
there is a spacious dining-room, but it is overcrowded; there are
clean European waiters, but they are few and far between.

At the hotel, in its garden, or elsewhere in the town, all the
world and his wife are residing—particularly the wife.

We used to think, in the Army of Natal, that Lord Roberts's
operations in the Free State had been a model of military skill and
knowledge, and, in a simple way, we regarded French as one of the
first cavalry soldiers of the age.

All this was corrected at Capetown, and I learned with painful
disenchantment that "it" (the said operations) had all been a
shameful muddle from beginning to end; that the Field-Marshal

had done this and that and the other "which no man in his senses", &c., that French was utterly . . . and as for Lord Kitchener, Capetown—let us be just, imported social Capetown—was particularly severe on Lord Kitchener.

It was very perplexing; and besides it seemed that these people ought to know, for they succeeded in making more news in the twenty-four hours than all the correspondents at the front put together. The whole town was overrun with amateur strategists and gossiping women. There were more colonels to the acre than in any place outside the United States, and if the social aspect was unattractive, the political was scarcely more pleasing.

Party feeling ran high. Some of the British section, those tremendous patriots who demonstrate but do not fight—not to be on any account compared with the noble fellows who fill the volunteer corps—pot-house heroes, and others of that kidney, had just distinguished themselves by mobbing Mr. Schreiner in the streets.

The Dutch section, some of them the men who, risking nothing themselves, had urged the Republics to their ruin, all of whom had smiled and rubbed their hands at the British reverses, sat silent in public, but kept a strict watch on incoming steamers for members of Parliament and others of more influence than guile, and whispered honeyed assurances of their devotion to the Empire, coupled with all sorts of suggestions about the settlement—on the broad general principle of "Heads I win, tails you lose".

British newspapers advocated short shrift to rebels—"Hit 'em hard now they're down"; "Give them a lesson this time, the dirty Dutchmen!" Dutch papers recorded the events of the war in the tone, "At the end of the battle the British, as usual, fled precipitately, leaving 2,000 killed, *our* loss"—no, not quite that, but very nearly; everything, in fact, but the word "our"—"one killed, two slightly wounded".

Let no one stay long in Capetown now who would carry away a true impression of the South Africans. There is too much shoddy worn there at present.

Only at Government House did I find the Man of No Illusions, the anxious but unwearied Proconsul, understanding the faults and the virtues of both sides, measuring the balance of rights and wrongs, and determined—more determined than ever; for is it not the only hope for the future of South Africa?—to use his knowledge and his power to strengthen the Imperial ties.

All this time the reader has been left on a siding at Naauwpoort; but does he complain of not being taken to Capetown? We will hasten back together to the healthier atmosphere of war.

Indeed, the spell of the great movements impending in the Free State began to catch hold of me before I had travelled far on the line towards Bloemfontein. Train loads of troops filled every station or siding. A ceaseless stream of men, horses, and guns had been passing northwards for a fortnight, and on the very day that I made the journey Lord Kitchener had ordered that in future all troops must march beyond Springfontein, because the line must be cleared for the passage of supplies, so that, besides the trains in the sidings, there were columns by the side of the railway steadily making their way to the front.

The one passenger train in the day stopped at Bethany. I got out. To go on was to reach Bloemfontein at midnight. Better, then, to sleep here and proceed at dawn.

"Are there many troops here?" I asked. They replied, "The whole of the Third Division." "Who commands?" "Gatacre." That decided me.

I knew the general slightly, having made his acquaintance up the Nile in pleasant circumstances, for no one was allowed to pass his mess hungry or thirsty. I was very anxious to see him and hear all about Stormberg and the rest of the heavy struggle along the eastern line of rail. I found him in a tin house close to the station. He received me kindly, and we had a long talk. The General explained to me many things which I had not understood before, and after we had done with past events he turned with a hopeful eye to the future. At last, and for the first time, he was going to have the division of which he had originally been given the command.

"You know I only had two and a half battalions at Sterkstroom and a few colonial horse; but now I have got both my brigades complete."

I thought him greatly altered from the dashing, energetic man I had known up the river, or had heard about on the frontier or in plague-stricken Bombay. Four months of anxiety and abuse had left their mark on him. The weary task of keeping things going with utterly insufficient resources, and in the face of an adroit and powerful enemy in a country of innumerable kopjes, where every advantage lay with the Boer, had bowed that iron frame and tired

the strange energy which had made him so remarkable among
soldiers. But when he thought of the future his face brightened.
The dark days were over. The broken rocky wilderness lay behind,
and around rolled the grassy plains of the Free State. He had his
whole division at last. Moreover, there was prospect of immediate
action. So I left him, for it was growing late, and went my way.
Early next morning he was dismissed from his command and
ordered to England, broken, ruined, and disgraced.

I will not for one moment dispute the wisdom or the justice of
his removal. In stormy weather one must trust to the man at the
helm, and when he is such a man as Lord Roberts it is not a very
hard thing to do. But because General Gatacre has been cruelly
persecuted in England by people quite ignorant of the difficulties
of war or of the conditions under which it is carried on in this
country, it is perhaps not out of place to write a few words of
different tenor.

Gatacre was a man who made his way in the army, not through
any influence or favour which he enjoyed, but by sheer hard work
and good service. Wherever he had served he had left a high record
behind him. On the Indian frontier he gained the confidence of so
fine a soldier as Sir Bindon Blood, and it was largely to his reputation won in the Chitral Expedition that his subsequent advance-
ment was due. At Bombay in 1897 he was entrusted with the duty
of fighting the plague, then first gripping its deadly fingers into
the city. No one who is at all acquainted with the course of this
pest will need to be told how excellent was his work. After the late
Soudan campaign I travelled from Bombay to Poona with a
Parsee gentleman, a wealthy merchant of the plague-stricken town,
and I well remember how he dilated on the good which Gatacre
had done.

"He was our only chance," said the black man. "Now he is gone,
and the sickness will stay for ever."

Gatacre's part in the Soudan campaign has been described at
length elsewhere. His courage has never been questioned, because
the savage critics did not wish to damage their cause by obvious
absurdities. If I were to discuss his tactics in the Boer war here I
should soon get on to ground which I have forbidden myself. It
is sufficient to observe that Gatacre retained the confidence and
affection of his soldiers in the most adverse circumstances. When
the weary privates struggled back to camp after the disastrous

day at Stormberg they were quite clear on one point: "No one could have got us out but him." Two days before he was dismissed the Cameron Highlanders passed through Bethany, and the men recognised the impetuous leader of the Atbara charge; and, knowing he had fallen among evil days, cheered him in the chivalry of the common man. The poor general was much moved at this spontaneous greeting, which is a very rare occurrence in our phlegmatic, well-ordered British Army. Let us hope the sound will long ring in his ears, and, as it were, light a bright lamp of memory in the chill and dreary evening of life.

Exit General Gatacre. "Now," as my Parsee merchant remarked, "he is gone"; and I suppose there are, here and there, notes of triumph. But among them I will strike a note of warning. If the War Office breaks generals not so much for incapacity as for want of success with any frequency, it will not find men to fight for it in brigade and divisional commands. Every man who knows the chances of war feels himself insecure. The initiative which an unsympathetic discipline has already killed, or nearly killed, in younger officers, will wither and die in their superiors. You will have generals as before, but they will not willingly risk the fruits of long years of service in damnable countries and of perils of all kinds. They will look at the enemy's position. They will endeavour to divide responsibility. They will ask for orders or instructions. But they will not fight—if they can possibly help it, and then only on the limited liability principle, which means the shedding of much blood without any result. Besides, as an irreverent subaltern remarked to me: "If you begin with Gatacre, where are you going to end? What about poor old ——?"

But I dare not pursue the subject further.

CHAPTER THREE

AT HALF-WAY HOUSE

Bloemfontein: April 16, 1900

AFTER A decent interval let the curtain rise on a new act. The scene and most of the characters are different, but it is same play. The town—a town of brick and tin—stands at the apparent edge of a vast plain of withered grass, from whose inhospitable aspect it turns and nestles, as if for protection, round the scrub-covered hills to northward. From among the crowd of one-storied dwelling-houses, more imposing structures, the seats of Government and commerce, rise prominently to catch the eye and impress the mind with the pleasing prospect of wealthier civilisation. Here and there are towers and pinnacles, and, especially remarkable, a handsome building surrounded in the classic style by tall white pillars, and, surmounted by a lofty dome, looks like a Parliament House, but for the Red Cross flag which flies from the summit and proclaims that, whatever may have been its former purposes, the spacious hall within is at last devoted to the benefit of mankind. The dark hills—their uncertain outline marked at one point by the symmetrical silhouette of a fort—form the background of the picture: Bloemfontein, April, 1900.

It is five o'clock in the afternoon. The Market-square is crowded with officers and soldiers listening to the band of the Buffs. Every regiment in the service, every Colony in the Empire is represented; all clad in uniform khaki, but distinguished by an extraordinary variety of badges.

Each group is a miniature system of Imperial Federation. The City Volunteer talks to a Queensland Mounted Infantryman, who hands his matchbox to a private of the Line. A Bushman from New Zealand, a Cambridge undergraduate, and a tea-planter from Ceylon stroll up and make the conversation general. On every side all kinds of men are intermingled, united by the sympathy of a common purpose and soldered together in the fire of war. And this will be of great consequence later on.

The inhabitants—bearded burghers who have made their peace, townsfolk who never desired to make a quarrel—stand round and watch complacently. After all, there are worse things than to be defeated. Demand is keen, the army is wealthy, and prices are high. Trade has followed hard on the flag which waves from every building; and, whether it be for merchandise or farm produce, the market is buoyant.

The officers congregate about the pretentious building of the club, and here I find acquaintances gathered together from all the sentry beats of the Empire, for the regular army usually works like a kaleidoscope, and, new combinations continually forming, scatter old friends in every direction. But here all are collected once more, and the man we met on the frontier, the man we met "up the river", the man we met at manœuvres with the comrade of Sandhurst, the friend or enemy of Harrow days, and the rival of a Meerut tournament, stand in a row together. Merry military music, laughing faces, bright, dainty little caps, a moving throng, and the consciousness that this means a victorious British Army in the capital of the Free State, drive away all shadows from the mind.

One cannot see any gaps in the crowd; it is so full of animation that the spaces where Death has put his hand are not to be seen. The strong surges of life have swept across them as a sunny sea closes over the foundered ship. Yet they are not quite forgotten.

"Hullo, my dear old boy, I am glad to see you. When did you get up here? Have you brought —— with you? Oh, I am sorry. It must have been a fever-stricken hole, that Ladysmith. Poor chap! Do you remember how he . . . Charlie has gone home. He can never play polo again—expanding bullet smashed his arm all to bits. Bad luck, wasn't it? Now we've got to find a new back . . . and —— was killed at Paardeberg . . . spoiled the whole team." The band struck into a lively tune. "How long is it going to last?"

"With luck it ought to be over by October, just a year from start to finish."

"I thought you said something about Pretoria the third week in March."

"Ah, I must have meant May, or, perhaps, June."

"Or August."

"Who can tell? But I think this is the half-way house."

The conversation stops abruptly. Everyone looks round. Strolling across the middle of the square, quite alone, was a very small grey-haired gentleman, with extremely broad shoulders and a most unbending back. He wore a staff cap with a broad red band and a heavy gold-laced peak, brown riding boots, a tightly-fastened belt, and no medals, orders, or insignia of any kind. But no one doubted his identity for an instant, and I knew that I was looking at the Queen's greatest subject, the commander who had in the brief space of a month revolutionised the fortunes of the war, had turned disaster into victory, and something like despair into almost inordinate triumph.

Other soldiers of career and quality mingle with the diversified throng. Macdonald sits on a bay pony near the club verandah talking to Martyr of the Mounted Infantry and of Central African repute. Pole-Carew, who came to the Cape as Sir Redvers Buller's camp commandant, and passed at a bound to brigadier-general, and by another still greater leap to the command of the Eleventh Division, canters across the square. General French and his staff have just ridden up. But the central figure holds all eyes, and everyone knows that it is on him, and him alone, that the public fortunes depend.

Such was the scene on the afternoon of my arrival in Bloemfontein. What of the situation? The first thing to be done after the occupation of the town was to re-open the railway. The presence of a large army in their rear and the swift advance of Gatacre and Clements compelled the invaders to withdraw from Cape Colony, so that Norval's Pont and Bethulie bridges were once more in British hands. Both were, however, destroyed or partially destroyed. Besides these, various other smaller bridges and culverts had been blown up. All these were forthwith repaired by the engineers, and through communication by rail was established between the advanced Field Army in the Free State and the sea bases at East London, Port Elizabeth, and Capetown.

In the meantime the army at Bloemfontein lived on the reserve of rations it had carried from Modder River. When the railway was opened the line from Modder River was dropped. A broad-gauge railway, even though it be only a single line, is usually capable of supplying an army of at least 50,000 men with considerable ease, and the reader may remember how the Natal

Government Railway was able to support 30,000 men through January and February, to transport reinforcements and sick, and to run all its ordinary traffic in addition. But the repaired or provisional bridges on the Bloemfontein line caused so much delay that the carrying power of the railway was seriously diminished. When a permanent bridge has been blown up two alternatives present themselves to the engineers: a high-level or a low-level substitute. The high-level bridge, such as was thrown across the Tugela after the relief of Ladysmith, takes much longer to build, but, when built, trains are run straight over it with very little diminution of speed. It is, moreover, secure against floods.

The low-level bridge must be approached by zigzag ramps, which impose frequent shuntings, and cause great delay; and it is, of course, only to be trusted when there are no floods. But it has this inestimable advantage in military operations: speed in construction. The army must be fed immediately. So the low-level bridges were chosen; hence an early but reduced supply. When this was further minimised by the passage of reinforcements the commissariat depots could scarcely make headway, but must be content to feed the army from day to day and accumulate at the rate, perhaps, of only one day in three, or even one in four. It was, therefore, evident that no offensive movement to the northward could be made for several weeks.

See how the stomach governs the world. By the rapid invasion of their territories, by the staggering blows which they had been dealt at Kimberley, Paardeberg, Poplar Grove, and Driefontein, and by the bad news from Natal, the Boers in the Free State were demoralised. If we could have pressed them unceasingly the whole country would have been conquered to the Vaal River. Encouraged by Lord Roberts's Proclamation, and believing that all resistance in the Southern Republic was at an end, great numbers of Free Staters returned to their homes, took the oath of neutrality, and prepared to accept the inevitable.

But while the army waited, as it was absolutely forced to wait, to get supplies, to get horses—to get thousands of horses—to give the infantry new boots, and all arms a little breathing space, the Boers recovered from their panic, pulled themselves together, and, for the moment, boldly seized the offensive.

Great, though perhaps temporary, were the advantages which they gained. The belief that the war in the Free State was at an end, which had led so many of the burghers to return to their farms, was shared to some extent by the British commander, and loudly proclaimed by his colonial advisers. To protect the farmers who had made their peace the Imperial forces were widely extended. A line was drawn across the Free State from Fourteen Streams, through Boshof, Bloemfontein, and Thabanchu, south of which it was assumed that the country was pacified and conquered.

Meanwhile Olivier and the southern commando, recalled from their operations in the Cape Colony, were making a hurried and, as it seemed, a desperate march to rejoin the main Boer forces. They expected the attack of the same terrible army which had already devoured Cronje; nor was it until they reached Ladybrand and found only Pilcher with a few hundred men snapping at their heels that they realised that the bulk of the British troops were for the moment practically immobile at Bloemfontein. Then they turned.

Pilcher fled warily before them, and fell back on Broadwood's Brigade, near Thabanchu. With renewed courage and strong reinforcements from their friends north of the line of occupation they pressed on. Broadwood was compelled to fall back on the Ninth Division, which was camped west of the waterworks. He made a twenty-mile march at night and laagered in the small hours of the morning, thinking, as most people would think, that pursuit was for the time being shaken off. Morning broke, and with it a Boer cannonade.

I do not intend to be drawn into a detailed description of the action that followed. For many reasons it deserves separate and detailed consideration, chiefly because it shows the Boer at his very best: crafty in war and, above all things, deadly cool. In a word, what happened was this: The shells crashed into the laager. Everyone said, "Take the blasted waggons out of the shell fire. We will cover their retreat"; which they did most beautifully: Broad-wood displaying all the skill which had enabled him to disentangle the reconnaissance of the 5th of April near the Atbara from the clutches of the Dervishes. The said waggons hurried out of the shell fire only to fall into the frying-pan of an ambuscade. Guns, prisoners and much material fell into the hands of the Boers. The Ninth Division retreated suddenly—too suddenly, say the army, with other remarks which it is not my business to transcribe—on Bloemfontein, and the force of the storm fell on Gatacre.

Gatacre had a post at Dewetsdorp: three companies of the Royal Irish Rifles, two of Mounted Infantry. So soon as he heard of the retirement of the Ninth Division he sent orders by many routes for his post to fall back too. They fell back accordingly; but at Reddersburg the net closed round them. Let us judge no man harshly or in ignorance. Fighting followed. With a loss of eight killed and thirty-one wounded, the retreating troops surrendered when relief was scarcely five miles away. Everything curled back on to Bloemfontein and the railway line, which it was *vital* to hold. Reinforcements were thrust to the front to meet the emergency: Rundle, with the Eighth Division, was diverted from Kimberley to Springfontein; Hunter, with the Tenth Division (our old friends the Irish and Fusilier Brigades), started from Natal, thus condemning Buller to the strict defensive, and the Boers swept southward.

Now, in accordance with the terms of Lord Roberts's Proclamation, many farmers of the Free State, fighting men of the Boer Army—that is to say, who had thought that all was up: deserters, in other words—had come into the British posts, made their submission, taken the oath, and returned to their farms. The Boers were very angry with these people. What protection could we give them? Some, it is said—it may be a lie—were shot by the enemy. Most of them, from fear or inclination, rejoined their commandos.

The whole of the right-hand bottom corner of the Free State was overrun. Southward still hastened the Boer forces. Brabant was the next to feel the tempest. His garrison in Wepener was assailed, surrounded, fought well—perhaps is now fighting desperately. Other Boers approached the rebel districts of Cape Colony. The lately penitent rebels stirred, are stirring.

Mark, by the way, this sedition is not the result of misplaced generosity but of military misfortunes. No one expects beaten men to be grateful; but, under certain conditions, they will be loyal. An enemy at their throats is not one of those conditions. Southward still sweep the commandos *with empty carts*, for this is the most fertile of all the Republican territories; and, in the meanwhile, what are we doing? Divisions and brigades are being moved by a strong yet deliberate hand. The hope—general and special idea in one—is to catch these bold fellows who have thrust their heads thus far into the lion's mouth and enjoyed until now such immunity. Wepener making a brave defence; Brabant marching through

Rouxville to bar their advance; Rundle, Chermside, and Brabazon striking east from Edenburg to shut the door behind them with two infantry divisions, twenty-four guns, and 2,000 yeomanry; and, further north, the great Bloemfontein Army—four infantry divisions, Hamilton's 10,000 mounted men, French's four cavalry brigades, and many guns—is almost ready to move. Assuredly these Boers are in a dangerous place. Will they escape? Will they, perhaps, carry some part of the intercepting lines with them as a trophy of victory? "Qui vivra verra", and, if these letters continue, "who runs may read", for I purpose to journey via Edenburg to Reddersburg tomorrow, and thence on to the point of collision, which must mark the climax of this extremely interesting event henceforward to be called "The Operations in the Right-hand Bottom Corner of the Free State".

CHAPTER FOUR

TWO DAYS WITH BRABAZON

Before Dewetsdorp: April 21, 1900

WHEN THE incursion of the Boers into the recently pacified districts became known, the Eighth Division (Rundle) was diverted from Kimberley, whither it was proceeding, and concentrated at Springfontein. The Third Division (Chermside, in supersession of Gatacre) massed at Bethany. Still more troops were needed to guard the line and clear the country.

Sir Redvers Buller was asked whether he could co-operate by forcing Van Reenen's Pass and bringing pressure on the enemy's line of retreat. His position in the centre of the triangle of Natal was, however, an inconvenient one. The strategic advantages possessed by the Boers in this scene of the war have before been noticed. But it may be worth while to explain them again.

The enemy possess the superiority of an enveloping frontier. If Sir Redvers Buller moves west through Van Reenen's Pass to make the diversion required in the Free State, down will come the Boers from the Biggarsberg on his communications and into South Natal. If he moves north to attack the Biggarsberg positions in order to clear Natal he will cut the Boers on his left flank and line.

According to the best information there are three thousand Boers on the Drakensberg Passes, and ten thousand on the Biggarsberg. Buller, therefore, would have preferred to mask Van Reenen's with the Ladysmith Division (Fourth, Lyttelton), which was getting well and strong again, and move northwards with the Second, Fifth, and Tenth Divisions. He did not consider until northern Natal should be cleared that he could safely move westward. On the other hand, the need in the Free State was urgent, and it was therefore arranged that the Tenth Division (Hunter) should come by sea to East London—one brigade to replace the division diverted from Kimberley, one brigade to Bethulie, and that the rest of the Natal Field Army should remain strictly on the defensive until the situation was materially altered.

Practically, therefore, five brigades of troops were available for the operations in the right-hand bottom corner: Hart, with a brigade of Hunter's Division at Bethulie, the Third and Eighth Divisions under Chermside and Rundle at Springfontein and Bethany. Besides these powerful bodies, which were quite independent of the communication troops or the Bloemfontein Army, there were fourteen hundred yeomanry and mounted infantry under General Brabazon, and Brabant's Colonial Brigade, about two thousand five hundred strong.

It is scarcely necessary to follow all the movements in exact detail. Rundle formed a column at Edenburg, and, marching to Reddersburg, joined his force to part of Chermside's Division from Bethany, thus having under his immediate command eight battalions, four batteries, and Brabazon's Mounted Brigade. Another brigade was collecting at Edenburg under Campbell. Hart was moved north-east towards Rouxville, where was also Brabant with a thousand horse. The rest of Brabant's force, some fifteen hundred strong, were blockaded in Wepener by the enemy. Such was the situation when I left Bloemfontein on the morning of the 17th.

I travelled prosperously; came by rail to Edenburg, trekked from there in drenching rains, most unusual for this time of year, and greatly increasing the difficulties of supply; and, resting for the night at Reddersburg, caught up the marching column in its camp, about eleven miles from Dewetsdorp, on the night of the 19th.

The position of the various troops was then as follows: Rundle, with eight battalions, four batteries, and fifteen hundred horse at Oorlogs Poort, about twelve miles from Dewetsdorp; Campbell, with two battalions and a battery near Rosendal, marching to join him; the Grenadier Guards double marching through Reddersburg to catch up the main force; Hart, with four battalions in Rouxville; Brabant, with one thousand horsemen eight miles north of Rouxville; Dalgety, with a garrison of fifteen hundred men, holding Wepener.

So far as could be learned the enemy had about seven thousand men with twelve guns south of the Bloemfontein-Thabanchu line under Commandants Olivier and De Wet, and with this force, which made up in enterprise and activity what it lacked in numbers or material, they were attempting to blockade and attack Wepener, to bar the road of Rundle's column to Dewetsdorp, and to check Brabant and Hart at Smithfield. Besides proposing this ambitious programme, the Boers sent their patrols riding about the country commandeering all pacified farmers under threats of death.

We had a very pleasant ride from Reddersburg, and it was evening when we rounded the shoulder of a grassy hill and saw the camp of the main British column before us. It lay about the foot of

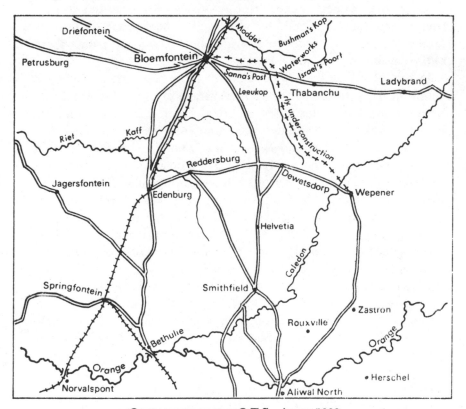

OPERATIONS IN THE O.F.S., APRIL 1900

a prominent knoll rising from a broad plain, which was in striking contrast to the mountains of Natal, and seemed to promise ample opportunity to the regular soldier. "Camp" is, perhaps, an inaccurate description, for there were scarcely any tents to be seen, and the rolling ground was littered with swarms of grazing horses and oxen, and overspread with an immense canopy of white smoke from the hundreds of gleaming grass fires lighted to cook the soldiers' suppers. I presented myself to Sir Leslie Rundle, who received me courteously, and briefly explained the outlines of the situation. We had arrived in the nick of time. The whole force would march at dawn. The scouts had exchanged shots during the day. The Kaffir spies reported that the enemy would fight on the morrow. What could be better? So with much satisfaction we went to bed.

There was a biting chill in the air when the first light of dawn began to grow in the sky, nor was I the only one who searched a modest kit for some of those warm clothes which our friends at home have thoughtfully been sending out. The South African winter was drawing near. But the sun soon rose, and we shivered no longer. The cavalry were early astir. Indeed their mounted squadrons in silhouette against the morning sky was my first waking impression, and by half-past five all were in motion. I started a little later, but it was not long before I overtook them. Though the command was not a large one, it presented several interesting features.

For the first time I saw the Imperial Yeomanry in the field. Trotting across the beautiful green pasture land in a most extended formation, to which they seemed readily to adapt themselves, were seven hundred yeomen, all good men and true, who had volunteered to fight because they understood the main causes of the quarrel, and from personal conviction earnestly desired to be of some assistance to the State, and who were, moreover, excellently mounted on smart, short-docked cobs, which they sat and rode like the sportsmen they mostly were.

We were moving along in a wide formation, which secured us against all possibilities of surprise, when suddenly I noticed that the scouts far in front were halted.

"Tit-tat, tit-tat": two shots from a high plateau to the right. Shots fired towards you, I must explain, make a double, and those fired away from you a single, report.

We had flushed one of the enemy's outposts. Riding nearer, I could see their figures—seven in all—exposed on the skyline. This showed they were only an outpost, and wished to make us believe they were more. When the Boer is in force he is usually invisible. Still, the position was a strong one, and it is always a possibility worth considering with the Boer that he may foresee your line of thought, and just go one step further, out of contrariness. General

Brabazon therefore halted his centre squadrons and detached a turning force of three companies of Yeomanry to the right.

We waited, watching the scouts exchange shots with the Boer picket, and watching—for it was a very pretty sight—the Yeomanry spread out and gallop away to the flank like a pack of hounds in full cry, each independent, yet the whole simultaneous. In a quarter of an hour they were scrambling up the steep sides of the plateau almost in rear of the obstructive picket, which hurriedly departed while time remained. Then the centre swung forward, and the whole cavalry force advanced again, the greater part of it moving on to the plateau, where a running fight with the Dutch outposts now commenced at long range.

Several times we thought that we had unmasked their main position, and that the cavalry work for the day was over; but each time Brabazon's turning movement on the right, the execution of which was entrusted to Colonel Sitwell, a very dashing officer of Egyptian note, compelled them to fall back. After an hour of this sort of thing we were in possession of practically the whole of the plateau, which turned out to be of large extent.

Beyond it, commanding it, essential to it, yet not of it, was a steep rocky kopje. The swift advance and the necessity of pressing the enemy had left the infantry a long way behind. The General felt, however, that this point must be secured. McNeill made a dash for it with the scouts. The yeomanry galloped off to the right again, as if about to surround it, and the Boers allowed themselves to be bounced out of this strong and important position, and scampered away to a smooth green hill a mile in rear. Brabazon made haste to occupy the captured kopje in force, and did so just in time, for as soon as the turning force—two companies (I am going to call them squadrons in future) of yeomanry and a company of mounted infantry—approached the green hill, the musketry suddenly grew from an occasional drip into a regular patter, and there was the loud boom of a field gun. We had found the main Boer position, and the cavalry came to a standstill.

The enemy now directed a very sharp fire on the captured kopje, which, it seems, they originally intended to hold had they not been hustled out of it as has been described. They also shelled the yeomanry—who were continuing the flank movement—rather heavily as they retired, inflicting some loss.

We had now to wait for the Infantry, and they lagged on the

road. The Boer fire began to take effect. Several soldiers were carried wounded off the top of the hill—one poor fellow shot through both cheek-bones. Others had to lie where they were struck because it was not possible to move them while the fire was so accurate.

On the reverse slope, however, there was good cover for man and horse. Some of the men were engaged for the first time, and, though their behaviour was excellent, the General thought it necessary to walk along the firing line and speak a few words here and there.

The infantry still lagged on the road, but at about two o'clock Sir Leslie Rundle himself arrived. The firing about the kopje had been loud, and a rumour—who starts these tales?—ran back along the marching columns that the cavalry were hard pressed, were running short of ammunition, and that the Boers were turning both flanks. At any rate, I found anxious faces in the divisional staff.

Rundle considered that the retention of the kopje was of first importance, and Sir Herbert Chermside, his second in command, fully agreed with him. But the Infantry of the advanced guard were alone near enough. It was decided to push them on. At this moment a reassuring message arrived from Brabazon engaging that he could hold his own, and hoping the Infantry would not be hurried so as to lose their breath.

Everyone was very cheerful after this, and when at last the leading battalion—the Worcester Regiment—marched to the kopje all were able to admire the fine cool way in which they crossed the dangerous ground behind it; and I myself saw three pom-pom shells strike all around a young officer, who waved his rifle thereat in high delight, and shouted out loudly, "By the left!" an order the purport of which I am as uncertain as the reader, but which, doubtless, was encouraging in spirit. When the infantry had relieved the mounted men the latter withdrew to safer positions, and as the evening was drawing on the action came to an end—by mutual consent and by the effective intervention of the British artillery.

The events of the next day, though according to the scale of the war unimportant, were nevertheless instructive from the military point of view, and, so far as they concerned me, sufficiently exciting to require, if not to deserve, a letter to themselves.

CHAPTER FIVE

TWO DAYS WITH BRABAZON (*continued*)

Camp before Dewetsdorp: April 22, 1900

WHETHER I am to see the white cliffs of Dover again I know not, nor will I attempt to predict. But it seems that my fortunes in this land are to be a succession of adventures and escapes, any one of which would suffice for a personal experience of the campaign. I acquit myself of all desire to seek for these. Indeed, I have zealously tried to avoid all danger except what must attend a War Correspondent's precarious existence. This I recognise as a necessary evil, for the lot of the writer in the field is a hard and heavy one. "All the danger of war and one-half per cent. the glory": such is our motto, and that is the reason why we expect large salaries. But these hazards swoop on me out of a cloudless sky, and that I have hitherto come unscathed through them, while it fills my heart with thankfulness to God for His mercies, makes me wonder why I must be so often thrust to the brink and then withdrawn.

However, I will tell the tale of the doings of the Army, and what happened to me shall fill its proper place, so that the reader may himself be the judge of the matter.

The night of the 20th passed quietly, but the Boers were awake with the sunrise and saluted us with discharges of the pom-pom, which, as far as I could see, did no harm to anyone. We could not press the attack on the previous day because the Infantry were tired out and the enemy's position of sufficient natural strength to make an assault a serious business. In the night the Dutchmen had been busy, and the black lines of entrenchments marked the hillsides. When I inquired whether there would be a battle or not that day, staff officers pointed over the veldt to a column of dust which was coming slowly nearer.

General Campbell, with three battalions (including two of Her Majesty's Guards) and a battery, was marching to join the main column. It was necessary, in view of the entrenchments and the approaching reinforcements, to wait until the force was complete. The event would be decided on the morrow, and meanwhile Brabazon and the mounted troops—cavalry, I shall call them— were to make a reconnaissance of the Boer left.

The brigade, which included the mounted infantry, and was about a thousand strong, moved southward behind the outpost line and, making a rapid and wide circuit, soon came on the enemy's left flank. Here we waited while patrols were pushed out and while Brabazon was clearing his own right by a still wider turning movement. The patrols soon drew the fire of the Boer pickets, and the rifle shots began to ring out in the clear cool air of the morning. Presently a party of a dozen Boers appeared in the distance, galloping down towards a farm whence they might fire on the gradually advancing cavalry. The General asked the subaltern in charge of our two guns whether they were within range. The young officer was anxious to try. We watched the experiment with attention.

The practice was extremely good. The first shell burst in the middle of the Boer horsemen, who at once spread into a looser formation. The next exploded in front of them, and all the seven shells that were fired fell within measurable distance of someone. For the first time in this war I saw the Boers show what I consider cowardice; for without anyone being killed or wounded the whole party turned back and, abandoning their intention or duty, scurried away to cover behind the long swell of ground over which they had come. The Boer Army in Natal was not thus easily dissuaded from its objects.

Meanwhile the flanking movement was in progress, and as the ground to our right was gradually made good and secured by Colonel Sitwell, Brabazon pushed his centre forward until McNeill's scouts were cantering all over the slopes where the Boers had just been shelled, and hunting such of the enemy as tarried to safer and more remote positions. At last we arrived at the edge of the swell of ground. It fell steeply towards a flat basin, from the middle of which rose a most prominent and peculiar kopje. Invisible behind this was Dewetsdorp. Round it stood Boers, some mounted, some on foot, to the number of about two hundred.

Our rapid advance, almost into the heart of their position, had disturbed and alarmed them. They were doubtful whether this was reconnaissance or actual attack. They determined to make certain by making an attempt to outflank the outflanking Cavalry; and no sooner had our long-range rifle fire compelled them to take cover behind the hill than a new force, as it seemed, of two hundred rode into the open and, passing across our front at a distance of, perhaps, 2,000 yards, made for a white stone kopje on our right.

Angus McNeill ran up to the General: "Sir, may we cut them off? I think we can just do it." The scouts pricked up their ears. The General reflected. "All right," he said, "you may try."

"Mount, mount, mount, the scouts!" cried their impetuous officer, scrambling into his saddle. Then, to me, "Come with us, we'll give you a show now—first-class."

A few days before, in an unguarded moment, I had promised to follow the fortunes of the scouts for a day. I looked at the Boers: they were nearer to the white stone kopje than we, but, on the other hand, they had the hill to climb, and were probably worse mounted. It might be done, and if it were done—I thought of the affair of Acton Homes—how dearly they would have to pay in that open plain. So, in the interests of the *Morning Post*, I got on my horse and we all started—forty or fifty scouts, McNeill and I, as fast as we could, by hard spurring, make the horses go.

It was from the very beginning a race, and recognised as such by both sides. As we converged I saw the five leading Boers, better mounted than their comrades, out-pacing the others in a desperate resolve to secure the coign of vantage. I said, "We cannot do it"; but no one would admit defeat or leave the matter undecided. The rest is exceedingly simple.

We arrived at a wire fence 100 yards—to be accurate, 120 yards—from the crest of the kopje, dismounted, and, cutting the wire, were about to seize the precious rocks when—as I had seen them in the railway cutting at Frere, grim, hairy, and terrible—the heads and shoulders of a dozen Boers appeared; and how many more must be close behind them?

There was a queer, almost inexplicable, pause, or perhaps there was no pause at all; but I seem to remember much happening. First the Boers—one fellow with a long, drooping, black beard, and a chocolate-coloured coat, another with a red scarf round his neck. Two scouts cutting the wire fence stupidly. One man taking aim across his horse, and McNeill's voice, quite steady: "Too late; back to the other kopje. Gallop!"

Then the musketry crashed out, and the "swish" and "whirr" of the bullets filled the air. I put my foot in the stirrup. The horse, terrified at the firing, plunged wildly. I tried to spring into the saddle; it turned under the animal's belly. He broke away, and galloped madly off. Most of the scouts were already 200 yards off. I was alone, dismounted, within the closest range, and a mile at least from cover of any kind.

One consolation I had—my pistol. I could not be hunted down unarmed in the open as I had been before. But a disabling wound was the brightest prospect. I turned, and, for the second time in this war, ran for my life on foot from the Boer marksmen, and I thought to myself, "Here at last I take it." Suddenly, as I ran, I saw a scout. He came from the left, across my front; a tall man, with skull and crossbones badge, and on a pale horse. Death in Revelation, but life to me.

I shouted to him as he passed: "Give me a stirrup." To my surprise he stopped at once. "Yes," he said shortly. I ran up to him, did not bungle in the business of mounting, and in a moment found myself behind him on the saddle.

Then we rode. I put my arms round him to catch a grip of the mane. My hand became soaked with blood. The horse was hard hit; but, gallant beast, he extended himself nobly. The pursuing bullets piped and whistled—for the range was growing longer—overhead.

"Don't be frightened," said my rescuer; "they won't hit you." Then, as I did not reply, "My poor horse, oh my poor — horse; shot with an explosive bullet. The devils! But their hour will come. Oh, my poor horse!"

I said, "Never mind, you've saved my life." "Ah," he rejoined, "but it's the horse I'm thinking about." That was the whole of our conversation.

Judging from the number of bullets I heard I did not expect to be hit after the first 500 yards were covered, for a galloping horse is a difficult target, and the Boers were breathless and excited. But it was with a feeling of relief that I turned the corner of the further kopje and found I had thrown double sixes again.

The result of the race had been watched with strained attention by the rest of the troops, and from their position they knew that we were beaten before we ever reached the wire fence. They had heard the sudden fierce crackle of musketry and had seen what had passed. All the officers were agreed that the man who pulled up in such a situation to help another was worthy of some honourable distinction. Indeed, I have heard that Trooper Roberts—note the name, which seems familiar in this connection—is to have his claims considered for the Victoria Cross. As to this I will not pronounce, for I feel some diffidence in writing impartially of a man who certainly saved me from a great danger.

Well satisfied with my brief experience with the scouts, I returned to General Brabazon. While we had been advancing deeply into the Boer flank, they had not been idle, and now suddenly, from the side of the solitary kopje behind which they had collected, three guns came into action against us. For ten minutes the shell fire was really hot. As these guns were firing with black powder, the smoke springing out in a thick white cloud from the muzzle warned us whenever a projectile was on its way, and, I think, added to the strain on the nerves. You could watch the distant artillery. There was the gun again; four or five seconds to wonder whether the shell would hit you in the face; the approaching hiss rushing into a rending shriek; safe over; bang! right among the horses a hundred yards behind. Here comes the next—two guns fired together this time. Altogether, the Boers fired nearly thirty shells—several of which were shrapnel—on this small space of ground. But fate was in a merciful mood that day, for we had but one man killed and five or six—including the General's orderly—wounded by them.

It was, however, evident that this could not endure. Brabazon had not cared to bring his own two guns into such an advanced position, because they were not horse guns, and might not be able to get away safely if the Boers should make a strong counter-attack. Indeed, so long as the loss of guns is considered a national disaster instead of only an ordinary incident of war, cavalry officers will regard them rather as sources of anxiety than as powerful weapons.

Without guns it was useless to stay, and as, moreover, Sir Leslie Rundle's orders were that the cavalry were not to be severely engaged, Brabazon decided to withdraw the reconnaissance, and did so most successfully, after an instructive little rearguard action. He had penetrated far into the enemy's position; had compelled him to move his guns and disturb his frontal dispositions; had reconnoitred the ground, located the laagers, and come safely away with the loss of little more than a dozen men. Had there been on this day an infantry support behind the cavalry we should have hustled the enemy out of his whole position and slept triumphantly in Dewetsdorp.

Sir Leslie Rundle was much impressed by the vigour and success of the cavalry, whose fortunes were watched from the plateau, and as evening came the report spread through the camp that a general engagement would be fought on the next day. He also decided to entrust the direction of the actual turning attack to General Brabazon, who, besides his cavalry force, was to have twelve guns and an infantry brigade under his command.

With every feeling of confidence in the issue the army went to bed, impatient for the dawn. But in the dead of night a telegram arrived from Lord Roberts, instructing Rundle not to press his attack until he was in touch with Pole-Carew and other reinforcements; and it thus became evident that the operations had grown to an altogether larger scale.

CHAPTER SIX

THE DEWETSDORP EPISODE

Bloemfontein: May 1, 1900

SOMETIMES IT happens that these letters are devoted to describing small incidents, and often personal experiences, in a degree of detail which, if the rest of the campaign were equally narrated, would expand the account to limits far beyond the industry of the writer or the patience of the reader. At others many important events must be crowded into a few pages. But though the proportions of the tale may vary, I shall not deserve criticism so long as the original object of conveying a lively impression of the war is strictly pursued; nor should the reader complain if, for his instruction or amusement, he is made one day to sit with the map of the Orange Free State spread before him, and move little flags to show the course of the operations, and on another day is invited to share the perils of a scout's patrol or try the chances of a cavalry skirmish. Today there is much to tell, and we must remain almost beyond the sound of the cannon watching a distant panorama.

The object of the operations was in any case to relieve Wepener, and to clear the right-hand bottom corner of the Orange Free State of the Boers, and, if the enterprise prospered and the fates were kind, to cut off and capture some part of their forces. In all five columns were in motion. There were to be demonstrations along the east of the railway line, increasing in earnestness according as they were nearer the south, and the lowest columns were to actually push the matter through. Ian Hamilton, with 2,000 mounted infantry, was ordered to demonstrate against the waterworks position. French, supported by Pole-Carew, was instructed to move on Leeukop. Rundle, in conjunction with Hart and Brabant from the southward, was to force his way to Dewetsdorp and to relieve Wepener. What befell his column on April 20 and 21 has already been described. The attack on the Boer position in front of Dewetsdorp had not been made on the 20th because Sir Herbert Chermside pointed out that the infantry were fatigued with marching. The next morning the smooth hills were crowned with entrenchments, and it was thought better to wait for Campbell's Brigade, which would arrive at sundown.

The 22nd was to be the day of battle. Meanwhile Sir Leslie Rundle had telegraphed to Lord Roberts describing the horseshoe position of the enemy, and its strength, explaining that with the small mounted force at his disposal any attack which he might make would develop into something very like a frontal attack, and would be costly. A strong memorandum had previously been circulated among divisional and brigade commanders condemning, almost prohibiting, frontal attacks, and the General, not un-naturally, wished to assure himself that the price of victory would not be grudged. When this telegram reached Bloemfontein it was apparently misunderstood. "Rundle is hung up," they said. "He can't get on"; and hence the reply which arrived in the dead of night and prevented the attack of the 22nd. "Wait till you get into touch with Pole-Carew," or words to that effect. So the powerful force —almost equal in strength to that with which Sir George White had resisted the first fury of the Boers when, with 25,000 men under the Commandant-General himself, they burst into Natal—was relegated to some days of pusillanimous waiting in front of a position held by scarcely 2,500 men.

After breakfast on the morning of the unfought battle I climbed to the top of the hill the cavalry had seized two days before, and which the soldiers had christened "Brab's kopje". A fifteen hundred yards musketry duel was proceeding, and it was dangerous to put one's head over the stone shelters even for a minute to look at the Boer entrenchments on the green slope opposite. But such was not my purpose. I scanned the northern horizon. Far away on a peak of the misty blue hills there flashed a diamond. It was Pole-Carew. Half an hour later another star began to twinkle further to the eastward. French and his cavalry were riding steadily forward, "fighting, too," said the heliograph, "but pushing them back". The scale of the operations had grown indeed. No less than five infantry and three cavalry brigades, with more than seventy guns, were involved in the business of dislodging 2,500 Boers from their position in front of Dewetsdorp.

The 23rd passed quietly, except for an intermittent bombardment of our camp by the Dutch guns and Vickers-Maxim and the usual patter of musketry along the outposts. The diamond points on the distant hills seemed nearer and more to the east than before, and in the afternoon Brabazon was sent to reconnoitre towards them. As the yeomanry emerged from the shelter of the plateau the Boer Creusot gun espied them. Brabazon, with half a dozen officers or orderlies, was riding fifty yards in front of his brigade.

"See there," said the Dutch gunners, "there is the Hoofd Commandant himself; take good aim." So they did, and from a range of 5,000 yards burst their shell within two yards of the General's horse. "Wonderful," said Brabazon; "why can't our forsaken artillery shoot like that?" and he ordered the brigade to canter by troops across the dangerous ground. I watched the scene that followed from comparative safety, 600 yards nearer the Boer gun. Troop by troop the yeomanry emerged from shelter. As each did so the men opened out to dispersed order and began to gallop; and for every troop there was one shell. From where I stood the spectacle was most interesting. Between the shrieking of the shell overhead and its explosion among the galloping horsemen there was an appreciable interval, in which one might easily have wagered whether it would hit or miss.

The yeomanry were very steady, and for the most part ran the gauntlet at a nice, dignified canter, pulling into a walk as soon as the dangerous space was crossed. After all no one was hurt, except three men who broke their crowns through their horses falling on the rocky ground. Indeed, I think, speaking from some experience, that we can always treat these Creusot 9-pounders with contempt. They fling a small shell an immense distance with surprising accuracy, but unless they actually hit someone they hardly ever do any harm. An ordinary bullet is just as dangerous, though it does not make so much noise.

At Vaal Krantz, in Natal, Dundonald's Brigade and other troops lived quite comfortably for three days under the fire of a 98-pounder gun, which in all that time only killed one soldier of the Dublin Fusiliers, two natives, and a few beasts. The wholesale aspect of artillery fire is not obtained unless at least a dozen guns are firing percussion shell or unless shrapnel can be used. At present the Boers often cause us a great deal of trouble with single guns, which, though they do scarcely any material harm, disturb everyone, so that camps are shifted and marching columns ordered to make long *détours*; whereas we ought to shrug our shoulders, as Ladysmith did, pay the small necessary toll, and go our ways uninterruptedly. But I am being drawn into detail and discussion, which, if I am ever to catch up the swift march of events, must be rigorously excluded.

The 23rd passed quietly for times of war, and the Boer riflemen and artillerists fired busily till dusk without doing much harm. We wondered how much they knew of the "increased scale" of the operations. Did they realise the enormous strength of the forces closing round them? Were they going to be caught as Cronje was caught? It was hardly likely. Yet they were certainly holding all their positions in force at nightfall, and meanwhile the spring of the trap was compressed, and the moment for releasing it arrived.

The morning of the 24th was unbroken by a single shot. Rundle, now in touch with Pole-Carew, swung his division to the left, pivoting on Chermside, to whom he entrusted the defence of the plateau. Brabazon with his Mounted Brigade formed the extreme outer flank of this sweeping movement. His orders were to join French, who drove inward from the north, somewhere behind Dewetsdorp on the Modder River. So we started, and, with much caution and the pomp of war, turned the enemy's left, and in solemn silence bore down on the flank and rear of his position.

Meanwhile, Chermside on the plateau was struck by the entire cessation of fire from the Boer lines opposite to him. He sent scouts to reconnoitre. Single men crept up the hill, looked into the trenches, and found—nothing. The Boers had retreated swiftly in the night. They enjoyed good information of all our movements and designs: had foreseen the impossibility of withstanding the great forces operating against them. They delayed us with the appearance of strength until the last minute. On the night of the 22nd they sent off their waggons towards Thabanchu. On the 23rd they made their effort against Wepener, and attacked the garrison heavily, and on the night of the 24th, having failed at Wepener, they performed a masterly retreat, the assailants of Wepener marching northwards *via* Ladybrand, the covering force at Dewetsdorp moving on Thabanchu.

And so it was that when, as directed, Brabazon circled round the enemy's left flank and struck the Modder River—here only a rocky ditch with occasional pools of mud—and when French, moving from Leeukop round and behind their right flank, met him, they found the Dutch already departed, and Dewetsdorp again under the Union Jack. The strong jaws of the rat-trap shut together with a snap. I saw them—black across the open plain—two great horns of cavalry and guns; but the rat had walked comfortably away some hours before. Chermside moving over the empty trenches occupied the town. Rundle, reaching it an hour later, owing to his turning movement, hurried on through it to the Modder, and laid Brabazon's dusty squadrons on the retreating enemy. Indeed, the latter officer was already at the trot towards Thabanchu when French himself arrived—a large and magnificent staff, "pom-poms", horse artillery, and two cavalry brigades—and assumed supreme command.

He immediately stopped the pursuit, sent Brabazon back to relieve Wepener—which place had by its plucky defence, like Jellalabad, relieved itself—and entered Dewetsdorp, where he remained until the next day.

Such is the story of Dewetsdorp, which cannot be contemplated with feelings of wild enthusiasm. The Wepener situation was cleared up, and the Boers were persuaded to retire from the right-hand bottom corner of the Free State towards Ladybrand and Thabanchu at an exceedingly small price in blood. On the other hand, the enemy might boast that 2,500 burghers with six runs had contained 13,000 troops with thirty guns for a week, while their brethren worked their wicked will on Wepener, and had only been dislodged by the setting in motion of more than 25,000 men and seventy guns.

The movements which followed the occupation of Dewetsdorp need not take long in the telling. French's occupation of the town instead of pursuing the enemy was not in accordance with the Commander-in-Chief's ideas, and the cavalry leader was forthwith ordered to follow the Boers at his best pace to Thabanchu. He started accordingly at daylight on the 25th, and Rundle with the Eighth Division followed at noon. Chermside remained at Dewetsdorp with part of the Third Division, and was entrusted with the re-establishment of order through the disturbed districts.

Brabazon marched on Wepener and collected the garrison. Their defence of seventeen days, under continual rifle and shell fire, in hastily dug trenches, which they were unable to leave even at night; exposed to several fierce attacks; in spite of heavy losses and with uncertain prospects of relief, will deserve careful attention when full accounts are published, and is a very honourable episode in the history of Brabant's Colonial Brigade, and particularly in the records of the Cape Mounted Rifles, who lost nearly a quarter of their strength.

Bringing the defenders with him, and having communicated with Hart and Brabant, Brabazon returned to Dewetsdorp, and was ordered to move thence to Thabanchu, which he did in an exceedingly convenient hour, as it turned out, for a certain convoy with an escort of Scots Guards and yeomanry. Pole-Carew and the Eleventh Division returned to Bloemfontein to take part in the main advance.

The Boers made good their retreat. They took with them twenty-five prisoners of the Worcester Regiment, who had blundered into their camp before Dewetsdorp, armed only with cooking pots, which they meant to carry to their regiment on "Brab's kopje", and great quantities of sheep and oxen. They halted in Ladybrand, and to the north and east of Thabanchu, in a most pugnacious mood. Indeed, they had no reason to be discontented with the result of their southern incursion.

They had captured seven guns and nearly 1,000 prisoners. They had arrested and carried off a good many farmers who had laid down their arms and made their peace with the British Government. They had harried all who received the troops kindly, had collected large quantities of supplies, which they had sent north, and, lastly, had delayed the main advance by more than five weeks.

Owing to the great disproportion of the forces, the fighting had not been of a severe nature, and the losses were small. In the skirmishes before Dewetsdorp about forty men were killed and wounded, mostly in Brabazon's Brigade. In the action at Leeukop and the subsequent fighting which attended French's march several officers and fifty men were stricken, and a squadron of the 9th Lancers, which was required to attack a kopje, suffered severely, having nearly twenty casualties, including Captain Stanley, a very brave officer, who died of his wounds, and Victor Brooke (of whom more will be heard in the future) who had his left hand smashed. Captain Brazier-Creagh, 9th Bengal Lancers, commanding Roberts's Horse, was killed at Leeukop, and his many friends along the Indian frontier will not need to be told that by his death Lord Roberts's Army suffered a loss appreciable even among the great forces now in the field.

IAN HAMILTON'S MARCH

Winburg: May 8, 1900

T HE UNSATISFACTORY course of the operations in the
south-eastern corner of the Free State, and the indecisive
results to which they led, were soon to be arrested and reversed by a series of movements of surprising vigour and remarkable success. Of all the demonstrations which had been intended
against the enemy to the east of the railway, Hamilton's advance
towards the waterworks position, being the most northerly, was
to have been the least earnestly pressed. The orders were: "If you
find the waterworks weakly held, which is not likely, you may try
to occupy them, and, in the event of success, may call up Smith-
Dorrien's Brigade to strengthen you."

On this, General Ian Hamilton, who now commanded the imposing, but somewhat scattered, Mounted Infantry Division,
started from Bloemfontein on the 22nd of April with about 2,000
Light Horse, Australians, and mounted infantry, and one battery
of Horse Artillery.

On the 23rd he arrived before the waterworks, reconnoitred
them, found them weakly held, or, at any rate, thought he could
take them, attacked, and before dark made himself master of the
waterworks themselves, and of the drift over the river which led to
the hills beyond, into which the enemy had retired. Smith-Dorrien's
Brigade was called up at once, arrived after dark, and the next
morning the force crossed at the drift, and the whole position was
occupied. The enemy offered a slight resistance, which was attributed by some to a deep design on their part to lure the column into
a trap further to the east, and by others to the manner in which
the attack was delivered. The news of the capture of this strong and
important place, which secures the Bloemfontein water supply,
was received with great satisfaction at headquarters.

Meanwhile the operations round Dewetsdorp came to their abortive conclusion, and it became evident that the Boers had evaded the intercepting columns and were making their way northwards by Thabanchu. What was to be done? Had the officer commanding at the waterworks any suggestion to make? Most certainly, and the suggestion was that he should be permitted to advance himself and occupy Thabanchu. This was the answer that was expected and desired. Permission, and with it a field battery, was accordingly given, and, on the 25th of April, the column moved out of the waterworks position towards Thabanchu. It consisted of Ridley's Brigade of Mounted Infantry, which included a large proportion of colonials—Australians and New Zealanders—Smith-Dorrien's Infantry Brigade (Gordons, Canadians, Shropshires, and Cornwalls), with twelve guns.

The country to the east of Bloemfontein is at first smooth and open. Great plains of brownish grass stretch almost to the horizon, broken to the eye only by occasional scrub-covered hills. To anyone unaccustomed to the South African veldt they appear to offer no obstacle to the free movement of cavalry or artillery; nor is it until one tries to ride in a straight line across them that the treacherous and unimagined donga or the awkward wire fence interposes itself. But beyond the Modder River, on which the waterworks are situated, the surface of the ground becomes rocky and hilly, and the features increase in prominence until Thabanchu Mountain is reached, and thereafter the country uprears itself in a succession of ridges to the rugged and lofty peaks of Basutoland.

Thabanchu, a small village, as we should regard it in England, a town of comparative commercial importance in the Orange Free State, and of undoubted strategic value during this phase of the operations, stands at the foot of the precipitous feature that bears its name. It is approached from the direction of Bloemfontein by a long, broad, flat-bottomed valley, whose walls on either side rise higher and higher by degrees as the road runs eastward. The eastern end of this wide passage is closed by a chain of rocky kopjes, whose situation is so curious and striking that they seem to be devised by nature to resist the advance of an invader. The kopjes, rising abruptly from the flat glacis-like ground, are a strong rampart, and the whole position, resting on apparently secure flanks, creates a most formidable barrier, which is called locally Israel's Poorte.

Along the valley, on the 25th of April, Hamilton proceeded to march with his entire force, Ridley and the mounted infantry being a considerable distance in front of the main body. At ten o'clock a heavy fire of musketry and artillery was opened at an extreme range from the hills on the left-hand side of the column.

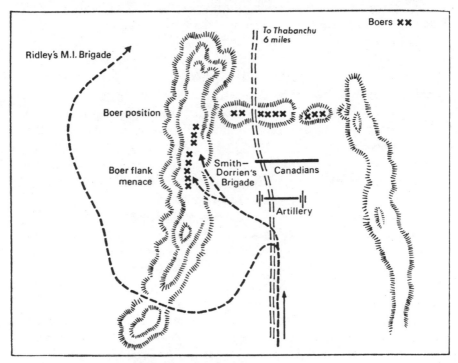

Boers ✗✗

To Thabanchu
6 miles

Ridley's M.I. Brigade

Boer position

Boer flank
menace

Smith–
Dorrien's
Brigade

Canadians

Artillery

DIAGRAM EXPLAINING HAMILTON'S ACTION AT ISRAEL'S
POORTE, THE 25TH OF APRIL

Ignoring this, which proved afterwards to be only a Boer demonstration, Ridley continued his march, and Hamilton followed, until, at a little after eleven o'clock, both were brought to a standstill before the Israel's Poorte position, which was found to be occupied by the enemy, estimated at 800 strong, with several guns.

After a personal reconnaissance, and in spite of a most disquieting report that the Boers had just been reinforced by "two thousand men in four lines", the General resolved to attack. His plan was simple but effective. It resembles very closely Sir Bindon Blood's forcing of the "Gate of Swat" at Landakai in 1897. The front was to be masked and contained by a sufficient force of Infantry and all the guns. The rest of the troops were to stretch out to the left and swing to the right, the infantry along the left-hand wall of the valley, the mounted men actually the other side of the wall.

Accordingly, the Canadian Regiment and the Grahamstown Volunteers (Marshall's Horse) moved forward in extended order— 25 yards interval between men—to within about 800 yards of the enemy's position, and here, just out of the range of serious harm, they lay down and opened a continuous musketry fire. Both batteries came into action forthwith and shelled the crest line with satisfactory energy. Smith-Dorrien, with the remaining three battalions of his brigade, moved to the left, and began working along the ridges. Ridley, breaking out of the valley into the more open ground beyond, began to move against the enemy's line of retreat.

Four hours passed, during which the Boers indulged the hope that the frontal attack would be pushed home, and at the end of which they found their right flank turned and their rear threatened. Immediately, with all the hurry of undisciplined troops who feel a hand on their communications, they evacuated the position, and, running to their horses, galloped away. The Canadians and Grahamstown Volunteers thereupon arose and occupied the line of kopjes, and thus the door was opened and the road to Thabanchu cleared. Our losses in this smart action were about twenty killed and wounded, among whom were no less than five officers of the Grahamstown Volunteers. The Dutch left five corpses on the field, and doubtless carried away a score of wounded.

General Hamilton, pushing on, entered Thabanchu the same night, and the British flag was again hoisted over the town. The Imperialist section of the community, who had in the interval between the evacuation and reoccupation of the town been subjected to much annoyance at the hands of the Boers, were naturally shy, and afraid to make any sign of welcome. The southern commandos from Dewetsdorp and Wepener had by hard marching already passed behind Thabanchu with their convoys. On the 26th French and his cavalry, covering the march of Rundle's (Eighth) Division, arrived, and, since he was a lieutenant-general, took the command out of Hamilton's hands for a time.

I had come northwards from Dewetsdorp with the cavalry brigades, and was an eye-witness of the operations round Thabanchu which occupied the 26th and 27th. Thabanchu Mountain is a lofty and precipitous feature of considerable extent, and, towards the south, of indefinite shape. To the north, however, it presents a wide bay, on whose grassy shores rising from the more arid plain the Boer laagers were reported to stand. The enemy held the crest of the crescent-shaped mountain with guns and riflemen, and in order that no one should pry behind it they extended on their right a few hundred trustworthy fellows, who, working in the most scattered formation, gave to their position an enormous front of doubtful strength.

On the afternoon of the 26th, with a view to further operations on the following day, a force of mounted infantry, supported by galloping Maxims and a horse battery, was sent to reconnoitre, and if possible to hold the hill, henceforward called "Kitchener's Horse Hill". The troops gained possession of the feature without fighting, though a few Boers were seen galloping along the ridges to the right and left, and an intermittent musketry fire began. A garrison to hold the hill was detailed, consisting of Kitchener's Horse, a company of the Lincoln Mounted Infantry, and two Maxim guns; but just as the sun sank this plan was changed by the officer commanding the force, and the whole were ordered to retire into Thabanchu. On the Indian frontier it is a cardinal rule to retire by daylight and sit still when overtaken by night in the best position at hand. In this war experience has shown that it is usually better to remain on the ground, even at a heavy cost, until it is quite dark, and then to retreat, if necessary. The reason of the difference is that while close contact with an Afridi armed with a four-foot knife, active as a cat and fierce as a tiger, is to be avoided as much as possible, no soldier asks better than the closest contact with a Dutchman. But though the teaching of both wars may seem contradictory on many points, on one point it is in complete agreement: twilight is the worst time of all to retire.

The consequences of this ill-timed change of plan were swift. The Boers saw the retrograde movement, and pressed boldly forward, and Kitchener's Horse, finding themselves closely engaged, were unable to move. A sharp and savage little fight followed in the gloom. The Boers crept quite close to the soldiers, and one fierce greybeard was shot through the head eight paces from the British firing line, but not until after he had killed his man. The reports which reached the town, that Kitchener's Horse were "cut off" on a kopje four miles from the camp, induced General French to send the Gordon Highlanders to their relief. This batta-

lion started at about ten o'clock, and were put on their road to the
northward. But in the darkness and the broken ground they lost
their way, marched five miles to the south, occupied another hill,
and did not rejoin the command until the afternoon of the next
day, an absence which, since no inquiries could discover them,
caused much anxiety. Kitchener's Horse meanwhile, under Major
Fowle, of the 21st Lancers, made a plucky defence, beat off the
Boers, and managed at about eleven o'clock to effect their retreat
undisturbed. The losses in the affair were twelve or fourteen men
killed and wounded, including one officer, who was shot through
the head.

Very early the next morning the whole force marched out of the
town, and French's operations were this day designed to compel
the enemy to retreat from his positions in rear of Thabanchu
Mountain, and if possible to surround some part of his force. The
information at General French's disposal could not, however, have
been very accurate, for in my telegram of the 26th I wrote that
"more than 2,000 Boers" were collected to the north of Thabanchu,
and the Press Censor erased this and substituted the words "small
parties". If this latter view had been correct it is probable that
the operations of the following day would have been attended by a
greater measure of success.

The plan was clear and vigorous. Gordon's Cavalry Brigade was
to move to the right, round the east of Thabanchu Mountain, and
force their way into the plains behind it. It was hoped that the
Lancers, of which this brigade is entirely composed, would find
some opportunity for using their dreaded weapon. Hamilton was
to push back the weak Boer right, and open the way for Dickson's
Cavalry Brigade to pass through and join hands with Gordon.
Rundle, whose infantry were tired from their long march from
Dewetsdorp, was to demonstrate against the Boers' centre and
hold the town.

The action opened with the re-oc upation of Kitchener's Horse
Hill by Smith-Dorrien's Infantry Brigade, who advanced in determined style, and by a sweeping movement of Ridley's Mounted
Infantry. Both these undertakings, which were directed by Hamilton, prospered. The Boer right, which was very thin, was brushed
aside, and the road for the Cavalry was opened. At, and not until,
nine o'clock, French's leading squadrons began to appear on the
plain, and by ten the whole of Dickson's Brigade had passed

through the gap and were safely extended in the undulating plains beyond.

Wishing to see, for the first time, cavalry and horse artillery working in suitable country, I rode down from my post of observation on Kitchener's Horse Hill and trotted and cantered until I caught up the squadrons. It was evident that the left enveloping arm was making good progress. Already we could almost look into the bay behind Thabanchu Mountain. If Gordon were only getting on as well we might join hands with him, and enclasp a goodly catch of prisoners. So the brigade continued to advance from ridge to ridge, and presently Boers began to gallop across the front to escape, as was thought, from the net we were drawing round them. At all of these the horse artillery and the pom-poms— British pom-poms at last—fired industriously. But as the enemy kept a respectful distance and an open formation, only a few were seen to fall. The others did not fly very far, but gathered together in what soon became considerable numbers outside the net, near a peaked hill, which does not appear in my sketch, but which the reader may bear in mind as lying to the left rear of the turning cavalry.

At last Dickson's advance reached a point between Thabanchu Mountain and the peaked hill, so that no more Boers could escape by that road; and we saw the others, three or four hundred in number, riding about, up and down, or round and round in the bay, like newly-caught rats in a cage.

At this everyone became very excited. "Gordon must have headed them back," it was said. "Only a few more men and we might make a bag." Where could men be found? Somebody suggested asking Hamilton. The helio twinkled: "Come and help us make a bag", it said, in somewhat more formal language. And Hamilton came forthwith, leaving positions which were of much value; collecting every man he could lay his hands on—weary mounted infantry, a tired-out battery, and all of Smith-Dorrien's Brigade that could march fast at the end of a long day—he hurried to seize and line the northern spurs of Thabanchu Mountain, prepared to risk much to strike a heavy blow.

The movement of infantry and guns to support him encouraged Dickson to press still further forward, and the whole brigade advanced nearly another mile. At length we overtopped a smooth ridge, and found ourselves looking right into the bay or horseshoe of mountains. Now at last we must see Gordon. "There he is," cried several voices, and looking in the direction shown I saw a majestic body of horse streaming out of the centre of the bay towards the north-west. But was it Gordon? At least 4,000 mounted men were riding across our front, hardly two miles away. Surely no brigade was so numerous. Yet such was the precision of the array that I could not believe them Boers.

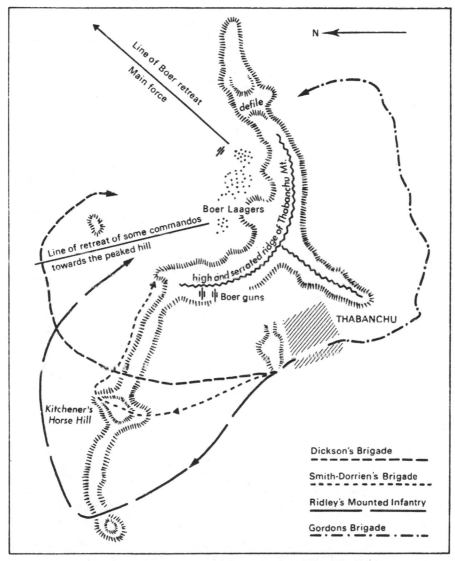

DIAGRAM EXPLAINING FRENCH'S OPERATIONS ROUND
THABANCHU, THE 26TH AND 27TH APRIL

Boers their numbers, however, proved them to be; and not their numbers alone, for before we had watched this striking spectacle long, two large puffs of smoke leapt from the tail of the hostile column, and two well-aimed shells burst near our horse battery. At the same time patrols from the left rear hurried in with the news that the Boers who had already escaped from our imagined "trap" were advancing in force, with two more guns, to cut us from the rest of the army.

As for Gordon, there was no longer any doubt about his fortunes. Far away to the eastward the horseshoe wall of mountains dipped to a pass, and on the sides of this gateway little puffs of smoke, dirty brown against the darkening sky, showed that Gordon was still knocking with his artillery at the door, and had never been able to debouch in the plains behind it. Moreover, the dangerous hour of twilight was not long distant. Dickson determined to retreat while time remained, and did so without any unnecessary delay. Whereat the Boers came down on our rear and flank, opening furious fire at long range, and galloping eagerly forward, so that the brigade and its guns, so far from entrapping the enemy, were all but entrapped themselves; indeed, the brigadier's mess cart, the regimental water carts, and several other little things, which, being able only to trot, could not "conform to the general movement", were snapped up by the hungry enemy, who now pressed on exulting.

Meanwhile Hamilton had taken some risks in order to promote the expected entrapping. He had now to think of himself. First, the Boer advance must be stopped, and, secondly, the force which had, in the hopes of grasping the Boers, let go its hold on Kitchener's Horse Hill, must be withdrawn within the Thabanchu picket line. The General, however, was equal to both requirements. Judiciously arranging some force of infantry and guns, he peppered the advancing Boers heavily, so that at 800 yards they wheeled about and scurried to the shelter of adjacent kopjes. This advantage restored the situation. Hamilton remained on the ground till dark, and then, with the whole of Ridley's and Smith-Dorrien's commands, returned safely into Thabanchu.

During the day rifle and artillery fire had been constant; but as the fighting had been conducted at extreme ranges, which neither side showed much anxiety to diminish, the slaughter was small. Indeed, I do not think that a dozen men were stricken in either army. So far as the British were concerned, the result of the day's operations was a qualified success.

The Boers were evidently prepared to retreat from Thabanchu, but they proposed to do so in their own time and at their most excellent discretion, and it was quite evident that we had not succeeded in any way in hindering or preventing them. It was also clear that, far from being "in small parties", their strength was nearly 6,000, so that on the whole we might congratulate ourselves on having moved in ignorance and taken no great hurt. The only point about the action difficult to understand was the behaviour of the Boers who had ridden about like caged rats. Why should they do so when they knew that their line of retreat to the north-east was perfectly secure? I can only conclude that this particular commando had arranged to retire northwards towards the peaked hill, and were annoyed at being prevented from joining their comrades at the point where their waggons, and, consequently, their dinners, were awaiting them.

On the evening of this instructive, but unsatisfactory, day, Hamilton received orders from Lord Roberts to march north on Winburg in conformity with the general advance of the army. For this purpose his force was to be largely increased, and the operations which followed require the space of another letter. French remained for some days at Thabanchu, but attempted no further serious operations against the enemy.

Only one other incident of interest occurred in the neighbourhood of Thabanchu. After his relief of Wepener, Brabazon was ordered thither *via* Dewetsdorp. On the 28th, dusty and tired at the end of a long march, he arrived with his Yeomanry at the foot of a pass among the hills. A Kaffir lounged into the bivouac and asked the General whether he would like to see some pretty shelling, for that there was a fine show at the top of the valley. Brabazon, much interested, mounted his horse forthwith, and, guided by the Kaffir through devious paths, reached a point which afforded an extensive view.

There, in the twilight, lay a British convoy, stoutly defended by a company of the kiddies and a few yeomanry, and shelled—as the Kaffir had said—with great precision by two Boer guns. The General thereupon gave the Kaffir a "fiver" to carry a letter through the Boer lines to the commander of the convoy, telling that officer to hold out manfully, and promising that with the dawn Brabazon and the Imperial Yeomanry would come to his aid.

The Kaffir succeeded in his mission. The convoy was encouraged, and, good as his word, with the daylight came the General, at whose approach the Boers fled incontinently, so that Brabazon, the yeomanry, and the convoy came in safety and triumph into Thabanchu together.

CHAPTER EIGHT

IAN HAMILTON

London: August 10, 1900

IAN STANDISH MONTEITH HAMILTON was born at Corfu in
1853. His father, the late Colonel Christian Monteith Hamilton—
then a captain, but who eventually commanded the 92nd
Highlanders—was the eldest son of John George Hamilton and
of Christina Cameron Monteith, daughter of Henry Monteith of
Carstairs, sometime Member of Parliament for Lanarkshire. His
mother, the late Maria Corinna Vereker, was daughter of John,
third Viscount Gort, by Maria O'Grady, daughter of Viscount
Guillamore.* The Hamilton family is one of the elder branches
of the Scottish Hamiltons, and represents the male line of the
Hamiltons of Westport. One of his ancestors on his father's side,
a Colonel Hamilton, was for several years an aide-de-camp of the
first Duke of Marlborough, and it was therefore something in the
nature of a coincidence when Ian Hamilton found the present
Duke of Marlborough serving in a similar capacity on his staff. It
would not be quite correct to call him a pure Celt, but some notice
should be taken by those interested in these questions that his
blood is mostly Celtic: both of his grandmothers, Monteith and
O'Grady, being of Celtic stock, Scottish and Irish respectively.

When Ian Hamilton was born his father was serving with a
detachment of the 92nd Highlanders at Corfu. His mother died in
1856, and for the next ten years, the father being constantly on
duty with the regiment, he and his younger brother, Vereker
Hamilton, who was born in 1856, lived with their grandparents
at Hapton, in the Holy Loch in Argyllshire. Such a childhood on
moor and loch in a fine wild country was likely to develop and
brace nerve and muscle, and stir the keen blood inherited from

---

* *Vide* Peerage, Gort and Guillamore.

many generations of warlike ancestors. He was educated first at Cheam, and as he grew sufficiently old at Wellington College. Here he was very happy, and although he was not especially noted for industry, his success in the examinations at the end of each term excused any neglect in its course. In 1872 he passed the tests for the army, and, according to the system at that time in force, was offered the choice of going to Sandhurst or living for a year abroad to learn a foreign language thoroughly. The cadet chose the latter, and was sent to Germany. Here he had the good luck to make the close friendship of a most distinguished old man. General Dammers was a Hanoverian who had fought against the Prussians at Lange-salze, and who, refusing a very high command under the Prussians, lived at Dresden. Although he himself remained the aide-de-camp to the ex-King of Hanover, he became the centre of a group of Hanoverian officers who had entered the Saxon service. He was thus in touch with the latest school of military thought, stimulated to its utmost activity by the lessons of the great war which had lately been concluded. From General Dammers, Ian Hamilton learned the German language, military surveying, something of military history, and something doubtless of strategy and the art of war. The year thus passed very profitably. On his return to England, however, the War Office announced that they had changed their minds and that for the future everybody must go through Sandhurst. Such protests as his father, himself an officer, was entitled to make were overruled by the authorities, and Ian Hamilton embarked upon his military career having lost, through no fault of his own, one year of seniority—a year which Fortune had perhaps even then determined to restore to him manifold.

In 1873 he entered the 12th Foot, and after some months joined his father's old regiment, the 92nd. At first with the 92nd, and after 1881 with the 2nd battalion of the regiment, the Gordon Highlanders, Ian Hamilton followed the drum from garrison to garrison, going through the military routine, and plodding slowly up the first few steps of the long ladder of promotion. From the very first he interested himself in musketry. He became himself a keen and good rifle shot, and not with the military rifle alone. He spent a long leave in Kashmir on the fringe of the snows, and made a remarkable bag. Indeed, some of his heads attained nearly to the record dimensions, and one big single-horned markhor enjoyed the actual supremacy for several months.

Then came the Afghan war. Ian Hamilton, although only an infantry soldier, became aide-de-camp, with Brabazon as Brigade Major, to the unfortunate commander of the British Cavalry Brigade. Early in the campaign he was stricken down with fever, and so avoided being drawn into the controversy which raged for several years in military circles around the actions in the Chardeh valley. It would indeed have been unfortunate if at this early stage in his career he had been led into any antagonism to the great General with whom his fortunes were afterwards so closely associated.

The Boer war of 1881 found Hamilton still a subaltern. He was ordered to South Africa with his regiment, and went full of eager anticipation. The regiment, composed almost entirely of soldiers inured to the hardships and disdainful of the dangers of war, was in the most perfect condition to encounter the enemy, and, as is usual in British expeditions on the outward voyage, they despised him most thoroughly. It was not to be dreamed of that a parcel of ragged Boers should stand against the famous soldiers of Kabul and Kandahar. They discussed beforehand the clasps which would be given upon the medal for the campaign. They were to be Laing's Nek, Relief of Potchefstroom, and Pretoria 1881. No one had then ever heard the name of Majuba Mountain. Yet there was to be the first encounter between Highlanders and Dutchmen.

The dismal story of Majuba is better known than its importance deserves. Had that action been fought in this war it would perhaps have gone down to history as the affair of the 27th of February. Instead, it was accepted as a stricken field, and might, such was the significance that was attached to it, have changed the history of nations. It needs no repetition here save in so far as it is concerned with Ian Hamilton. Majuba Mountain may in general terms be described as a saucer-topped hill. Sir George Colley and his six hundred soldiers, picked from various units (that all might share the glory), sat themselves down to rest and sleep, and dig a well in the bottom of the saucer. One weak picket of Gordon Highlanders was thrust forward over the rim on to the outer slope of the hill to keep an eye on those silent grey patches which marked the Boer laagers far below. Hamilton was the subaltern in command. As the day gradually broke and the light grew stronger, he saw from the very lifting of the curtain the course of the tragedy. Boers awoke, bustled about their encampments; looked up just as Symons's Brigade looked up on the morning of Talana Hill, and saw the sky-line fringed with men. More bustle, long delay, much argument and hesitation below, a little boasting rifle fire from some of the British soldiers: "Ha, ha! got you this time I think!"—and then, straggle of horsemen riding in tens and twenties towards the foot of the mountain. Hamilton reported accordingly. The action of Majuba Hill had begun. Pause.

There was—so it has been described to me—a long donga that led up the steep slope. Into the lower end of this the Boer horsemen disappeared. Hamilton moved his score of men a little to their right, where they might command this zig-zag approach as much as the broken ground would allow, and reported again to the General or whoever was directing affairs—for Colley, wearied with the tremendous exertion of the night climb, was sleeping—"Enemy advancing to attack." He also made a few stone shelters. Pause again. Suddenly, quite close, darting forward here and there among the rocks and bushes of the donga—Boers! Fire on them, then. The Gordons' rifles spluttered accordingly, and back came the answer hot and sharp—a close and accurate musketry fire pinning the little party of Regulars to the earth behind their flimsy shelters. No one could show his head to fire. Soldiers would hold a helmet up above the sheltering stone and bring it down with two and three bullets through it. Could half a company fight a battle by itself? What were others doing? Hamilton felt bound to send another report. He left the half company in charge of the sergeant, got up, ran up the slope, and dropped into safety the other side of the saucer-shaped rim. The distance was scarcely forty yards, yet two bullets passed through his kilt in crossing it. Where was the General? A staff officer, ignorant and therefore undisturbed, said that the General was sleeping. "He knew," said the staff officer, "what was going on. No need for a subaltern of Highlanders to concern himself." Hamilton returned, running the gauntlet again, to his men. The fire grew hotter. The Boers began to creep gradually nearer. Their front of attack widened and drew around the contours of the hill. Were all the force asleep? One more warning at any rate they should have. Again he darted across the open space with the swish of bullets around him. Again he found the staff. But this time they were annoyed. It is such a bore when young officers are jumpy and alarmist. "It's all right," they said: and so it was within the saucer. The bullets piped overhead as the wind howls outside the well warmed house. But a sudden change impended.

Hamilton rejoined his men just as the Boers attacked at all points. The little picket of Highlanders, utterly unable to withstand the weight of the enemy's advance, ran back to the rim of the saucer intermingled with the Boers, who fired their rifles furiously at them, even putting the muzzles to the men's heads and so destroying them. In Sir William Butler's book, written almost entirely with the view of exonerating Sir George Colley, it is suggested that his advanced picket fell back in a panic. The truth is that they were swept backward by overwhelming force after they had three times reported to the General the development of a heavy attack. Of the seventeen men under Ian Hamilton in this advanced position twelve were shot dead.

The survivors of the picket with the pursuing Boers reached the rim together, and became visible to the main force. Astounded by this apparition, the troops who were lying down in the saucer rose up together, and, some accoutred, some with their coats off, Highlanders, sailors, and linesmen, ran forward and fired a ragged volley. The Boers immediately lay down and replied, causing heavy loss. A furious musketry fight followed between the Dutch in cover along the rim and the British among the rocks across the centre of the saucer. This was ended by the appearance of other Boers on the high ground at the northern end of the plateau. Without orders or order, exposed to a terrible fire, ignorant of what was required of them, the soldiers wavered. One last chance presented itself. Hamilton rushed up to the General in the impetuosity of youth: "I hope you'll forgive my presumption, sir, but will you let the Gordon Highlanders charge with the bayonet?"

"No presumption, young gentleman," replied Colley, with freezing calmness. "We'll let them charge us, and then we'll give them a volley and a charge."

On the word the whole scene broke into splinters. The British troops abandoned their positions and fled from the ground. The Boers, standing up along the rim, shot them down mercilessly— sporting rifles, crack shots, eighty yards' range. Hamilton saw a figure scarcely ten yards away aiming at him, raised the rifle he found himself somehow possessed of to reply. Both fired simultaneously. The British officer went down with his wrist smashed to pieces. He rose again: the rear crest was near. The last of the fugitives were streaming over it. One dash for liberty! The fire was murderous. Before the distance was covered his tunic was cut by one bullet, his knee by another, and finally a splinter of rock striking him behind the head brought him down half stunned to the ground—luckily behind the shelter of a small rock.

The firing stopped. The Boers began to occupy the position. Two discovered the wounded man. The younger, being much excited, would have shot him. The elder restrained him. "Are you officer, you damned Englishman?" said they.

"Yes."

"Give your sword."

Now Hamilton's sword had belonged to his father before him. He replied by offering them money instead.

"Money!" they cried; "give it up at once," and were about to snatch it away when a person of authority—it is said Joubert himself—arrived. "Voorwärts," he said to the burghers, and in spite of their desire to plunder he drove them on. Hamilton thanked him. "This is a bad day for us."

"What can you expect," was the answer characteristic of the Boer—the privileged of God—"from fighting on a Sunday?"

Then they collected the prisoners and helped Hamilton to walk back to the British position. Colley lay dead on the ground. The Boers would not believe it was the General. "Englishmen are such liars." Hector Macdonald—grim and sad—hero of the Afghan war, now a prisoner in the enemy's hand, watched the proceedings sullenly. The Boers picked out the surrendered prisoners. They looked at Hamilton. He was covered with blood from head to foot. They said: "You will probably die. You may go." So he went; staggered, and crawled back to camp, arrived there delirious the next morning. The wrist joint is composed of eight separate bones. The bullet, breaking through, had disarranged them sadly, had even carried one or two away. If he had consented to amputation he would soon have been convalescent. But a soldier must preserve all he can. What with fever and shock he nearly died. For six months he was an invalid. But the hand was saved, so that now the General can hold an envelope between its paralysed and withered fingers, and sometimes hold a cigarette. For all other purposes it is useless, and when he rides it flaps about helplessly—a glorious deformity.

After some months of doubt as to whether he should leave the army and throw himself entirely into the literary pursuits which had always possessed for him a keen attraction, Hamilton decided to remain a soldier.

He next saw service in the Soudan: he was not intended to make this campaign, for the battalion to which he belonged was serving in India, and there has always been much jealousy between the Indian and the Egyptian British officer. But he happened to be coming home on leave, and when the steamer reached Suez it occurred to him to ask himself why he should not go up the Nile with the columns which were being formed. He got out of the ship accordingly and ran across the sands to the train which was standing in the station. Had he not caught it he would have returned to the ship. But he was in time. Next day he arrived in Cairo, and while waiting there for his luggage he applied for employment. It was refused, officers were not allowed to volunteer. The Gordon Highlanders, his only hope, had their full complement of officers. They had no vacancy for him. Hamilton did not, however, give up his idea easily. He resolved to travel as far as Wady Halfa and renew his application there. He journeyed south with Colonel Burnaby, and after a week of train and river-boat arrived at the whitewashed mud huts in the midst of a vast circle of sand which marked the base of the British Expeditionary forces, both desert and river columns.

What followed has happened so often that it is well worth the attention of young officers. Be it always remembered that the regulations of the army are formed to make all people quite alike one uniform pattern and on one level of intelligence—not yet the highest. You do not rise by the regulations, but in spite of them. Therefore in all matters of active service the subaltern must never take "No" for an answer. He should get to the front at all costs. For every fifty men who will express a desire to go on service in the mess or the club, and will grumble if they are not selected, there is only about one who really means business and will take the trouble and run the risk of going to the front on the chance. The competition is much less keen when you get there. I know something of this myself, and am convinced of its truth.

The subaltern really stands on velvet in the matter. If he succeeds all is well. If he gets rebuked and ordered down, he must try again. What can the authorities do? They cannot very well shoot him. At the worst they can send him back to his regiment, stop his leave for six months, and some choleric old martinet who was a young man once, though he had half forgotten it, will write in some ponderous book in Pall Mall against the offender's name: "Keen as mustard—takes his own line—to be noted for active service if otherwise qualified."

Of course everyone was delighted to see Hamilton at Wady Halfa. They appointed him to a vacancy which had meanwhile occurred in the Gordon Highlanders, and gave him a company and a boat in the River Column. Through all the hard campaign that followed he served with credit. The fortunes of the troops who worked their way up the Nile have not been so closely studied as those of the columns which plunged into the desert and fought at Abu Klea and Abu Kru. But it was nevertheless one of the most picturesque enterprises of our military history. The broad boats toiling forward against the current of the river, making perhaps three miles a day, obstructed by frequent cataracts and menaced continually by the enemy, the scouts on the banks, the lines of men on the tow ropes, the red sand of the desert, the hot steel sky, and the fierce sunlight slanting in between rocks of the Nile gorge, are materials from which a fascinating sketch might be painted. Hamilton's boat became somehow the head of the rear column. At length there came a day when they were told of expected opposition, dervish encampments, and a certain rocky ridge said to be lined with riflemen. The leading column of boats was hurried forward. By some mischance Hamilton's boat became the rear boat of the leading column. At any rate, his company alone of the Gordon Highlanders fought in the action of Kirbeckan next day. Nothing succeeds like success. Hamilton received the Distinguished Service Order for his services.

After the Nile Expedition of 1885 had reached its sad conclusion, Hamilton returned to India and became an aide-de-camp on the staff of Lord Roberts, who was then commanding the Madras Army. The question of musketry training for infantry was at that time much discussed, and Lord Roberts was determined to do something to improve the shooting of the British army. In his book "Forty-one Years in India" he tells us how he and his staff formed themselves into a team and had many exciting rifle matches with the regiments in the Madras command. In all this Hamilton's skill with the rifle and the keen interest he had always shown for musketry—his first regimental appointment had been to be Musketry Instructor—stood him in good stead, and when Lord Roberts became Commander-in-Chief in India his aide-de-camp, who had meanwhile served in the Burmah campaign, was made Assistant Adjutant-General for Musketry.

In 1886 he married Jean, daughter of Sir John Muir, Baronet, of Deanston, Perthshire. He had now determined to persevere in the military profession, and devoted himself to it with great assiduity. His literary talents were turned to military subjects. He published a book on musketry in the army entitled "The Fighting of the Future". It was strong and well written. The introduction of the magazine rifle has modified many of his conclusions, but at the time the book attracted a great deal of attention. He found time, however, to write on other things, and there are still extant from his pen: "A Jaunt in a Junk", an account of a cruise which he made with his brother down the west coast of India; a volume of verses, "The Ballad of Hadji and the Boar"; and one or two other writings. He preserved and extended his acquaintance with literary men, particularly with Andrew Lang, whom he powerfully impressed, and who inscribed a volume of poems to him in the following compulsive lines:

TO COLONEL IAN HAMILTON

To you, who know the face of war,
You, that for England wander far,
You that have seen the Ghazis fly
From English lads not sworn to die,
You that have lain where, deadly chill,
The mist crept o'er the Shameful Hill,
You that have conquered, mile by mile,
The currents of unfriendly Nile,
And cheered the march, and eased the strain
When Politics made valour vain,
Ian, to you, from banks of Ken,
We send our lays of Englishmen!

After doing much useful work in the Musketry Department he became one of the Assistant Quartermaster-Generals in India. From this office he managed to sally forth to the Chitral Expedition, for his services in which on the lines of communication he was made Commander of the Bath. He next became Deputy Quartermaster-General, and it was evident that if he chose to continue to serve in India he would ultimately become the head of the department. In 1897 the Great Frontier War broke out. Hamilton was appointed to command one of the brigades of the Tirah Expeditionary Force. He was at the time on leave in England. He returned at speed, assumed command, and led his brigade through the Kohat Pass in the first movement of the general advance. It looked as if his chance in life had come. He had a magnificent force under him. He enjoyed the confidence of the General-in-chief, Sir William Lockhart, and only a few miles away the enemy awaited the advancing army on the heights of Dargai. The next morning his horse shied suddenly. He was thrown to the ground and broke his leg. They carried the brigadier away in a doolie, his brigade passed to another, and the campaign in Tirah was fought without him.

Ian Hamilton took this bitter disappointment with philosophical composure. "Perhaps", he said to me one day in Calcutta, "I should have lost my reputation had I held my command." But it was easy to see how much he felt the lost opportunity and the enforced inaction. At length his leg was mended—after a fashion. He persuaded a medical board to pass him as sound. The campaign continued. There was, however, no vacancy at the front. For several weeks he waited. Presently Sir Bindon Blood—who was preparing for his invasion of Buner, and who knew Hamilton well—applied for him to command his lines of communication. Obstacles were, however, raised by the Indian War Office, and the proposal fell through. At last, in February, when it seemed certain that a spring campaign must be undertaken against the Afridis, Sir William Lockhart decided to replace General Kempster by some other brigadier, and Ian Hamilton was again sent to the front. The hopes or fears of a further campaign proved unfounded. The Afridis gradually paid their toll of rifles, and their jirgahs made submission. The fighting was practically over. Yet in such skirmishing as occurred while Hamilton's brigade were holding the advanced posts in the Bara valley his care and eagerness attracted attention, and, small as was his share in the campaign, Sir William Lockhart gave him an honourable mention in the despatches.

On the restoration of order along the North-West Frontier Hamilton was offered the temporary position of Quartermaster-General in India. Anxious, however, for home employment, and fully alive to the importance of not becoming too closely identified with any particular military set, he declined this important office and proceeded to England on a year's leave. After some delay he was appointed commandant of the School of Musketry at Hythe, and from this post he was twice withdrawn to command brigades at the Manoeuvres. When Sir George White was sent to Natal in September 1899 Hamilton accompanied him as Assistant Adjutant-General. The War Office are therefore entitled to plume themselves upon his successes, for he is one of the few men originally appointed who have increased their reputation.

Ian Hamilton's part in the Boer war is so well known that it will be unnecessary to do more than refer to it here. He displayed a curious facility for handling troops in close contact with the enemy, and practically from the beginning of the fighting he held the command of a brigade. It was Hamilton whose influence went so far to counteract the astounding optimism of the gallant Penn Symons. It was Hamilton who was to have led the bayonet attack by night on the Boer laagers two days before Talana Hill was fought. It was Hamilton to whom French entrusted the entire disposition of the infantry and artillery at Elandslaagte, who arranged the attack, rallied the struggling line, and who led the final charge upon the Boer entrenchment. Again after Lombard's Kop, when the army reeled back in disorder into Ladysmith, it was Hamilton's brigade which, judiciously posted, checked the onset of the victorious enemy. During the defence of Ladysmith Hamilton's section of the defence included Ceasar's Camp and Waggon Hill. He was censured in the Press for not having fortified these positions on their outer crests, and it was said in the army after the 6th of January that this neglect caused unnecessary loss of life. How far this criticism may be just I do not now propose to examine. The arguments against entrenching the outer crest were that heavy works there would draw the enemy's artillery fire, and that the Imperial Light Horse, who were to have defended this section, said they preferred to avail themselves of the natural cover of rocks and stones. The reader would be well advised to defer judgement until some serious and historical work on the campaign in Natal is published. At present all accounts are based on partial and imperfect evidence, nor do I think that the whole true account of a single action has yet been written.

Whatever the rights of this question may be, it is certain that on the 6th of January Ian Hamilton, by his personal gallantry and military conduct, restored the situation on Wagon Hill. Indeed, the Homeric contest, when the British General and Commandant Prinsloo of the Free State fired at each other at five yards' range, the fierce and bloody struggle around the embrasure of the naval gun, and the victorious charge of the Devons, may afterwards be found to be the most striking scene in the whole war.

After the relief of Ladysmith, Roberts, who knew where to find the men he wanted, sent for Hamilton, much to the disgust of Sir Redvers Buller, who proposed to keep this good officer for the command of one of his own brigades. On reaching Bloemfontein he was entrusted with the organisation of the mounted infantry division, a post from which he could conveniently be drawn for any service that might be required. Of the rest some account will be found in these letters.

Ian Hamilton is, as the fine portrait by Sargent, reproduced as the frontispiece of this book, shows him, a man of rather more than middle height, spare, keen eyed, and of commanding aspect. His highly nervous temperament animating what appears a frail body imparts to all his movements a kind of feverish energy. Two qualities of his mind stand forward prominently from the rest. He is a singularly good and rapid judge of character. He takes a very independent view on all subjects, sometimes with a slight bias towards or affection for their radical and democratic aspects, but never or hardly ever influenced by the set of people with whom he lives. To his strong personal charm as a companion, to his temper never ruffled or vexed either by internal irritation or the stir and contrariness of events, his friends and those who have served under him will bear witness. He has a most happy gift of expression, a fine taste in words, and an acute perception of the curious which he has preserved from his literary days. But it is as a whole that we should judge. His mind is built upon a big scale, being broad and strong, capable of thinking in army corps and if necessary in continents, and working always with serene smoothness undisturbed alike by responsibility or danger. Add to all this a long experience in war, high military renown both for courage and conduct, the entire confidence and affection of the future Commander-in-Chief, the luck that has carried him through so many dangers, and the crowning advantage of being comparatively young, and it is evident that here is a man who in the years that are to come will have much to do with the administration of the British Army in times of peace and its direction in the field.

CHAPTER NINE

THE ACTION OF HOUTNEK

Winburg: May 8

IAN HAMILTON'S orders were to march north from Thabanchu on Winburg by the Jacobsrust road, and he was expected, if no opposition was encountered, to reach his destination by the 7th of May. The column with which he started from Thabanchu was composed of Smith-Dorrien's 19th Infantry Brigade, Ridley's Mounted Infantry Brigade, and two batteries of artillery; but at Jacobsrust he would receive a strong reinforcement, consisting of Bruce-Hamilton's 21st Brigade of Infantry, Broadwood's Cavalry Brigade, two batteries of field and one of horse artillery, and two 5-in. guns. This accession would raise his force to a total of 7,500 infantry, 4,000 mounted men, and thirty-two guns—an imposing command for an officer who had not yet had time to take the badges of a colonel off his shoulders. The first thing, however, was to reach Jacobsrust, and effect the junction with Bruce-Hamilton's force.

The Thabanchu column started at daybreak on the 30th of April, and when it was within three or four miles of Houtnek Poort the enemy suddenly unmasked field guns and "pom-poms", and opened a long-range fire with them from the east on the right flank of the marching troops. Colonel Bainbridge, with the 7th Corps of mounted infantry, wheeled up to contain this force of the enemy, and at the same time De Lisle—of polo fame—pushed forward boldly at a gallop with the 6th Corps and the New Zealanders, and seized a commanding position about 2,000 yards south of the actual nek. Colonel Legge, meanwhile advancing on the left front, noticed that Thoba Mountain was weakly held by the enemy, and thereupon ordered Kitchener's Horse to attack it, thus anticipating the order which the General was himself about to send. These dispositions, which were made on their own initiative by the various mounted infantry officers, enabled a deliberate view of the situation to be taken.

The pass of Houtnek consists of two parallel grassy ridges separated by a smooth shallow valley a little more than a mile across, and devoid of cover. On the east the pass runs up into sharp rocky kopjes, strengthened by successive lines of stone walls trailing away towards the main laagers of the enemy. Both the centre and the left flank of the Boer position refused all opportunity of attack. The Dutch right was scarcely more encouraging. On the west of the pass rose the great mountain of Thoba, an uneven battlefield, better suited to Boers than to British troops. Yet as it was on Hamilton's safer flank, dominated the rest of the enemy's position, could be turned by mounted troops making a very wide detour, and being, moreover, the only way, the General resolved to attack it.

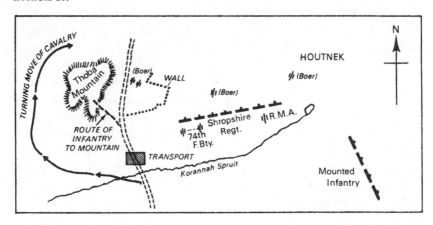

At 9.30 the infantry began to come up, and at ten o'clock the approaches to the Boer position were strongly occupied. As soon as Kitchener's Horse were seen to have made good their footing on Thoba Mountain, Hamilton ordered General Smith-Dorrien to support them with part of his brigade, which was accordingly done, two companies of the Shropshires, the Gordon Highlanders, and four companies of the Canadians being successively worked up on to the hill under a heavy shell fire from the enemy. This practically disposed of the whole force, which was soon engaged all along the line, the mounted infantry holding the enemy off the right and right rear, the Cornwalls guarding the baggage, one-half

Smith-Dorrien's Brigade containing the front, and the other half
with Kitchener's Horse pushing the flank attack on Thoba Mountain.

As soon as the Boers understood the designs of the British on
Thoba they made a strong effort to regain and hold that important
feature. At first the troops made good progress; but as the enemy
received continual reinforcements the resistance became more
severe, until, presently, far from gaining ground, they began to lose
it. At last, about two o'clock, some one hundred and fifty of the
German corps of the Boer force advanced from the northern point
of Thoba in four lines across the table top to drive the British off
the hill. So regular was their order that it was not until their
levelled rifles were seen pointing south that they were recognised
as foes, and artillery opened on them. In spite of an accurate shell
fire they continued to advance boldly against the highest part of
the hill, and, meanwhile, cloaked by a swell of the ground, Captain
Towse, of the Gordon Highlanders, with twelve men of his own
regiment and ten of Kitchener's Horse, was steadily moving
towards them. The scene on the broad stage of the Thoba plateau
was intensely dramatic. The whole army were the witnesses.

The two forces, strangely disproportioned, drew near to each
other. Neither was visible to the other. The unexpected collision
impended. From every point field glasses were turned on the
spectacle, and even hardened soldiers held their breath. At last,
with suddenness, both parties came face to face at fifty yards'
distance. The Germans, who had already made six prisoners,
called loudly on Captain Towse and his little band to surrender.
What verbal answer was returned is not recorded; but a furious
splutter of musketry broke out at once, and in less than a minute
the long lines of the enemy recoiled in confusion, and the top of the
hill was secured to the British. Among the foreigners wounded in
this encounter was Colonel Maximoff.

Captain Towse, for his conspicuous gallantry, and for the extraordinary results which attended it, has been awarded the Victoria
Cross; but, in gaining what is above all things precious to a soldier,
he lost what is necessary to a happy life, for in the moment when
his military career was assured by a brilliant feat of arms, it was
terminated by a bullet which, striking him sideways, blinded him
in both eyes. Thus do Misery and Joy walk hand in hand on the
field of war.

All this time the rifle and gun fire along the whole front had been continuous, and as the day wore on without the British making good their hold on Thoba Mountain the enemy gathered in a more and more threatening attitude on the right of the column, and by four o'clock at least 1,500 men were collected, with guns and "pom-poms", which threw shell into the rearguard and transport. Hamilton, however, was determined to fight the matter out. He therefore directed that all troops should post guards on their front, lie down wherever darkness found them, and prepare to renew the action at daybreak. He then telegraphed to General French for some assistance, the need of more mounted troops being painfully felt.

At dawn on May-day fighting recommenced, and soon after six o'clock parties of the Gordons and Canadians succeeded in gaining possession of the two peaks of Thoba Mountain. Besides this, half a company of the Shropshires, under Colour-Sergeant Sconse, managed to seize the nek between them, and though subjected to a severe cross-fire, which caused in this small party ten casualties out of forty, maintained themselves stubbornly for four hours. The points which dominate the flat top of the mountain were thus gained.

Meanwhile reinforcements, consisting of the 8th Hussars, a composite Lancer regiment, the East Yorkshires, and a field battery, had arrived from Thabanchu, and the approach of Bruce-Hamilton's force from the direction of Kranz Kraal was also felt. General Ian Hamilton now ordered Colonel Clowes, commanding the Cavalry, to move right round Thoba Mountain and threaten the Boer line of retreat as a preliminary and accompaniment of the main Infantry assault, which had now become inevitable. Clowes's force was strengthened by the addition of a horse battery. The newly-arrived Infantry and the field battery had to be diverted to support the right and right rear, where the pressure was now very strong.

At about 8 a.m. General Smith-Dorrien had himself gone up to the top of Thoba Mountain to direct personally the decisive move-ment when the time should come. A little before one o'clock, the progress of the Cavalry being satisfactory, he determined to settle the matter, so that if successful the force might get its baggage over the pass before dark. He therefore formed a line of infantry right across the plateau, two companies of the Shropshires in the centre, and one and a half companies of the Gordons on either flank. The advance was sounded.

The troops moved forward with alacrity. For a few moments the fire was heavy, but the Boers knew themselves bested, and on the soldiers raising the cheer that precedes the actual assault they rushed to their horses, and the whole of Thoba Mountain was won. The rest of the position now became untenable, and the enemy, to the number of 4,000, promptly evacuated it, galloping swiftly back in the direction of Jacobsrust.

A few troops of the 8th Hussars alone got near enough to charge; half-a-dozen Dutchmen were sabred, and one was shot dead by an officer, Lieutenant Wylam. The Boers who were making the attack on the right retreated at the same time as their comrades, and the transport, no longer molested, passed safely over the pass and parked for the night on the northern side. No trustworthy estimate can be formed of the enemy's loss; but a score of prisoners were taken, and an equal number of bodies were found on the position.

The British casualties were fortunately slight considering the fire and its duration, and did not exceed a hundred officers and men.

The next day the junction between the columns was effected, and Ian Hamilton's force formed, with reference to the main advance, the Army of the Right Flank, and was composed as follows:*

Infantry	{ 19th Brigade 21st Brigade }	Smith-Dorrien Bruce-Hamilton
Mounted Infantry	{ 1st M.I. Brigade }	Ridley
Cavalry	{ 2nd Cavalry Brigade }	Broadwood
Artillery	{ 3 Batteries F.A. 2 Batteries H.A. 2 5-in. Guns }	Waldron

The force was supported by the Highland Brigade and two 4·7 naval guns, under General Colvile, who was directed to follow the leading column at a distance of ten miles. Hamilton proposed to march forward on the 2nd of May, but an order from headquarters enjoined a halt; nor was it until the afternoon of the 3rd

* For full composition see Appendix.

that the force reached Jacobsrust, as it is called by the inhabitants.
Isabellasfontein, as our maps record. A little cavalry skirmishing
in the neighbourhood of the camp resulted in the death of one
Lancer.

On the 4th of May the whole army moved forward again, Lord
Roberts passing through Brandfort towards Smaldeel, Hamilton
continuing his march on Winburg. This day did not pass without
fighting, for scarcely had the troops left camp when a patter of
musketry warned the General that his cavalry had become engaged. Riding forward, he was the witness of a very dashing
cavalry exploit. Across the line of advance was drawn up a strong
force of the enemy, estimated at 4,000 men and thirteen guns.
These, in a good position along a range of wooded bluffs, promised
a sufficient task for the troops during the day. But now, suddenly,
from the direction of Brandfort, a new army of Boers began to
appear, riding swiftly down to join hands with their comrades
athwart the road, and fall on the left flank of the column.

The thing was urgent, and perhaps vital. But between the fast
converging Boer forces, at the angle where they would meet, ran a
long ridge of indefinite extent. General Broadwood at once, without
a moment's delay, galloped forward, and with two squadrons of
the Guards' Cavalry and two of the 10th Hussars seized it. The
Boers were already scrambling up its lower slopes. A sharp fight
immediately opened. Kitchener's Horse, hurrying up in support,
occupied a further point of the ridge, and the Dutch, after a
determined but futile attempt to clear the hill, fell back. The
junction of the two Boer columns was prevented. It seems that
the whole of their plan for the day was based on this first condition, and in an army where every individual soldier must have
the details of any plan explained to him it is not easy to make
fresh dispositions on the field.

Indeed, a sort of panic seems to have taken hold of the enemy,
for without waiting for the infantry attack to develop they fled
forthwith at great speed, galloping madly across the drift—as the
British proprietor of Welcome Farm told me—horsemen and guns,
pell-mell, in downright rout, pursued, so swift was their departure,
only by the shells of the horse artillery.

The losses in this brief affair were not large, and almost entirely
among the cavalry. In those few minutes of firing on the ridge
about a dozen troopers had been hit. Lord Airlie was slightly

wounded in the arm, and Lieutenant Rose, Royal Horse Guards, was killed. He had been sent forward to see what lay beyond the further crest of the hill, and found that deadly riflemen lay there waiting for a certain victim. He fell pierced by several bullets, and lived only for half an hour.

This officer was a most zealous soldier. Though possessed of private means which would have enabled him to lead a life of ease and pleasure, he had for several years devoted himself assiduously to the military profession. He went to India as a volunteer during the Tirah Campaign, and served with distinction on Sir Penn Symons's staff—general and aide-de-camp both vanished now, as the foam fades in the wake of a fast ship! From India he hastened to West Africa, and in that vile and pestilential region won a considerable reputation; indeed, he was to have received the Distinguished Service Order for his part in recent operations there had not another war intervened. He arrived at the Cape scarcely a month ago, full of hope and energy. This is the end; and while it is one which a soldier must be ready to meet, deep sympathy will be felt for the father, from whom the public necessities have now required two gallant sons.

Though the disorderly and demoralised nature of the Boer flight through Welcome Farm was known throughout the British Army, it was not expected that so strong a position as the bluffs behind the Vet River would be yielded without a shot fired. This, nevertheless, proved to be the case, for when, on the morning of the 6th, Hamilton resumed his advance, he found that no force of the enemy stood before him and Winburg.

He therefore sent, shortly after noon, a staff officer, Captain Balfour to wit, under flag of truce, with a letter to the mayor of the town summoning him forthwith to surrender the town and all stores therein, and promising that if this were done he would use every effort to protect private property, and that whatever food-stuffs were required by the troops should be paid for. This message, which was duly heralded by the sound of a trumpet, concluded by saying that unless an acceptance was received within two hours the General would understand that his offer had been declined.

Thus accredited, Captain Balfour made his way into the town and was soon the centre of an anxious and excited crowd of burghers and others who filled the market square. The mayor, the landdrost, and other prominent persons—indeed, all the inhabitants—were eager to avail themselves of the good terms, and a satisfactory settlement was almost arranged when, arriving swiftly from the north-east, Philip Botha and a commando of 500 men, mostly Germans and Hollanders, all very truculent since they were as yet unbeaten, entered the town.

A violent and passionate scene ensued. Botha declared he would never surrender Winburg without a fight. Dissatisfied with the attentions paid him by Captain Balfour, he turned furiously on him and rated him soundly. Several of the Free Staters had asked what would be done to them if they laid down their arms. Balfour had replied that they would be permitted to return to their farms, unless actually captured on the field. This Botha held to be a breach of the laws of war, and he thereupon charged the officer with attempting to suborn his burghers. What had he to say that he should not be made a prisoner? "I ask no favours of no Dutchman," replied Balfour, sternly.

"Arrest that man!" shouted Botha, in a fury; "I shall begin shooting soon." At these shameful words a great commotion arose. The women screamed, the mayor and landdrost rushed forward in the hopes of averting bloodshed. The Boers raised their rifles in menace, and the unarmed British envoy flourished his white flag indignantly.

For several minutes it seemed that an actual scuffle, possibly a tragedy, would occur. But the influence of the townsfolk, who knew that their liberty and property lay in the hands of the Imperial General, and that the great siege guns were even then being dragged into effective range, prevailed, and Philip Botha, followed by his men, galloped furiously from the square towards the north.

That afternoon General Ian Hamilton entered Winburg at the head of his troops. Under a shady tree outside the town the mayor and landdrost tendered their submission and two large silver keys. The Union Jack was hoisted in the market-place amid the cheers of the British section of the inhabitants, and, as each battalion marching through the streets saw the famous emblem of pride and power, bright in the rays of the setting sun, these feeble or interested plaudits were drowned in the loud acclamations of the victorious invaders.

Hamilton was expected to arrive on the 7th, if no opposition was encountered. He had fought nearly every day, and reached the town on the evening of the 5th.

CHAPTER TEN

THE ARMY OF THE RIGHT FLANK

Kroonstadt: May 16, 1900

ON THE same day that Ian Hamilton's force won their fight at Houtnek, to wit, the 1st of May, the advance of the main army towards Pretoria, long expected, long prepared, long delayed, began, and the Eleventh Division marched north from Bloemfontein to join the Seventh, which was entrenched at Karree Siding. On the 3rd both infantry divisions moved forward along the railway, their left protected by Gordon's Cavalry Brigade and Hutton's Mounted Infantry, and after a sharp cannonade drove the Boers from their positions covering Brandfort and entered the town. The advance was resumed on the 5th, and the enemy were again met with, this time holding the line of the Vet River. Another artillery action ensued, in which the British 5-inch and naval 4·7 guns were very effective, and at the end of which the West Australians and other parts of Hutton's Mounted Infantry force, pushed across the river in gallant style and captured an important kopje. The Dutchmen then retreated, and the Field Marshal's headquarters on the 6th were fixed in Smaldeel. His losses since leaving Bloemfontein had not amounted to twenty-five men.

Ian Hamilton, in spite of the long marches his troops had made, was impatient to push on from Winburg without delay, and, following the track to Ventersburg, to seize the drifts across the Sand River, twenty miles to the north. The great speed of his last movement had outpaced the Boers, and their convoys were struggling along abreast of, and even behind, the British column, trying vainly to slip across our front, and join the burgher forces accumulating for the defence of Kroonstadt. By marching forthwith—great though the strain might be—the General hoped to secure the bloodless passage of the river, and perhaps cut up some of these same toiling convoys. Accordingly, having collected from the town about three days' stores—Sir Henry Colvile helping him unselfishly with mule waggons—he set his brigades in motion on the afternoon of the 6th, and marched nine miles towards the Sand.

But Lord Roberts had decided to remain at Smaldeel until his temporary bridge over the Vet River was made and the trains running, and he did not choose to run the risk of the Boers concentrating all their forces upon any single division of his army, such as would be incurred if Hamilton pushed forward alone. The principle was indisputable; but, of course, in practice it resolved itself into another instance of balancing drawbacks, for delay gave the enemy time to get his breath, and meant that the Sand River passage would be opposed. Besides, if the Boers had flung all their strength upon Hamilton, we were 7,000 bayonets, 3,000 horse, and nearly forty guns, and would have beat them off with a shocking slaughter. To us it seemed a great pity to wait; but to the Chief, in whose eyes the Army of the Right Flank was but one column of that far-flung line which stretched from Rundle near Senekal, along the front of the main army to Methuen near Boshof, Hunter at Warrenton, and Mahon far away on the fringe of the Kalahari desert, it must have been a very small matter, and certainly not one justifying any loss of cohesion in the general scheme. So I have no doubt that it was right to make us halt on the 7th and 8th.

On the former of these two days of rest Lord Roberts sent for General Hamilton to meet him at a point on the branch railway line midway between Winburg and Smaldeel, and they had a long private conference together. On the 9th, the whole army marched forward again towards the Sand River. I rode with the General, who managed somehow to find himself among the cavalry patrols of the right flank guard, and we watched with telescopes three long lines of dust in the eastward, which, under examination, developed into horsemen and waggons marching swiftly north and turning more and more across our front. It was clear that if we had pushed on without halting, all these commandos would have been prevented from reaching Kroonstadt. The General contemplated them hungrily for some time, but they were too far off to attack, bearing in mind the great combination of which we were a part. The flanking patrols, however, exchanged a few shots.

The march was not a long one, and by mid-day we reached the halting-place, a mile south of the river. The headquarters were fixed in a large farm which stood close to the waggon-track we followed.

This farmhouse was certainly the best purely Dutch homestead I have ever seen in the 500 miles I have ridden about the Free State. It was a large square building, with a deep verandah, and a pretty flower-garden in front, and half a dozen barns and stables around it. The construction of a dam across the neighbouring spruit had formed a wide and pleasant pool, in which many good fat ducks and geese were taking refuge from the wandering soldier. At the back, indeed, on all sides but the front of the farm, rose a thick belt of fir-trees. Within the house the ground-floor was divided into three excellent bedrooms, with old-fashioned feather-beds and quaint wooden bedsteads, a prim but spacious parlour, a kitchen, pantry, and store-room. The parlour deserved the greatest attention. The furniture was dark and massive. The boards of the floor were deeply stained. In the middle was a good carpet upon which an ample oval table stood. The walls were hung with curious prints or coloured plates, and several texts in Dutch. One pair of plates I remember represented the ten stages of man's life and woman's life, and showed both in every period from the cradle to the grave, which latter was not reached until the comfortable age of one hundred. The woman's fortunes were especially prosperous. At birth she sprawled contentedly in a cradle, whilst loving parents bent over her in rapture, and dutiful angels hung attendant in the sky. At ten she scampered after a hoop. At twenty she reclined on the stalwart shoulder of an exemplary lover. At thirty she was engaged in teaching *seven* children their letters. At forty, she celebrated a silver wedding. At fifty, still young and blooming, she attended the christening of a grandchild. At sixty, it was a great-grandchild. At seventy she enjoyed a golden wedding. At eighty she was smilingly engaged in knitting. Even at ninety she was well preserved, nor could she with reason complain of her lot in life when, at a hundred, the inevitable hour arrived. "Be fruitful and multiply", was the meaning of a Dutch text on the opposite wall, and a dozen children black and white (little Kaffirs, the off-spring of the servants, playing with the sons and daughters of the house) showed that the spirit of the injunction was observed; and these are things with which the statesman will have to reckon.

The inmates of the farm consisted of the old man, a venerable gentleman of about sixty years, his dame, a few years younger, three grown-up daughters, a rather ill-favoured spinster sister, and seven or eight children or grandchildren of varying ages. There were in all seven sons or grandsons—two were married and had farms of their own; but all, including even one of fourteen, were "on commando" at the wars, some, perhaps, looking at us and their home from the heights across the river.

The General politely requested shelter for the night, and a bed-room and the parlour were placed at his disposal; not very en-thusiastically, indeed, but that was only natural. The staff settled down in the verandah so as not to disturb the family. Ian Hamilton, keenly interested in everything, began at once to ask the old lady questions through an interpreter. She gave her answers with no good grace, and when the General inquired about her youngest fighting son—he of fourteen—her sour face showed signs of emotion, and the conversation ended for the day. On the morrow, however, just before he crossed the river, he had to come back to the tele-graph-tent pitched near the farm, and found time to see her again.

"Tell her," he said to the interpreter, "that we have won the battle to-day."

They told her, and she bowed her head with some dignity.

"Tell her that the Dutch will now certainly be beaten in the war."

No response.

"Perhaps her sons will be taken prisoners."

No answer.

"Now tell her to write down on a piece of paper the name of the youngest, and give it to my aide-de-camp; and then when he is captured she must write to me or to the Hoofd-General, and we will send him back to her, and not keep him a prisoner."

She thawed a little at this, and expressed a hope that he had been comfortable while beneath her roof, and then—for the guns were still firing—he had to hurry away. But the aide-de-camp remained behind for the paper.

During the time we spent in this homely place I made a thorough inspection of the farm, especially the parlour, where I found one very curious book. It was a collection of national songs and ballads, compiled, and in part written, by Mr. Reitz. I afterwards succeeded in buying another copy in Ventersburg; indeed, it has been widely disseminated. The first part consists of patriotic Boer poems—the

Volkslied, the Battle of Majuba, the Battle of Laing's Nek, and other similar themes. The second half of the book is filled with Reitz's translations of English songs and well-known ditties into the *taal*. John Gilpin, besides being a burgher of credit and renown, was eke a Field-Cornet of famous Bloemfontein. Young Lochinvar had come from out of the Boshof district. The Landdrost's daughter of Winburg found a lover no less faithful than a famous swain of Islington. The pictures were mightily diverting. The old Field-Cornet Gilpin—"Jan Jurgens", as he called himself now—was shown galloping wildly along, on a pulling Basuto pony, through the straggling streets of, let us say, Ventersburg, his slouch hat crammed over his eyes, his white beard flapping in the wind, while a stately *vrouw*, four children, and a Kaffir, flung up their hands in mingled wonder and derision.

One piece began:

> Engels! Engels! alles Engels! Engels wat jij siet en hoor.
> Ins ons skole, in ons kerke, word ons modertaal vermoor.

I cannot read Dutch, but the meaning and object of the book were sufficiently clear without that knowledge.

F. W. Reitz, sometime President of the Free State, now State Secretary of the Transvaal, looked far ahead, and worked hard. This, the foundation-stone of a vernacular literature, was but one act in the long scheme of policy, pursued, year in year out, with tireless energy, and indomitable perseverance, to manufacture a new Dutch nation in South Africa—the policy which, in the end, had brought a conquering army to this quiet farm, and scattered the schemers far and wide. But what a game it must have been to play! Only a little more patience, a little less pride and over-confidence, concessions here, concessions there, anything to gain time, and then, some day—a mighty Dutch Republic, "the exchange of a wealthier Amsterdam, the schools of a more learned Leyden", and, above all—no cursed Engels.

I was considering these matters, only suggested here, when messengers and the sound of firing came in from the eastward. The news that small parties of Boers were engaging our right flank guard did not prevent Hamilton riding over to meet the Chief, nor tempt us to quit the cool verandah of the farm; but when, suddenly, at about three o'clock, fifty shots rang out in quick succession, scarcely 500 yards away, every one got up in a hurry, and snatching pistols and belts, ran out to see what mischance had occurred. The scene that met our eyes was unusual. Down the side of the hill there poured a regular cascade of antelope—certainly not less than 700 or 800 in number—maddened with fear at finding themselves in the midst of the camp, and seeking frantically for a refuge. This spectacle, combined with the hope of venison, was too much for the soldiers, and forthwith a wild and very dangerous fire broke out, which was not stopped until fifteen or twenty antelopes were killed, and one Australian mounted infantryman wounded in the stomach. The injury of the latter was at first thought to be serious, and the rumour ran that he was dead; but, luckily, the bullet only cut the skin.

Thus disturbed, I thought it might be worth while to walk up to the outpost line and see what was passing there. When I reached the two guns which were posted on the near ridge, the officers were in consultation. Away across the Sand River, near two little kopjes, was a goodly Boer commando. They had just arrived from the east of our line of march, and having skirted round our pickets had set themselves down to rest and refresh. Spread as they were on the smooth grass, the telescope showed every detail. There were about 150 horsemen, with five ox-waggons and two guns. The horses were grazing, but not off-saddled. The men were lying or sitting on the ground. Evidently they thought themselves out of range. The subaltern commanding the guns was not quite sure that he agreed with them. Some Colonial mounted infantry officers standing near were almost indignant that the guns should let such a chance slip. The subaltern was very anxious to fire—"really think I could reach the brutes"; but he was afraid he would get into trouble if he fired his guns at any range greater than artillery custom approves. His range finders said "6,000". Making allowances for the clear atmosphere, I should have thought it was more. At last he decided to have a shot. "Sight for 5,600, and let's see how much we fall short." The gun cocked its nose high in the air and flung its shell accordingly. To our astonishment the projectile passed far over the Boer commando, and burst nearly 500 yards beyond them: to our astonishment and to theirs. The burghers lost no time in changing their position. The men ran to their horses, and, mounting, galloped away in a dispersing cloud. Their guns whipped up and made for the further hills. The ox-waggons sought the shelter of a neighbouring donga. Meanwhile, the artillery subaltern, delighted at the success of his venture, pursued all these objects with his fire, and using both his guns threw at least a dozen shells among them. Material result: one horse killed. This sort of artillery fire is what we call waste of ammunition when we do it to others, and a confounded nuisance when they do it to us. After all, who is there who enjoys being disturbed by shells just as he is settling himself comfortably to rest, after a long march? And who fights the better next day for having to scurry a mile and a half to cover with iron pursuers at his heels? Even as it was an opportunity was lost. We ought to have sneaked up six guns, a dozen if there were a dozen handy, all along the ridge, and let fly with the whole lot, at ranges varying from 5,000 to 6,000 yards with time shrapnel. Then there would have been a material as well as a moral effect. "Pooh," says the scientific artillerist, "you would have used fifty shells, tired your men, and disturbed your horses, to hit a dozen scallawags and stampede 150. That is not the function of artillery." Nevertheless function or no function, it is war, and the way to win war. Harass, bait, and worry your enemy until you establish a funk. Once he is more frightened of you than you are of him, all your enterprises will prosper; and if fifty shells can in any way accelerate that happy condition, be sure they are not wasted.

The afternoon passed uneventfully away, though the outposts were gradually drawn into a rifle duel with the Dutch sharpshooters in the scrub across the river. In the evening the General returned from his conference with Lord Roberts, and told us the passage was to be forced on the morrow all along the line. The Army of the Right Flank would cross by the nearest drift in our present front. The Seventh Division inclining to its right would come into line on our left. The Field-Marshal, with the Guards and the rest of Pole-Carew's Division, would strike north along the line of the railway. French, with two cavalry brigades and Hutton's Mounted Infantry Brigade, was to swing around the enemy's right and push hard for Ventersburg siding. Broadwood from our flank, with the Second Cavalry Brigade, and such of the Second Mounted Infantry Brigade as could be spared, was to be thrust through as soon as the Boer front was broken, and try to join hands with French, thus, perhaps, cutting off and encircling the Boer right. The diagram—it is not a map—on page 800 will help to explain the scheme.

The operation of the next day was one of the largest and most extended movements of the war, although, probably from this cause, it was attended by very little loss of life. Upon the British side six infantry and six mounted brigades, with rather more than 100 guns, were brought into action along a front of over twenty-five miles. The Boers, however, still preserved their flanks. Upon the west they succeeded in holding up French, and on the east they curled round Hamilton's right and rear so that his action here,

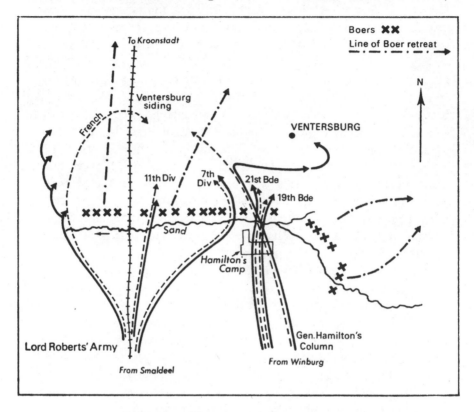

DIAGRAM TO EXPLAIN THE PASSAGE OF THE
SAND RIVER, 10TH OF MAY, 1900
The dotted lines show what was proposed; the
continuous lines show what was done
The crosses indicate the Boers

which in its early stages resembled that afterwards fought at Diamond Hill, was of a piercing rather than a turning nature. But in thus amazingly extending their scanty forces, which, altogether, did not number more than 9,000 men, with twenty-five guns, the enemy became so weak all along their front that the attacking divisions broke through everywhere, as an iron bar might smash thin ice, with scarcely any shock.

On the evening of the 10th, the British forces, in their extended line, lay spread along the south bank of the river, just out of cannon-shot of the Boer positions on the further side. French, indeed, did not rest content with securing his ford twelve miles to the west of the railway, but pushed his two brigades across before dark. The wisdom of this movement is disputed. On the one hand, it is contended that by crossing he revealed the intention of the Commander-in-Chief, and drew more opposition against himself the next day. On the other, it is urged that he was right to get across unopposed while he could, and that his purpose was equally revealed, no matter which side of the river he stayed. During the night Ian Hamilton, at the other end of the line, seized the drift in his front with a battalion, which promptly entrenched itself. Tucker, who proposed to cross near the same point, despatched the Cheshire Regiment for a similar purpose. The single battalion was sufficient; but the importance and wisdom of the movement was proved by the fact that the enemy during the night sent 400 men to occupy the river bank and hold the passage, and found themselves forestalled.

At daybreak the engagement was begun along the whole front. I am only concerned with Ian Hamilton's operations; but, in order that these may be understood, some mention must be made of the other forces. French advanced as soon as it was light, and almost immediately became engaged with a strong force of Boers, who barred his path, and prevented his closing on the railway as intended. A sharp cavalry action followed, in which the Boers fought with much stubbornness; and the Afrikander Horse, a corps of formidable mercenaries, even came to close quarters with Dickson's brigade, and were charged. French persevered through the day, making very little progress towards the railway, but gaining ground gradually to the north. Although his casualties numbered more than a hundred, he was still some distance from Ventersburg siding at nightfall. The centre attack properly awaited the progress of the flanking movements, and was, during the early part of the day, contented with an artillery bombardment, chiefly conducted by its heavy guns. Tucker and Hamilton, however, fell on with much determination, and were soon briskly engaged.

Ian Hamilton began his action at half-past five, with his heavy guns, which shelled the opposite heights leisurely, while the infantry and cavalry were moving off. The Boer position before us ran along a line of grassy ridges, with occasional kopjes, which sloped up gradually and reached their summits about a mile from the river. But besides this position, which was the objective of the force, the Boers, who held all the country to the east, began a disquieting attack along our right and right rear, and although the mounted infantry, and principally Kitchener's Horse, under Major Fowle, held them at arm's length throughout the day, the firing in this quarter caused the General some concern, and occupied the greater part of his attention.

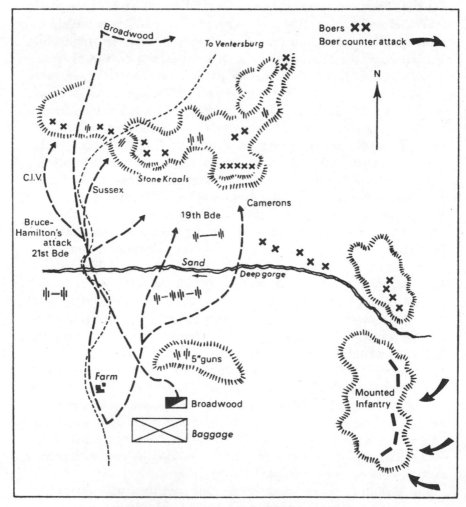

IAN HAMILTON'S ACTION AT THE SAND RIVER,
10TH OF MAY, 1900

The crosses indicate the Boers

At six o'clock the Twenty-first Brigade began to cross the river, and Bruce-Hamilton, stretching out to his left, soon developed a wide front. The Boers now opened fire with two or three field-guns and a "pom-pom", which latter was quickly silenced by our heavy pieces. At the same time, the Nineteenth Brigade, who were containing the enemy's left, became engaged with their skirmishers in the scrub by the river. The four batteries of field artillery also came into action, and were pushed forward across the drift as soon as sufficient space was gained by the Infantry. At a little after seven the head of General Tucker's Division appeared on the plain to our left, and that determined officer thrust his men over the river in most vigorous style. Moreover, seeing Bruce-Hamilton committed to an assault, he swung two of his own batteries round to the eastward, and so rendered us material assistance.

Both Smith-Dorrien, who directed the two infantry brigades, and Ian Hamilton were fully alive to the grave dangers of crowding too many troops on to a narrow front, and the infantry attack was very sparingly fed with supports, until it became completely extended. This condition was attained about eleven o'clock, when the Camerons were sent across the river to clear the scrub and prolong the line to the right. Bruce-Hamilton now had his deployment completed, and with an admirable simultaneity the whole of the assaulting Infantry rose up and advanced together upon the enemy's position, covered by the heavy fire of twenty-six guns. The panorama was now very extensive. Far away to the left the smoke of lyddite shells, and the curious speck of the war-balloon high in the clear air, showed that the centre was engaged. The whole of the Seventh Division had crossed the Sand, and were now curving to the north-west amid a crackle of fire. Before us the slopes were sprinkled with brown dots moving swiftly upwards. The crest of the ridge was fringed with exploding shells. For a few minutes the Boers fired steadily, and the dust jumped amid the Sussex Regiment and the City Imperial Volunteers. But both infantry and artillery attacks were far beyond the capacity of the defence to resist, and by noon the whole of the heights beyond the Sand were in British possession.

Ian Hamilton had meanwhile ordered baggage and cavalry to cross. Broadwood was over the enemy's position almost as soon as the infantry. He proceeded to move in the direction of Ventersburg siding. The enemy, however, had covered themselves with a strong rearguard, and the cavalry were soon opposed by three guns and a force of riflemen of considerable numbers. Whether Broadwood would have thought it worth while to make here the effort which he afterwards made in the action of Diamond Hill, and order a charge, is uncertain; for at this moment a misunderstanding arose which induced him to change his plans altogether.

The Boer pressure on our right rear had been growing stronger and stronger all the morning, and at length Hamilton, wishing to check the enemy sharply, so as to draw his rearguard over the river after his baggage, told his chief of artillery to find him a battery. Now it happened that only one of the two horse batteries, P, had been able to go with the Cavalry, the other, Q, being too tired to keep up. The chief of artillery therefore proposed to send for the tired battery. Unfortunately, by some mistake, either in giving or taking the order, the orderly was sent for P instead of Q. The man, a sergeant-major, galloped across the river, and, understanding that the matter was urgent, hurried after Broadwood, overtook him just as he was becoming engaged, and demanded the battery. Broadwood, who knew that Hamilton would never deprive him of his guns except for some very urgent reason, sent them at once, abandoned his movement to the north-west, which indeed was now impracticable without artillery, and concluding that the rearguard was seriously involved, turned sharply to the east to assist them. Explanations arrived too late to make it worth while to revert to the original plan, and, perhaps, seeing that French was unable to make Ventersburg siding, it was just as well that Broadwood did not try alone.

Broadwood's latest movement, or the action of the artillery, or the knowledge that the British had successfully forced the passage of the river at all points, induced the Boers who were assailing the rearguard to desist, and the musketry in that quarter gradually died away. Meanwhile, by the exertions of Lieutenant-Colonel Maxse, the baggage had mostly been dragged across the river, and Ian Hamilton made haste to overtake his victorious Infantry, who had already disappeared into the valley beyond the enemy's position. By the time that we reached the top of the high ground, Bruce-Hamilton's leading battalions were nearly a mile further on, and the tail of Broadwood's brigade was vanishing in a high cloud of dust to the eastward. The City Imperial Volunteers, who had lost a few men in the attack, were resting on the hill after their advance, and eating their biscuits. Several dead Boers had been found lying among the rocks, and a burial party was at work digging a grave for these and for four of our own men who had fallen close by. There were also a few prisoners—Transvaalers for the most part —who had surrendered when the troops fixed bayonets. Four miles away to the north-east the trees and houses of Ventersburg rose from a grassy hollow.

The General decided to bivouac in the valley beyond the enemy's position, and to set his pickets upon the hills to the northward. He also sent an officer with a flag of truce into Ventersburg to demand the surrender of the town, and directed Broadwood to detach a regiment and some mounted infantry to occupy it, should the enemy comply. In case they should desire to hold the town the 5-inch guns were brought into position on the captured heights.

Hoping to secure some supplies, particularly bottled beer, before everything should be requisitioned by the army, I rode forward after the flag of truce had gone in and waited where I could see what followed. When, about an hour later, a cavalry force began to advance from the direction of Broadwood upon the town, I knew that all was well, and trotted on to join them. My road led me within a few hundred yards of the town, but, luckily for me, I did not enter it alone, and hurried to join the troops. All of a sudden the ominous patter of rifle shots broke the stillness of the evening, and, turning to where the sound came, I saw a score of Boers standing on the sky-line about a mile away and firing at the advancing cavalry, or, perhaps, for I was much nearer, at me. The next minute there galloped out of the town about a score of Dutchmen, who fled in the direction of their friends on the western sky line. Had I ridden straight into the town I should have run into these people's jaws. I lost no time in joining the cavalry, and entered the streets with the squadron of Blues. It was a miserable little place, not to be compared with Winburg. There were a few good stores and a small hotel, where I found what I sought; but the whole town was very dirty and squalid. Thirty or forty troopers of Roberts's Horse were firing at the fugitive burghers from the edge of the buildings and gardens, while a score of reckless fellows were galloping after them in excited pursuit. The Boers on the hill kept up a brisk fire to help their comrades in, and not a few of the bullets kicked up the dust in the village streets, without in the least disturbing the women and children who crowded together to look at the war, in blissful ignorance of their danger. When some of these people were told that they would perhaps be killed if they came out of their houses while the fighting was going on, they clutched their children and sought shelter with an energy at which, since, after all, nobody was hurt, it was pardonable to laugh.

Night put an end to all skirmishing, and under its cover the Boers retreated—the greater part to Kroonstadt, which, be it remembered, they meant to hold to the death; but a considerable proportion to the east, where they collected with the commandos under Christian de Wet. Broadwood's brigade had captured about a dozen waggons and thirty prisoners. In all there were fifty-two unwounded and seven wounded Boers in our hands at the end of the day. The casualties in Hamilton's force were under fifty. Tucker and Pole-Carew may have lost the same number between them. French, who encountered the most stubborn resistance, had a little over 120. But, in any case, the passage of the Sand River in this long straggling action was cheaply won at a cost of under 250 officers and men.

All our beasts were so exhausted by the labour of dragging the waggons through the steep and rocky drift of the Sand, and by the long pull up the hills on the opposite side, that few of the regiments got their baggage that night, and hence it was impossible to make an early start next morning. But it was known that the Field-Marshal meant to reach Kroonstadt on the next day, and as all the information at our disposal indicated that the Boers were entrenching a strong position along a line of wooded bluffs called the Boschrand, just south of the town, every minute of halt was grudged.

We moved at eleven o'clock, heading direct for Kroonstadt, and persevered for two hours after the sun had set, making in all nearly seventeen miles. The country to our left was flat and open, and as we converged upon the main army we could see, like red clouds with the sunset behind them, the long parallel lines of dust which marked the marches of the Seventh and Eleventh Divisions; and we knew besides, that, beyond both columns and west of the railroad, French was driving his weary squadrons forward upon another wide swoop. The army drew together in the expectation of a great action. But for all our marching we could never make up the extra distance we had to cover in coming diagonally from the flank, and as darkness fell we realised that the Seventh Division was drawing across our front, and that Pole-Carew with the guard was striding along ahead of us all. That night Lord Roberts slept at America siding, scarcely six miles from the Boschrand position.

Ian Hamilton marched on again at dawn, transport and convoys struggling along miles behind, and the fine-drawn yet eager infantry close upon the heels of the cavalry screen. At times we listened for the sound of guns, for if the enemy stood, the Field-Marshal must come into contact with them by eight o'clock. And when, after nine o'clock, no cannonade was heard, the rumour ran through the army that the Boers had fled without giving battle, the pace slacked off, and the Infantry began to feel the effects of their exertions.

At eleven a message from Lord Roberts reached General Broad-wood to say that it did not matter by which road Hamilton's column marched in, as the enemy was not holding his positions. Thereupon I determined, since there was to be no battle, to see the capture of Kroonstadt, and being mounted on a fresh pony I had bought at Winburg, a beautiful and tireless little beast, by an English blood sire out of a Basuto mare, I soon left the cavalry behind, caught up the rear of Tucker's transport, pushed on four or five miles along the line of march of his division, struck the tail of the Eleventh Division, and finally overtook the head of the Infantry columns about three miles from the town.

Lord Roberts entered Kroonstadt at about mid-day with all his staff. The Eleventh Division, including the Guards' Brigade, marched past him in the market square, and then, passing through the town, went into bivouac on the northern side. The rest of the army halted south of Kroonstadt. Gordon's Cavalry Brigade a mile from the town; the Seventh Division and Ian Hamilton's force three miles away, in a wide valley among the scrub-covered, trench-rimmed hills the Boers had not dared defend. French, whose turning movement had again been obstinately opposed, reached the railway line north of the town too late to intercept any rolling stock. Indeed, Major Hunter-Weston, a daring and enterprising engineer, arrived at the bridge he had hoped to blow up only to find that it had been blown up by the enemy.

Thus, by one long spring from Bloemfontein, Kroonstadt, the new capital of the Free State, was captured. It has the reputation of being one of the prettiest places in the Republic, but even when allowances are made for the circumstances under which we saw it, it does not seem that its fame is just. The town looked a little larger than Winburg, though not nearly so clean and well-kept, and the whole place was smothered in reddish dust, and dried up by the sun. The Boers retreated northward along the railway, in spite of all President Steyn's exhortations, which included the public sjambokking of several unwilling burghers, and did not stop except to wreck the permanent way until they reached Rhenoster kopjes. The President, with the members of the Executive Council and the seat of Government—which needs to have a good pair of legs beneath it in times like these—withdrew to Lindley, whither, for various reasons, it soon became desirable to follow them.

CHAPTER ELEVEN

LINDLEY

Heilbron: May 22, 1900

HAVING ARRIVED thus prosperously at Kroonstadt, Lord Roberts determined to halt until his supplies were replenished and the railway line from Bloemfontein in working order. Moreover, in the expectation of a general action outside the town, he had concentrated all his troops and had drawn the Army of the Right Flank close in to the main force. Before he advanced again towards the enemy's position on the Rhenoster River, he wished to extend his front widely, as he had done in the previous operation. The scheme of advance by converging columns required a pause after each concentration before the movement could be repeated; so that while the Field-Marshal himself remained stationary his energetic lieutenant was again on the move.

General Ian Hamilton, with the same troops as before and an addition of four "pom-poms", started from his camp outside Kroonstadt on the 15th, and after a short march encamped on the eastern side of the town preparatory to moving on Lindley, whither President Steyn had withdrawn. The question of supplies was a very troublesome one, and it was no light matter to thrust out fifty miles into a hostile country with only three and a half days' food and forage in hand. Suppose anything should happen to the convoys which were to follow. Meat in plenty could be found everywhere, but the stores of flour and other farinaceous goods which the farmhouses might contain were insufficient and precarious. Even the benefits of the abundant meat supply were to some extent discounted by the scarcity of wood, for it is not much satisfaction to a soldier to be provided with a leg of mutton if he has no means of cooking. The deficiencies were hardly made good by the arrival of a small convoy, the greater part of which consisted of disinfectants

for standing camps, and the rest—so valuable in a grass country—
of compressed hay.

Nevertheless, being determined, and trusting, not without reason,
in his supply officer, Captain Atcherley, Hamilton started on the
16th, and the infantry bivouacked eighteen miles from Kroonstadt
on the Lindley road—it would perhaps be less misleading to write
track. The cavalry brigade with one corps of mounted infantry
under Broadwood were pushed ten miles further on, and seized a
fine iron bridge, not marked on any map, which spans an important
spruit at Kaalfontein. Here trustworthy information was received
that a large force of Boers with guns was retreating before Rundle's
column (Eighth Division) northwards upon Lindley, and deeming
it important to occupy the town before they arrived, Hamilton
ordered the cavalry to hurry on and take possession of the heights
to the north of it. It was a double march when ordinary marches
were long. The result, however, justified the effort. Broadwood
"surprised"—the word is taken from the Boer accounts—Lindley
on the 17th. Scarcely fifty Boers were at hand to defend it. A waggon with 60,000*l.* in specie barely escaped from the clutches of the
cavalry. After a brief skirmish the town surrendered. The British
loss was three men wounded. Broadwood then retired as directed by
his chief to the commanding hill to the north to bivouac. This hill
may for convenience be called "Lindley Hill" in the subsequent
narrative.

The infantry and baggade also made a long march on the 17th,
but as the road was obstructed by several bad spruits or *dongas*,
they were still fourteen miles from Lindley when night closed in.
Even then the transport was toiling on the road, and a large part of
it did not come in, and then in an exhausted condition, until after
midnight. I wonder how many people in England realise what a
spruit is, and how it affects military operations. Those who live in
highly developed countries, where the surface of the earth has been
shaped to our convenience by the patient labour of many years, are
accustomed to find the road running serenely forward across the
valleys, and they scarcely notice the bridges and culverts over
which it passes. All is different in South Africa. The long column of
transport trails across the plain. The veldt in front looks smooth
and easy going. Presently, however, there is a block. What is the
matter? Let us ride forward to see: and so onward to where the
single string of waggons merges in a vast crowd of transport, twenty

rows abreast, mule carts, Cape carts, ox waggons, ambulances, and artillery, all waiting impatiently, jostling each other, while drivers and conductors swear and squabble. Here is the spruit—a great chasm in the ground, fifty feet deep, a hundred yards from side to side. The banks are precipitous and impassable at all points except where the narrow single track winds steeply and unevenly down. The bottom is a quagmire, and though the engineers are doing their best to level and improve the roadway, it is still a combination of the Earl's Court water chute and the Slough of Despond. One by one, after a hot dispute for precedence, the waggons advance. The brakes must be screwed up to their tightest grip lest the ponderous vehicles rush forward down the slope and overwhelm their oxen. Even with this precaution the descent of each is a crash, a scramble, and a bump. At the bottom like a feather bed lies the quagmire. Here one waggon in every three sticks. The mules give in after one effort—unworthy hybrids. The oxen strain with greater perseverance. But in the end it is the man who has to do the hauling. Forthwith come fatigue parties of weary men—it has been a long march already to soldiers fully equipped. Drag ropes are affixed, and so with sweat, blood, and stretching sinew, long whips cracking and whistling, white men heaving and natives yelping encouragement, another waggon comes safely through. And there are seven miles of transport!

On the morning of the 18th the infantry were about to move off, when a pattern of rifle shots to the north of the road reminded us of the presence of the enemy. A foraging party of Major Rimington's Guides had ridden up to a farm, which stood in full view of the camp and flew (or was it hoisted afterwards?) a white flag. Arrived there, they were received by a volley from five Boers in hiding near. Conceive the impudence of these people: five Boers, within a mile of eight thousand British and a powerful cavalry force, fire on a foraging party! Luckily no harm done; cavalry gallop out angrily; Boers vanish among remoter kopjes. "But," said the General, "what about my convoys?"

So it was arranged that Smith-Dorrien should be left where he was (twelve miles west of Lindley) with his own brigade, one battery, and a corps of mounted infantry to help in the expected convoy, and should cut off the corner and rejoin the column at the end of its first march towards Heilbron. Ian Hamilton with the rest of the troops then moved on to Lindley. The march lay through the same class of country hitherto traversed—a pleasant grassy upland which, if not abundantly supplied with water by nature, promised a rich reward to man, should he take the trouble to construct even the simplest irrigation works. Spruits ran in all directions, and only required an ordinary dam, like the *bunds* the peasants build in India, to jewel each valley with a gleaming vivifying lake. The husbanding of water would repair the scarcity of wood, and the tenth year might see the naked grass clothed and adorned with foliage. But at present the country-side is so sparsely populated that the energies of its inhabitants could not produce much effect upon the landscape. The unamiable characteristic of the Boer, to shun the sight of his neighbour's barn, has scattered the farms so widely that little patches of tillage are only here and there to be seen, and the intervening miles lie neglected, often not more than twenty acres of a six thousand acre property being brought into cultivation, which seems rather a pity.

The fair face of the land under its smiling sky was not unmarked by the footprints of war. In the dry weather the careless habits of the soldiers were the constant cause of grass fires. The half-burnt match, tossed idly aside after a pipe was lighted, or an unguarded spark from a cooking fire kindled at once an extensive conflagration. The strong winds drove the devouring blaze swiftly forward across the veldt, clouding the landscape by day with dense fumes of smoke and scarring the scene by night with vivid streaks of flame. So frequent were these grass fires that they became a serious nuisance, wasting in an hour many acres of grazing, proclaiming the movement and marking the track of the army, stifling the marching columns with pungent odours, destroying the field telegraph, and only extinguished by the heavy dews of the early morning. But in spite of repeated injunctions in the daily orders, the accidents—for which, indeed, there was every excuse—continued, and the plains of brownish grass were everywhere disfigured with ugly patches of black ashes which, as the fires burnt outwards, would spread and spread, like stains of blood soaking through khaki.

At length the track, which had been winding among the smooth undulations, rounded an unusually steep hillock of kopje character, and we saw before us at the distance of a mile the pretty little town of Lindley. The cavalry bivouacs covered the nearer slopes of the high hill to the northward. The houses—white walls and blue-grey roofs of iron—were tucked away at the bottom of a regular cup, and partly hidden by the dark green Australian trees. We rode first of all to Broadwood's headquarters, following the ground wire which led thither. Arrived there we learned the news. Boer laagers and Boer patrols had been found scattered about the country to the south-east and north-east. There was occasional firing along the picket line. The town had upon most searching requisition yielded nearly two days' supply, and, most important of all, Piet De Wet, brother of the famous Christiaan, had sent in a message offering to surrender with such of his men as would follow his example, if he were permitted to return to his farm. Broadwood had at once given the required assurance, and Hamilton on his arrival had wired to Lord Roberts fully endorsing the views of his subordinate, and requesting that the agreement might be confirmed. The answer came back with the utmost despatch, and was to the effect that surrender must be unconditional. De Wet, it was remarked, was excluded from the favourable terms of the Proclamation to the Burghers of the Orange Free State, by the fact that he had commanded part of the Republican forces. He could not therefore be permitted to return to his farm. I need not say with what astonishment this decision was received. The messenger carrying the favourable answer was luckily overtaken before he had passed through our picket line and the official letter was substituted. Piet De Wet, who awaited the reply at a farmhouse some ten miles from Lindley, found himself presented with the alternative of continuing the war or going to St. Helena, or perhaps Ceylon; and as events have shown he preferred the former course to our loss in life, honour, and money.

In the afternoon I rode into Lindley to buy various stores in which my waggon was deficient. It is a typical South African town with a large central market square and four or five broad unpaved streets radiating therefrom. There is a small clean-looking hotel, a substantial gaol, a church and a school-house. But the two largest buildings are the general stores. These places are the depots whence the farmers for many miles around draw all their necessaries and comforts. Owned and kept by Englishmen or Scotchmen, they are built on the most approved style. Each is divided into five or six large well-stocked departments. The variety of their goods is remarkable. You may buy a piano, a kitchen range, a slouch hat, a bottle of hair wash, or a box of sardines over the same counter. The two stores are the rival Whiteley's of the country-side; and the diverse tastes to which they cater prove at once the number of their customers, and the wealth which even the indolent Boer may win easily from his fertile soil.

Personally I sought potatoes, and after patient inquiry I was directed to a man who had by general repute twelve sacks. He was an Englishman, and delighted to see the British bayonets at last. "You can't think", he said, "how we have looked forward to this day."

I asked him whether the Dutch had ill-used him during the war.

"No, not really ill-used us; but when we refused to go out and fight they began commandeering our property, horses and carts at first and latterly food and clothing. Besides, it has been dreadful to have to listen to all their lies and, of course, we had to keep our tongues between our teeth."

It was evident that he hated the Boers among whom his lot had been cast with great earnestness. This instinctive dislike which the British settler so often displays for his Dutch neighbour is a per-plexing and not a very hopeful feature of the South African prob-lem. Presently we reached his house (where the potatoes were stored). Above the doorway hung a Union Jack. I said—

"I advise you to take that down."

"Why?" he asked, full of astonishment. "The British are going to keep the country, aren't they?"

"This column is not going to stay here for ever."

"But," with an anxious look, "surely they will leave some soldiers behind to protect us, to hold the town."

I told him I thought it unlikely. Ours was a fighting column. Other troops would come up presently for garrison duty. But there would probably be an interval of at least a week. Little did I foresee the rough fighting which would rage round Lindley for the next three months. He looked very much disconcerted; not altogether without reason.

"It's very hard on us," he said after a pause. "What will happen when the Boers come back? They're just over the hill now."

"That's why I should take the flag down if I were you. If you don't fight, keep your politics till the war is over!" He looked very disappointed, and I think was asking himself how much his en-thusiasm had compromised him. After we had settled the potato question to his satisfaction and I had sent the sack away upon my pack pony, he perked up. "Come and see my garden," he said, and nothing loth I went. It was not above a hundred yards square, but its contents proclaimed his energy and the possibilities of the soil. He explained how he had dammed a marshy sluit in the side of the hills to the eastward. "Plenty of water at all seasons: this pipe you see, only a question of piping: as much water as ever I want: twenty gardens: grow anything you like, potatoes mostly, cabbages (they were beauties), tomatoes and onions, a vine of sweet white grapes, a bed of strawberries over there—anything: it only wants water, and there's plenty of that if you take the trouble to get it."

The signs of industry impressed me. "How long", I asked, "have you been here?"

"Eight years last February," he replied; "see those trees?"

He pointed to a long row of leafy trees about twenty feet high, which gave a cool shade and whose green colour pleased the eye after looking at so much brown grass. I nodded.

"I planted those myself when I came: they grow quickly, don't they? Only a question of water, and that is only a question of work."

Then I left him and returned to the camp with my potatoes and some information thrown in.

The next morning before breakfast-time there was firing in the picket line south of Lindley. The patter of shots sounded across the valley, and upon the opposite slopes the British patrols could be seen galloping about like agitated ants. I was at the moment with General Hamilton. He watched the distant skirmish from his tent door for a little while in silence. Then he said:

"The scouts and the Kaffirs report laagers of the enemy over there, and over there, and over there" (he pointed to the different quarters). "Now either I must attack them today or they will attack me tomorrow. If I attack them today, I weary my troops; and if I don't we shall have to fight an awkward rear-guard action to get out of this place tomorrow."

He did not say at the time which course he meant to follow, but I felt quite sure he would not take his troops back very far to the south or south-east to chastise impalpable laagers. We were running on schedule time and had to make our connections with the main army, to securing whose smooth and undisturbed march all our efforts must be directed. So I was not surprised when the day passed without any movement on our part.

Very early on the 20th the brigades were astir, and as soon as the light was strong Broadwood's Cavalry began to stream away over the northern ridges. The guns and the greater part of the Infantry followed them without delay, so that by seven o'clock the great column of transport was winding round the corner of Lindley Hill on the road to Heilbron. The fact that parties of the enemy had been observed on all sides except the west, made the operation of disentangling the force from Lindley difficult and dangerous. Broadwood's duty was to clear the way in front. Legge's corps of Mounted Infantry guarded the right flank: and Ian Hamilton himself watched the movement of the rearguard, which consisted of the Derbyshire Regiment, Bainbridge's corps of Mounted Infantry and, as a special precaution, the 82nd Field Battery.

The full light of day had no sooner revealed the march of the troops than the watching Boers began to feel and press the picket line: and an intermittent musketry spread gradually along the whole threequarter circle round Lindley. At eight o'clock our troops evacuated the town itself, at nine, the convey being nearly round Lindley Hill, the pickets commenced to draw in. This was a signal for a decided increase in the firing. No sooner were the outposts clear of the town than the Boers in twos and threes galloped into it and began to fire from the houses. All kinds of worthy old gentlemen, moreover, who had received us civilly enough the day before, produced rifles from various hiding-places and shot at us from off their verandahs. Indeed, so quickly did the town revert to the enemy's hands that Somers Somerset, the despatch-rider of *The Times*, was within an ace of being caught. He had arrived late the night before, and having found a comfortable bed at the hotel went to sleep without asking questions. The next thing he remembers is the landlord rushing into his room and crying in great excitement that the Boers were in the town. He scrambled into his clothes and, jumping on his horse, galloped through the streets and was not fired at till he was more than a quarter of a mile away. History does not record whether among such disturbing events he retained his presence of mind sufficiently to settle his hotel bill.

The General and his staff had watched the beginnings of the action from the now deserted camping ground, a dirty waste, littered with rubbish and dotted with the melancholy figures of derelict horses and mules. So soon as the retiring pickets drew north of the town, he mounted and made his way to the top of Lindley Hill. From this commanding table-top the whole scene of action, indeed the whole surrounding country, was visible. At our

feet beyond the abandoned bivouac lay the houses of Lindley
giving forth a regular rattle of musketry. On either side, east and
west, rose two prominent kopjes held by companies of mounted
infantry briskly engaged. The tail of the transport serpent was
twisting away into safety round the base of our hill. Far away on
the broad expanse of down parties of Dutch horsemen cantered
swiftly forward; and along a road beyond the eastern kopje rose a
steady trickle of mounted men. They moved in true Boer fashion—
little independent groups of four and five, now and then a troop of
ten or a dozen, here and there a solitary horseman riding back
against the general flow. At no particular moment were more than
thirty to be seen on the mile of dusty road. Yet to an experienced
eye the movement seemed full of dangerous significance. One became conscious of a growing accumulation of force somewhere
among the hills to the eastward. The General, who had served on
the Indian frontier, understood rearguard actions, and his face was
grave, as I had not seen it when larger operations were toward; and
at this moment the boom of a heavy gun told us that the advanced
troops were also engaged. The Boers knew what they wanted.
There was an air of decision about their movements which boded no
good to rear or right flank guard. Gallopers were sent off, one to
warn the right corps of mounted infantry, another to bid the main
body of the force go dead slow, another to the threatened eastern
kopje to learn the state of affairs there. The rearguard battery was
brought up on to the table-top, and came into action. This was, I
think, the key of the situation. The battery planted on Lindley
Hill, and casting its shells now in one direction, now in another,
compelled the assailants to keep their distance, and helped the
pickets into safety and new positions further back. It called to
mind some famous knight of history or romance holding an angry
rabble back beyond the sweep of his long sword, while his comrades
made good their retreat. Under this good protection the pickets,
having dutifully held their positions until the convoy was well on its
road, scampered in, and the battery itself began to think about
retiring. But the trickle of Boers along the eastern roadway had
not stopped. Seven or eight hundred men must have passed already;
and those that now came galloped as if they had some very tangible
objective. "Look out, the right flank!"

But now, the rearguard having disengaged itself from Lindley
town, the General's place was with his main body, and we set off to

trot and gallop the seven miles that intervened between the head
and tail of our force. The firing in front had ceased before we came
up. Indeed, the affair had not been of any importance. About seven
hundred Boers with three or four guns had obstructed the advance
near the Rhenoster River; had even checked the Cavalry screen;
Tenth Hussars had two officers wounded; a dozen other casualties
in the Brigade; Infantry and guns wanted to clear the way. A
Cavalry brigade is not a kopje-smashing machine. "Never mind,
here come the cow-guns. Now we shall see." Indeed, as soon as the
head of the 21st Brigade began to deploy, the five-inch guns and a
field battery opened on the enemy, who thereupon fled incontinently
across the river, pursued by the fire of the guns and of the Cavalry
"pom-poms".

We were just congratulating ourselves upon the success of these
curious operations—curious because the drill books do not contemplate both sides fighting rearguard actions at the same time—
when half a dozen riderless horses galloped in from somewhere miles
away on the right flank. Evidently sharp fighting was proceeding
there; the flow of Boers had meant mischief. The peaceful landscape
told no tale. No sound of musketry nor sign of action could be distinguished. Indeed, in this scattered warfare one part of a force may
easily be destroyed without the rest even knowing that a shot has
been fired. "Why scatter them?" asks the armchair strategist.
"Because if you don't scatter, and haven't got soldiers who are
good enough to act when scattered, you will all get destroyed in a
lump together."

The General sent directions to the rearguard to communicate
with the flank guard; kept another corps of Mounted Infantry
handy to support either if necessary, and turned his attention to
getting his brigades across the Rhenoster River. While this was
proceeding the head of Smith-Dorrien's column, which had marched
prosperously from their bivouac near Kaalfontein, came into view,
and the Army of the Right Flank stood again united, a fact which
suggests some consideration of its functions in the general scheme of
Lord Roberts's advance.

After Kroonstadt had been captured the republican forces on the
railway retreated to the line of the Rhenoster. Half a mile to the
north of this river there rises abruptly from the smooth plain a long
line of rocky hills, and in this strong position the Boers had determined to make a stubborn stand. Any force advancing along the

railway would indeed have found it a difficult and costly business to cross the river and dislodge an enemy so posted. Other low hills trending away to either flank would have made any turning movement an exceedingly extended and probably a useless operation, for the enemy being on the inside of the circle would have been able to confront the attack wherever it might fall. But the Rhenoster River, as the reader will see by a glance at the map (p. 260), rises considerably south of the point where it intersects the railway; and so soon as Ian Hamilton's force was across it, the Boers holding the kopjes position were in considerable danger of being cut off. The effect of our crossing the Rhenoster between Lindley and Heilbron should therefore be to clear the march of the main army. All fell out as Lord Roberts had expected; although the Boers had made great preparations to defend Rhenoster, had constructed strong entrenchments and made sidings to detrain their heavy guns, they evacuated the whole position without a shot being fired, compelled by the movement of a column forty miles away to their left flank.

All who understood the scope and cohesion of the operations were delighted at the prospect of getting across the Rhenoster River. The General was determined, rear and flank guard actions notwithstanding, to have his army and transport over that night: and two practicable crossings having been found, infantry, cavalry, guns and baggage began to push across. The last was now increased by the arrival of Smith-Dorrien, who brought with him a much needed convoy with sufficient supplies to carry us on to Heilbron and a march beyond. It was midnight before all the waggons were across; but though this cruel day of march and sun tore the hearts out of the transport animals, and the flocks of sheep were so weary they could scarcely be driven along, we knew that the exertions had not been made in vain.

Late in the evening came the news from the right flank guard. They had waited, fearing to expose the rearguard to a flank attack. The rearguard had made good its retreat. A gap had sprung up between the two bodies. The vigilant Boers had pounced in and stampeded the horses of one mounted infantry company. A sharp, fierce fight followed; rearguard hearing the fusillade swung in to help. Ultimately the Boers were checked sufficiently to enable rear and flank guard to draw inwards together and draw off: but it was by general agreement of participants a very unpleasant affair. The officer commanding the company whose horses were stampeded had.

particularly interesting experiences. The Boers galloped right in among his men, and a confused scrimmage followed: officer was running towards stampeded horses; on the way he passed a burgher; "Surrender," cried the Dutchman. "No," retorted the officer—an Irishman—(with suitable emphasis) and ran on, whereupon burgher dismounted and began shooting; had four shots and missed every one. Meanwhile officer reached shelter of a convenient rock, turned in just indignation, fitted his Mauser pistol together and fired back. The burgher, finding his enemy behind cover, and himself in the open—by no means the situation for a patriot—jumped on his horse, and would have galloped away but that the officer managed to hit him in the leg with his pistol, and so he dropped, according to the account of an eye-witness, "like a shot rook".

The local advantage, however, rested with the Boers, who hit or captured the greater part of the squadron, including twenty wounded. Concerning these latter, Piet De Wet sent in a flag of truce during the night offering to hand them over if ambulances were sent, and several wounded Boers whom we had taken were given up. This was accordingly done. Our total losses during the 20th were about sixty, some of whom were officers. The Boers admitted a loss of twenty killed and wounded, and it may easily have been more. The army bivouacked on the north bank of the Rhenoster within two marches of the town of Heilbron, upon which it was now designed to move.

CHAPTER TWELVE

CONCERNING A BOER CONVOY

Heilbron: May 22, 1900

HEILBRON LIES in a deep valley. About it on every side rolls the grassy upland country of the Free State, one smooth grey-green surge beyond another, like the after-swell of a great gale at sea; and here in the trough of the waves, hidden almost entirely from view, is the town itself, white stone houses amid dark trees, all clustering at the foot of a tall church spire. It is a quiet, sleepy little place, with a few good buildings and pretty rose gardens, half-a-dozen large stores, a hotel, and a branch line of its own.

For a few days it had been capital of the Free State. The President, his secretaries, and his councillors arrived one morning from Lindley, bringing the "seat of Government" with them in a Cape cart. For nearly a week Heilbron remained the chief town. Then, as suddenly as it had come, the will-o'-the-wisp dignity departed, and Steyn, secretaries, councills, or Cape cart, hurried away to the eastward, leaving behind them rumours of advancing hosts—and (to this I can testify) three bottles of excellent champagne. That was on Sunday night. The inhabitants watched and wondered all the next day.

On the Tuesday morning, shortly after the sun had risen, Christiaan De Wet appeared with sixty waggons, five guns, and a thousand burghers, very weary, having trekked all night from the direction of Kroonstadt, and glad to find a place of rest and refreshment. "What of the English?" inquired the newcomers, and the Heilbron folk replied that the English were coming, and so was Christmas, and that the country to the southward was all clear for ten miles. Thereat the war-worn commando outspanned their oxen and settled themselves to coffee. Forty minutes later the leading patrols of Broadwood's Brigade began to appear on the hills to the south of the town.

Looked at from any point of view, the British force was a formidable array: Household Cavalry, 12th Lancers and 10th Hussars, with P and Q Batteries Royal Horse Artillery (you must mind your P's and Q's with them), two "pom-poms", and two galloping Maxims; and, hurrying up behind them, light horse, mounted infantry, Nineteenth and Twenty-first Brigades, thirty field-guns, more "pom-poms", two great 5-in. ox-drawn siege pieces ("cow guns" as the army calls them), and Ian Hamilton. It was an army formidable to any foe; but to those who now stared upwards from the little town and saw the dark, swift-moving masses on the hills— an avalanche of armed men and destructive engines about to fall on them—terrible beyond words.

"And then," as the poet observes, "there was mounting in hot haste," saddling up of weary ponies, frantic inspanning of hungry oxen cheated of their well-earned rest and feed, cracking of long whips, kicking of frightened Kaffirs; and so pell-mell out of the town and away to the northward hurried the commando of Christiaan De Wet.

The cavalry halted on the hills for a while, the General being desirous of obtaining the formal surrender of Heilbron, and so preventing street-fighting or bombardment. An officer—Lieutenant M. Spender-Clay, of the 2nd Life Guard—was despatched with a flag of truce and a trumpeter; message most urgent, answer to be given within twenty minutes, or Heaven knows what would happen; but all these things take time. Flags of truce (prescribe the customs of war) must approach the enemy's picket line at a walk; a mile and a half at a walk—twenty minutes; add twenty for the answer, ten for the return journey, and nearly an hour is gone. So we wait impatiently watching the two solitary figures with a white speck above them draw nearer and nearer to the Boer lines; "and", says the brigadier, "bring two guns up and have the ranges taken."

There was just a chance that while all were thus intent on the town, the convoy and commando might have escaped unharmed, for it happened that the northern road runs for some distance eastward along the bottom of the valley, concealed from view. But the clouds of dust betrayed them.

"Hullo! what the deuce is that?" cried an officer.

"What?" said everyone else.

"Why that! Look at the dust. There they go. It's a Boer convoy. Gone away."

And with this halloa the chase began. Never have I seen anything in war so like a fox hunt. At first the scene was uncertain, and the pace was slow with many checks.

Before us rose a long smooth slope of grass, and along the crest the figures of horsemen could be plainly seen. The tail of the waggon train was just disappearing. But who should say how many rifles lined that ridge? Besides, there were several barbed-wire fences, which, as anyone knows, will spoil the best country.

Broadwood began giving all kinds of orders—Household Cavalry to advance slowly in the centre; 12th Lancers to slip forward on the right, skirting the town, and try to look behind the ridge, and with them a battery of horse guns; 10th Hussars, to make a cast to the left, and the rest of the guns to walk forward steadily.

Slowly at first, and silently besides; but soon the hounds gave tongue. Pop, pop, pop—the advanced squadron—Blues—had found something to fire at, and something that fired back, too; pip-pop, pip-pop came the double reports of the Boer rifles. Bang—the artillery opened on the crest-line with shrapnel, and at the first few shells it was evident that the enemy would not abide the attack. The horsemen vanished over the sky-line.

The leading squadron pushed cautiously forward—every movement at a walk, so far. Infantry brigadiers and others, inclined to impatience, ground their teeth, and, thinking there would be no sport that day, went home criticising the master. The leading squadron reached the crest, and we could see them dismount and begin to fire.

We were over the first big fence, and now the scent improved. Beyond the first ridge was another, and behind this, much nearer now, dust clouds high and thick. The General galloped forward himself to the newly-captured position and took a comprehensive view. "Tell the brigade to come here at once—sharp."

A galloper shot away to the rear. Behind arose the rattle of trotting batteries. The excitement grew. Already the patrols were skirting the second ridge. The Boer musketry, fitful for a few minutes, died away. They were abandoning their second position. "Forward, then." And forward we went accordingly at a healthy trot.

In front of the jingling squadrons two little galloping Maxims darted out, and almost before the ridge was ours they were spluttering angrily at the retreating enemy, so that four burghers, as I saw myself, departed amid a perfect hail of bullets, which peppered the ground on all sides.

But now the whole hunt swung northward towards a line of rather ugly-looking heights. Broadwood looked at them sourly. "Four guns to watch those hills, in case they bring artillery against us from them." Scarcely were the words spoken, when there was a flash and a brown blurr on the side of one of the hills, and with a rasping snarl a shell passed overhead and burst among the advancing cavalry. The four guns were on the target without a moment's delay.

The Boer artillerists managed to fire five shots, and then the place grew too hot for them—indeed, after Natal, I may write, even for them. They had to expose themselves a great deal to remove their gun, and the limber and its six horses showed very plainly on the hillside, so that we all hoped to smash a wheel or kill a horse, and thus capture a real prize. But at the critical moment our "pom-poms" disgraced themselves. They knew the range, they saw the target. They fired four shots; the aim was not bad. But four shots—four miserable shots! Just pom-pom, pom-pom. That was all. Whereas, if the Boers had had such a chance, they would have rattled through the whole belt, and sent eighteen or twenty shells in a regular shower. So we all saw with pain how a weapon, which is so terrible in the hands of the enemy, may become feeble and ineffective when used on our side by our own gunners.

After the menace of the Boer artillery was removed from our right flank, the advance became still more rapid. Batteries and squadrons were urged into a gallop. Broadwood himself hurried forward. We topped a final rise.

Then at last we viewed the vermin. There, crawling up the opposite slope, clear cut on a white roadway, was a long line of waggons—ox waggons and mule waggons—and behind everything a small cart drawn by two horses. All were struggling with frantic energy to escape from their pursuers. But in vain.

The batteries spun round and unlimbered. Eager gunners ran forward with ammunition, and some with belts for the "pom-poms". There was a momentary pause while ranges were taken and sights aligned, and then——! Shell after shell crashed among the convoys. Some exploded on the ground; others, bursting in the air, whipped up the dust all round mules and men. The "pom-poms", roused at last from their apathy by this delicious target and some pointed observations of the General, thudded out strings of little bombs. For a few minutes the waggons persevered manfully. Then one by one they came to a standstill. The drivers fled to the nearest shelter, and the animals strayed off the road or stood quiet in stolid ignorance of their danger.

And now at this culminating moment I must, with all apologies to "Brooksby", change the metaphor, because the end of the chase was scarcely like a fox hunt. The guns had killed the quarry, and the cavalry dashed forward to secure it. It was a fine bag—to wit, fifteen laden waggons and seventeen prisoners. Such was the affair of Heilbron, and it was none the less joyous and exciting because, so far as we could learn, no man on either side was killed, and only one trooper and five horses wounded. Then we turned homewards.

On the way back to the town I found, near a fine farmhouse with deep verandahs and a pretty garden, Boer ambulance waggons, two German doctors, and a dozen bearded men. They inquired the issue of the pursuit; how many prisoners had we taken? We replied by other questions. "How much longer will the war last?"

"It is not a war any more," said one of the Red Cross men. "The poor devils haven't got a chance against your numbers."

"Nevertheless," interposed another, "they will fight to the end."

I looked towards the last speaker. He was evidently of a different class to the rest.

"Are you", I asked, "connected with the ambulance?"

"No, I am the military chaplain to the Dutch forces."

"And you think the Free State will continue to resist?"

"We will go down fighting. What else is there to do? History and Europe will do us justice."

"It is easy for you to say that, who do not fight; but what of the poor farmers and peasants you have dragged into this war? They do not tell us that they wish to fight. They think they have been made a catspaw for the Transvaal."

"Ah," he rejoined, warmly, "they have no business to say that now. They did not say so before the war. They wanted to fight. It was a solemn pledge. We were bound to help the Transvaalers; what would have happened to us after they were conquered?"

"But, surely you, and men like you, knew the strength of the antagonist you challenged. Why did you urge these simple people to their ruin?"

"We had had enough of English methods here. We knew our independence was threatened. It had to come. We did not deceive them. We told them. I told my flock often that it would not be child's play."

"Didn't you tell them it was hopeless?"

"It was not hopeless," he said. "There were many chances."

"All gone now."

"Not quite all. Besides, chances or no chances, we must go down fighting."

"You preach a strange gospel of peace!"

"And you English", he rejoined, "have strange ideas of liberty."

So we parted, without more words; and I rode on my way into the town. Heilbron had one memory for me, and it was one which was now to be revived. In the hotel—a regular country inn—I found various British subjects who had been assisting the Boer ambulances—possibly with rifles. It is not my purpose to discuss here the propriety of their conduct. They had been placed in situations which do not come to men in quiet times, and for the rest they were mean-spirited creatures.

While the Republican cause seemed triumphant they had worked for the Dutch, had doubtless spoken of "damned rooineks", and used other similar phrases; so soon as the Imperial arms predominated they had changed their note; had refused to go on commando in any capacity, proclaimed that Britons never should be slaves, and dared the crumbling organism of Federal government to do its worst.

We talked about the fighting in Natal which they had seen from the other side. The Acton Homes affair cropped up. You will remember that we of the irregular brigade plumed ourselves immensely on this ambuscading of the Boers—the one undoubted score we ever made against them on the Tugela.

"Yes," purred my renegades, "you caught the damned Dutchmen fairly then. We were delighted, but of course we dared not show it." (Pause.) "That was where De Mentz was killed."

De Mentz! The name recalled a vivid scene—the old field cornet lying forward, grey and grim, in a pool of blood and a litter of empty cartridge cases, with his wife's letter clasped firmly in his stiffening fingers. He had "gone down fighting"; had had no doubts what course to steer. I knew when I saw his face that he had thought the whole thing out. Now they told me that there had been no man in all Heilbron more bitterly intent on the war, and that his letter in the *Volksstem*, calling on the Afrikanders to drive the English scum from the land, had produced a deep impression.

"Let them", thus it ran, "bring 50,000 men, or 80,000 men, or even"—it was a wild possibility—"100,000, yet we will overcome them." But they brought more than 200,000, so all his calculations were disproved, and he himself was killed with the responsibility on his shoulders of leading his men into an ambush which, with ordinary precautions, might have been avoided. Such are war's revenges. His widow, a very poor woman, lived next door to the hotel, nursing her son who had been shot through the lungs during the same action. Let us hope he will recover, for he had a gallant sire.

CHAPTER THIRTEEN

ACTION OF JOHANNESBURG

Johannesburg: June 1, 1900

ON THE 24th of May, Ian Hamilton's force, marching west from Heilbron, struck the railway and joined Lord Roberts's main column. The long marches, unbroken by a day's rest, the short rations to which the troops had been restricted, and the increasing exhaustion of horses and transport animals seemed to demand a halt. But a more imperious voice cried "Forward!" and at daylight the travel-stained brigades set forth, boots worn to tatters, gun horses dying at the wheel, and convoys struggling after in vain pursuit—"Forward to the Vaal."

And now the Army of the Right Flank became the Army of the Left; for Hamilton was directed to move across the railway line and march on the drift of the river near Boschbank. Thus, for the first time it was possible to see the greater part of the invading force at once.

French, indeed, was already at Parys, but the Seventh and Eleventh Divisions, the Lancer Brigade, the corps troops, the heavy artillery, and Hamilton's four brigades were all spread about the spacious plain, and made a strange picture; long brown columns of infantry, black squares of batteries, sprays of cavalry flung out far to the front and flanks, 30,000 fighting men together, behind them interminable streams of waggons, and, in their midst, like the pillar of cloud that led the hosts of Israel, the war balloon, full blown, on its travelling car.

We crossed the Vaal on the 26th prosperously and peacefully. Broadwood, with his cavalry, had secured the passage during the previous night, and the infantry arriving found the opposite slopes in British hands. Moreover, the engineers, under the indefatigable Boileau, assisted by the strong arms of the Blues and Life Guards, had cut a fine broad road up and down the steep river banks.

Once across we looked again for the halt. Twenty-four hours' rest meant convoys with full rations and forage for the horses. But in the morning there came a swift messenger from the Field-Marshal: main army crossing at Vereeniging, demoralisation of the enemy increasing, only one span of the railway bridge blown up, perhaps Johannesburg within three days—at any rate, "try", never mind the strain of nerve and muscle or the scarcity of food.

Forward again. That day Hamilton marched his men eighteen miles—("ten miles", say the text-books on war, "is a good march for a division with baggage", and our force, carrying its own supplies, had ten times the baggage of a European division!)—and succeeded besides in dragging his weary transport with him. By good fortune the cavalry discovered a little forage—small stacks of curious fluffy grass called manna, and certainly heaven-sent—on which the horses subsisted and did not actually starve. All day the soldiers pressed on, and the sun was low before the bivouac was reached. Nothing untoward disturbed the march, and only a splutter of musketry along the western flank guard relieved its dullness.

At first, after we had crossed the Vaal, the surface of the country was smooth and grassy, like the Orange River Colony, but as the column advanced northwards the ground became broken—at once more dangerous and more picturesque. Dim blue hills rose up on the horizon, the rolling swells of pasture grew sharper and less even, patches of wood or scrub interrupted the level lines of the plain, and polished rocks of conglomerate or auriferous quartz showed through the grass, like the bones beneath the skin of the cavalry horses. We were approaching the Rand.

On the evening of the 27th, Hamilton's advance guard came in touch with French, who, with one mounted infantry and two cavalry brigades, was moving echeloned forward on our left in the same relation to us as were we to the main army.

The information about the enemy was that, encouraged by the defensive promise of the ground, he was holding a strong position either on the Klip Riviersberg, or along the line of the gold mines crowning the main Rand reef. On the 28th, in expectation of an action next day, Hamilton made but a short march. French, on the other hand, pushed on to reconnoitre, and if possible—for the cavalry were very ambitious—to pierce the lines that lay ahead.

I rode with General Broadwood, whose brigade covered the advance of Hamilton's column. The troops had now entered a region of hills which on every side threatened the march and limited the view.

At nine o'clock we reached a regular pass between two steep rocky ridges. From the summit of one of these ridges a wide land-scape was revealed. Northwards across our path lay the black line of the Klip Riviersberg, stretching to the east as far as I could see, and presenting everywhere formidable positions to the advancing force. To the west these frowning features fell away in more grassy slopes, from among which, its approach obstructed by several rugged under-features, rose the long smooth ridge of the Wit-watersrand reef. The numerous grass fires which attend the march of any army in dry weather—the results of our carelessness, or, perhaps, of the enemy's design—veiled the whole prospect with smoke, and made the air glitter and deceive like the mirages in the Soudan. But one thing showed with sufficient distinctness to attract and astonish all eyes. The whole crest of the Rand ridge was fringed with factory chimneys. We had marched nearly 500 miles through a country which, though full of promise, seemed to Euro-pean eyes desolate and wild, and now we turned a corner suddenly, and there before us sprang the evidences of wealth, manufacture, and bustling civilisation. I might have been looking from a distance at Oldham.

The impression was destroyed by the booming of shotted guns, unheard, by God's grace, these many years in peaceful Lancashire. French was at work. The haze and the distance prevented us from watching closely the operations of the cavalry. The dark patches of British horsemen and the white smoke of the Dutch artillery were the beginning and the end of our observations. But, even so, it was easy to see that French was not making much progress.

As the afternoon wore on the loud reverberations of heavy cannon told that the Boers had disclosed their real position, and we knew that something more substantial than cavalry would be required to drive them from it. In the evening French's brigades were seen to be retiring across the Klip River, and the night closed in amid the rapid drumming of the Vickers-Maxims covering his movement, bringing with it the certainty of an Infantry action on the morrow.

At twelve o'clock a despatch from the Cavalry Division reached Hamilton. French's messenger said that the cavalry were having a hot fight and were confronted by several 40-pounder guns, but the stout-hearted commander himself merely acquainted Hamilton with his orders from headquarters, to march *via* Florida to Drie-fontein, and made no allusion to his fortunes nor asked for assistance. Indeed, as we found out later, his operations on the 28th had been practically confined to an artillery duel, in which, though the expenditure of ammunition was very great and the noise alarming, the casualties—one officer and eight men—were fortunately small.

But the Boers, seeing the cavalry retire at dusk, claimed that they had repulsed the first attack; their confidence in the strength of the Rand position was increased; their resistance on the next day was consequently more stubborn; and the *Standard and Diggers' News* was enabled to terminate a long career of exaggeration and falsehood by describing one more "bloody British defeat with appalling slaughter."

The event of the next day admitted of no such misinterpretation.

The orders from headquarters for the 29th were such as to involve certain fighting should the enemy stand. French, with the Cavalry Division, was to march around Johannesburg to Driefontein; Ian Hamilton was directed on Florida; the main army, under the Field-Marshal, would occupy Germiston and seize the junctions of the Natal, Cape Colony, and Potchefstroom lines. These movements, which the chief had indicated by flags on the map, were now to be executed—so far as possible—by soldiers on the actual field.

The operations of the main army are not my concern in this letter; but it is necessary to state the result, lest the reader fail to grasp the general idea, and, while studying the detail, forget their scale and meaning.

Advancing with great speed and suddenness through Elands-fontein, Lord Roberts surprised the Boers in Germiston, and after a brief skirmish drove them in disorder from the town, which he then occupied. So precipitate was the flight of the enemy, or so rapid the British advance, that nine locomotives and much other rolling stock were captured, and the line from Germiston south-ward to Vereeniging was found to be undamaged. The importance of these advantages on the success of the operations can scarcely be over-estimated. The problem of supply was at once modified, and though the troops still suffered privations from scarcity of food the anxieties of their commanders as to the immediate future were removed.

French had camped for the night south of the Klip River, just out of cannon shot of the enemy's position, and at eight o'clock on the morning of the 29th he moved off westward, intending to try to penetrate, or, better still, circumvent, the barrier that lay before him.

Such ground as he had won on the previous day he held with mounted infantry, and thus masking the enemy's front he attempted to pierce if he could not turn his right. For these purposes the force at his disposal—three horse batteries, four "pom-poms", and about 3,000 mounted men—was inadequate and unsuited. But he knew that Ian Hamilton, with siege guns, field guns, and two infantry brigades, was close behind him, and on this he reckoned.

Firing began about seven o'clock, when the Boers attacked the Mounted Infantry Corps holding the positions captured on the 28th, and who were practically covering the flank movement of the rest of the Cavalry Division and the march of Hamilton's column. The mounted infantry, who were very weak, were gradually compelled to fall back, being at one time enfiladed by two Vickers-Maxims and heavily pressed in front.

But their resistance was sufficiently prolonged to secure the transference of force from right to left. By ten o'clock French had gone far enough west to please him, and passing round the edge of a deep swamp turned the heads of his regiments sharply to their right (north), and moved towards the Rand ridge and its under features.

By the vigorous use of his horse artillery he cleared several of the advanced kopjes, and had made nearly two miles progress north of the drainage line of the Klip River, when he was abruptly checked. A squadron sent forward against a low fringe of rocks, clumping up at the end of a long grass glacis, encountered a sudden burst of musketry fire, and returned, pursued by shell, with the information that mounted men could work no further northwards.

Meanwhile Hamilton, who had determined to lay his line of march across the Doornkop ridges (of inglorious memory), and whose infantry, baggage, and guns were spread all along the flat plain south of the Klip, was drawing near. French halted his brigades and awaited him. The instructions from headquarters defined very carefully the relations which were to be observed between the two generals. They were to co-operate, yet their commands were entirely separate. Should they attack the same hill at once, French, as a lieutenant-general and long senior to Hamilton, would automatically assume command. But this contingency was not likely to arise from the military situation, and the good feeling and mutual confidence which existed between these two able soldiers, and which had already produced golden results at Elandslaagte, made the possibility of any misunderstanding still more remote.

French was joined by Hamilton at one o'clock, and they discussed the situation together. French explained the difficulty of further direct advance. He must move still more to the west. On the other hand, Hamilton, whose force was eating its last day's rations, could make no longer detour, and must break through there and then—frontal attack, if necessary. So all fitted in happily. The Cavalry Division moved to the left to co-operate with the infantry attack by threatening the Boer right, and, in order that this pressure might be effective, Hamilton lent Broadwood's Brigade and two corps of mounted infantry to French for the day. He himself prepared to attack what stood before him with his whole remaining force.

By two o'clock the cavalry in brown swarms had disappeared to the westward, both infantry brigades were massed under cover on the approaches of the Rand ridge, and the transport of the army lay accumulated in a vast pool near the passage of the Klip—here only a swamp, but further east a river. The artillery duel of the morning had died away. The firing on the right, where the mounted infantry still maintained themselves, was intermittent. The reconnaissance was over. The action was about to begin, and in the interval there was a short, quiet lull—the calm before the storm. The soldiers munched their biscuits silently under the sun blaze. The officers and staff ate a frugal luncheon. Ian Hamilton with his aide-de-camp, the Duke of Marlborough, shared the contents of my wallets. I watched the General closely. He knew better than the sanguine people who declared the Boers had run away already. No one understood better than he what a terrible foe is the rock-sheltered Mauser-armed Dutchman. In spite of its cavalry turning movement, and other embellishments, the impending attack must be practically frontal. Supply did not allow a wider circle: to stop was to starve; and the position before us—half-a-dozen clusters of rock, breaking from the smooth grass upward slopes, except in colour, like foam on the crest of waves, natural parapet and glacis combined, and, beyond all, the long bare ridge of the Rand lined with who should say what entrenchments or how many defenders— a prospect which filled all men who knew with the most solemn thoughts.

For my part, having seen the infantry come reeling back in bloody ruin two or three times from such a place and such a foe, though I risked no repute on the event—scarcely my life—I confess to a beating heart. But the man who bore all the responsibility, and to whom the result meant everything, appeared utterly unmoved. Indeed, I could almost imagine myself the General and the General the Press Correspondent, though perhaps this arrangement would scarcely have worked so well.

At three o'clock precisely the Infantry advanced to the attack. Major-General Bruce-Hamilton directed the left attack with the Twenty-first Brigade, and Colonel Spens the right with the Nineteenth Brigade. The whole division was commanded by General Smith-Dorrien. The lateness of the hour gave scarcely any time for the artillery preparation, and the artillery came into action only a few minutes before the infantry were exposed to fire.

It must be noticed that the combination of the batteries and the support which they afforded to the attack were scarcely so effective as might have been expected from the number of guns available. But the General commanding a mixed force is bound to trust the various specialists under him, at least until experience has shown them to be deficient in energy or ability.

The infantry advance was developed on the most modern principles. Each brigade occupied a front of more than a mile and three-quarters, and the files of the first line of skirmishers were extended no less than thirty paces. Bruce-Hamilton, with the left attack, started a little earlier than the right brigade, and, with the City Imperial Volunteers in the fire line, soon had his whole command extended on the open grass.

A few minutes after three, French's guns were heard on the extreme left, and about the same time the firing on the right swelled up again, so that by the half-hour the action was general along the whole front of battle—an extent of a little over six miles.

The left attack, pressed with vigour, and directed with skill by General Bruce-Hamilton, led along a low spur, and was designed to be a kind of inside turning movement to assist the right in conformity with the cavalry action now in full swing. The City Imperial Volunteers moved forward with great dash and spirit, and in spite of a worrying fire from their left rear, which increased in proportion as they moved inwards towards the right, drove the Boers from position after position. While there is no doubt that

French's pressure beyond them materially assisted their advance, the rapid progress of this Twenty-first Brigade entitled them and their leader to the highest credit. The Cameron Highlanders and the Sherwood Foresters supported the attack. The Boers resisted well with artillery, and their shells caused several casualties among the advancing lines; but it was on the right that the fighting was most severe.

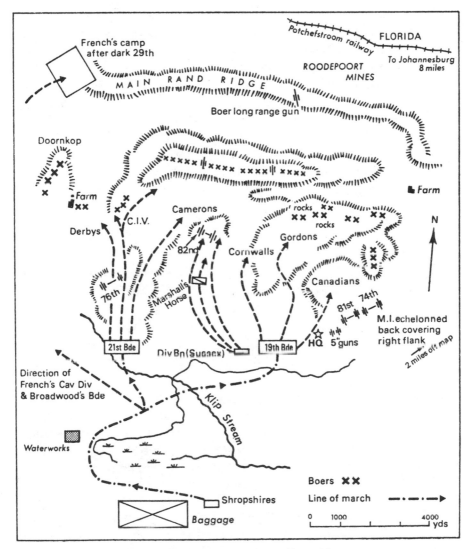

IAN HAMILTON'S ACTION BEFORE JOHANNESBURG

The leading battalion of the Nineteenth Brigade chanced—for there was no selection—to be the Gordon Highlanders; nor was it without a thrill that I watched this famous regiment move against the enemy. Their extension and advance were conducted with machine-like regularity. The officers explained what was required to the men. They were to advance rapidly until under rifle fire, and then to push on or not as they might be instructed.

With impassive unconcern the veterans of Chitral, Dargai, the Bara Valley, Magersfontein, Paardeberg, and Houtnek walked leisurely forward, and the only comment recorded was the observation of a private: "Bill, this looks like being a kopje day." Gradually the whole battalion drew out clear of the covering ridge, and long dotted lines of brown figures filled the plain. At this moment two batteries and the two 5-in. guns opened from the right of the line, and what with the artillery of French and Bruce-Hamilton there was soon a loud cannonade.

The Dutch replied at once with three or four guns, one of which seemed a very heavy piece of ordnance on the main Rand ridge, and another fired from the kopje against which the Gordons were marching. But the Boer riflemen, crouching among the rocks, reserved their fire for a near target. While the troops were thus approaching the enemy's position, the two brigades began unconsciously to draw apart. Colonel Spens's battalions had extended further to the right than either Ian Hamilton or Smith-Dorrien had intended. Bruce-Hamilton, pressing forward on the left, found himself more and more tempted to face the harassing attack on his left rear. Both these tendencies had to be corrected. The Gordons were deflected to their left by an officer, Captain Higginson, who galloped most pluckily into the firing line in spite of a hail of bullets. Bruce-Hamilton was ordered to bear in to his right and disregard the growing pressure behind his left shoulder. Nevertheless a wide gap remained. But by this mischance Ian Hamilton contrived to profit. Smith-Dorrien had already directed the only remaining battalion—the Sussex—to fill up the interval, and the General-in-Chief now thrust a battery forward through the gap, almost flush with the skirmish line of the Infantry on its left and right.

The fire of these guns, combined with the increasing pressure from the turning movements both of Bruce-Hamilton and French, who was now working very far forward in the west, weakened the enemy's position on the kopje which the Gordons were attacking.

Yet, when every allowance has been made for skilful direction and bold leading, the honours, equally with the cost of the victory, belong more to the Gordon Highlanders than to all the other troops put together.

The rocks against which they advanced proved in the event to be the very heart of the enemy's position. The grass in front of them was burnt and burning, and against this dark background the khaki figures showed distinctly. The Dutch held their fire until the attack was within 800 yards, and then, louder than the cannonade, the ominous rattle of concentrated rifle fire burst forth. The black slope was spotted as thickly with grey puffs of dust where the bullets struck as with advancing soldiers, and tiny figures falling by the way told of heavy loss. But the advance neither checked nor quickened.

With remorseless stride, undisturbed by peril or enthusiasm, the Gordons swept steadily onward, changed direction half left to avoid, as far as possible, an enfilade fire, changed again to the right to effect a lodgment on the end of the ridge most suitable to attack, and at last rose up together to charge. The black slope twinkled like jet with the unexpected glitter of bayonets. The rugged sky-line bristled with kilted figures, as, in perfect discipline and disdainful silence, those splendid soldiers closed on their foe.

The Boers shrank from the contact. Discharging their magazines furiously, and firing their guns twice at point-blank range, they fled in confusion to the main ridge, and the issue of the action was no longer undecided.

Still the fight continued. Along the whole infantry front a tremendous rifle fire blazed. Far away to the left French's artillery pursued the retreating Boers with shells. The advanced batteries of Hamilton's force fired incessantly. The action did not cease with the daylight. The long lines of burning grass cast a strange, baleful glare on the field, and by this light the stubborn adversaries maintained their debate for nearly an hour.

At length, however, the cannonade slackened and ceased, and the rifles soon imitated the merciful example of the guns. The chill and silence of the night succeeded the hot tumult of the day. Regiments assembled and reformed their ranks, ambulances and baggage waggons crowded forward from the rear, the burning veldt was beaten out, and hundreds of cooking fires gleamed with more kindly meaning through the darkness.

The General rode forward, to find the Gordons massed among the rocks they had won. The gallant Burney, who commanded the firing line, was severely wounded. St. John Meyrick was killed. Nine officers and eighty-eight soldiers had fallen in the attack; but those that remained were proud and happy in the knowledge that they had added to the many feats of arms which adorn the annals of the regiment—one that was at least the equal of Elandslaagte or Dargai; and, besides all this, they may have reflected that by their devotion they had carried forward the British cause a long stride to victory, and, better than victory, to honourable peace. Ian Hamilton spoke a few brief words of thanks and praise to them—"the regiment my father commanded and I was born in"—and told them that in a few hours all Scotland would ring with the tale of their deeds. And well Scotland may, for no men of any race could have shown more soldier-like behaviour.

Then we rode back to our bivouac, while the lanterns of searching parties moved hither and thither among the rocks, and voices cried "Bearer party this way!" "Are there any more wounded here?" with occasional feeble responses.

Owing to the skilful conduct of the attack, the losses, except among the Gordons, were not severe—in all about 150 killed and wounded. The result of the fight—the action of Johannesburg, as we called it—was the general retreat of all the enemy west of the town under Delarey and Viljoen northwards towards Pretoria, and, in conjunction with the Field-Marshal's movements, the surrender of the whole of the Witwatersrand.

French, continuing his march at dawn to Driefontein, captured one gun and several prisoners. Ian Hamilton entered Florida, and found there and at Maraisburg sufficient stores to enable him to subsist until his convoys arrived.

CHAPTER FOURTEEN

THE FALL OF JOHANNESBURG

Johannesburg: June 2

MORNING BROKE and the army arose ready, if necessary, to renew the fight. But the enemy had fled. The main Rand ridge still stretched across our path. Its defenders had abandoned all their positions under the cover of darkness. Already French's squadrons were climbing the slopes to the eastward and pricking their horses forward to Elandsfontein (North). So Hamilton's force, having but six miles to march to Florida, did not hurry its departure, and we had leisure to examine the scene of yesterday's engagement. Riding by daylight over the ground of the Gordon's attack, we were still more impressed by the difficulties they had overcome. From where I had watched the action the Boers had seemed to be holding a long black kopje, some forty feet high, which rose abruptly from the grass plain. It now turned out that the aspect of steepness was produced by the foreshortening effects of the burnt grass area; that in reality the ground scarcely rose at all, and that what we had thought was the enemy's position was only a stony outcrop separated from the real line of defence by a bare space of about 200 yards.

Looking around I found a Highlander, a broad-shouldered, kind-faced man, with the Frontier ribbon, which means on a Gordon tunic much hard fighting; and judging with reason that he would know something of war, I asked him to explain the ground and its effect.

"Well, you see, sir," he said, in quick-spoken phrases, "we was regularly tricked. We began to lose men so soon as we got on the burnt grass. Then we made our charge up to this first line of little rocks, thinking the Boers were there. Of course they weren't here at all, but back over there, where you see those big rocks. We were all out of breath, and in no order whatever, so we had to sit tight here and wait."

"Heavy fire?" I asked. He cocked his head like an expert.

"I've seen heavier; but there was enough. We dropped more than forty men here. 'Tis here poor Mr. —— was wounded; just behind this stone. You can see the blood here yet, sir—this mud's it."

I looked as required, and he proceeded:

"We knew we was for it then; it didn't look like getting on, and we couldn't get back—never a man would ha' lived to cross the black ground again with the fire what it was, and no attack to fright them off their aim. There was such a noise of the bullets striking the rocks that the officers couldn't make themselves heard, and such confusion too! But two or three of them managed to get together after a while, and they told us what they wanted done . . . and then, of course, it was done all right."

"What was done? What did you do?"

"Why, go on, sir, and take that other line—the big rocks—soon as we'd got our breath. It had to be done."

He did not seem the least impressed with his feat of arms. He regarded it as a piece of hard work he had been set to do, and which—this as a matter of course—he had done accordingly. What an intrepid conquering machine to depend on in the hour of need!—machine and much more, for this was a proud and intelligent man, who had thought deeply upon the craft of war, and had learnt many things in a severe school.

I had not ridden a hundred yards further, my mind full of admiration for him and his type, when a melancholy spectacle broke upon the view. Near a clump of rocks eighteen Gordon Highlanders—men as good as the one I had just talked with—lay dead in a row. Their faces were covered with blankets, but their grey stockinged feet—for the boots had been removed—looked very pitiful. There they lay stiff and cold on the surface of the great Banket Reef. I knew how much more precious their lives had been to their countrymen than all the gold mines the lying foreigners say this war was fought to win. And yet, in view of the dead and the ground they lay on, neither I nor the officer who rode with me could control an emotion of illogical anger, and we scowled at the tall chimneys of the Rand.

General Ian Hamilton, General Smith-Dorrien, all their staffs, and everyone who wished to pay a last tribute of respect to brave men, attended the funerals. The veteran regiment stood around the grave, forming three sides of a hollow square—Generals and staff filled the other. The mourning party rested on their arms, reversed; the Chaplain read the Burial Service, the bodies were lowered into the trench, and the pipes began the lament. The wild, barbaric music filled the air, stirring the soldiers, hitherto quite unmoved, with a strange and very apparent force. Sad and mournful was the dirge wailing of battles ended, of friendships broken, and ambitions lost; and yet there were mingled with its sadness many notes of triumph, and through all its mourning rang the cry of hope.

The whole of Hamilton's force had marched by ten o'clock, but even before that hour the advanced guard had passed through Florida and picketed the hills beyond. Florida is the Kew Gardens of Johannesburg. A well-built dam across a broad valley has formed a deep and beautiful lake. Carefully planted woods of Australian pines offer a welcome shade on every side. The black and white pointed chimneys of the mine buildings rise conspicuous above the dark foliage. There is a small but comfortable hotel, called "The Retreat", to which on Sundays, in times of peace, the weary speculators whose minds were shattered by the fluctuations of the Exchange were wont to resort for rest or diversion. Everywhere along the reef the signs of industry and commerce were to be seen. Good macadamised roads crossed each other in all directions; flashy advertisements caught the eye. A network of telegraphs and telephones ran overhead. The ground was accurately marked out with little obelisks of stone into "Deeps" and "Concessions", and labelled with all the queer names which fill the market columns of the newspapers. In a word, it seemed—to us dirty, tattered wanderers—that we had dropped out of Africa and War, and come safely back to Peace and Civilisation.

Since the soldiers had eaten their last day's rations, and the only food they had had that morning came from any odds and ends the regiments might have saved, it was imperative to find some supplies. The Field-Marshal had ordered that no troops should enter Johannesburg until he should specially direct; but, finding little to eat in Florida, Hamilton sent his supply officer and a squadron as far as Maraisburg; whence they presently returned with a quantity of tinned rabbit and sardines, and with the news that the Boers were said to be occupying a position near Langlaagte mine.

During the morning we caught a train and some prisoners. The train was returning from Potchefstroom, guarded by six armed burghers, and on rifles being pointed, it stopped obediently and surrendered. The other prisoners were brought in by the cavalry and mounted infantry, who had caught them wandering about without their horses. Among them was Commandant Botha—not Louis or Philip—but Botha of the Zoutspansberg commando, a brave and honest fellow, who had fought all through the war from Talana Hill until the last action; but who was quite content that Fate had decided he should fight no more. Hearing of him under guard, and near headquarters, I went to see him. He displayed no bitterness whatever, and seemed quite prepared to accept the decision of war. He inquired anxiously whether he would be sent to St. Helena, and evinced a childish horror of the sea. While we were chatting, one of the other Boer prisoners, who had been looking hard at us, said, suddenly, in very good English:

"The last time I saw you, you were in my position and I in yours."

He then went on to tell me that he had been in the commando that destroyed the armoured train. "I felt very sorry for you that day," he said.

I remarked that it was much worse to be taken prisoner at the beginning of a war than near the end, as he was.

"Do you think this is the end?" asked the Commandant quickly.

"I should ask you that."

"No, no—not yet the end. They will fight a little more. Perhaps they will defend Pretoria—perhaps you will have to go to Lydenburg; but it will not be very long now."

And then, since both he and his companion had been through the Natal campaign, we fell to discussing the various actions. Ian Hamilton came up while we were talking. I had just told the Commandant that we considered the Boers had made a fatal strategic mistake in throwing their main strength into Natal, instead of merely holding the passes, masking Mafeking and Kimberley, and marching south into the colony with every man and gun they could scrape together. He admitted that perhaps that might be so; "but," said he, "our great mistake in Natal was not assaulting Ladysmith —the Platrand position, you know—the day after our victory at Lombard's Kop. We blame Joubert for that. Many of us wanted to go on then. There were no fortifications; the soldiers were demoralised. If once we had taken the Platrand (Cæsar's Camp) you could not have held the town. How many men had you on top of it?"

"Only a picket for the first week," said the General.

"Ah! I knew we could have done it. What would have happened then?"

"We should have had to turn you out."

The Commandant smiled a superior smile. The General continued: "Yes—with the bayonet—at night; or else, as you say, the town could not have been held."

"Presently," said Botha, "you pulled yourselves together, but for three days after Nicholson's Nek there was no fear of bayonets. If we had stormed you then—(then we had all our men and no Buller to think about)—you would not have been able to turn us out."

Hamilton reflected. "Perhaps not," he said, after a pause. "Why didn't Joubert try it?"

"Too old," said Botha, with complete disdain; "you must have young men for fighting."

That was, so far as I remember, the end of the conversation; but, a fortnight later, I met Botha a free man in the streets of Pretoria. He told me he had been released on parole, so that evidently his frank manliness had not been lost upon the General.

After lunch I became very anxious to go into, and, if possible, through Johannesburg. An important action had been fought, witnessed by only two or three correspondents; and since the enemy lay between the force and the telegraph wire no news could have been sent home. Hamilton, indeed, had sent off two of Rimington's Guides early in the morning with despatches; but they were to make a wide sweep to the south, and it was not likely, if they got through at all, that they would reach Lord Roberts until late. The shortest, perhaps the safest, road lay through Johannesburg itself. But was the venture worth the risk? While I was revolving the matter in my mind on the verandah of the temporary headquarters, there arrived two cyclists from the direction of the town. I got into conversation with one of them, a Frenchman, Monsieur Lautré by name. He had come from the Langlaagte mine, with which undertaking he was connected. There were no Boers there, according to him. There might or might not be Boers in the town. Could a stranger get through? Certainly, he thought, unless he were stopped and questioned. He undertook there and then to be my guide if I wished to go; and it being of considerable importance to get the telegrams through to London, I decided, after a good many misgivings, to accept his offer. The General, who wanted to send a more detailed account of his action, and to report his arrival at Florida, was glad to avail himself even of this precarious channel. So the matter was immediately settled. Lautré's friend, a most accommodating person, got off his bicycle without demur and placed it at my disposal. I doffed my khaki and put on a suit of plain clothes which I had in my valise, and exchanged my slouch hat for a soft cap. Lautré put the despatches in his pocket, and we started without more ado.

The tracks were bad, winding up and down hill, and frequently deep in sand; but the machine was a good one, and we made fair progress. Lautré, who knew every inch of the ground, avoided all highways, and led me by devious paths from one mine to another, around huge heaps of tailings, across little private tram lines, through thick copses of fir trees, or between vast sheds of machinery, now silent and idle. In three-quarters of an hour we reached Lang-laagte, and here we found one of Rimington's scouts pushing cautiously forward towards the town. We held a brief parley with him, behind a house, for he was armed and in uniform. He was very doubtful of the situation ahead; only knew for certain that the troops had not yet entered Johannesburg. "But," said he, "the Correspondent of *The Times* passed me more than two hours ago."

"Riding?" I asked.

"Yes," he said, "a horse."

"Ah," said my Frenchman, "that is no good. He will not get through on a horse. They will arrest him." And then, being quite fired with the adventure: "Besides, we will beat him, even if, un-happily, he escape the Boers."

So we hurried on. The road now ran for the most part downhill, and the houses became more numerous. The day was nearly done and the sun drew close to the horizon, throwing our long shadows on the white track before us. At length we turned into a regular street.

"If they stop us," said my guide, "speak French. *Les Français sont en bonne odeur ici.* You speak French, eh?"

I thought my accent might be good enough to deceive a Dutch-man, so I said yes; and thereafter our conversation was conducted in French.

We avoided the main thoroughfares, bicycling steadily on through the poorer quarters. Johannesburg stretched about me on every side, silent, almost deserted. Groups of moody-looking people chatted at the street corners, and eyed us suspiciously. All the shops were shut. Most of the houses had their windows boarded up. The night was falling swiftly, and its shades intensified the gloom which seemed to hang over the town, on this the last day of its Republican existence.

Suddenly, as we crossed a side lane, I saw in the street parallel to that we followed three mounted men with slouch hats, bandoliers, and that peculiar irregular appearance which I have learned to associate with Boers. But to stop or turn back was now fatal. After all, with the enemy at their gates, they had probably concerns of their own to occupy them. We skimmed along unhindered into the central square, and my companion, whose coolness was admirable, pointed me out the post-office and other public buildings, speaking all the time in French. The slope now rose against us so steeply that we dismounted to push our machines. While thus circumstanced I was alarmed to hear the noise of an approaching horse behind me. With an effort I controlled my impulse to look back.

"*Encore un Boer*," said Lautré lightly. I was speechless. The man drew nearer, overtook and pulled his horse into a walk beside us. I could not help—perhaps it was the natural, and, if so, the wise, thing to do—having a look at him. He was a Boer sure enough, and I think he must have been a foreigner. He was armed *cap-à-pié*. The horse he rode carried a full campaigning kit on an English military saddle. Wallets, saddle-bags, drinking-cup, holsters—all were there His rifle was slung across his back, he wore two full bandoliers over his shoulders and a third round his waist—evidently a dangerous customer. I looked at his face and our eyes met. The light was dim, or he might have seen me change colour. He had a pale, almost ghastly visage, peering ill-favoured and cruel from beneath a slouch hat with a large white feather. Then he turned away carelessly. After all, I suppose he thought it natural a poor devil of a towns-man should wish to look at so fine a cavalier of fortune. Presently he set spurs to his horse and cantered on. I breathed again freely. Lautré laughed.

"There are plenty of cyclists in Johannesburg," he said. "We do not look extraordinary. No one will stop us."

We now began to approach the south eastern outskirts of the town. If the original scheme of advance had been carried out, Lord Roberts's leading brigade should be close at hand. Lautré said,

"Shall we inquire?" But I thought it better to wait. As we progressed the streets became still more deserted, and at last we found ourselves quite alone. For more than half a mile I did not see a single person. Then we met a shabby-looking man, and now, no one else being in sight, the night dark, and the man old and feeble, we decided to ask him.

"The English," he said with a grin, "why, their sentinels are just at the top of the hill."

"How far?"

"Five minutes—even less."

Two hundred yards further on three British soldiers came in sight. They were quite unarmed, and walking casually forward into the town. I stopped them and asked what brigade they belonged to. They replied Maxwell's.

"Where is the picket line?"

"We haven't seen no pickets," said one of them.

"What are you doing?"

"Looking for something to eat. We've had enough of 'arf rations."

I said, "You'll get taken prisoners or shot if you go on into the town."

"Wot's that, guvnor?" said one of them, deeply interested in this extraordinary possibility.

I repeated, and added that the Boers were still riding about the streets.

"Well, then, I ain't for it," he said with decision. "Let's go back and try some of them 'ouses near the camp."

So we all proceeded together.

I discovered no picket line at the edge of the town. Maxwell must have had one somewhere, but it certainly did not prevent anyone from passing freely; for we were never challenged, and, walking on, soon found ourselves in the middle of a large bivouac. I now became of some use to my companion, for if he knew the roads I knew the army. I soon found some officers of my acquaintance, and from them we learned that Lord Roberts's headquarters were not at Elandsfontein (South), but back at Germiston, nearly seven miles away. It was now pitch dark, and all signs of a road had vanished; but Lautré declared he knew his way, and, in any case, the messages —press and official—had to go through.

We left the camp of Maxwell's Brigade and struck across country in order to cut into the main southern road. A bicycle now became a great encumbrance, as the paths wound through dense fir woods, obstructed by frequent wire fences, ditches, holes, and high grass. Lautré, however, persisted that all was well, and, as it turned out, he was right. After about an hour of this slow progress we reached the railway, and, seeing more camp fires away to the left, turned along it. Half a mile in this direction brought us to another bivouac, which we likewise entered unchallenged. I asked a soldier whose brigade he belonged to, but he did not know, which was painfully stupid of him. A group of officers were gathered round an enormous fire a few yards away, and we went up to them to ask. Chance had led me to General Tucker's mess. I had known the commander of the Seventh Division in India, when he was stationed at Secunderabad, and he welcomed me with his usual breezy courtesy. He had been sent off with his leading brigade late in the afternoon to try to join hands with French, and so complete the circle round Johannesburg; but darkness had curtailed his march. Besides this, no communications having yet come through from the cavalry, he was uncertain where French was. Naturally he was interested to hear what had passed on the west of the town, and about the stirring action of the previous day. From him I got some whisky and water, and clear directions to the Field-Marshal's headquarters. They were, it appeared, two miles beyond Germiston, a mile and a half west of the road, in a solitary house on a small hill which stood beyond a large tank. And in case these indications might have been of little avail in the dark, he led us a few feet up the slope, and there we saw that, on the blackness of the night, flamed a regular oblong of glittering lights. It was the camp of the Eleventh Division. Somewhere near that were the Chief's headquarters. Thus instructed, we resumed our journey.

Another half-hour of walking brought us, as Lautré had promised, to a good firm road, and the bicycles quickly made amends for their previous uselessness. The air was cold, and we were glad to spin along at a fair ten miles an hour. At this rate twenty minutes brought us into Germiston. Not knowing where I should be likely to find dinner, or a bed, I dismounted opposite the hotel, and, seeing lights and signs of occupation, went inside. Here I found Mr. Lionel James, the principal Correspondent of *The Times*. I asked him if his subordinate had arrived from Hamilton's force. He said "No"; and when I told him he had started two hours in front of me, looked much concerned; whereat the Frenchman could not conceal a heartless grimace. I offered to give him some account of the action for his own use (for what is more detestable than a jealous journalist?), but he said that I had had the good luck to come through, and that he would not think of depriving me of my advantage. Alas! the days of newspaper enterprise in war are over. What can one do with a censor, a forty-eight hours' delay, and a fifty-word limit on the wire? Besides, who can compete with Lord Roberts as a special correspondent? None against the interest of his daily messages; very few against their style and simple grace. Never mind. It is all for the best.

We dined hastily and not too well, secured the reversion of half the billiard table, should all other couches fail, and set out again, this time tired and footsore. After two miles of dusty track the camp was reached. I found more officers who knew where Army Headquarters were, and at last, at about half past ten, we reached the solitary house. We sent the despatches in by an orderly, and after a few minutes Lord Kerry came out and said that the Chief wanted to see the messengers.

Now, for the first time in this war, I found myself face to face with our illustrious leader. The room was small and meanly furnished, and he and his staff, who had just finished dinner, sat round a large table which occupied the greater part of the floor. With him were Sir William Nicholson (who arranges all the transport of the army, a work the credit of which is usually given to Lord Kitchener) and Colonel Neville Chamberlayne, his private secretary, both of them soldiers of the practical Indian school, where you have real fighting, both of them serving once more under their commander of Afghan days. There, too, was Sir Henry Rawlinson, whom I had last seen round Sir George White's table, the night Dundonald broke into Ladysmith; and Sir James Hills-Johnes, who won the Victoria Cross in the Indian Mutiny, and aides-de-camp and others whom I cannot remember.

The Field-Marshal rose from his place, shook hands, and bade us, in most ceremonious fashion, to be seated. He had read half of Hamilton's despatch.

"The first part of this," he said, "we knew already. Two guides—Rimington's, I think—got in here about an hour ago. They had a dangerous ride, and were chased a long way, but escaped safely. I am glad to hear Hamilton is at Florida. How did you get through?"

I told him briefly. His eye twinkled. I have never seen a man before with such extraordinary eyes. I remember to have been struck with them on several occasions. The face remains perfectly motionless, but the eyes convey the strongest emotions. Sometimes they blaze with anger, and you see hot yellow fire behind them. Then it is best to speak up straight and clear, and make an end quickly. At others there is a steel grey glitter—quite cold and uncompromising—which has a most sobering effect on anyone who sees it. But now the eyes twinkled brightly with pleasure or amusement or approbation, or, at any rate, something friendly.

"Tell me about the action," he said.

So I told him all I knew, much as it is set down in these pages, though not nearly at such length; but I don't think the tale lost in the telling. From time to time he asked questions about the Artillery concentration, or the length of front of the Infantry attack, and other technical matters, on which I was luckily well-informed. The fact that the troops had no rations seemed to disturb him very much. He was particularly interested to hear of Hamilton's novel attack "at thirty paces extension"; of the manner in which the batteries had been rammed almost into the firing line; but most of all he wanted to hear about the Gordons' charge. When I had done he said: "The Gordons always do well." Then he asked what we proposed to do. Lautré said he would go back forthwith; but the Chief said, "Much better stay here for the night; we will find you beds"; so of course we stayed. He asked me whether I meant to go back next morning. I said that as I had got my messages to the telegraph office I thought, upon the whole, that I would not run any more risks, but wait and see the British occupation of the town. He laughed at this, and said that I was quite right, and would be very ill-advised to be caught again. Then he said that he would send a letter to Hamilton in the morning, bade us all "good-night", and retired to his waggon. I, too, found a comfortable bed—the first for a month—and being thoroughly worn out soon fell asleep.

Part of Lord Roberts's letter that he wrote to Ian Hamilton next day was published in the orders of the flanking column. In some ways it explains why the private soldier will march further for "Bobs Bahadur" than for anyone else in the world.

"I am delighted at your repeated successes, and grieve beyond measure at your poor fellows being without their proper rations. A trainful shall go to you to-day. I expect to get the notice that Johannesburg surrenders this morning, and we shall then march into the town. I wish your column, which has done so much to gain possession of it, could be with us.

"Tell the Gordons that I am proud to think I have a Highlander as one of the supporters on my coat-of-arms."

CHAPTER FIFTEEN

THE CAPTURE OF PRETORIA

Pretoria: June 8, 1900

THE COMMANDER-IN-CHIEF had good reasons—how good we little knew—for wishing to push on at once to the enemy's capital, without waiting at Johannesburg. But the fatigue of the troops and the necessities of supply imposed a two days' halt. On the 3rd of June the advance was resumed. The army marched in three columns. The left, thrown forward in echelon, consisted of the Cavalry Division under French; the centre was formed by Ian Hamilton's force; and the right or main column nearest the railway comprised the Seventh and Eleventh Divisions (less one brigade left to hold Johannesburg), Gordon's Cavalry Brigade, and the Corps Troops all under the personal command of the Field-Marshal.

The long forward stride of the 3rd was, except for a small action against French, unchecked or unopposed by the Boers, and all the information which the Intelligence Department could collect seemed to promise a bloodless entry into the capital. So strong was the evidence that at dawn on the 4th of June Hamilton's column was diverted from its prescribed line of march on Elandsfontein* and drawn in towards the main army, with orders to bivouac on Pretoria Green, west of the town. French, whom the change of orders did not reach, pursued his wide turning movement, and encountered further opposition in a bad country for cavalry.

At ten o'clock it was reported that Colonel Henry, with the corps of mounted infantry in advance of the main column, was actually in the suburbs of Pretoria without opposition. The force continued to converge, and Ian Hamilton had almost joined Lord Roberts's force when the booming of guns warned us that our anticipations were too sanguine. The army had just crossed a

* Yet another Elandsfontein, situated to the west of Pretoria.

difficult spruit, and Colonel Henry with the mounted infantry had obtained a lodgment on the heights beyond. But here they were sharply checked. The Boers, apparently in some force, were holding a wooded ridge and several high hills along the general line of the southern Pretoria forts.

Determined to hold what he had obtained, Lord Roberts thrust his artillery well forward, and ordered Ian Hamilton to support Colonel Henry immediately with all mounted troops. This was speedily done. The horsemen galloped forward, and, scrambling up the steep hillsides, reinforced the thin firing line along the ridge. The artillery of the Seventh Division came into action in front of the British centre. The Boers replied with a brisk rifle fire, which reached all three batteries, and drew from them a very vigorous cannonade.

Meanwhile the infantry deployment was proceeding. The 14th Brigade extended for attack. Half an hour later Pole-Carew's batteries prolonged the line of guns to the right, and about half past two the corps and heavy artillery opened in further prolongation. By three o'clock fifty guns were in action in front of the main army, and both the Seventh and Eleventh Divisions had assumed preparatory formations. The balloon ascended and remained hanging in the air for an hour—a storm signal.

During this time Hamilton was pushing swiftly forward, and Smith-Dorrien's 19th Infantry Brigade occupied the line of heights, and thus set free the mounted troops for a turning movement. The 21st Brigade supported. The heights were so steep in front of Hamilton that his artillery could not come into action, and only one gun and one "pom-pom" could, by great exertion, be dragged and man-handled into position. The fire of these pieces, however, caught the Boers holding the wooded ridge in enfilade, and was by no means ineffective.

So soon as Hamilton had collected the mounted troops he sent them to reinforce Broadwood, whom he directed to move round the enemy's right flank. The ground favoured the movement, and by half past four the cavalry were seen debouching into the plain beyond the Boer position, enveloping their flank and compromising their retreat.

Colonel de Lisle's corps of mounted infantry, composed mainly of Australians, made a much shorter circuit, and reaching the level ground before the cavalry espied a Boer Maxim retreating towards the town. To this they immediately gave chase, and the strong

Waler horses were urged to their utmost speed. The appearance of this clattering swarm of horsemen must have been formidable to those below. But we who watched from the heights saw what Ian Hamilton, who was in high spirits, described as "a charge of infuriated mice" streaming across the brown veldt; so great are the distances in modern war.

Towards four o'clock the cannonade all along the front had died away, and only the heavy artillery on the right of Pole-Carew's Division continued to fire, shelling the forts, whose profile showed plainly on the sky-line, and even hurling their projectiles right over the hills into Pretoria itself. So heavy had the artillery been that the Boers did not endure, and alarmed as well by the flank movement they retreated in haste through the town; so that before dusk their whole position was occupied by the Infantry without much loss. Night, which falls at this season and in this part of the world as early as half past five, then shut down on the scene, and the action—in which practically the whole Army Corps had been engaged—ended.

The fact that the forts had not replied to the British batteries showed that their guns had been removed, and that the Boers had no serious intention of defending their capital. The Field-Marshal's orders for the morrow were, therefore, that the army should advance at daybreak on Pretoria, which it was believed would then be formally surrendered. Meanwhile, however, Colonel de Lisle, with the infuriated mice—in other words, the Australians—was pressing hotly on, and at about six o'clock, having captured the flying Maxim, he seized a position within rifle shot of the town. From here he could see the Boers galloping in disorder through the streets, and, encouraged by the confusion that apparently prevailed, he sent an officer under flag of truce to demand the surrender. This the panic-stricken civil authorities, with the consent of Commandant Botha, obeyed, and though no British troops entered the town until the next day, Pretoria actually fell before midnight on the 4th of June.

As soon as the light allowed the army moved forward. The Guards were directed on the railway station. Ian Hamilton's force swept round the western side. Wishing to enter among the first of the victorious troops the town I had crept away from as a fugitive six months before, I hurried forward, and, with the Duke of Marlborough, soon overtook General Pole-Carew, who, with his staff, was advancing towards the railway station. We passed through a narrow cleft in the southern wall of mountains, and Pretoria lay before us—a picturesque little town with red or blue roofs peeping out among masses of trees, and here and there an occasional spire or factory chimney. Behind us, on the hills we had taken, the brown forts were crowded with British soldiers. Scarcely two hundred yards away stood the railway station.

Arrived at this point, General Pole-Carew was compelled to wait to let his Infantry catch him up; and while we were delayed a locomotive whistle sounded loudly, and, to our astonishment—for had not the town surrendered?—a train drawn by two engines steamed out of the station on the Delagoa Bay line. For a moment we stared at this insolent breach of the customs of war, and a dozen staff officers, aides-de-camp, and orderlies (no mounted troops being at hand) started off at a furious gallop in the hopes of compelling the train to stop, or at least of shooting the engine-driver, and so sending it to its destruction. But wire fences and the gardens of the houses impeded the pursuers, and, in spite of all their efforts, the train escaped, carrying with it ten trucks of horses, which might have been very useful, and one truck-load of Hollanders. Three engines with steam up and several trains, however, remained in the station, and the leading company of Grenadiers, doubling forward, captured them and their occupants. These Boers attempted to resist the troops with pistols, but surrendered after two volleys had been fired, no one, fortunately, being hurt in the scrimmage.

After a further delay, the Guards, fixing bayonets, began to enter the town, marching through the main street, which was crowded with people, towards the central square, and posting sentries and pickets as they went. We were naturally very anxious to know what had befallen our comrades held prisoners all these long months. Rumour said they had been removed during the night to Waterfall Boven, 200 miles down the Delagoa Bay line. But nothing definite was known.

The Duke of Marlborough, however, found a mounted Dutchman who said he knew where all the officers were confined, and who undertook to guide us, and without waiting for the troops, who were advancing with all due precautions, we set off at a gallop.

The distance was scarcely three-quarters of a mile, and in a few minutes, turning a corner and crossing a little brook, we saw before us a long tin building surrounded by a dense wire entanglement.

Seeing this, and knowing its meaning too well, I raised my hat and cheered. The cry was instantly answered from within. What followed resembled the end of an Adelphi melodrama.

The Duke of Marlborough called on the commandant to surrender forthwith. The prisoners rushed out of the house into the yard, some in uniform, some in flannels, hatless or coatless, but all violently excited. The sentries threw down their rifles. The gates were flung open, and while the rest of the guards—they numbered fifty-two in all—stood uncertain what to do, the long-penned-up officers surrounded them and seized their weapons. Someone— Grimshaw of the Dublin Fusiliers—produced a Union Jack (made during imprisonment out of a Vierkleur). The Transvaal emblem was torn down, and, amid wild cheers, the first British flag was hoisted over Pretoria. Time 8.47, June 5.

The commandant then made formal surrender to the Duke of Marlborough of 129 officers and 39 soldiers whom he had in his custody as prisoners of war, and surrendered, besides himself, 4 corporals and 48 Dutchmen. These latter were at once confined within the wire cage, and guarded by their late prisoners; but, since they had treated the captives well, they have now been permitted to take the oath of neutrality and return to their homes. The anxieties which the prisoners had suffered during the last few hours of their confinement were terrible, nor did I wonder, when I heard the account, why their faces were so white and their manner so excited. But the reader shall learn the tale from one of their number, nor will I anticipate.

At two o'clock Lord Roberts, the staff, and the foreign attachés entered the town, and proceeded to the central square, wherein the Town Hall, the Parliament House, and other public buildings are situated. The British flag was hoisted over the Parliament House amid some cheers. The victorious army then began to parade past it, Pole-Carew's Division, with the Guards leading, coming from the south, and Ian Hamilton's force from the west. For three hours the broad river of steel and khaki flowed unceasingly, and the townfolk gazed in awe and wonder at those majestic soldiers, whose discipline neither perils nor hardships had disturbed, whose relentless march no obstacles could prevent.

With such pomp and the rolling of drums the new order of things was ushered in. The former Government had ended without dignity. One thought to find the President—stolid old Dutchman—

seated on his stoep reading his Bible and smoking a sullen pipe. But he chose a different course. On the Friday preceding the British occupation he left the capital and withdrew along the Delagoa Bay Railway, taking with him a million pounds in gold, and leaving behind him a crowd of officials clamouring for pay, and far from satisfied with the worthless cheques they had received, and Mrs. Kruger, concerning whose health the British people need not further concern themselves.

I cannot end this letter without recalling for one moment the grave risks Lord Roberts bravely faced in order to strike the decisive blow and seize Pretoria. When he decided to advance from Vereeniging without waiting for more supplies, and so profit by the enemy's disorder, he played for a great stake. He won, and it is very easy now to forget the adverse chances. But the facts stand out in glaring outline: that if the Boers had defended Pretoria with their forts and guns they could have checked us for several weeks; and if, while we were trying to push our investment, the line had been cut behind us, as it has since been cut, nothing would have remained but starvation or an immediate retreat on Johannesburg, perhaps on the Vaal. Even now our position is not thoroughly secure, and the difficulties of subjugating a vast country, though sparsely populated, are such that the troops in South Africa are scarcely sufficient. But the question of supplies is for the present solved. The stores of Johannesburg, and still more of Pretoria, will feed the army for something over a fortnight, and in the meanwhile we can re-open our communications, and perhaps do much more. But what a lucky nation we are to have found, at a time of sore need and trouble, a General great enough to take all risks and overcome all dangers.

CHAPTER SIXTEEN

"HELD BY THE ENEMY"

Extracts from the Journal of Lieutenant H. Frankland, Royal Dublin Fusiliers, lately prisoner of war at Pretoria.

LIEUTENANT FRANKLAND was captured by the Boers when the armoured train was destroyed at Chieveley, in Natal, on the 15th of November, 1899. He was carried as a prisoner to Pretoria, where he arrived on the 19th of November, and where he remained until the 5th of June, 1900, when Pretoria fell and the greater part of the prisoners were set free by their victorious comrades.

*　　*　　*　　*　　*

"*November* 19th.—To wake up and find oneself enclosed in the space of a few acres for an indefinite period is scarcely pleasant; however, one cannot always be miserable. The monotony will, I have no doubt, become very trying, but for the first few days I have a good deal to do. The State Model School, which has been turned into a prison for the officers, is a building of rectangular shape. A long corridor runs through the centre, and on both sides of this are the rooms, where the officers sleep. They are supplied with a spring bed and two blankets apiece, while the whole place is lighted by electricity. At one end is the dining-room and gymnasium.

"In front is the road, from which the building is separated by iron railings. Behind there is a sort of back garden where the police and soldier servants live in tents, and where the kitchen and the bathroom are situated. This piece of ground is surrounded on three sides by a six-foot fence of corrugated iron, and the whole place is watched by a cordon of armed police, about fifteen being on duty always. The Government here generously supplies the officers with bread and water, half a pound of bully beef a day, and groceries. We have a small piece of ground and a gymnasium for exercise. As there are, alas! about fifty officers here, we have formed a sort of mess, and for the sum of three shillings a day we improve our scanty allowance of food. They have supplied us with a suit of clothes each, but mine was much too big for me. I began to write my diary this evening, and had a long talk with Garvice in my regiment, who told me how he had been captured. Dinner 7.30; bed, and sleep.

"*November 20th.*—It looks as if the rest of my diary for several months would contain each day the words, 'the same as usual'. I have only been here forty-eight hours, but the monotony has already begun to show itself. Not the monotony only, but the want of freedom, the want of news, the knowledge that the rest of the war will be carried out without my share in its victories, when, had it not been for some unhappy fate, I might yet have seen many an action —all these combine to oppress and irritate my mind. I tried to make a sketch of the armoured train, but it was not a success, and I must begin again tomorrow. The very length of empty time in front of me makes me quite patient.

"*November 21st.*—It is getting extremely hot. The lack of open space to walk in makes me feel lazy, and one gets quite tired after going a few times around the building. What one most looks forward to are the meals, and these are not very satisfying. But of course I am still suffering from the appetite of freedom, and I have no doubt that a month or so of this sort of life will make me feel less ravenous. I wrote some of my diary, and commenced another sketch of the armoured train, which I hope to be able to send to the *Graphic*. Churchill has written asking to be released, but he does not expect any result. The mosquitoes here are very troublesome, and I have been constantly bitten.

"*November 23rd.*—The mail was supposed to go to-day, so I found occupation in a few letters. It is still very sultry. I succeeded in getting through a good deal of my diary, and, after writing nearly all day, played a game of rounders in the evening. This last occupation appears to cause much annoyance to the police, who frequently get hit by the ball. Another game here is fives, which we play with a tennis ball in the gymnasium. There seems to be some news about, but we can get nothing out of these people. By these people I mean Malan—a spiteful, objectionable animal—who ought to be at the front, were he not a coward; Opperman, a slightly more agreeable person, of large dimensions, and Dr. Gunning, a much more amiable fellow. It seems absurd that they do not allow us to buy papers. What harm could we do with them?

"Some of the restrictions are so childish, and tend to make life here so sickening, that I am sure if curses could harm the Transvaal Government it would not be long-lived.

"This morning Churchill was visited by De Souza, the Secretary of War, by the Under-Secretary for Foreign Affairs, and others, and there followed a very animated discussion about the causes and the justice of the war. It was a drawn game, and they all talked at once at the end, especially Churchill. I am afraid for his sake he is not likely to be exchanged or released. The Boers have got to hear of the part he played in the armoured train episode.

"*November 24th.*—There is some news abroad today. The Free Staters have been attacked at Belmont by the British, probably under Buller, but the result is uncertain. Of course the Boers report a victory on their side, but one gets quite accustomed to their 'victories'. Dundee was a victory, likewise Elandslaagte. I am getting on slowly with my diary, and manage to make it occupy a great deal of time.

"*November 25th.*—Evidently we have won a victory at Belmont; its results are immediately apparent here. They have suddenly become much more lenient and complacent. We are actually allowed newspapers, and the President is considering the question of beer. The papers admit that the British drove the Free Staters from their position at Belmont, but with great loss, while that of the Boers is practically *nil*. Rumours say that General Joubert is cut off between Estcourt and Mooi River; how I hope it is true!

"*November 26th.*—The Rev. Mr. Hofmeyr is a prisoner here, and held service this morning, when he delivered a most eloquent address. There is a harmonium in one of the rooms, and Mr. Hofmeyr, who sings very well, gives us some very good music. He knows a lot of old English songs, which are pleasant to hear, although they rather suggest the Psalm beginning 'By the waters of Babylon'. Hofmeyr, though a Dutchman, is an ardent supporter of the Imperial cause, and he has in consequence been very cruelly treated by the Boers before he came here.

"It is quite touching to see how the Boers try to hide their defeat. All the accounts are cooked, but even De Souza acknowledges that if things go on as at present the war will soon be over. There have been several days' fighting south of Kimberley, and Buller is advancing steadily. On the Natal side Joubert passed Estcourt, and reached Mooi River, where he was attacked by the new division and defeated. In retiring he was attacked by part of the Estcourt garrison, result unknown. He will probably retire on Colenso.

"*November 27th.*—Not much news today. According to the *Volksstem* British lost fifteen hundred at Belmont, and the Boers nine killed and forty wounded. However, they can't deny that the Free Staters were licked, and De Souza admits that Kimberley will probably be relieved shortly. Moreover, Khama is said to have risen. This has disturbed them all exceedingly, and Opperman is highly indignant.

"*November 30th.*—I find nothing to record here except the scraps of news one gets in the newspapers, all else is monotonous—appalling monotony. In the evening one feels it most, and sometimes I don't think I can endure it for another month. All sorts of absurd rumours are spread about here by that intelligent paper the *Volksstem*. The latest is that four British regiments have refused to fight, being in sympathy with the Republican cause. I wonder whether Buller will desert to the Boer side? The fact remains that the papers give no news whilst there must be plenty, and this looks as if the untold news must be bad for them. We hear that General Forestier-Walker has been killed, and that Lord Methuen is seriously wounded. This morning the rumour runs that our troops have occupied Colenso. The regiment is sure to be there. How I wish I were with it!

"*December 4th.*—No real news, but various and contradictory rumours. The Boers have begun to acknowledge their losses, and the papers have long lists of killed and wounded. Major ——, of the West Yorks, arrived today, having been captured near Estcourt. From him I learned that all was well there. A few days ago three battalions—West Yorks, Borderers and Second Queen's—went out and attacked the Boers. Apparently the engagement was indecisive, and the losses on either side not very great. The rumour goes that Buller is in Natal, and not in the Free State after all. Of course he is advancing to the relief of Ladysmith. We all think that his plan will be to hold the Boers in front at Colenso while he takes a large force around by the flank. The Boers have retired beyond the river, and have blown up the Tugela railway bridge. On the other side, Lord Methuen's Division is having severe fighting; he has defeated the Boers at Modder River, and the relief of Kimberley is imminent. The papers do not publish much news themselves, but occasionally publish some of the English cuttings with sarcastic editorial comments. In the Dutch version of the *Volksstem* they slate the Free Staters unmercifully for having run away at Modder River.

"Oh, that we might be exchanged. Joubert has wired *via* Buller to England advocating such a step.

"*December* 15*th.*—'*Tempus fugit*', and it has not been quite so dull as usual. First, and most important of all, Churchill has escaped. Whether he has made it good or not is still uncertain; but he has now been gone two days, and I have great hopes. Besides the excitement there has been a very amusing side to the affair. Of course Churchill was the very last person who ought to have gone. He was always talking and arguing with the officials, and was therefore well known, and, indeed, scarcely a day passed without Dr. Gunning or Mr. de Souza inquiring for him. His plans for escape were primitive; but, being still in prison, I must not write anything about this part of the affair. Let it suffice that Churchill got away without any trace left behind. Next morning, as it chanced, it was the day for the barber to come and shave him, and having only just woke up I put the barber off rather feebly by saying that Churchill had gone to the bath-room, and would not need shaving. What should the detective who accompanied the barber do but wait outside the bath-room, and, finding no Churchill, began to suspect. Gunning then came upon the scene, closely followed by Opperman, both asking and seeking anxiously for their captive. Their distress at finding him gone was really pathetic. They immediately put on all kinds of restrictions. No papers, calling rolls, not allowing anyone into the yard outside the building after 8 p.m., and stopping all beer. I am reminded of the fable 'Le Corbeau et le Renard', which ends, '*Le Corbeau . . . jura, mais un peu tard, qu'on ne l'y prendroit plus*'. Curiously enough, the day after Churchill had escaped an order is said to have come from General Joubert for his release. However, I have no doubt but that this was all made up to excuse themselves for not being able to catch him. I do hope he gets away.

"Our spirits are constantly on the rise and fall. At one time we are about to be exchanged, at another nothing has been heard of it; at one time there is a brilliant British success, greatly modified, of course, by the enlightened *Volksstem* editor, at another a crushing British defeat, with all the Generals and thousands of soldiers killed and wounded. Yesterday we heard of the splendid achievement of the British troops in Ladysmith in smashing up the 84-pounder at

Lombard's Kop, several Howitzers and a Maxim. Then came the defeat of General Gatacre at Stormberg, and the capture of 600 prisoners, and on the top of this the victory which the Boers claim at Magersfontein. All this is very terrible. I think I feel almost as miserable as I did the night I was captured. Are the British troops ever going to drive the Boers back? Will they ever come and take Pretoria? or will they, on the other hand, be driven back, and the people at home get sick of the war, like in '81, and—no, impossible—and yet who will dare predict? It is too awful to hear all these shocking reports, and to be able to do nothing oneself. One always imagines on these occasions one's presence at the scene of fighting absolutely indispensable if there is to be a victory. However, these miserable days cannot last for ever. Perhaps they are even now at an end. De Souza, with a faltering voice, has confessed that Buller is advancing at last in great force. He must win.

"*December* 19*th*.—Worse than ever. Buller has attacked in full strength at Colenso and has been defeated with a loss of ten guns and many hundred men. This is too awful—I could have cried. The hand of fate seems to be raised against us. The only thing to do is to wait patiently till the next disaster. The Stormberg prisoners have arrived, the Colenso prisoners are expected tomorrow. Everybody is cursing the Generals; but they always think they could do better themselves. I hear that Hart's Brigade, with our regiment in it, were caught in quarter column at close range. They must have suffered terribly. Never mind; Methuen has relieved Kimberley. The officials all deny it, but it must be true.

"*December* 23*rd*.—No more news. The authorities are getting more and more silly and disagreeable; all kinds of babyish restrictions are invented to annoy us. Churchill has got to Delagoa Bay, and has wired his safe arrival to De Souza. Hurrah!

* * * * *

"I have not dared until now, when all is a failure, to set down in this book any account of the one occupation that has prevented us from going mad with disappointment in these sad times. About the middle of the month Haldane devised a plan of making a tunnel from under our room across the road. The five fellows in our dormitory and Le Mesurier, who shifted his abode for the purpose, began about ten days ago. First, we thought of cutting a hole in the floor, but, on looking round, we suddenly found a trap-door already made. Beneath the floor there is a curious place. The rafters are supported by stone walls, so that underneath there is a series of compartments about twenty-four feet by four, with access from one to another by means of man-holes in each wall. We commenced digging in the compartment next to the one under the trap-door. The ground at first was very hard, but with chisels and implements taken from the gymnasium, we managed to get down four feet of the shaft in about four days. It was a queer sight to see two half-naked figures digging away by candle light, for we used to work in reliefs of two—one to dig and the other to cast away the earth in boxes or jugs. Suddenly, one day, we broke through the hard crust and came to some soft clay soil. We were delighted at this, and expected to get through it in no time; but, alas! with the soft earth came water, and without pumps, bale as we would, we could not get rid of it. Every morning the shaft was completely bilged; so, having dug down six feet, our plan was brought to an end, and we had to screw up our trap-door again in bitter disappointment. The officers of the Gloucester Regiment are digging too, but they are sure to find the same difficulties.

"*Christmas Day*, 1899.—I can scarcely realise that it is Christmas, the day I have hitherto spent at home with family and friends. I can see the rooms decorated with holly and 'Merry Christmas' cut in white paper and pasted on red Turkish twill hanging over the doorway. A Merry Christmas! What irony! The time, of course, was bound to come when the circle at home would be broken; but little did I dream where or under what unhappy circumstances. A Merry Christmas! to a prisoner—not when his countrymen, victorious and full of enthusiasm, are marching rapidly to his release, but when the armies of his country, beaten back, lie far away; when, helpless himself, despair seizes his heart; when reverses grow into disasters and the might of the dear old land in which he trusted seems to have weakened and died. A Happy Christmas! with the New Year black, uncertain, and unknown. Of course we drank the health of the Queen at dinner—in lime-juice. 'Twas all we had; but we meant it none the less.

"*December 30th*.—They say there were only 1,200 casualties at Colenso; but we have just heard that —— and —— of our regiment have been killed. O God! it seems too awful. To hear of all one's friends crippled or dead; all the best are picked off, and here are we tied up quite safely with our beastly skins unhurt, and not likely to run into the slightest danger while our comrades are losing their lives. We must win this war.

*   *   *   *   *

"*January 1st.*—I have had many arguments as to whether this is the commencement of a new century or not, and after much reasoning I have decided that as it is the year 1900, or the nineteen hundredth year, it is the last of the nineteenth century and not the beginning of the twentieth. Whatever it may be, this is a hateful place to spend the beginning of anything in. The *Volksstem* printed a list of casualties today, and I see that our regiment lost forty-two killed at Colenso. What must the numbers of the wounded have been? [Here follows a list of wounded officers.] Sergeant Gage was killed, and they say he was one of the first to cross the waggon bridge. This looks as if the regiment had stormed the bridge, which is much better than being mown down in quarter column. All these losses are terrible, but I believe that Colenso is only a reconnaissance in force. What must a battle be like?

"The last week has been, if possible, more dreary than usual. One of the fellows in our room has made himself very obnoxious lately, and has had to be sat upon severely. I have never met such an ungentlemanlike creature. It is all the more unpleasant in a place like this, where we are so closely packed. There are rumours of fighting near Colesberg, probably by General French. The Boers say the action is indecisive, which means a victory for us.

"*January 7th.*—Nothing of importance has occurred lately. There has been a bit of a fight with Opperman, who tried to take away from Boshof, the local grocer, his contract for the supply of our mess, on the ground that Boshof had helped Churchill to escape: Result a complete victory for us and the reinstatement of Boshof. More Zarps, as the policemen who guard us are called, and poor little Gunning have been commandeered. He prepares himself to go. His reason is peculiar. Should his children, in after years, ask him if he fought for the freedom of the State, he would like to be able to say 'Yes'. However, if he goes I hope he will find a large rock to get behind and so come back safely.

"This afternoon a most alarming rumour was started by somebody, namely: that Ladysmith had fallen. Though I did not actually believe it, we are always having such frightful disasters that I felt very uncomfortable. Later, however, we learned that all was well.

"*January* 10*th.*—Ladysmith has not fallen. The news of the defeat of the Boers on the Platrand has been confirmed, and, in spite of their lies, we know their losses were heavy. At Colesberg there was a night attack, and a half battalion of the Suffolks got much knocked about. Two of their officers came in as prisoners yesterday; they say the Boers have received large reinforcements at Colesberg. There is a rumour that Dr. Leyds has been arrested in Germany for trying to enlist German Reservists. A British force is said to be at Douglas, west of Kimberley. They made a night attack and captured some stores and ammunition. The Transvaalers in their excitement succeeded in firing into the Free Staters, shooting, among others, Opperman's nephew. We offered our sympathies, but after all it is one the less. This evening we received a most excellent rumour that the Boers had lost 900 men near Colenso. I hope it is true, and that the Tugela has, therefore, been crossed. This will be a step towards the relief of Ladysmith. At Colesberg the Boers are in a critical position. Things seem to be looking up a bit. I wish that we could get just a little truth. These rumours torture and deceive.

"*January* 14*th.*—All kinds of startling rumours have been about today: The British fighting in overwhelming numbers around Ladysmith; Buller surprised and taken prisoner at Pieters Station. Boers in a tight corner at Colesberg. What can one believe? All men are liars—in Africa! Life is getting very unbearable. I am sure we shall be a lot of lunatics when we are set free.

"*January* 29*th.* How we clamour for news, and how our spirits rise and fall as the rumours are favourable or bad. The other day the prisoners arrived from the Spion Kop fight. The result of the attack on Spion Kop is not known. We took the hill, but, for some reason, the rumour goes that we have left it again and re-crossed the river. Can this be another lie? We hear that the regiment did not cross the waggon bridge, but tried to swim the river at Colenso last month. Very few got over. Hensley was killed the other day at Spion Kop. One can scarcely realise these losses, and I don't think we shall until we join the mess and see the sad gaps among familiar faces.

"*February* 5*th.*—We have been getting a fair share of good news lately, or, at least, good rumours. The relief of Kimberley is an established fact. Colesberg is on its last legs, though news of its surrender to French needs confirmation. There is fighting at the Tugela, concerning which the latest bulletin is 'British have taken a position—Vaal Krantz'. Nor is this all, other factors are at work

besides the British Army. There is considerable dissension between
the Transvaalers and the Free Staters. The former complain that
they are always put in the forefront of the battle, while the latter
rejoin that not only are they invariably sent to the more exposed
kopjes, but that while they are aiding the Transvaalers to fight in
Natal they are receiving no help in the defence of the Free State.

"*February* 12th.—It would take too long, even when time is
nothing but a curse, to record all the items of news we have lately
received. So many startling rumours have been confirmed and
denied that I long to know what is the real truth, but in the Capital
of this doomed country—in the very metropolis of lies and liars—
we shall never learn the truth until our friends come to bring it
with them.

"I have just finished reading *Esmond*, which I enjoyed very much.
One advantage of my forced sojourn in this country is that I may
improve my education. Indeed, reading occupies the greater part of
our time though I myself cannot fix my attention on a book for
very long under these miserable circumstances. The State Library
has a fair selection of books, and by paying a small subscription the
prisoners are allowed to take out books therefrom. The only forbidden fruits are the books of South Africa; for these volumes,
recording the evil wrought by the British race on this chosen people,
are carefully stowed away for fear of the English trying to destroy
the histories of their crimes.

"This morning an officer of the South African Light Horse was
buried. To all intents and purposes he was murdered by the Transvaal Government. Although he had typhoid fever he was thrown
into prison, and not until the authorities were pretty certain he
would die was he sent to the hospital. Ten officers on parole went as
pall-bearers and we all subscribed for a very pretty wreath.

"Patience is played as a game here largely by ancient Colonels
and Majors, and practised by us all with indifferent success as a
cruel necessity.

"*February* 17th.—Good news at last! Kimberley has been
relieved! Boers are retiring in all directions. Lord Roberts, with the
British Army, has entered the Free State. Warrenton has been
occupied, there is great consternation in Pretoria. Opperman is
furious. Perhaps the tide has begun to turn.

"To explain how we get news: Brockie, a Sergeant-Major in the
Imperial Light Horse, knows a Zarp here and gets a certain amount

of news from him, which is not, however, very trustworthy. When we first came here an Englishman named Patterson, employed in the Government telegraph office, used to pass by the railings and whisper the news. He only used to come when there was good news to tell, and generally ended with the words, Hurrah, hurrah! Since he was always accompanied on these occasions by a large St. Bernard, we called him the Dogman. Lately he has elaborated and improved his system of giving us news and has begun to signal with a flag from the passage of Mr. Cullingworth's house opposite. Either he or one of the Misses Cullingworth stands some way back in the passage so as not to be visible to the Zarps and sends messages, which are read by Captain Burrows from the gymnasium window. As he is in the telegraph office and sees all that passes, the Dogman sends very truthful information.

"*February* 18*th*.—More good news this morning. Cronje is lost, strayed or stolen. The Boers have been driven back at Dordrecht. The British Army is within forty miles of Bloemfontein. Buller has taken the Tugela position. All this needs no comment. '*Quo plus—eo plus* ——'. I meant to quote a Latin phrase—the only one I ever knew—but I cannot risk the tenses and moods of the verbs. It means, however, the more we have the more we want. We live, as it were, from news to news. Two officers arrived from Colesberg this morning. They say Colesberg has never been quite surrounded, only hemmed in on three sides. General French began to withdraw his cavalry about three weeks ago, sending away detachments every night until only an infantry brigade was left to sit in front of Colesberg, occupying exactly the same extent of front as before. The Boers never spotted this, so that French and his cavalry succeeded in joining the Free State column, and the infantry brigade, by making a great show of their forces, was able to keep up the ruse until the other day, when it was decided to retire. Everything went well with the retirement except for two companies of the Wiltshires who were cut off and captured after a gallant fight. I suppose all Governments lie to a certain extent about their defeats, but this Boer one takes the cake.

"*February* 19*th*.—I have caught the patience disease. I spent most of the day at this interesting game, but found by 7 p.m. I was rather sick of it. Le Mesurier told me today that Haldane, Brockie, Grimshaw and he had thought of a plan of escape. The idea was to put out the electric light in the house and in the yard by cutting the wire as it entered the building in the roof above the entrance. The sudden extinguishing of the lights on a dark night would enable them to creep to the back wall and climb over unobserved by the Zarps, whose eyes would not have become accustomed to the sudden darkness. They had made small ladders, by means of which they could climb over the corrugated iron more easily and with less noise. Once outside, they were going to trek for Mafeking, which is only about one hundred and eighty miles off. They had meant to go tonight, but, though it was wet, there was too much lightning.

"*February 21st.*—More good news both from Stormberg and the Tugela. Our friend Opperman is getting excessively polite. I think one can best describe him as a greasy, unwashed bully, oily physically and morally, cruel to anyone in his power, cringing to those he fears.

"*February 22nd.*—We hear that Cronje is completely surrounded. De Wet tried to break the encircling cordon, but was defeated with great loss. Buller has taken the Boschkop and all the British troops have crossed the Tugela.

"A very amusing article appeared in one of the papers the other day, in which Napoleon was termed 'the Botha of the early '10's.' Botha the Napoleon of these days is presumption, but Napoleon, the Botha of the early '10's! I cannot help pitying the editor of the *Volksstem*, as he is only allowed to publish good news, and must really be at his wit's-end to know what to put in now.

"Haldane and the others had arranged to go tonight, but unfortunately the sentry was walking about the place which had been chosen for getting over, so that the escape was prevented.

"*February 24th.*—Haldane and Co. have tried again. This time they were determined to go. Clough, the servant, was sent up *via* the gymnasium on to the roof to cut the wire. I gave the signal by going into the room under the main switch and asking for a map. The light went down temporarily but came up again almost immediately. We were much alarmed lest Clough should have got a shock, but he came down all right, surprised that the lights had not gone out. Of course the escape was off.

"*February 25th.*—We were all sure that Clough had not cut the wires at all last night. He had received a slight shock and then left it, so it was arranged that Cullen should try. However, the position of the sentry again prevented any attempt.

"*February 26th.*—Best, of the Inniskilling Fusiliers, arrived today from the Tugela. He said that all were well down there, though the fighting had been very severe, and that the troops were beyond Pieters. Cronje had no food and must surrender shortly.

"This evening the lights went out without any mistake. Opperman was greatly alarmed, and the electrician could not find out what was up. They all believe a football must have hit the wire outside and put the light out. Probably Clough had partially severed the wires, and the football had completed the damage. Now, however, the wire being broken before it was quite dark, the advantage of surprise would be lost. It was, moreover, a bright night, and we noticed that the light in the streets shone on the wall where we had meant to climb over it. The sentries were doubled, so we finally gave up the plan and tried to think of another. We are told that they will remove us to a new place on the 1st of March, and, perhaps, this will give us a better chance.

*   *   *   *   *

"When I went into my room at about 9.30 I found that Le Mesurier, Haldane, and Brockie were having a discussion. As we were to move in two days to the new prison they argued 'why not go to earth now'. The authorities would think they had escaped under cover of the light going out and would, if anything, hasten the removal of the prisoners, leaving these three under the floor to depart in peace when opportunity offered.

"*February 27th.*—This morning Opperman came into our room as usual to count the number of prisoners in bed, and on seeing three beds empty he fairly staggered with astonishment. I was looking at him with one eye and chuckled to myself at his dismay. He went and asked Brett if he knew anything about it. Brett asked innocently, 'About what?' Then I pretended to wake up and ask Opperman what the hell he meant by disturbing us at this hour. He left the room in a fury, but presently returned with Gunning and later with Du Toit, the Chief of the Police, who examined everything à la Sherlock Holmes, and expressed, with a smile, his confidence in the recapture of the flown birds. After breakfast the whole house was cleared and searched. The rooms, the cupboards, the roof—everywhere except under the floor. Then they brought in a dark lantern, and I really thought they had discovered the fugitives at last, but Sherlock Holmes never thought of the floor; his reasoning did not carry him there. He found Haldane's saw made out of a table knife, and connecting this with the hole in the roof of the gymnasium, and the wires cut, he was sure they had gone away in the darkness. The rest, such is their mutual trust of one another in this country, were quite sure somebody had been bribed. The theories of the other officers in the prison are diverting. The discussions as to how the escaped had got out and where they had gone were full of imagination, but quite off the mark. In the afternoon Opperman and Sherlock Holmes came in with a hat and said the prisoners had been seen going over the hills towards Mafeking and had dropped the hat in question. By nightfall they had been tracked to Koodoosberg, about thirty miles out; and, indeed, the remains of their midday meal had been found. O wise detectives! This evening the Dogman went into Cullingworth's house in a great state of excitement and lit a candle at the verandah—a sign of good news, and on Majuba day too!

"*February 28th.*—We received the good news which the Dogman's excitement last night portended. Cronje has surrendered. This was received through the British Consul at Delagoa Bay. Buller has also driven back the Boers, and Botha wired: 'No use; burghers here won't face British.' In the afternoon we received the following wire: 'Cronje's surrender unconditional. Boers retreating on the Biggarsberg,' and in the evening we heard that the British were entering Ladysmith.

"Three more officers replaced the three escaped in my room. We did not let them know about those underground, but I managed to send food, news, and water down as usual, also some hot cocoa at night.

"*March 1st.*—Ladysmith is relieved. Joubert wires: 'On Lancers coming out of Ladysmith my mounted men retired leaving waggons and stores behind them.' This afternoon the Cullingworth signalled over: 'No more news, furthest telegraph station Elandslaagte.' Kruger has gone to the front to exhort his burghers with texts. He was preceded by a telegram which was sent to all laagers. It is too long and too profane for me to copy out. Nothing but texts and psalms, showing that they are bound to win 'though the enemy compass them about', as the Almighty is their own exclusive and peculiar property. The *Volksstem* says: 'There seems to be some foundation for the rumour that Cronje has surrendered, but the report that Ladysmith has been relieved is quite untrue, our burghers are still fighting bravely south of that town. Should, however, Ladysmith be relieved, the war will only enter upon a new phase. We will then have to defend our borders against the greedy grasp of an unholy race. Now will the British see what fighting with the Boers really is. Now will the war begin in earnest.'

"(Sherlock Holmes & Co. are completely off the track and all is well below.)

"*March 2nd.*—There are no signs of our moving into our new prison. This is very disconcerting as our friends cannot stay below much longer without getting ill. The Zarps' tents have been moved into the road. Opperman says because the yard was damp, but I fancy they are afraid of an attack on the Zarps. With the dumbbells in the gymnasium it might be possible to overpower them. The day was wet and dreary; I wrote letters, Mr. Hofmeyr prayed for the escaped. I have had to divulge the secret to No. 12 room, owing to one of them unfortunately seeing the trap-door open. They were very nice about it, and will do nothing to compromise the chances of success.

"*March 6th.*—Our signals this morning informed us that the President had wired to Lord Salisbury, 'Is it not time bloodshed ceased? Will send peace proposals.' These people have got some nerve. First they declare war against an Empire, and then they expect that when they have had enough they can demand a cessation of hostilities. There are no signs of moving.

"*March 7th.*—The Ides of March, but I don't expect Kruger will be murdered in the forum of Pretoria. Those below are still all right, though their condition is not enviable.

"*March 8th.*—The following telegrams were received today by our signaller-in-chief Burrows: (1) fighting with De Wet; (2) Occupation of Bloemfontein on the 6th. I busied myself by drawing a picture of Kruger going to the front to exhort his burghers, on the wall of my room. There seems no chance of moving. Opperman says they have not even put down the floor in our new abode. Haldane wants to try to make them move. He thought that if Grimshaw vanished too it might alarm the authorities, and make them anxious to move us to a more secure place, but I feel sure—and Grimshaw agrees with me—this would only lead to the discovery of everything.

"*March 11th.*—I drew another large picture on my wall, a sequel to the first. It represents Kruger just escaping from Lord Roberts, who with drawn sword appears to be running after him at a good pace. My picture No. 1 is entitled 'President Kruger goes to front to exhort his burghers'; No. 2, 'But returns on urgent business'.

"As chances of a move seem so uncertain and they are all determined below not to give in, it has been decided to try to get out by making a shallow tunnel, roofed in with cupboard shelves, into the hospital. Haldane is making arrangements with No. 12 room, who, it appears, are following the same plan.

"*March* 12th.—The man who came for grocery orders reported this morning that Bloemfontein had fallen, but our signal was that the British were within seven miles of the Free State capital. Opperman saw my portraits of Kruger this morning; I am afraid he did not appreciate them as he should have done. However, I told him that with a pail of whitewash and a brush he might obliterate them if he chose. (N.B.—Such is the procrastinating nature of these Boer-Hollander people that Opperman never had the pictures removed, and this with other things had, I believe, a good deal to do with his own eventual removal.)

"No. 12 decided to have nothing more to do with the digging plan. We have therefore arranged that Grimshaw, Garvice, and I shall take part in the operation. Garvice has not been informed of Le Mesurier's whereabouts, but has decided to dig. The Colonials in No. 20 room are also digging, but theirs is to be a deep tunnel and I doubt if they can master the water question.

"*March* 13th.—Tragedy. The Dogman and Cullingworth have been commandeered as undesirables, but intend, I fancy, to escape to the British lines. We signalled to him, 'Good-bye, eternal gratitude; God bless you!' The Dogman replied, 'British twenty miles north of Bloemfontein; Goodbye; speedy release; will return with Bobs.'

"We started our shaft under the big room No. 16. Apparently we made a good deal of noise, for the old Colonels were very much alarmed and threatened to stop all digging, though they did not know who the culprits were. Opperman came into the room when mining was in full swing below, and it was all the occupants could do to hustle him outside, drowning the noise of the pick by stamping. We were rather distressed and decided to wait a few days. Garvice was very much startled when he saw Le Mesurier. He describes his feelings vividly. On going down by the trap-door he remarked what an awful hole it was. Suddenly, in the flickering candle-light he saw a gaunt, bearded, unwashed face, and a half-naked body. At first he could not make out what it was, but when he at last realised it was a brother officer he said you could have knocked him down with a feather had it not been that he was already crawling on his stomach. The new shaft is a long way off; when I went down I had to crawl on hands and knees along passages and through man-holes, backwards and forwards in a regular maze of compartments, and, indeed, had the candle gone out one could easily have been lost. Haldane looked very ill, but the others, except for being covered with dirt, seemed well enough.

"*March* 14*th*.—Grimshaw went down this evening to hold a confab. They have managed to dig without making a noise by wetting the earth. Grimshaw and I made the trap-door into one piece by securing the planks together, and also made it so as to batten down from underneath. I sent them down jugs of water during the day to wash in.

"*March* 15*th*.—All went as usual this morning. Grimshaw descended and did a little digging. In the afternoon Opperman brought the news that we were to be moved tomorrow! Most of the officers were very annoyed, but Grimshaw and I sent the information below with gladness. Well, there was no time to be lost. Food enough to last them a week, all the bottles filled with water, and everything that could possibly be of any use to the cave-men was sent down. We heard, however, and not to our surprise, that others were thinking of going into their respective holes so as to escape after we had moved. As this could have had no other effect than to cause the discovery of all, we were determined if possible to stop it. We told Colonel Hunt, and he managed to persuade all concerned to abandon their schemes.

"This settled, we set to work, after final goodbyes and hand-shakings, to putty up the cracks between the boards of the trap-door, which had already been fastened down from underneath. This we succeeded in doing to perfection, and after covering the place well with dust, the trap-door could scarcely have been located by anyone; certainly not by those who did not know of its existence.

    *   *   *   *   *

"*March* 16*th*.—The State Model School at an early hour was more than usually busy. We were all packing up such belongings as we had. I rolled everything in my mattress and rugs, and secured with rope. Then the gates were opened and all baggage was moved out on the road ready to be packed on the trolleys provided for the occasion. To be outside those gates was to breathe fresh air; to pass those barriers which had so long defied our efforts and our wits was like going out into another world. I went back into my room, and by pre-arranged taps on the floor Grimshaw signalled that all was well. I then sang 'For Auld Lang Syne' as a parting farewell.

"The Government had generously provided cabs for the convenience of the officers (who afterwards found they had to pay), and at about 10 a.m. the first cabs rolled off amid the friendly farewells of many neighbours. The long column of vehicles was escorted by a motley guard, consisting of very old men and tiny boys armed with Sniders and sporting guns of ancient pattern.

"We soon passed out of the town and, crossing a small river, began to crawl up a steep hill. The roads outside of Pretoria appear very much neglected, but, of course, the money that should have been devoted to general improvements was all spent in secret service or in preparations for the war. We soon arrived at our destination. The building stands halfway up the side of a hill, and is probably a much healthier place than the Model School. Besides, the view is really pretty. To the north, indeed, it is limited by the tops of two hills. Southward lies Pretoria, a collection of large Government buildings and of small villas amid masses of trees, nestling beneath a high range of hills, along the crest of which rise the famous forts. The view on the west is merely a vast plain which reaches to the horizon, and a large hill obliterates any view to the east.

"The place itself consists merely of a long white shanty with a fairly large compound enclosed by formidable barbed-wire entanglements. Outside are Opperman's house and the Zarps' tents. There are electric lights all round the enclosure, making escape a matter of considerable difficulty. Inside, the place looked more like a cattle-shed than anything else. A long galvanised-iron building, divided into sleeping-room, and four small bath-rooms, a servants' compartment and kitchen, eating-rooms. The sleeping-hall is eighty-five by thirty yards long and accommodates 120 officers, our beds being, roughly, a yard apart. There is no flooring. The drains consist of open ditches, while the sanitary arrangements are enough to disgust any civilised being. A strong protest was at once sent in to the authorities, but I doubt that it will have any effect.

"*March* 18*th*.—The greatest disadvantage of this place over the State Model School is that we can get no news.

"*March* 22*nd.*—Gunning gave us a small baboon the other day, which was very fierce at first, but has tamed wonderfully. There are many different kinds of curious insects here—not curious for this country, of course, but which I have never seen before. The 'Praying Mantis' or 'Kaffir God' is one of the queerest. The whole place seems to be a large ants' nest, and we have often witnessed great fights between the different kinds. Snakes also abound. A night-adder was killed the other day. It was about thirteen or fourteen inches long and very poisonous, so Gunning says.

"We hear Gunning and Opperman are going to the front to-morrow. I am very sorry for the former, though the departure of the latter is a great advantage.

"*March* 23*rd.*—The Zarps and Opperman departed for the front this morning. Their place was taken by a new guard selected from the Hollander Corps. The Commandant is a pleasant fellow and a great improvement on Opperman.

"*March* 25*th.*—We had service as usual this morning. This evening an attempt to escape was going to be made by Ansell and Co., but it never came off. There has been no news of Haldane and the others, so I suppose they are well away by now. This evening the new Commandant had roll-call. We call him 'Pyjamas', because he wears a suit of clothes for all the world like a pair of pyjamas. His real name is Westernant.

"*March* 30*th.*—There has not been anything very important to record for some days. On Tuesday an attempt to escape was made by Best. While one sentry was gossiping with another he crept under the barbed wire. As luck would have it, when Best had got half way through, the sentry finished his *tête-à-tête* and returned to his post. At first he thought Best was a dog and called out *footsack,** but seeing he was a human being, merely told him to go back. He might have shot him with some excuse, so Best was lucky in striking a kind-hearted man.

"On Wednesday Joubert died. In respect to him we sent a wreath. I don't think this will have any effect on the war, as (and the papers say as much) his moderate attitude in the recent crisis had taken away much of his popularity.

"*April* 3*rd.*—Hurrah! the papers this evening report the safe arrival of Haldane, Le Mesurier and Brockie at Lourenço Marques, having travelled through Swaziland. We were so glad to hear this

* Be off.

news. Alas! We also hear that sixteen officers arrive tomorrow, and that seven guns were captured with them.

"The Cullingworth girls came up this evening and signalled with a handkerchief that Mafeking had been relieved. I hope it is true. We all admire the pluck of those girls. We have already collected a large subscription to get them and the Dogman handsome presents.

"There was a large swarm of locusts yesterday. So thick was the cloud that it quite obliterated the view of the distant hills. They continued passing over nearly all day.

"*April 5th.*—The prisoners arrived this morning. They mostly belong to 'U' Battery, R.H.A.; some to the M.I. and cavalry. I have not quite gathered the circumstances of their capture, but they seem to have been caught in a trap, owing to the want of the ordinary precautions. The convoy and one battery were practically held up without firing a shot, but the other battery got away. When marched off they heard that another British force was pursuing so that the guns may be recaptured.

"They bring very little news; apparently they have heard nothing about the relief of Mafeking, though Warren was on his way thereto. Roberts has been delayed in his advance for the want of horses, but as this has been remedied the forward movement should begin shortly. Had the horses not been so done after Abram's Kraal, they say De Wet would have been caught and the war over. Such is the fashion of war. If so-and-so had happened—always 'if'!

"There was great excitement this evening caused by an attempted escape. The electric wires had been tampered with, and at about 10.30, by some device, Horne, a colonial, who is also an electrician, made the current travel on a shorter circuit, thus blowing out the main fuse and extinguishing all the lights round the building. Hardly had this happened than two shots were fired in quick succession, and then another. The escape failed, but all got back into the building unwounded. Apparently the lights had gone down, then up for a second, then finally out.

"During the momentary flash Hockley, of the escapees, had been seen and fired at. However, 'All's well that ends well', though some say that two bullets went through the dining-room. Sentries were doubled for the night and patrols sent out.

"*April 6th.*—How the fortunes of war vary! We seem to be going through a series of small disasters. Today the papers have the report of a 'Brilliant Boer Victory, thirty-six miles south-east of

Bloemfontein; 450 prisoners!!!' The only hope is that the account is not 'official'. But we must be ready for the worst. The leading article says: 'Within a few days Roberts will be forced to evacuate the Free State. *His retreat from Bloemfontein will be like Napoleon's retreat from Moscow.*'

"*April 11th.*—The prisoners reported captured some time ago have not arrived yet. They always seem to be 'expected to arrive somewhere', but apparently have not yet been actually seen by anybody. On Saturday their capture was reported officially. On Thursday English wires said that 300 Royal Irish were surrounded. Today they say the prisoners are expected at Pretoria tomorrow! Well, we shall see.

"The last few days we have had many good rumours about the capture of Boers and British victories. Today the papers say that Lord Methuen is advancing on Boshof (he must be there by now), and that Colonel de Villebois has been killed. He, apparently, and his men (100, so they say—probably 500) were all killed, wounded, or taken prisoners. A distinguished ex-French officer and his foreign legion is a good bag.

"The next piece of information is, quoting from Boer paragraphs or headlines, 'Fifteen hundred English in a corner'; 'Brabant's Horse in a trap'. Then, again, 'There is every hope of their surrender'. So much for this. But on the Dutch side we read that all telegraphic communication with Ladybrand and the south has been cut, so I rather fancy the Boers have over-reached themselves for once.

"The Boers have attacked our camps at Elandslaagte, and because, when they shelled, our camp tents were struck, they report that the British fled. I wonder if Le Mesurier was in this show.

"In all these fights, as usual, the Boers 'By the grace of God had (about) one man killed and four wonded.' This is heavy; generally it is one horse and three mules. 'The enemy', of course, 'must have lost heavily.' So the paragraphs run on. Many are the funny expressions. 'One brave burgher succumbed to the explosion of a bomb.' 'One of our guns *in firing* damaged its sight and one of its wheels!' They always end up with 'Our burghers are full of courage, and determined to withstand the enemy to the last.'

"Various officials came up the day before yesterday to inquire into the causes of the protest we had sent in, signed by all the officers here. They promised that everything would be seen to; but they are all—well they are Boer officials, and I doubt if our lot is to be in any way improved.

"The weather is getting much colder now, though the sun is still hot by day. A few stray shots whistled over the building today, probably 'accidentally on purpose'. I hope they do not begin sniping regularly.

"*April 12th.*—Alas! my hopes were doomed to disappointment. Eight prisoners arrived. They are mostly of the Irish Rifles; unlucky regiment, twice the victims of misfortune! There is among them a gunner who was acting on the staff. As usual, they bring little news, except a vivid account of their own 'show', which happened when they were on a bill-posting expedition.* A cart-load of packing cases came in today for the prisoners of war. Seven tons have already been sent to Waterval. These cases contained papers, books, cigars, cigarettes, tobacco and groceries, of which we were very thankful, the more so to feel that the people at home had not forgotten the unhappy prisoners of war.

"Since the new year one of the chief topics of discussion and bets has been: 'When the war will be over.' We have, alas! always underestimated the length of our stay here; had the prophecies of the more sanguine come true, we would have been free long ago. Some put the date of our release at the Queen's birthday; others later, and a few earlier. Personally, I have learnt since I have been here the impossibility of predicting what the future has in store. The day will surely come, though would that we knew the date, be it months hence, for we might then cross off the days as they passed.

"*April 17th.*—The papers have given no news for a considerable time. But rumours of the wildest description have been spread. Ever since Friday last rumour has persisted in De Wet's capture, and, indeed, it seems possible, even probable; having succeeded in two captures, General De Wet was not likely to be allowed to take another bag without some counter move on Lord Roberts's part. The papers today say nothing on the English side about De Wet, except that no news has been received from him for a considerable time; but the Dutch columns express anxiety as to his whereabouts. He had surrounded Brabant, they say, but strong columns came out of Bloemfontein, and today no news has been got, or, indeed, can be got, from the lost General. Rumour also has it that Lukas Meyer has been captured on the Natal side.

* Distributing the proclamation.

"I have been continuing my sketches and caricatures pretty regularly. I have also been reading more lately. Being Easter week, Mr. Hofmeyr held a service on Good Friday, and administered the Holy Communion on Easter Sunday. Easter Sunday! If somebody had told me when first captured that I should still be in prison on Easter Sunday, I should have thought him mad, or expected to go mad myself. 'Tis well we know not the future, but always live on hopes of early release.

"I have written and received a good many letters. I think I am quite reforming in the way of letter writing—that is, I am getting into the way of writing four pages of tolerably sensible stuff on nothing at all, which is a sure sign of a good correspondent.

"Talking of being a prisoner, we have heard more of those fortunate escaped. Fortunate! One cannot but think them lucky, and envy them, now they are free, with the just credit for their escape. But how many hardships had they to suffer? Well, to come to the point. Davy has just returned from hospital, where he saw Haldane's account of his escape in the *Standard and Diggers' News*. The trains did not seem to fit in, and our friends had a lot of walking to do. Le Mesurier sprained his ankle; food ran out, and they had to live on Kaffir food. Finally, getting into a coal truck, where they were nearly discovered, they crossed the border at Komati Poort. I envy them; but such success cannot be got without daring. Luck has certainly followed them, but I think their patience underground won Fortune's favour.

"We hear from Davy that the Dogman and Cullingworth are prisoners, having been arrested when trying to escape to the British lines. Poor fellows! Though, as our friends at home say of us, 'They are safer in prison than at the front.' This saying always irritates me. Every letter hints at it, as if safety were the chief reward one hoped to get during a war; one cannot help feeling bitter, though our imprisonment is only the payment for our very lives.

"*April 19th.*—Roulette is in full swing here. The arrangements are most ingenious and the dining-room after dinner is a regular Monte Carlo.

"We had a large mess meeting today to appoint a new mess committee, and to discuss various questions as regards the expenses, &c. It was a very amusing assembly, rather too frivolous to carry any real motions. Most of the speeches wandered off the point, and we finally dispersed without deciding anything of importance. One thing was, however, serious. Colonel Hunt appealed for further subscriptions for the sick soldiers in hospital. They are apparently entirely supported by charity, and by our subscriptions. The Transvaal Government (although boasting to be civilised) does not even supply beds! This fact might, perhaps, disillusion some who are so taken in by Boer cant.

"*May 8th.*—We have had an immense amount of news lately. Roberts has begun his big advance. Brandfort is in our hands also Winburg. The force advancing *via* Boshof has reached Hoopstad, while the British have crossed the Vaal at Fourteen Streams. De Wet has not been heard of for a considerable time. So much is acknowledged in the papers. Rumours say that we are behind Kroonstadt!! That De Wet, Steyn, and 8,000 Boers have been taken!! The English in the town think we shall be released by the 24th of May. A panic seems to have seized the Boers, and excited meetings have been held. Kruger summoned the Volksraad on Sunday, and addressed them in stirring words, which, while acknowledging the serious nature of the situation, exhorted the burghers to continue the struggle trusting in the Lord. General Schalk Burger, while addressing the townspeople, said that a stand might yet be made, if not, the independence of the Republic was at an end. The Church of Pretoria has addressed petitions for peace to the Churches of Great Britain and of Europe and America. They pray that this unholy bloodshed may cease. Kruger says 'Continue the struggle to the end.' Is it for England or for Kruger to give in?

"We have started a newspaper; it is progressing. We call it the *Gram,* because at the State Model School all our news came in under the popular names of signal-gram (when news was signalled), Kaffir-gram (when brought through the Kaffir). Brockie-gram (when Brockie succeeded in getting information from the Zarps), and so forth. Rosslyn is editor; Major Sturges sub-editor. White, R.A., Wake, 5th Fusiliers, and I, are the artists. The paper has been all written out by Rosslyn, and is now being hektographed. We hope to bring out seventy good copies of the first number.

"*May 13th.*—Though two or three prisoners have arrived lately, we can get no particular details of the news. There is no doubt that a general advance has been begun, but what point our troops have reached is uncertain. Also, it is still a question whether De Wet is captured or not. This morning the most serious rumour came in, to the effect that Mafeking had fallen, but I can scarcely believe it.

"Yesterday Mr. Hofmeyr received the welcome order to pack up his things and go. He seemed very affected at saying goodbye and nearly broke down. We all liked him very much, and bade him a hearty farewell, cheering him as he left the enclosure, and singing 'He's a jolly good fellow.' We shall miss him as well as his services.

"Our paper came out yesterday and was a great success. We hope to bring out a new one on the Queen's Birthday, though it is an awful labour.

"Life has not been so bad lately. Buoyed up with hope of a speedy release, and occupied with the *Gram*, time has passed, in my case, more quickly. We had a selling lottery the other day for the day of our release. The dates ranged from the 15th of May to the 15th of August. The Queen's Birthday was much in request, while 'the field' (any day after August 15th) went for six pounds.

"The *Volksstem*, of course, progresses as usual. Having exhausted all other insults on England, they commenced lately on the Queen! During the present British advance the mendacious powers of the editor are once more brought to trial, and once more he has not been found wanting. The burghers are full of courage (running everywhere); even the women wish to fight! There was, indeed, a rumour that our present guard was to be commandeered and the women put here to look after us. Poor time for us! I fancy we should be all shot! The Volksraad sat the other day, and after Kruger and others quoting a few scriptures the session of 1900 was closed after sitting two days!

"*May 14th.*—So much news has arrived today that I think I had better inscribe it, while I remember. This morning came the rumour that a good many Boers actually did get into Mafeking, but, being unsupported, still remain there. This evening's *Volksstem* is truly a wonder. It gives more news than it ever has given before. An attack was made on Mafeking. The Boers took a 'fort', but were attacked by night, and lost seven killed and 'some' wounded and prisoners. At present Carrington and Plumer are proceeding to Mafeking by train, so that it must have been relieved. Everywhere the Boers fly, and the British troops entered Kroonstadt on the 11th inst. Hunter, with his 25,000 men, drove the enemy back at Warrenton, and 'the Boers are unable to resist the advance of the forces at Vryberg'.

" 'But,' says the *Volksstem*, 'the fact that Kroonstadt is in the hands of the enemy need create no alarm. As we retire our line of defence becomes less and our commandos can be concentrated to resist more effectually the advance of the British forces. Besides, many things may happen which will put an entirely new face on the war. Our delegation has reached America, &c., &c. Lord Roberts's hastened advance is said to be caused by his desire to reach Pretoria on the Queen's Birthday, but might not the real reason be the fear of foreign intervention? Lord Roberts wishes to strike a decisive blow before his forces are needed elsewhere. Every day's delay is, therefore, an advantage to our cause. Courage is all that is needed, &c., &c.'

"The above is a précis of the *Volksstem* leading article. Still they harp on foreign intervention, but from what I gather from recent Continental criticisms on the war, I fancy their chances in this line are less than at the beginning of the war. As to the burghers' courage, I doubt if the majority of them have much left. For many months the Transvaal Government have whipped their subjects to the fight; but even the worm will turn, and to the simplest, or the most ignorant, the Government promises and hopes must seem vain.

"The day of our release is, perhaps, approaching; but it does not do to be too sanguine; one never knows where a check may occur. Still I 'plump' on the end of the present month.

"*May* 20*th*.—The month is drawing to a close, and the day of our release is still a matter of speculation. News is pretty plentiful; even the *Volksstem* tries to hide nothing. Roberts has made a great advance, but whether he has halted at Kroonstadt or not is uncertain. We all hoped he would not stop until he had reached Pretoria.

"We have been very much alarmed lately at the rumoured intention of the Government to move us to Lydenburg, but at present it is only a rumour. If we are moved we shall have every prospect of being shunted about the country with guerilla bands of Boers who would keep us merely as hostages. If, however, we are kept here we shall have every chance of being released during the siege of Johannesburg. The Boers, it is said, have decided to hold that place and are not going to blow up the mines. The defence of Pretoria would be impossible with the troops at their disposal.

"Life goes on as usual. The only diversion that has lately occurred was the athletic sports, which were got up by some energetic people.

The event took place yesterday, and, on the whole, was a decided success. The chief feature, however, of the day was the betting. Several enterprising officers kept books, but Haig, of the Inniskilling Dragoons, cut the best figure in that line, and it was chiefly owing to his amusing performance that the day was a success. White has made an excellent sketch of 'Our Bookie' for the next *Gram* number.

"The sermon this morning is worth recording. The Rev. Mr. Bateman delivered a most extraordinary speech as part of his service. Whether it was meant for our spiritual edification, or merely intended to convey news to us under the disguise of a text, was not quite certain; but, by preaching on the text that begins 'As cold water is to the thirsty soul, so is good news, &c.', he led us to believe that we were to be released in a very short time.

"Roulette has been going very strong. Large sums have been lost and won.

"*May 25th.*—Yesterday we prisoners of war joined with the British Empire all over the world in the celebration of the Queen's Birthday. In our little enclosure we have quite a representative British Empire—English, Scotch, and Irish soldiers, Colonials, South Africans, Australians, and civilians, and, indeed, we only require a Canadian to complete the list.

"Yesterday evening we drank the Queen's health in light port (rather nasty). The first drops of wine or spirit I had tasted since the 18th of November. This was followed by 'God Save the Queen,' sung by all with a heartiness and feeling that I never heard before. It must have sounded very well outside. To us it was as it were 'giving vent' to our imprisoned feelings, while we also found in it a link with our country, from which we have for so many months been severed.

"It is now pretty certain that Roberts is resting his troops, and rumours have it that the Boers have asked for an armistice. Whether Lord Roberts celebrated the Queen's Birthday by a victory or a peaceful armistice remains to be seen.

"The *Volksstem* considered that it would be a graceful act on the part of the State President if he were to wire the Queen and offer her as a birthday present the unconditional release of all the British prisoners of war. As the *Volksstem* is the official organ, this may quite possibly be merely a feeler to the public (if public there be in this country). At any rate it would be an act worthy of the wily Boer. He finds it a source of trouble and expsne feeding and guarding 5,000 prisoners, so he gives them away with a pound of tea—I mean as a graceful act. Whether the offer would be accepted is uncertain. But we at any rate will be very happy if the Transvaal Government puts us over the border.

"The weather (by day) is simply perfect. Every morning the lovely air makes one long for a walk or ride, and causes one to chafe at the inability to roam beyond the one hundred yards' enclosure. We are henceforth to be allowed to have wine, but personally I shall wait for freedom before I indulge in that luxury again. The second number of the *Gram* came out yesterday, and, I believe, was much appreciated.

"*May 26th.*—Two prisoners of war arrived this morning. They were caught at Lindley, which the Boers have apparently re-occupied. They were taken across country to the Natal railway, and then conveyed straight to Pretoria. They say they have heard firing at the Vaal, so I suppose Lord Roberts is there. The Boers hold a strong position south of Johannesburg, and they also intend defending that town. One of the De Wets is still on the right rear of our army, but will be dealt with by Rundle's division which is coming up that way. It is said that De Wet at one time offered to surrender on condition that he himself should not be made a prisoner. But Roberts would receive none but an unconditional surrender. Buller has been ordered to force Laing's Nek at all costs. The *Volksstem* says that Lord Roberts's headquarters are at Honningspruit, some way north of Kroonstadt, but this is probably news of some days' standing. There is also a rumour that our troops have occupied Potchefstroom.

"*May 29th.*—At last our release seems near at hand. Yesterday and today big guns were heard plainly in the direction of Johannesburg, which is now in our hands. Boshof, the grocer, has just arrived, having come up by the last train. He says that the Dragoons were actually in the streets when he left. I fancy tomorrow or next day will see us out. Everybody is in the best of spirits and full of excitement.

"Greatest excitement during dinner. Mr. Hay and Mr. Wood came in and asked Colonel Hunt to send twenty-four officers to Waterval to look after the men. Kruger has gone to Holland. The British are expected here tomorrow, and we shall be free! We sang 'God Save the Queen' and cheered Hay and the Commandant, who made a very nice speech, saying he hoped to shake hands with us outside. Oh! how I longed to see the old regiment once more! The Commandant says that there is still fighting at Klipdrift, but a force of 4,000 men has broken through and come here. I believe there is a lot of looting going on in the town now. Roulette is at an end. I can scarcely write coherently, so excited am I. Fancy being free; I can scarcely believe it! Six and a half months' imprisonment, and about to be freed! Thank God!

"*May 31st.*—Too premature were our hopes. Yesterday and today have been spent in awful suspense. Distant guns have been heard, Boers have been seen riding about, and rumours of all kinds and descriptions are rife. It is too awful this final suspense. We do nothing in hope of a speedy release, and we pass the day anxiously scanning the horizon for the approach of troops.

"All day commandos have gone through the town, and one was seen on the plain coming in from Mafeking. One commando came up our way, and we were rather surprised that they made no attempt to shoot us. Indeed there was nothing to prevent them. Three prisoners came in. They were caught in or near Johannesburg. That town was officially surrendered at 10 a.m. this morning. The Boers intend making a sort of stand (one of their usual ten-minute affairs I suppose) at Irene, a place six miles south of Pretoria, and a fight is expected there tomorrow. Their line of flight is past our abode and Waterval, and I should not be surprised if, unable to face and shoot armed men, some of these foreign ruffians shoot a few prisoners.

"The town is evidently to be handed over quietly. The *Volksstem* is still covering a sheet of paper with print, but seems to take not the slightest interest in the war. They speak of giving up Pretoria as one of our papers might of a concert. Well, I suppose it will come at last, but I shall heave a sigh of relief when it does!

"*June 1st.*—No sign of the British! But we expect to hear guns tomorrow. There are plenty of rumours about—Roberts captured, French killed, &c. There was a good deal of looting in the town yesterday, and five men were shot. Our hopes of a few days ago have been somewhat damped, and most of us put our release down at a week hence.

"The *Volksstem* is remarkable. The editor is evidently wishful to avoid his tarring and feathering, and scarcely speaks of the war at all.

"*June 3rd.*—I have almost given up looking forward to our

release, and have fallen back into the ordinary monotonous life. No guns have been heard, and therefore no serious fighting can have taken place anywhere near Pretoria. Rundle has been reported as having received a check in the Free State, and Lord Roberts is said to be still in Johannesburg; otherwise there is no news at all. Botha has taken matters into his own hands, has kicked out the officials appointed by Kruger, chosen a committee of his own, and has arranged the defence of the positions outside the town. He has therefore made himself practically President of what remains of the Transvaal. Kruger went off with a million of hard gold, paying the Government officials with dishonoured cheques on the National Bank, from which he has removed all the money. Every one of his ministers thirsts for the old man's blood, and perhaps it were best for him to go further than Middelburg.

"*June 4th.*—At about 8.30 this morning firing was heard at no great distance, in the south-west direction—field guns, 'pom-poms', Maxims, and even musketry. At about nine o'clock a shell was seen to burst on an earthwork on a ridge of hills south of the town. Field-glasses and telescopes were immediately brought out, and we were well entertained for the rest of the day. Shrapnel burst all along the ridges, and presently lyddite shells were planted on the hills. The firing seemed very unmethodical, and the Boers made little or no reply. On the western kopjes shrapnel was seen bursting all over the place, and we expected the Infantry to attack them. But the lyddite shells were certainly the most interesting. They burst with a tremendous noise, throwing up clouds of brownish earth. For some time the forts seemed the mark our gunners were aiming at, and these costly erections certainly received their share—four shells pitching well inside the west fort; but, later, the shells were directed on the eastern outskirts of the town. Whether these were intended for the railway station, we could not make out; but, otherwise, they seemed to have no object. At about 4.30 the Boers were seen leaving the western ridges and trekking at a remarkable pace across the plain, disappearing along the northern road. The day's action was ended by a kind of *feu de joie* of lyddite shells, which struck the two forts and the surrounding hills. Then peace ensued. The last few shots seemed to have been fired by guns which were much closer than at the commencement of the bombardment, and the flight of the projectiles, which we could distinctly hear, passed from west to east, so that we hope our troops have occupied the hills on the west.

"The hills are burning tonight, and the scene is strangely illuminated in honour of our approaching rescue.

"*June 5th.*—A day of strangely mingled hopes and fears. This morning at about 1.30 the Commandant awoke us and ordered us to pack up at once and prepare to march to the railway, whence we were to be transported by train down the Delagoa Bay line to some station beyond Middelburg. All were filled with consternation. To be hurried away when release was so near at hand seemed too awful. Words cannot express my feelings. At last we decided to refuse to go. Let them massacre us if they dared. We reminded the Commandant of the promise made to the officers the week before that if they restrained the men in Waterval neither they nor the men should be transported. The Commandant replied that he had his orders and must execute them, and he rose to leave the building, but we refused to let him or his lieutenant go, and held them both prisoners. The Commandant said that the guards would soon come in to rescue him, but he eventually promised to do his best to save us from being deported, if we set him free. Then, by Colonel Hunt's advice, for we did not know when a commando might appear, we returned to bed—you cannot shoot men in their beds. And so passed the anxious hours away till dawn. With the first streaks of daylight we scanned the hills anxiously for the British troops. We could see lines of men moving on the race-course, but it was impossible to make out what they were. Presently, at about half-past eight, two figures in khaki came round the corner, crossed the little brook and galloped towards us. Were they Boers come to order our removal?— the advance scouts, perhaps, of a commando to enforce the order!— or were they our friends at last? Yes, thank God! One of the horsemen raised his hat and cheered. There was a wild rush across the enclosure, hoarse discordant yells, and the prisoners tore like madmen to welcome the first of their deliverers.

"Who should I see on reaching the gate but Churchill, who, with his cousin, the Duke of Marlborough, had galloped on in front of the army to bring us the good tidings. It is impossible to describe our feelings on being freed. I can scarcely believe it, after seven months' imprisonment, the joy nearly made up for all our former troubles, and, besides, the war is not yet over.

"To close the scene we hoisted the Union Jack which Burrows (one of the prisoners) had made by cutting up a Vierkleur, on the staff whence the Transvaal colours had so long reminded us of our condition. I will not write about the triumphal entry of Lord Roberts and the army into Pretoria, because that has been already told by so many others.

"The Dogman and Cullingworth shared our good fortune, both being speedily released from the gaol where they had languished since their attempt to get through to the British lines, and with this happy fact let me end my record of so many weary days passed in uncertainty, disappointment, and monotony, but borne, I hope, with patience, and ending at last in joy."

CHAPTER SEVENTEEN

ACTION OF DIAMOND HILL

Pretoria: June 14, 1900

THE FEEBLE resistance which the Boers offered to our advance from Bloemfontein favoured the hope that with the fall of Pretoria they would sue for peace, and after the almost bloodless capture of the town there was a very general tendency to regard the war as practically over. The troops who had been marching for so many days with Pretoria as their goal, not unnaturally hoped that when that goal was achieved a period of rest and refreshment would be given them. But the imperious necessities of war demanded fresh efforts.

The successes gained in the Free State by the redoubtable Christian De Wet, and the cutting of the communications near Rhenoster, awoke everyone to the fact that further exertions were required. Though the Boers under Botha had made but a poor resistance in front of their capital, they were encouraged by the news from the Free State to adopt a more defiant attitude, and to make what we hope has been almost a final effort. As to that I will not be sanguine; but it is certain that, whereas on the 7th and 8th of June the Boer leaders in the Transvaal were contemplating surrender, on the 9th and 10th they were making all kinds of bold schemes to harass and even entrap the British army.

On the 7th the news ran through the camp that Mrs. Botha had come through the lines with some mission on her husband's behalf, and General Schoeman had himself made very decided overtures. On the 8th, therefore, an armistice was observed by both sides, and a conference on Zwartskop, where Lord Roberts was to meet the Republican generals, was arranged for the 9th; but when the 9th came circumstances had changed. The Field-Marshal had actually his foot in the stirrup ready to ride to the meeting-place, when a

messenger arrived from Botha declining, unless Lord Roberts had
some new proposal to make, to enter into any negotiations. The
consequence of this was an immediate resumption of active operations.

The military situation was, briefly, that Lord Roberts's army
was spread around and in Pretoria in various convenient camping
grounds, with the greater part of its force displayed on the east and
north-east sides of the town; and that the Boers, under Botha and
De la Rey, to the number of about 7,000, with twenty-five guns,
held a strong position some fifteen miles to the east astride the
Delagoa Bay Railway. It was evident that on any grounds, whether
moral or material, it was not possible for the conquering army to
allow the capital to be perpetually threatened by the enemy in
organised force, and, indeed, to be in a state of semi-siege.

With the intention, therefore, of driving the enemy from the
neighbourhood, and in the hope of capturing guns and prisoners, a
large series of combined operations was begun. Practically all the
available troops were to be employed. But the army which had
marched from Bloemfontein had dwindled seriously from sickness,
from casualties, and, above all, from the necessity of dropping
brigades and battalions behind it to maintain the communications.
We have already seen how it was necessary to leave the Fourteenth
Brigade to hold Johannesburg, and now the Eighteenth Brigade
became perforce the garrison of Pretoria, thus leaving only the
Eleventh Division, the corps troops, and Ian Hamilton's force free
for field operations.

The Eleventh Division numbered, perhaps, 6,000 bayonets with
twenty guns. Ian Hamilton's force had lost Smith-Dorrien's
Brigade, which was disposed along the line between Kroonstadt and
Pretoria, and though strengthened by the addition of Gordon's
Cavalry Brigade did not number more than 3,000 bayonets, 1,000
sabres, and 2,000 rifle-armed cavalry, with thirty guns. But the
shrinkage had been greatest among the mounted troops. French's
command of a Cavalry Division, which should have been some 6,000
mounted men, was scarcely, even with part of Hutton's Brigade of
Mounted Infantry, 2,000. The two cavalry brigades with Ian
Hamilton mustered together only 1,100 men, and Ridley's Mounted
Infantry, whose nominal strength was at least 4,000, was scarcely
half that number in actuality. Brigades, therefore, were scarcely as
strong as regiments, regiments only a little stronger than squadrons,

and the pitiful—absurd if it had not been so serious—spectacle of troops of eight and ten men was everywhere to be seen. It must, therefore, be remembered that though the imposing names of divisions and brigades might seem to indicate a great and powerful force, the army at Lord Roberts's disposal was really a very small one.

The enemy's position ran along a high line of steep and often precipitous hills, which extend north and south athwart the Delagoa Bay line about fifteen miles east from Pretoria, and stretch away indefinitely on either side. The plan of the Field-Marshal was to turn both flanks with cavalry forces, and to endeavour to cut the line behind the Boers, so that, threatened by the attack of the Infantry in front, and their retreat compromised, they would have to fall back, probably without being able to save some, at least, of their heavy guns.

French was directed to make a wide sweep round the enemy's right flank north of the railway. Pole-Carew, with the Eighteenth Brigade and the Guards, was to advance frontally along the railway; Ian Hamilton to move parallel to him about six miles further south; and Broadwood, who, with the rest of the mounted troops, formed part of Hamilton's force, was to endeavour to turn the enemy's left. It was felt that, important as were the objects to be gained, they scarcely justified a very large sacrifice of life. But though the Field-Marshal would be content with the retreat of the enemy, both Cavalry forces were intended to press hard inward.

On the 11th, the whole army was in motion. French on the extreme left of the British front, which was extended from flank to flank about sixteen miles, soon came in contact with the Boers, occupying strong defensive positions, and he became sharply engaged. During the day he continued to persevere, but it was not until nightfall that he was able to make any progress. Pole-Carew, with the Eleventh Division, moved eastward along the railway, extended in battle formation, and engaged the enemy with his long-range guns, to which the Boers replied with corresponding pieces, including a 6-in. gun mounted on a railway truck. Though an intermittent bombardment continued throughout the day, the operations in the centre were confined to a demonstration.

Meanwhile Broadwood and Ian Hamilton, advancing on the right, found that the Boers, besides occupying the whole line of the Diamond Hill plateau, had also extended their left flank, which was composed of the Heidelberg commando and other South Transvaal burghers, far beyond the reach of any turning movement, and for this reason the operations to the British right and right centre became of a piercing rather than of an enveloping nature. Hamilton endeavoured to hold off the enemy's unduly extended left by detaching a battalion, two field guns, and Gordon's Cavalry Brigade with its horse battery, in the direction of the Tigerspoort ridges. Ridley's Brigade of Mounted Infantry curved inwards towards the railway, and while these two forces struck out, like the arms of a swimmer, Broadwood's Brigade was intended to push through the gap thus made.

A dropping musketry and artillery fire began shortly after eight o'clock along the front of the force engaged in containing the Boers near Tigerspoort, and half an hour later Ridley's Brigade was engaged along the southern slopes of Diamond Hill. Meanwhile, Broadwood was advancing steadily to the eastward, and crossing a difficult spruit debouched into a wide, smooth, grass plain, surrounded by hills of varying height, at the eastern end of which was a narrow gap. Through this the line of march to the railway lay. He became immediately engaged with the Boers round the whole three-quarters of the circle, and a scattered action, presenting to a distant observer no picturesque features, and yet abounding in striking incidents, began. The Boers brought seven guns, so far as we could observe, against him, and since the fire of these pieces was of a converging nature, the cavalry was soon exposed to a heavy bombardment.

In spite of this, Broadwood continued to push on. The country was well suited for cavalry action, and the gap or "poort", as it is called in this country, plainly visible among the hills to the eastward, encouraged him to try to break through. Accordingly, at about eleven o'clock, he brought two horse-guns, under Lieutenant Conolly,* into a very forward position, with the design of clearing his road by their fire. The Boers, however, fought with a stubbornness and dash which had long been absent from their tactics. They were in this part of the field largely composed of Germans and other foreigners, of colonial rebels, and of various types of irreconcilables.

* A younger brother of that brilliant officer of the Scots Greys, whose death at Nitral Nek a few weeks later was so great a loss to his friends, his regiment, and his country.

No sooner had these two guns come into action than a very ugly attack was made on them. The ridge from which they were firing was one of those gentle swells of ground which, curving everywhere, nowhere allows a very extended view; and the Boers, about 200 strong, dashed forward with the greatest boldness in the hope of

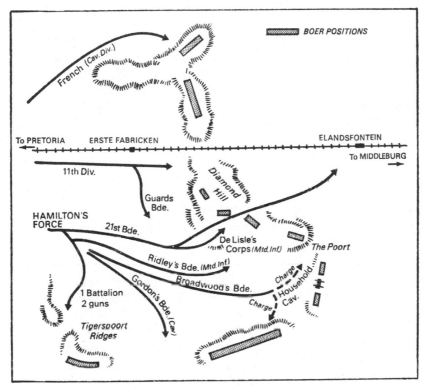

PLAN OF THE OPERATIONS OF 11TH AND 12TH JUNE, 1900

bringing a close musketry fire to bear on the gunners and of capturing their pieces. So sudden was the attack that their heads were seen appearing over the grass scarcely 300 yards away. In these circumstances the guns fired case shot, but though they prevented the Boers from coming nearer, it was evident that the position was still critical. Broadwood was compelled, therefore, to ask the 12th Lancers to charge.

The continual shrapnel fire of the last few hours had, in spite of their dispersed formation, caused a good deal of loss among the horses of the brigade. The Earl of Airlie, who was riding with the brigadier, had had his horse shot under him, and had gone away to find another. He returned to place himself at the head of his regiment just as it was moving forward to the attack, and, perhaps unacquainted with the latest development of the action, he gave a direction to the charge which was slightly more northerly than that which Broadwood intended; so that, in advancing, the regiment gradually came under the fire of the enemy holding the lower slopes of Diamond Hill, instead of falling on those who were directly threatening the guns. But it was a fine, gallant manœuvre, executed with a spring and an elasticity wonderful and admirable in any troops, still more in troops who have been engaged for eight months in continual fighting with an elusive enemy, and who must have regarded any action, subsequent to the capture of Pretoria, rather in the nature of an anti-climax.

Its effect was instantaneous. Though the regiment scarcely numbered 150 men, the Boers fled before them—those who were threatening the guns towards the south, and those immediately in the line of the charge eastward and northward, towards Diamond Hill. Had the horses been fresh and strong a very severe punishment would have been administered to the enemy; but with weary and jaded animals—many of them miserable Argentines, and all worn out with hard work and scanty food—they were unable to overtake the mass of fugitives who continued to fly before them. A few, however, stood boldly, and one man remained firing his rifle until the charge was close on him, when he shot Lieutenant Wright dead at only a few yards distance, and then, holding up his hands, claimed quarter. This was, however, most properly refused. Altogether ten Boers perished by the lance, and the moral effect on those who escaped must certainly have been considerable. But now in pursuit the regiment gradually came nearer to the enemy's main position, and drew a heavy fire on their left flank.

Seeing this, and having attained the object with which he had charged—the immediate relief of the guns—Lord Airlie gave the order "files about", and withdrew his regiment before it became too seriously involved. As he issued this command he was struck by a heavy bullet through the body, and died almost immediately. So fell, while directing his regiment in successful action, an officer of high and noble qualities, trusted by his superiors, beloved by his friends, and honoured by the men he led. The scanty squadrons returned in excellent order to the positions they had won, having lost in the charge, and mostly in the retirement, two officers, seventeen men, including a private of the 10th Hussars, who managed to join in, and about thirty horses.

Meanwhile the pressure on Broadwood's right had become very severe. A large force of Boers who were already engaging the 17th Lancers and the rest of Gordon's Brigade, but who were apparently doubtful of attacking, seeing the advance checked, now swooped down and occupied a kraal and some grassy ridges whence they could bring a heavy enfilading fire to bear. Broadwood, who throughout these emergencies preserved his usual impassive composure, and whose second horse had been shot under him, ordered the Household Cavalry to "Clear them out".

The troopers began immediately to dismount with their carbines, and the General had to send a second message to them, saying that it was no good firing now, and that they must charge with the sword. Whereon, delighted at this unlooked-for, unhoped-for opportunity, the Life Guardsmen scrambled back into their saddles, thrust their hated carbines into the buckets, and drawing their long swords, galloped straight at the enemy. The Boers, who in this part of the field considerably outnumbered the cavalry, might very easily have inflicted severe loss on them. But so formidable was the aspect of these tall horsemen, cheering and flogging their gaunt horses with the flat of their swords, that they did not abide, and running to their mounts fled in cowardly haste, so that, though eighteen horses were shot, the Household Cavalry sustained no loss in men.

These two charges, and the earnest fashion in which they were delivered, completely restored the situation; but though Broadwood maintained all the ground he had won, he did not feel himself strong enough, in face of the severe opposition evidently to be encountered, to force his way through the poort.

At about noon the Field-Marshal, who was with the Eleventh Division, observing an apparent movement of the enemy in his front, concluded that they were about to retreat, and not wishing to sacrifice precious lives if the strategic object were attained without, sent Ian Hamilton a message not, unless the resistance of the enemy was severe, to weary his men and horses by going too far. Hamilton, however, had seen how closely Broadwood was engaged, and fearing that if he stood idle the enemy would concentrate their whole strength on his Cavalry commander, he felt bound to make an attack on the enemy on the lower slopes of Diamond Hill, and so hold out a hand to Broadwood.

He therefore directed Bruce-Hamilton to advance with the Twenty-first Brigade. This officer, bold both as a man and as a general, immediately set his battalions in motion. The enemy

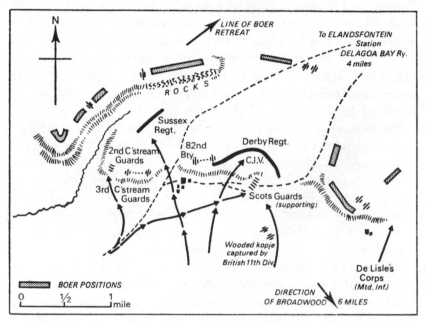

THE ACTION OF DIAMOND HILL

occupied a long scrub-covered rocky ridge below the main line of hills, and were in considerable force. Both batteries of artillery and the two 5-in. guns came into action about two o'clock. The Sussex Regiment, moving forward, established themselves on the northern end of the ridge, which was well prepared by shelling, and while the City Imperial Volunteers and some parts of the Mounted Infantry, including the Corps of Gillies, held them in front, gradually pressed them out of it by rolling up their right.

There is no doubt that our Infantry have profited by the lessons of this war. The widely-extended lines of skirmishers moving forward, almost invisible against the brown grass of the plain, and taking advantage of every scrap of cover, presented no target to the Boer fire. And once they had gained the right of the ridge it was very difficult for the enemy to remain.

Accordingly at 3.30 the Boers in twenties and thirties began to abandon their position. Before they could reach the main hill, however, they had to cross a patch of open ground, and in so doing they were exposed to a heavy rifle fire at 1,200 yards from the troops who were holding the front.

From where I lay, on the left of the Gillies' firing line, I could see the bullets knocking up the dust all round the retreating horsemen, while figures clinging to saddles or supported by their comrades, and riderless horses, showed that some at least of the bullets had struck better things than earth. So soon as they reached fresh cover, the Dutchmen immediately reopened fire, and two of the Gillies were wounded about this time.

The City Imperial Volunteers then occupied the whole of the wooded ridge. One poor little boy, scarcely fourteen years old, was found shot through the head, but still living, and his father, a very respectable-looking man, who, in spite of his orders from the field cornet, had refused to leave his son, was captured; but with these exceptions the Boers had removed their wounded and made good their retreat to the main position. It being now nearly dark the action was broken off, and having strongly picketed the ground they had won, the infantry returned to their waggons for the night.

It was now imperative to carry the matter through, and in view of the unexpected obstinacy of the enemy, the Field-Marshal directed Pole-Carew to support Hamilton with the brigade of Guards in his attack the next day.

Early the next morning Hamilton's infantry moved forward and re-occupied the whole of the ground picketed the previous night. On the right De Lisle's corps of mounted infantry prepared to attack; the cavalry maintained their wedge-like position, and exchanged shots all along their front with the Boers; but no serious operations were begun during the morning, it being thought better to await the arrival, or, at least, the approach, of the brigade which had been promised.

During this interval the Boers shelled our batteries heavily with their long range 30-pounder guns, and General Ian Hamilton, who was sitting on the ground with his Staff near the 82nd Field Battery, was struck by a shrapnel bullet on the left shoulder. Fortunately, the missile did not penetrate, but only caused a severe bruise with numbness and pain, which did not, however, make it necessary for him to leave the field. The case of this shell, which struck close by, ran twirling along the ground like a rabbit—a very peculiar sight, the like of which I have never seen before.

At one o'clock the leading battalion of the Guards was observed to be about four miles off, and Bruce-Hamilton's Brigade was therefore directed to attack. The Derbyshire Regiment, which had been briskly engaged during the morning, advanced up a flat tongue of land on the right. The City Imperial Volunteers moved forward in the centre, and the Sussex on the British left. Though this advance was exposed to a disagreeable enfilade fire from the Boer "pom-pom", the dispersed formations minimised the losses, and lodgments were effected all along the rim of the plateau. But once the troops had arrived here the fight assumed a very different complexion.

The top of the Diamond Hill plateau was swept by fire from a long rocky kopje about 1,800 yards distance from the edge, and was, moreover, partially enfiladed from the enemy's position on the right. The musketry immediately became loud and the fighting severe. The City Imperial Volunteers in the centre began to suffer loss, and had not the surface of the ground been strewn with stones, which afforded good cover, many would have been killed and wounded. Though it was not humanly possible to know from below what the ground on top of the hill was like—we were now being drawn into a regular rat-trap. It was quite evident that to press the attack to an assault at this point would involve very heavy loss of life, and, as the reader will see by looking at the rough plan I have made, the troops would become more and more exposed to enfilade and cross-fire in proportion as they advanced.

After what I had seen in Natal the idea of bringing guns up on to the plateau to support the Infantry attack when at so close a range from the enemy's position seemed a very unpleasant one. But General Bruce-Hamilton did not hesitate, and at half-past three the 82nd Field Battery, having been dragged to the summit, came into action against the Boers on the rocky ridge at a distance of only 1,700 yards.

This thrusting forward of the guns undoubtedly settled the action. The result of their fire was immediately apparent. The bullets, which had hitherto been whistling through the air at the rate of perhaps fifteen or twenty to the minute, and which had compelled us all to lie close behind protecting stones, now greatly diminished, and it was possible to walk about with comparative immunity. But the battery which had reduced the fire, by keeping the enemy's heads down, drew most of what was left on themselves. Ten horses were shot in the moment of unlimbering, and during the two hours they remained in action, in spite of the protection afforded by the guns and waggons, a quarter of the gunners were hit. Nevertheless, the remainder continued to serve their pieces with machine-like precision, and displayed a composure and devotion which won them the unstinted admiration of all who saw the action.

About four o'clock General Ian Hamilton came himself to the top of the plateau, and orders were then given for the Coldstream Guards to prolong the line to the left, and for the Scots Guards to come into action in support of the right. Two more batteries were also brought forward, and the British musketry and artillery being now in great volume, the Boer fire was brought under control. Ian Hamilton did not choose to make the great sacrifices which would accompany an assault, however, nor did his brigadier suggest that one should be delivered, and the combatants therefore remained facing each other at the distance of about a mile, both sides firing heavily with musketry and artillery, until the sun sank and darkness set in.

General Pole-Carew, who with the Eighteenth Brigade was still responsible for containing the Boer centre across the railway, now rode over to Hamilton's force, and plans were made for the next day. It must have been a strange experience for these two young commanders, who, fifteen years ago, had served together as aides-de-camp on Lord Roberts's staff, to find themselves now under the same chief designing a great action as lieutenant-generals. It was decided that Hamilton's force should move further to the right and attack on the front, which, on the 12th, had been occupied by De Lisle's corps of Mounted Infantry, that the Brigade of Guards should take over the ground which the Twenty-first Brigade had won and were picketing, and that the Eighteenth Brigade, which was now to be brought up, should prolong the line to the left. But these expectations of a general action on the morrow were fortunately disappointed. Worsted in the fire fight, with three parts of their position already captured, and with the lodgment effected by Colonel De Lisle's corps on the left threatening their line of retreat, the Boers shrank from renewing the conflict.

During the night they retreated in good order from the whole length of the position which they occupied, and marched eastward along the railway in four long columns. When morning broke and the silence proclaimed the British the victors, Hamilton, in order to carry out his original orders, marched northward and struck the railway at Elandsfrontein station, where he halted. The mounted infantry and cavalry were hurried on in pursuit, but so exhausted were their horses that they did not overtake the enemy.

Such were the operations of the 11th, 12th, and 13th of June, by which, at a cost of about 200 officers and men, the country round Pretoria for forty miles was cleared of the Boers, and a heavy blow dealt to the most powerful force that still keeps the field in the Transvaal.

After the action of Diamond Hill the whole army returned to Pretoria, leaving only a mounted infantry corps to hold the positions they had won to the eastward. French and Pole-Carew, whose troops had marched far and fought often, were given a much-needed rest. Ian Hamilton, whose force had marched further and fought more than either, was soon sent off on his travels again. The military exigencies forbade all relaxation, and only three days' breathing space was given to the lean Infantry and the exhausted horses. By the unbroken success of his strategy Lord Roberts had laid the Boer Republics low. We had taken possession of the Rand, the bowels whence the hostile Government drew nourishment in gold and munitions of war. We had seized the heart at Bloemfontein, the brain at Pretoria. The greater part of the railways, the veins and nerves, that is to say, was in our hands. Yet, though mortally injured, the trunk still quivered convulsively, particularly the left leg, which, being heavily booted, had already struck us several painful and unexpected blows.

To make an end two operations were necessary: first, to secure the dangerous limb, and, secondly, to place a strangling grip on the windpipe somewhere near Komati Poort. The second will, perhaps, be the business of Sir Redvers Buller and the glorious Army of Natal. The first set Hamilton's Brigades in motion as part of an intricate and comprehensive scheme, which arranged for the permanent garrisoning of Frankfort, Heilbron, Lindley, and Senekal, and directed a simultaneous movement against Christiaan De Wet by four strong flying columns.

I had determined to return to England; but it was with mixed feelings that I watched the departure of the gallant column in

whose good company I had marched so many miles and seen such
successful fights. Their road led them past Lord Roberts's headquarters, and the old Field-Marshal came out himself to see them
off. First the two cavalry brigades marched past. They were
brigades no longer; the Household Cavalry Regiment was scarcely
fifty strong: in all there were not a thousand sabres. Then Ridley's
1,400 Mounted Infantry, the remnants of what on paper was a
brigade of nearly 5,000; thirty guns dragged by skinny horses; the
two trusty 5-inch "cow-guns" behind their teams of toiling oxen;
Bruce-Hamilton's Infantry Brigade, with the City Imperial Volunteers, striding along—weary of war, but cheered by the hopes of
peace, and quite determined to see the matter out; lastly, miles of
transport: all streamed by, grew faint in the choking red dust, and
vanished through the gap in the southern line of hills. May they all
come safely home.

APPENDIX

COMPOSITION OF
LIEUT.-GENERAL IAN HAMILTON'S FORCE

DIVISIONAL STAFF

LIEUTENANT-GENERAL IAN HAMILTON, C.B., D.S.O.

A.D.C.s—Captain de Heriez Smith.
Captain Balfour, late 11th Hussars.
Captain Maddocks, R.A.
Captain Duke of Marlborough, I.Y.
A.A.G.—Lieut.-Colonel Le Gallais, 8th Hussars.
D.A.A.G.s—Captain Vallentin, Somerset L.I.
Captain Gamble, Lincoln Regiment.
Captain Atcherley, A.S.C.
Captain Kirkpatrick, R.E.
Provost Marshal—Captain Sloman, East Surrey Regiment.
Div. Signalling Officer—Captain Ross, Norfolk Regiment.
P.M.O.—Colonel Williams, N. S. Wales A.M.C.
Divisional Troops—Rimington's Guides under Major Rimington,
Inniskilling Dragoons.

2nd MOUNTED INFANTRY BRIGADE

BRIGADIER-GENERAL R. RIDLEY

A.D.C.—Captain Hood, Coldstream Guards.
Brigade Major.—Lieut.-Colonel Mitford, East Surrey Regiment.
Staff Officers—Captain Sir T. MacMahon, Royal Welsh Fusiliers.
Captain Eustace Crawley, 12th Lancers.

2ND MOUNTED INFANTRY CORPS

Lieut.-Colonel de Lisle, Commanding Durham Light Infantry.

Staff Officer—Captain Fanshawe, Oxford L.I.
6th M.I. Battalion—Captain Pennefather, Welsh Regiment.
New South Wales Mounted Rifles.
West Australians.
1 Pom-pom.

5TH MOUNTED INFANTRY CORPS
Lieut.-Colonel Dawson, I.S.C.

Staff Officer—Captain Ballard, Norfolk Regiment.
5th M.I. Battalion—Major Lean, Warwick Regiment.
Roberts' Horse—Captain Baumgartner, East Lancashire Regiment.
Marshall's Horse—Captain Corbett.
Ceylon M.I.—Major Rutherford.
1 Pom-pom.

6TH MOUNTED INFANTRY CORPS
Lieut.-Colonel Legge, 20th Hussars.

Staff Officer—Captain Hart, East Surrey Regiment.
2nd M.I. Battalion—Major Dobell.
Kitchener's Horse—Major Cookson, I.S.C.
Lovat's Scouts—Major A. Murray.
1 Pom-pom.

7TH MOUNTED INFANTRY CORPS
Lieut.-Colonel Bainbridge, Buffs.

Staff Officer—Captain Hamilton, Oxford L.I.
7th M.I. Battalion—Major Welch.
Burmah M.I.—Captain Copeman.
1 Pom-pom.

P. BATTERY

Ammunition Column—Major Mercer, R.H.A.
Bearer Company and Field Hospital—New South Wales Army Medical
    Corps.

2nd CAVALRY BRIGADE
BRIGADIER-GENERAL BROADWOOD

A.D.C.—Captain Aldridge, R.H.A.
Brigade Major—Captain Hon. T. Brand, 10th Hussars.
Signalling Officer—Captain Sloane Stanley, 12th Lancers.
Household Cavalry—Lieut.-Colonel Calley.
10th Lancers—Lieut.-Colonel Fisher.
12th Lancers—Lieut.-Colonel Earl of Airlie.
Q. Battery, R.A.
Ammunition Column—Captain Kincaid, R.A.
Bearer Company.
Field Hospital.

19th BRIGADE

MAJOR-GENERAL SMITH-DORRIEN

A.D.C.s—Captain Hood, R.M.L.I.
  Lieut. Dorrien Smith, Shropshire L.I.
Brigade Major—Major Inglefield, East Yorkshire Regiment.
74th Battery—Major MacLeod.
2nd Duke of Cornwall L.I.—Lieut.-Colonel Ashby.
Shropshire L.I.—Lieut.-Colonel Spens.
Gordon Highlanders—Lieut.-Colonel MacBean.
Royal Canadians—Lieut.-Colonel Otter.
Bearer Company and Field Hospital.

21st BRIGADE

MAJOR-GENERAL BRUCE-HAMILTON

A.D.C.—Lieut. Frazer, Cameron Highlanders.
Brigade Major—Major Shaw, Derbyshire Regiment.
76th Battery—Major Campbell.
1st Royal Sussex—Lieut.-Colonel Donne.
1st Derby—Major Gossett.
1st Cameron—Lieut.-Colonel Kennedy.
City Imperial Volunteers—Brigadier-Colonel Mac-Kinnon; Colonel The
  Earl of Albermarle.
Bearer Company.
Field Hospital.

DIVISIONAL ARTILLERY

LIEUT.-COLONEL WALDRON, R.F.A.

81st Battery.
82nd Battery—Major Conolly.
1 Section of Five-inch gun—Captain Massey.
Ammunition Column—Captain Hardman.

EFFECTIVE FIGHTING STRENGTH

11,000 Men.
4,600 Horses.
8,000 Mules.
36 Field guns.
2 Five-inch guns.
23 Machine guns.
6 Pom-poms.

The force left Bloemfontein, April 22.
Arrived at Pretoria on June 5.

Distance traversed, 401 miles in a straight line.
Time on the march, 45 days.
Halts, 10 days.

General actions on nine days:
 Israel's Poort, April 25.
 Houtnek, April 30 and May 1.
 Welkom, May 4.
 Sand River, May 10.
 Affair of Lindley, May 20.
 Doornkop (Florida) May 29.
 Six Mile Spruit (Pretoria), June 4.
 Diamond Hill, June 11 and 12.

Eighteen days' skirmishes.

Towns captured:
 Thabanchu.
 Winburg.
 Ventersburg.
 Kroonstadt.
 Lindley.
 Heilbron.
 Johannesburg.
 Pretoria.

THE INTERNATIONAL CHURCHILL SOCIETY

Founded 1968, the International Churchill Society is a worldwide, non-profit, charitable organization of scholars, historians, bibliophiles, professors, philatelists, collectors, students and others interested in the life and work of Winston Churchill, and the preservation of his memory. The Society has membership offices in five countries and additional local branches. An annual convention is held in either Canada, Great Britain or the United States, and many smaller events are hosted by national and local offices.

A quarterly journal, Finest Hour, *is professionally produced and printed, containing up to 50 pages of scholarly feature articles and regular columns. The Society has a commemorative cover program, in which special covers are issued on important anniversaries, bearing stamps and postmarks related to the event. Classified advertising is free to members but commercial advertising is restricted. A new book service, regular supplements to the Society's* Churchill Collector's Handbook, *and a calendar of coming events are included in the magazine.*

The Society stands foursquare behind Sir Winston's theme of amity and unity among the English-speaking Peoples. To this end, it sponsors a bi-annual visit to "Churchill's Britain," where Commonwealth and American members join UK members visiting homes and other sites closely related to Churchill. At these and other events, the Society welcomes speakers who either personally knew or have written extensively about Sir Winston, and a growing library of oral history now exits. ICS also engages in charitable endeavors. These include an Award in British History for students at York University; a Debating Award for Hart House, University of Toronto; and the perpetual care of the grave of Winston Churchill's famous nanny, Elizabeth Everest, in London. The Society is a registered charitable organization in Canada, Great Britain and the United States. ICS-UK, an autonomous British charity stressing Churchill's theme of "positive thinking," awards its "Young Winston" prizes in oratory, art and literature; all three charities sponsor educational programs.

ICS Branches in five countries welcome requests for further information, and will be pleased to send a membership application:

Australia: 8 Regnans Avenue, Endeavour Hills, Victoria 3802

Canada: 1079 Coverdale Road, Moncton, New Brunswick E1C 8J6

New Zealand: 3/1445 Great North Road, Waterview, Auckland 7

U.K.: 29 High Street, Shoreham, Sevenoaks, Kent TN14 7TD

U.S.A.: 1847 Stonewood Drive, Baton Rouge, Louisiana 70816

Bibliographic notes in the Foreword to this edition have been aided by kind assistance of the International Churchill Society, Richard M. Langworth and Ronald I. Cohen.